SEQUELS

Incorporating
Aldred & Parker's *Sequel Stories*

compiled by
FRANK M. GARDNER, F.L.A.

ASSOCIATION OF ASSISTANT LIBRARIANS
(*Group of the Library Association*)
1967

1st edition	1922
2nd edition	1928
3rd edition	1947
4th edition	1955
5th edition	1967

PREFACE TO THE FIFTH EDITION

This new edition of Sequels lists over 7,000 new titles, bringing the total to about 20,000. The general plan of the last edition has been retained, and the list includes:

    a. Series of novels with a connected narrative of events or a developing theme.

    b. Novels and stories in which the same character reappears.

    c. Non-fiction conceived as a single series, when the connection is not apparent from the titles.

    d. Series of novels with an interior connection, usually topographical or historical.

Series featuring a single character of group of characters are of course the largest section, and the establishment of a single character has become almost the keystone of the popular novel, particularly the thriller, detective story, or that revived convention, the spy story. Some quite interesting new trends can be discerned since the last edition of *Sequels*. The phenomenal cult of James Bond created two quite distinct new or revived types – a host of James Bond imitations with violence as the motivation, and the secret service novel, with the inevitable reaction and the creation of the anti-hero. Art, in popular fiction, appears to imitate art, or at least, success. By contrast, the pure detective story, the puzzle, is in a gentle decline, and the search for the unusual has brought up some bizarre characters – Judge Dee, the delightful medieval Chinese created by Robert Van Gulik, and Napoleon Bonaparte, the Australian aboriginal who is the hero of Arthur Upfield's series, to name but two. One curious byway in the history of the detective story, quite noticeable to the compiler, is the revival of the *Roman Policier*, in which often two or three separate investigations are joined in a single story. McBain's 87th *Precinct* stories; Creasey's *Gideon of the Yard* series; Freeling's untypical Dutchman, Van der Valk; the small town policemen, Sergeant Cluff and Chief of Police Fellows, and of course the unique Maigret, are some examples. However perishable the popular novel of today, most of it is good entertainment, and some of it rather more than entertainment.

Many more ambitious works appear here for the first time in this edition. The sequence novel is an important art form for the author who has a large canvas to cover, or a social theme to develop. Sir Charles Snow's *Strangers and brothers* series goes on, though more slowly, and his wife, Pamela Hansford Johnson has in three novels created a rather different group of characters. One wonders what Lewis Eliot would make of them. Anthony Powell's *Music of time* is developing into what looks like being a quadruple trilogy, and gains more critical acclaim with each new volume. Henry Williamson's enormous commentary *A chronicle of ancient sunlight* has now reached its twelfth volume. Two shorter series should also be noted, as almost perfect examples of the sequel and the trilogy, – Margaret Lane's *A smell of burning* and its sequel, and Olivia Manning's *Balkan trilogy*. And as one more example of the large canvas, Doris Lessing's *Children of violence* develops as a work of art of the first order.

Many titles appear here in translation, and some attempt has been made to solve the puzzles presented by partial translation and differing titles. Colette's *Claudine* series is a good example, but there are many others.

For various reasons, more bibliographical notes have been included than in previous editions, and it is hoped that they will be of help. An indication of theme or subject has also been given where it is thought it might be helpful.

In response to many requests, a start was made on including dates of first publication, omitted in previous editions. Regretfully, it was found that this was a bigger task than anticipated. To complete it would have further delayed publication, and it had to be abandoned. But the dates already listed, mainly for more recent books, have been retained.

As in previous editions, references have been kept to a minimum, consistent, I hope, with helping the user to find a particular series. Entry is under the best-known name, and pseudonyms are not noted unless they are at least as well-known as the real name.

Where an American title is known to vary from the British title, it is given in square brackets, but no indication is given for books published only in the U.S.A. Foreign books are only included if a series has been at least partially translated, and if the translation is not complete, I have tried to give an indication of the complete scope of the series.

As usual, I am greatly indebted to publishers, authors' agents, and authors themselves for assistance in clearing up points of difficulty, and many have gone to a great deal of trouble.

Mr F. B. Carruthers, of Edinburgh Public Libraries and Miss F. B. Cockroft, have maintained their own lists of additions and I am greatly indebted to them for these, which have been most useful for checking.

Other valuable notes have come from Mr E. Ellis, Reference Librarian, Buffalo, Mr F. Thibault, Montreal, Mr Richard White, of Dunedin, New Zealand and Mr G. B. Cotton. I am also greatly indebted to Mr Anthony Langman, who sent me some most erudite notes on early twentieth century fiction.

As a Librarian, I would also acknowledge my debt to the London Fiction Reserve collections. This is an increasingly valuable addition to our library resources.

Other contributors are too numerous to mention, but interest in *Sequels* is by no means confined to librarians, and some of my correspondence is from readers who show an extraordinary knowledge, particularly of older books. It has occasionally been suggested that *Sequels* should only note recent books, but in fact every edition contains notes on earlier books that were either wrongly listed or omitted altogether from previous editions, and most of these corrections come from correspondents.

From such corrections I am sadly aware of the deficiencies in this work that are almost inevitable. In preparing this edition, there have been considerable difficulties caused by the long interval since the last, and the speed with which popular novels go out of print. I should be grateful at any time for information on omissions or errors.

One major change in arrangement of this edition should be noted. The section on children's books has now got so large that it was thought more suitable that it should be included as a separate section, on blue paper.

FRANK M. GARDNER

Sequels

PART ONE : ADULT BOOKS

Aarons, E. S.
SAM DURELL SERIES:
1 Assignment suicide 1960
2 Assignment Stella Marni 1965

Abbot, A.
THATCHER COLT SERIES:
1 Murder of Geraldine Foster
2 Crime of the century
3 The night club lady
4 Murder of the circus queen
5 Murder of a startled lady
6 Murder of a man afraid of women
7 Murder at Buzzard's Bay
8 Deadly secret

Abdullah, A.
1 The red stain
2 The blue-eyed Manchu

Abetti, G. O. *and* **Hack, M.**
1 The sun
2 Stars and planets (not yet printed in English)
3 Nebulae and galaxies
N.F. Astronomy

Acheta
1 March winds and April showers
2 May flowers

Ackworth, J. *pseud.* [**Rev. F. R. Smith**]
CLOGSHOP CHRONICLES
1 Clogshop chronicles
2 Doxie Dent
3 Beckside lights

Adam, P.
1 Force
2 The child of the Austerlitz
3 The sun of July
   These are the only parts published in English of the series 'Le Temps et la vie' of about 20 volumes.

Adams, C. F.
REX MACBRIDE SERIES:
1 Murder at the dam [Sabotage]
2 And sudden death
3 Decoy
4 The black door
5 What price murder
6 The private eye
7 Up jumped the devil
8 The crooking finger

Adams, Herbert
JIMMY HASWELL SERIES:
1 The secret of Bogey House
2 The crooked lip
3 The Queen's Gate mystery
4 The empty bed
5 Rogues fall out
6 Oddways
7 The golden ape
8 The crime in the Dutch garden
9 The Paulton plot
10 The woman in black
ROGER BENNION SERIES:
1 The old Jew mystery
2 Death off the fairway
3 A single hair
4 The Bluff
5 The damned spot
6 Black death
7 The nineteenth hole mystery
8 The case of the stolen bridegroom
9 The chief witness
10 The stab in the back
11 Roger Bennion's double
12 The Araway oath
13 Sequel for invasion
14 Victory song
15 Four winds
16 The writing on the wall
17 Welcome home
18 Diamonds are trumps

19 Crime wave at Little Cornford
20 One to play
21 The Dean's daughters
22 The sleeping draught
23 Exit the skeleton
24 The spectre in brown
25 Slippery Dick
26 Death on the first tee 1957
27 Death of a viewer 1958

Adams, S. H.
THE RUYLAND FAMILY:
1 Siege
2 Piper's fee

Adamson, Joy
1 Born free
2 Living free
3 Forever free
N.F. Books about a lion cub adopted as a pet. Republished in one vol. 1966 'The story of Elsa'.

Afghan, *pseud.*
1 Exploits of Asaf Khan
2 The wanderings of Asaf

Agnew, E. C.
1 Geraldine
2 Rome and the Abbey

Agnus, Orme *pseud.* **[J. C. Higginbotham]**
SARAH TULDON SERIES:
1 Sarah Tuldon
2 Sarah Tuldon's lovers

Aguilar, G.
1 Home influence
2 The mother's recompense

Aicard, J.
1 Adventures of Maurin
2 Maurin, the illustrious

Aimard, G.
TALES OF INDIAN LIFE:
(*a*)
1 The adventurers
2 The Pearl of the Andes
3 The tiger-slayer
4 The gold seekers

5 The Indian chief
□
1 The Prairie Flower
2 The Indian scout
□
1 The trail hunter
2 The pirates of the Prairies
3 The trapper's daughter
□
1 The Border Rifles
2 The freebooters
□
(*b*) A suggested order of reading:
1 The trappers of the Arkansas
2 The Border Rifles
3 The freebooters
4 The white scalpers
5 Guide to the Desert; or, Life on the Pampas
6 The insurgent chief
7 The flying chief
8 The last of the Incas
9 The Missouri outlaws
10 The Prairie Flower
11 The Indian scout
12 Stronghand
13 The bee hunters
14 Stoneheart
15 The Queen of the Savannah
16 The buccaneer chief
17 The smuggler chief
18 The adventurers
19 The Pearl of the Andes
20 The trail hunter
21 The pirates of the Prairies
22 The trapper's daughter
23 The tiger-slayer
24 The gold seekers
25 The Indian chief
26 The red track

Ainsworth, E.
1 Second-lieut. Billie Impett and his orderly
2 Billie Impett and Doris

Ainwell, W. *pseud.* **[W. Simonds]**
1 Oscar
2 Clinton
3 Ella
4 Whistler
5 Marcus

6 Jessie
7 Jerrie

Aksakoff, S.
1 Years of childhood
2 A Russian schoolboy
3 A Russian gentleman
N.F. Autobiography

Aldanov, M. A.
THE THINKER SERIES:
1 The ninth Thermidor
2 The Devil's bridge
3 The conspiracy
4 Saint Helena, little island

Alden, Mrs. G. M. *see* Pansy, *pseud.*

Aldrich, B. S.
1 A lantern in her hand
2 A white bird flying

Aldrich, T. B.
1 Marjorie Daw and other people
2 The Queen of Sheba

Alington, A.
1 These our strangers
2 Those kids from town again

Alington, C. A.
ARCHDEACON SERIES
1 Archdeacons afloat
2 Archdeacons ashore
3 Blackmail in Blankshire
4 Gold and gaiters
   Some characters in 4 appear in 'Midnight wireless'.

Allain, M., *and* **Souvestre, P.**
See Souvestre, P.

Allan, J. M. *pseud.* [**Lennox Allan**]
1 And love thee evermore
2 The living sword

Allan, L.
BLUE PETE SERIES:
1 Blue Pete, half-breed
2 The return of Blue Pete

3 Blue Pete, detective
4 Blue Pete, horsethief
5 Vengeance of Blue Pete
6 Blue Pete, rebel
7 Blue Pete pays a debt
8 Blue Pete breaks the rules
9 Blue Pete, outlaw
10 Blue Pete's dilemma
11 Blue Pete's vendetta
12 Blue Pete to the rescue
13 Blue Pete and the Pinto
14 Blue Pete unofficially
15 Blue Pete Indian scout
16 Blue Pete works alone
17 Blue Pete at bay
18 Blue Pete rides the foothills
19 Blue Pete and the kid
20 Blue Pete in the Badlands

Allan, M.
1 Rose cottage
2 Base rumour

Allbury, A.
1 You'll die in Singapore
2 Bamboo and Busjido
N.F. War reminiscences

Allcard, E.
1 Single handed passage
2 Temptress returns
N.F. Two sea voyages

Allee, Mrs. M.
1 Judith Lankester
2 House of her own
3 Off to Philadelphia
   Nos. 2 and 3 are about younger sisters of Judith Lankester

Allen, H.
THE DISINHERITED SERIES:
1 The forest and the fort
2 Bedford village
3 Toward the morning
   This was to be a series of six novels. The above three together with a part of a fourth, were published in one volume in U.S.A. under the title 'City in the dawn'.

Allen, J. L.

CHRISTMAS SEASON SERIES:
1 The bride of the mistletoe
2 The doctor's Christmas Eve

KENTUCKY SERIES:
1 A Kentucky cardinal
2 Aftermath

Allingham, M.

ALBERT CAMPION SERIES:
1 The crime at Black Dudley [Black Dudley murder]
2 Mystery mile
3 The Gyrth chalice mystery
4 Police at the funeral
5 Sweet danger [Kingdom of death]
6 Death of a ghost
7 Flowers for the judge
8 The case of the late pig
9 Dancers in mourning
10 The fashion in shrouds
11 Mr. Campion and others
12 Black plumes
13 Traitor's purse
14 Coroner's pidgin [Pearls before swine]
15 More work for the undertaker
16 Tiger in the smoke
17 Beckoning lady 1955
18 Hide my eyes 1958
19 The china governess 1963
20 The mind readers 1965
The volume 'Mysterious Mr Campion' 1963, is an omnibus volume with one new short story.
The Second Allingham omnibus gives the inner sequence of the story of Campion and his wife Amanda, in nos. 5, 10, 13 above. It also includes a new Campion short story.

Allis, M.

ASHBEL FIELD SERIES:
1 Now we are free 1952
2 To keep us free 1953
3 Brave pursuit 1954
4 Rising storm 1955
5 Free soil 1960
A series of novels about an American family, beginning with the revolutionary war.

Almedingen, E. M.

1 Fair Haven 1959
2 Dark splendour 1961
Andrew Thorngold of 2 is the son of Hal Thorngold of 1. Scene is Russia in the 18th century.

☐
1 Tomorrow will come
2 The almond tree
3 Within the harbour
N.F. Autobiography

A.L.O.E. *pseud. see* Tucker, C.

Altsheler, J. A.

CIVIL WAR SERIES:
1 The guns of Bull Run
2 The guns of Shiloh
3 The sword of Antietam
4 The scouts of Stonewall
5 The star of Gettysburg
6 The rock of Chickamauga
7 The shades of the wilderness
8 The tree of Appomattox

FRENCH AND INDIAN WAR SERIES:
1 The hunters of the hills
2 The shadow of the North
3 The rulers of the Lakes
4 The masters of the Peaks
5 The lords of the wild
6 The Sun of Quebec

GREAT WEST SERIES:
1 The great Sioux trail
2 The lost hunters

TEXAN SERIES:
1 The Texan star
2 The Texan scouts
3 The Texan triumph

TRAILERS SERIES:
1 The young trailers
2 The forest runners
3 The keepers of the trail
4 The eyes of the woods
5 The free rangers
6 The rifleman of the Ohio
7 The scouts of the valley
8 The border watch

WORLD WAR SERIES:
1 The guns of Europe
2 The forest of swords
3 The hosts of the air

Ambler, E.
1 Uncommon danger
2 Cause for alarm
The character Zaleshoff appears in both books, but not otherwise connected.

Amery, L. S.
MY POLITICAL LIFE
1 England before the storm, 1896–1914.
2 War and peace, 1914–1929.
3 The unforgiving years
N.F. Autobiography

Ames, D.
DAGOBERT BROWN SERIES:
1 She shall have murder 1948
2 Murder begins at home 1949
3 Death of a fellow traveller 1950
4 Corpse diplomatique 1950
5 The body on page one 1951
6 Murder, maestro please 1952
7 No mourning for the Matador 1953
8 Crime, Gentlemen please 1954
9 Landscape with corpses 1955
10 Crime out of mind 1956
11 She wouldn't say who 1957
12 Lucky Jane 1959
SERGEANT JUAN LLORCA SERIES:
1 The man in the tricorn hat 1962
2 The man with three Jaguars 1963
3 The man with three chins 1964

Ames, F. T.
1 Between the lines in Belgium
2 Between the lines in France
3 Between the lines on the American front

Ames, J. B.
1 Curly of the Circle-bar in Texas
2 Curly and the Aztec gold
3 Curly Graham, cowpuncher

Aminoff, Madame [Baroness Leonine]
NAPOLEONIC SERIES:
1 Revolution
2 Love
3 Ambition
4 Success
5 Victory

6 Triumph
7 Glory
8 Arrogance
9 Storm
10 Retreat
Two final volumes 'Defeat' and 'The End' were projected but have not been published.

Ammers-Kuller, J. van, *see*
Kuller, J. van Ammers-

Amothy, Christine
1 I am fifteen and I do not want to die
2 It is not so easy to live
N.F. Autobiography

Anand, M. J.
STORY OF LAL SINGH:
1 The village
2 Across the black waters
3 The sword and the sickle

Anderson, H. M.
1 Kelston of Kells
2 Sons of the forge

Anderson, O.
GUY RANDOM SERIES:
1 Random at random 1958
2 Random rapture 1959
3 Random all round 1960

Anderson, S.
1 Story-teller's story
2 Tar: a Mid-West childhood
N.F. Autobiography

Anderson, V.
1 Spam tomorrow 1956
2 Our square 1957
3 Beware of children 1958
4 Daughters of divinity 1959
5 The Flo affair 1963
N.F. Autobiography

Anethan, Baroness A. d'.
1 The twin soul of O'Také-San
2 Her mother's blood

Annesley, M.
FENTON SERIES:
1 Room 14
2 Spies in the web
3 Spies in action
4 The missing agent
5 The vanished vice-consul
6 Unknown agent
7 Spy against the Reich
8 Suicide spies
9 An agent intervenes
10 Spies abounding
11 Spy counter-spy
12 Spy corner
13 Spy island

Annunzio, G. d'.
ROMANCES OF THE ROSE TRILOGY:
1 The triumph of death
2 The child of pleasure
3 The victim *same as* The intruder
Two other trilogies were projected, 'Romances of the lily', and 'Romances of the pomegranate' but were never written.

Anonymous stories
COMMUTER'S SERIES:
1 People of the whirlpool
2 Woman errant
SAUL WEIR SERIES:
1 Saul Weir
2 A modern minister
INDIANA SERIES:
1 Black Beauty
2 Strike at Shane's
DIARY SERIES:
1 The diary of a honeymoon
2 The indiscretion of Lady Usher
DAPHNE SERIES:
1 Daphne in the Fatherland
2 Daphne in Paris
FAUSTUS SERIES:
1 Faustus
2 The second report of Dr. Faustus
☐
1 WAAC – the woman's story of the war
2 WAAC demobilized
☐
1 The wiles of Lim Quong
2 The bamboo rod

Anstey, F. *pseud.* [T. A. Guthrie]
VOCES POPULI. TWO SERIES

Anstey, R.
1 Leopold's Congo 1964
2 King Leopold's legacy 1966
N.F. The history of the Congo

Anstruther, E. H. [Mrs. J. C. Squire]
1 The farm servant
2 The husband
3 Five in family

Anthony, E.
1 Imperial Highness
2 Curse not the King
3 Far fly the eagles

Anthony, L. R.
ANNE THORNTON SERIES – 2 VOLS.

Antony, J.
1 Mrs. Dale's bedside book
2 Mrs. Dale at home
with Surley, R.
3 The Dales of Parkwood Hill

Aragon, L.
THE REAL WORLD:
1 Bells of Basel
2 Residental quarter
3 Passengers of destiny
[The century was young]
4 Aurélien

Archibald, Mrs. G.
1 Lady Gay
2 A dozen good times
☐
1 Laura's holidays
2 Laura in the mountains

Armfelt, R.
1 County affairs
2 Village affairs
3 Shapton affairs

Armstrong, A.
1 Cottage into house
2 We like the country
3 Village at war
4 We keep going
5 The year at 'Margaret's'
The records of a house and family in Sussex.

Armstrong, A. (*contd.*)
1 Patrick, undergraduate
2 Patrick engaged
3 Patrick helps
JIMMY REZAIRE SERIES:
1 The secret trail
2 The trail of fear
3 The trail of the black king
4 The trail of the Lotto
5 The poison trail
□
1 Percival and I
2 Percival at play
3 Apple and Percival

Armstrong, R.
CHIEF INSPECTOR MASON SERIES:
1 Dangerous limelight
2 Sinister playhouse
3 Sinister widow
4 Sinister widow again
5 Sinister widow returns
6 Sinister widow comes back 1956
7 Widow and the cavalier 1956
8 Sinister widow at sea 1959
ROCKINGHAM STONE SERIES:
1 Cavalier of the night 1955
2 The widow and the cavalier 1956
2 is also in the previous series.

Armstrong, T.
THE CROWTHER CHRONICLES:
1 The Crowthers of Bankdam
2 Pilling always pays
3 Sue Crowther's marriage 1961
4 Our London office 1966
Edwin Crowther makes a brief appearance in 'A ring has no end'.

**Arnim, M. A. Baroness von
[Countess Russell]**
ELIZABETH SERIES:
1 Elizabeth and her German garden
2 The solitary summer
3 The benefactress
4 Adventures of Elizabeth in Rügen

Arnold, R.
1 A very quiet war
2 Orange Street and Brickhole Lane
N.F. Autobiography

Arnott, P.
1 This impertinence
2 More impertinence
N.F. Travel in India.

Aron, R.
THE LIBERATION OF FRANCE:
1 The Vichy regime
2 De Gaulle before Paris
3 De Gaulle triumphant
N.F. History

Arthur, F.
INSPECTOR SPEARPOINT:
1 Who killed Netta Maudê? [The Suva Harbour mystery]
2 Another mystery in Suva
3 Murder in the tropic night 1961
4 The throbbing dark 1962

Arthur, T. S.
HOME STORIES:
1 Hidden wings
2 Sowing the wind
3 Sunshine at home
4 Peacemaker
5 Not anything for peace
6 After a shadow
HOUSEHOLD LIBRARY:
1 Married life
2 Seed time and harvest
3 Stories for young housekeepers
4 Two wives
5 Woman's trials
6 Words for the wise
ANOTHER SERIES:
1 Nothing but money
2 What came afterwards

Asch, S.
1 The Nazarene
2 The Apostle
3 Mary
4 Moses
5 The Prophet 1955
First conceived as a 'New Testament' trilogy, and then expanded into a biblical series.

Ashe, G.
1 King Arthur's Avalon 1957
2 From Caesar to Arthur 1960
N.F.

Ashe, Gordon

PATRICK DAWLISH SERIES:
1 Speaker
2 Death on demand
3 Terror by day
4 Secret murder
5 'Ware danger
6 Murder most foul
7 There goes death
8 Death in high places
9 Death in flames
10 Two men missing
11 Rogues rampant
12 Death on the move
13 Invitation to adventure
14 Here is danger
15 Give me murder
16 Murder too late
17 Engagement with death
18 Dark mystery
19 A puzzle in pearls
20 Sleepy death
21 The long search
22 Death in the trees
23 Double for death
24 The kidnapped child
25 Day of fear
26 Wait for death
27 Come home to death
28 Elope to death
29 Don't let him kill
30 The crime haters
31 Rogue's ransom
32 Death from below 1963
33 The big call 1964
34 A promise of diamonds 1965
35 A taste of treasure 1965
From no. 30 the series is referred to as 'The crime haters'.

Ashford, J.

DETECTIVE-INSPECTOR DON KERRY:
1 Investigations are proceeding 1963
2 Enquiries are continuing 1964

Ashmun, M. E.
1 Isabel Carleton's year
2 The heart of Isabel Carleton
3 Isabel Carleton's friends

Ashton, Helen
WILCHESTER CHRONICLES:
1 Tadpole Hall

2 Joanna at Littlefold
3 Yeoman's hospital
4 Captain comes home
5 Half-crown house 1956
There are a few references to Wilchester in an earlier novel, 'Hornet's nest'.

Asimov, I.
1 Foundation 1951
2 Foundation, and empire 1952
3 Second foundation 1953
S.F. A trilogy on the far future.

Askew, A. *and* C.
1 The Shulamite
2 The woman Deborah

Aspinall, R.
THE MALINSON BROTHERS:
1 Yesterday's kingdom 1961
2 The promise of his return 1962
3 Echo sounding 1965

Asquith, Lady C.
1 Haply I may remember
2 Remember and be glad
N.F. autobiography

Atherton, G.
1 Transplanted. *Same as* American wives and English husbands
2 The Californians

Atkey, B.
1 The amazing Mr. Bunn
2 Smiler Bunn, gentleman crook
3 Smiler Bunn, manhunter
4 The man with the yellow eyes
□
1 Winnie O'Wynn and the wolves
2 Winnie O'Wynn and the dark horses

Attenborough, D.
1 Zoo quest to Guiana
2 Zoo quest for a dragon
3 Zoo quest in Paraguay
4 Zoo quest in Paradise
5 Zoo quest to Madagascar
6 Zoo quest under Capricorn
N.F. Travel

Audemars, P.
M. PINAUD SERIES:
1 The obligations of Hercule
2 Hercule and the gods
3 The temptations of Hercule
4 Confessions of Hercule
5 The two imposters
6 The fire and the clay
7 The turns of time
8 The crown of night 1962
9 The dream and the dead 1963
10 The wings of darkness 1963
11 Fair maids missing 1964
12 Dead with sorrow 1965
13 Time of temptation 1966
Nos. 1–4 were earlier translations.

Audoux, M.
1 Marie Claire
2 Marie Claire's workshop

Austen, J.
'Old friends and new fancies,' by S. G. Brinton, is an imaginary sequel to the novels of Jane Austen.
'The Watsons': a fragment, concluded. by L. Oulton (imaginative).
'The Watsons'. Completed in accordance with her intentions by Edith (her great grand-niece) and Francis Brown. 1928.
'The Watsons'. Completed by J. Coates 1958.
'The Younger sister'(a continuation of 'The Watsons'), by Mrs. Hubback 1850.
'The ladies', by E. Barrington.
Short stories continuing, 'Pride and prejudice'.
'Margaret Dashwood' and 'Susan Price', by Mrs. F. Brown are sequels to 'Sense and sensibility'.
'Pemberley Shades', by D. Bonavia-Hunt, is a sequel to 'Pride and prejudice'.
See also **Piper, W.**

Austin, A.
BONNIE DUNDEE SERIES:
1 Murder at bridge
2 Murder backstairs
3 The avenging parrot
4 The black pigeon
5 One drop of blood

Austin, F. B.
NAPOLEON BONAPARTE
1 The road to glory (Italy)
2 Forty centuries look down (Egypt)

Austin, H.
LIEUTENANT PETER D. QUINT SERIES:
1 It couldn't be murder
2 Murder in triplicate
3 Murder of a matriarch
4 The upside down murders
5 Lilies for Madame

Austin, J. G.
1 Dora Darling
2 Outpost. Later published as Dora Darling and Little Sunshine

Austin, Mrs. J. G.
1 A nameless nobleman
2 Dr. Le Baron and his daughters
□
1 Standish of Standish
2 Betty Alden
3 David Alden's daughter, etc.

Austwick, J.
1 The mobile library murders 1963
2 The Borough Council murders 1965

Avery, E.
1 The Margaret days 1959
2 The Marigold summer 1960

Avon, R. A. Eden, 1st Earl
1 Facing the dictators 1962
2 The reckoning 1965
3 Full circle 1960
N.F. Autobiography. Above is chronological order.

Ayres, R. M. [Mrs. R. W. Pocock]
1 Richard Chatterton, v.c.
2 The road that bends
3 The long lane to happiness

Bacchelli, R.
MILL ON THE PO TRILOGY
1 Mill on the Po
2 Nothing new under the sun
Originally published in Italy as three vols. in one. British edition contains first two vols. under title 'Mill on the Po'.

Bacheller, I.
1 Eben Holden
2 Eben Holden's last day a-fishing
  ☐
1 Keeping up with Lizzie
2 Charge it, *or* Keeping up with Harry
3 The Marryers
ABRAHAM LINCOLN:
1 A boy for the ages
2 A man for the ages
3 Father Abraham

Bacon, J. D.
1 Luck of Lowry
2 Kathy

Baerlein, H.
1 Mariposa
2 Mariposa on the way

Bagby, G.
INSPECTOR SCHMIDT SERIES:
1 Bachelor's widow
2 Murder at the piano
3 Murder half baked
4 Murder on the nose
5 Bird walking weather
6 Corpse with the purple thighs
7 The corpse wore a wig
8 Here comes the corpse
9 Red is for killing
10 Original carcase
11 Dead drunk 1954
12 The body in the basket 1956
13 Murder in wonderland 1965

Bagot, R.
1 The passport
2 Darneley Place

Bagster, H.
1 Country practice
2 Doctor's weekend
N.F. Autobiography

Bailey, H. C.
MR. FORTUNE SERIES:
1 Call Mr. Fortune
2 Mr. Fortune's practice
3 Mr. Fortune's trials
4 Mr. Fortune, please
5 Mr. Fortune speaking
6 Mr. Fortune explains
7 Case for Mr. Fortune
8 Mr. Fortune wonders
9 Shadow on the wall
10 Mr. Fortune objects
11 Clue for Mr. Fortune
12 Black land, white land
13 This is Mr. Fortune
14 The great game
15 Mr. Fortune here
16 The Bishop's crime
17 No murder [Apprehensive dog]
18 Mr. Fortune finds a pig
19 Dead man's effects
20 The life sentence
21 Saving a rope
22 Shrouded death
MR. CLUNK SERIES:
1 Garstons
2 The red castle
3 The sullen sky mystery
4 Clunk's claimant [Twittering bird mystery]
5 The Veron mystery
6 The little captain
7 Dead man's shoes
8 Slippery Ann
9 Honour among thieves
  "Fortune appears in 'Clunk's Claimant, and Clunk in 'The Great Game,' but they are not much concerned with each other." – Author

Bain, F. W.
INDIAN MYSTIC LOVE STORIES:
1 A digit of the moon
2 The descent of the sun
3 A heifer of the dawn
4 The Great God's heir
5 A draught of the blue
6 An essence of the dusk
7 An incarnation of the snow
8 A mine of faults
9 The ashes of a god
10 Bubbles of the foam
11 A syrup of the bees
12 The livery of Eve
13 The substance of a dream

Baines, F.
1 Look towards the sea
2 In deep
N.F. Autobiography

Baird, J. K.
1 The coming of Hester
2 Hester's counterpart
3 Hester's wage-earning

Baker, D. V.
1 The sea's in the kitchen
2 The door is always open
N.F. Autobiography

Baker, Mrs. E. I. A.
Fairmount series – 4 vols.

Baker, G.
1 Cry Hylas on the hills
2 Son of Hylas
3 Fidus Achates
A trilogy on the voyage of the Argonauts and the Trojan wars.

Baker, J.
1 The gleaming dawn
2 The Cardinal's page
Cardinal Henry Beaufort figures in both novels.

Baker, R. S. *see* Grayson, D., *pseud.*

Baker, R. St. B.
1 Kabongo
2 Kamiti

Balaam, *pseud.*
1 Chalk in my hair
2 Chalk gets in your eyes
N.F. Autobiography

Baldwin, F. *pseud.* [**F. B. Cuthrell**]
1 Conflict [American family]
2 The Puritan strain

Baldwin, J.
1 Notes of a native son
2 Nobody knows my name
N.F. Autobiography

Baldwin, M.
1 Granddad with snails
2 In step with a goat
N.F. Autobiography

Balgrave, R.
1 The wreck of the *Spa*
2 The burning of the *Spa* saloon

Ballew, C.
1 Rim-Fire rides
2 Rim-Fire sheriff
3 Rim-Fire detective
4 Rim-Fire of the Range
5 Rim-Fire and Six Guns
6 Rim-Fire roams
7 Rim-Fire ranchero
8 Rim-Fire fights
9 Rim-Fire horns in
10 Rim-Fire and Slats
11 Rim-Fire on the desert
12 Rim-Fire slips
13 Rim-Fire presides
14 Rim-Fire in Mexico
15 Rim-Fire gets them
16 Rim-Fire runs
17 Rim-Fire on the prod
18 Rim-Fire and the bear
19 Rim-Fire abstains

Balmer, E. *and* **P. Wylie**
1 When worlds collide
2 After worlds collide
Science Fiction

Balzac, H. de
THE HUMAN COMEDY
Balzac frequently altered the titles of his works and changed them from one division to another. Hereunder is the arrangement of works *actually written* as classified by the author in 1845. A slightly different arrangement with the volumes grouped as published in English, will be found in Baker & Packman Guide to the best fiction 1932.
SCENES OF PRIVATE LIFE:
1 At the sign of the Cat and Racket
2 The dance of Sceaux
3 Recollections of two young brides
4 The purse
5 Modeste Mignon
6 A start in life
7 Albert Savarus
8 The vendetta
9 A double family
10 The peace of the household

Balzac, H. de (*contd.*)

11 Madame Firmiani
12 A study of woman
13 The pretended mistress
14 A daughter of Eve
15 Colonel Chabert
16 The message
17 La Grenadière
18 The forsaken woman
19 Honorine
20 Béatrix
21 Gobseck
22 A woman of thirty
23 Old Goriot
24 Pierre Grasassou
25 The atheist's mass
26 The interdiction
27 The marriage contract
28 Another study of woman

SCENES OF PROVINCIAL LIFE:

1 The Lily of the Valley
2 Ursule Mirouet
3 Eugénie Grandet
4 The celibates
   Part 1. Pierrette
   Part 2. The Vicar of Tours
   Part 3. A bachelor's establishment
5 The Parisians in provincial France
   Part 1. Gaudissart the Great
   Part 2. Wrinkled people
   Part 3. The muse of the department
   Part 4. An actress abroad
6 The superior woman
7 The rivalries
   Part 3. The old maid. (Parts 1 and 2 not written).
8 The provincials in Paris
   Part 1. The cabinet of antiques (Part 2 not written).
9 Lost illusions
   Part 1. The two poets
   Part 2. A provincial great man in Paris.
   Part 3. An inventor's sufferings

SCENES OF PARISIAN LIFE:

1 History of the Thirteen
   Part 1. Ferragus
   Part 2. The Duchess of Langeais
   Part 3. The girl with the golden eyes
2 The employees
3 Sarrasine

4 Grandeur and downfall of César Birotteau
5 The house of Nucingen
6 Facino Cane
7 The secrets of the Princess of Cadignan
8 Splendours and miseries of courtesans
   Part 1. How harlots love
   Part 2. How much love costs old men
   Part 3. The end of bad roads
   Part 4. The last incarnation of Vautrin
9 The prince of Bohemia
10 The involuntary comedians
11 A sample of French familiar conversation
12 A petty bourgeois
13 The brothers of consolation: the seamy side of contemporary history

SCENES OF POLITICAL LIFE:

1 An episode under the Terror
2 A dark affair
3 The Deputy of Arcis
4 Z. Marcas

SCENES OF MILITARY LIFE:

1 The Chouans
2 A passion in the desert

SCENES OF COUNTRY LIFE:

1 The peasants
2 The country doctor
3 The village curé

PHILOSOPHIC STUDIES:

1 The wild ass's skin
2 Jesus Christ in Flanders
3 Melmoth reconciled
4 Massimilla Doni
5 The unknown masterpiece
6 Gambara
7 The quest of the absolute
8 A child accursed
9 Adieu
10 The Maranas
11 The conscript
12 The executioner
13 The seashore drama
14 Master Cornelius
15 The Red Inn
16 About Catherine de Medici
   Part 1. The Calvinist martyr
   Part 2. The confession of the Ruggieri
   Part 3. The two dreams
17 The elixir of long life

18 The exiles
19 Louis Lambert
20 Séraphita
POOR PARENTS SERIES:
1 Cousin Pons
2 Cousin Betty

Bamford, M. E.
1 The Look-out Club
2 The second year of the Look-out Club

Bancroft, F.
GERMANS IN SOUTH AFRICA SERIES:
1 An armed protest
2 Great possessions
SOUTH AFRICA TRILOGY:
1 The Veldt dwellers
2 Thane Brandon
3 Dalliance and strife

Banfield, E. J.
1 Confessions of a beachcomber
2 My tropic isle

Bangs, J. K. [A. W. Witherup]
HOUSEBOAT SERIES:
1 A houseboat on the Styx
2 The pursuit of the houseboat
MOLLIE SERIES:
1 Mollie and the unwisemen
2 Mollie and the unwisemen abroad

Baptist, R. H.
1 Four handsome negresses
2 Wild deer

Barbellion, W. N. P.
1 Journal of a disappointed man
2 Last diary
N.F. Autobiography

Barber, Mrs. H.
1 Drafted in
2 The bread winners

Barbette, J.
HARVEY BUTTEN SERIES:
1 Final copy
2 Dear dead days

Barclay, Mrs. F.
1 The rosary
2 Mistress of Shenstone
3 Following of the star

Barclay, V. C.
1 Danny, the detective
2 Danny again

Barcynska, Countess
1 The honey-pot
2 Love Maggy
3 Pretty dear
4 Back to the honey-pot

Bard, M.
1 Doctor wears three faces
2 Forty odd
3 Just be yourself 1957
N.F. Autobiography

Barea, A.
1 The track
2 The forge
3 The clash
Autobiography and source book of modern Spanish history.

Bark, C. V.
MR. HOLMES SERIES:
1 Mr. Holmes at sea 1962
2 Mr. Holmes goes to ground 1963
3 Mr. Holmes and the fair Armenian 1964
4 Mr. Holmes and the love bank 1964

Barke, J.
1 The wind that shakes the barley
2 The song in the green thorn tree
3 The wonder of all the gay world
4 The crest of the broken wave
5 The well of the silent harp
A series of novels on the life of Robert Burns.
6 Bonnie Jean 1958
Continues the Burns story with the story of his wife Jean Armour as a widow.

Barkeley, R.
THE DANUBIAN EMPIRE:
1 The Road to Mayerling
2 Sarajevo and Madeira

Barlow, J.
1 Irish idylls
2 Strangers at Lisconnel
3 From the East unto the West
☐
1 Kerrigan's quality
2 The founding of fortunes

Barnard, C.
1 The soprano
2 Money and music

Barnes, J. S.
1 Half a life
2 Half a life left
N.F. Autobiography

Barnum, P. T.
1 Lion Jack
2 Jack in the jungle

Baroja, P.
THE STRUGGLE FOR LIFE TRILOGY:
1 The quest
2 Weeds
3 Red dawn
There are many sequels by Baroja, but no others have been completely translated. The best known series is 'Memoirs of a Man of action.' 22 Vols.

Baron, A.
HARRYBOY BOAS:
1 The lowlife 1964
2 Strip Jack naked 1966

Barr, A. E.
NEW YORK IN 1756 SERIES:
1 The bow of orange ribbon
2 The maid of Maiden Lane
3 Song of a single note
SHETLAND SERIES:
1 Jan Vedder's wife
2 Sheila Vedder

Barr, R.
THE RHINE AND THE MOSELLE (14TH CENTURY) SERIES:
The Archbishop of Cologne appears in
1 The Countess Tekla
2 The strong arm
3 The sword maker

STRANLEIGH SERIES:
1 Young Lord Stranleigh
2 Stranleigh's millions
3 Lord Stranleigh, philanthropist
4 Lord Stranleigh abroad

Barren, C.
THE STEMSTON FAMILY:
1 Eighty North 1959
2 Jamestown 1960

Barrie, Sir J. M.
PETER PAN SERIES:
1 Peter Pan in Kensington Gardens
2 Peter and Wendy
THRUMS (FORFARSHIRE) BOOKS:
1 Auld licht idylls
2 A window in Thrums
3 The little minister
4 Sentimental Tommy
5 Tommy and Grizel (*sequel to* Sentimental Tommy)

Barringer, L.
NEUSTRICE SERIES:
1 Gerfalon
2 Sons of the rock
3 Shy leopardess

Barry, C.
INSPECTOR GILMARTIN SERIES:
1 The smaller penny
2 The detective's holiday
3 The Mauls house mystery
4 The witness at the window
5 The corpse on the bridge
6 The avenging ikon
7 The ghost of a clue
8 The boat train mystery
9 A case dead and buried
10 The dead have no mouths
11 Death in darkness
12 Death overseas
13 Nicholas Lattermole's case
14 Wrong murder mystery

Barry, J.
CHICK NOLAN SERIES:
1 Murder with your malted
2 Leopard's cats-cradle
3 Lady of night

Barstow, S.
1 A kind of loving 1962
2 The watchers on the shore 1965
Two novels on love and marriage.

Bartimeus *pseud.* [**L. A. da C. Ricci**]
1 Naval occasions
2 A tall ship
3 Unreality
4 Long trick
5 Sure shield
6 Awfully big adventure

Bartlett, V.
1 This is my life
2 And now, tomorrow 1962
3 Tuscan retreat 1964
N.F. Autobiography

Barton, G.
1 The strange adventures of Bromley Barnes
2 The Pembroke Mason affair
3 The ambassador's trunk

Baruch, B. M.
1 My own story
2 The public years
N.F. Autobiography

Bassani, G.
1 A prospect of Ferrara 1965
2 The gold-rimmed spectacles 1965
3 The garden of the Fingi-Continis 1965
4 Dietro la porta (not yet trans.)
*'In a sense they are all part of one book –
the protagonist, the "I" is recognisably
the same character. The city described
is always the same one, Ferrara in the
time of Signor Bassani's youth. More-
over the same characters appear over
and over again, sometimes as major
personages, sometimes as background
figures. This may give the impression
that Signor Bassani is engaged on a
"Roman Fleuve". This is not so since
his books have no consistent time
sequence.' Times Literary Supplement.*

Bassett, S. W.
CAPE COD SERIES:
1 The taming of Zenas Henry

2 The wayfarers at the Angels
3 The harbor road
4 Flood tide
5 Granite and clay
6 The green dolphin
7 Bayberry Lane
8 Twin lights
9 Shifting sands
10 Turning tide
11 Hidden shoals
12 Eternal deeps
13 Shining headlands
14 Ocean heritage
15 White sail
*Separate novels with locality as the
connection.*

Basso, H.
1 Light infantry ball 1959
2 Pompey's Head [The view from
Pompey's Head] 1954
*The connection is the town of Pompey's
Head. Some characters in 1 are ancestors
of those in 2.*

Batchelor, D.
DET.-INSPECTOR JOHNSON SERIES:
1 The man who loved chocolates 1962
2 On the brink 1964
3 The sedulous ape 1965

Bates, A.
1 The Pagans
2 The Philistines

Bates, D.
1 A Fly-switch from the Sultan
2 The Mango and the palm

Bates, H. E.
LARKIN FAMILY SERIES:
1 The darling buds of May 1958
2 A breath of French air 1959
3 When the green woods laugh 1961
4 Oh! to be in England 1963
□
1 My uncle Silas
2 Sugar for the horse

Bax, C.
1 Evenings in Albany
2 Rosemary for remembrance
N.F. Autobiography

Bayer, O. W.
1 Paper/chase
2 No little enemy

Bayley, E. B.
1 Zachary Brough's venture
2 Forestwyk

Bazan, Madame E. P.
1 The son of a bondwoman
2 La Madre Natureleza

Bazin, R.
1 The nun (L'isolée)
2 The coming harvest
3 Redemption (De toute son âme)

Beachcomber, *pseud. see* Morton, J. B.

**Beaconsfield, Benjamin Disraeli,
1st Earl of,** *see* Disraeli, B., 1st Earl of
Beaconsfield

Beale, A.
1 The Queen of the May
2 May Goldsworthy

Bearne, D.
1 A Ridingdale year
2 Lance and his friends

Beaton, C.
1 The wandering years
2 The years between
N.F. Autobiography

Beauvoir, S. de
1 Memoirs of a dutiful daughter
2 The prime of life 1963
3 Force of circumstance 1965
N.F. Autobiography

Beckett, S.
1 Molloy
2 Malone dies
3 The unnamable
Later published in one vol. 1959.

Beckwith, L.
1 The hills is lonely 1959
2 The sea for breakfast 1961

3 The loud halo 1964
N.F. Autobiography
*The story of a schoolteacher's retirement
to the Hebrides.*

Beecham, J. C.
1 The Argus pheasant
2 The yellow spider

Beeding, F.
COLONEL GRANBY SERIES:
1 One sane man
2 The two undertakers
3 Three fishers
4 Four armourers
5 Five flamboys
6 Six proud walkers
7 Seven sleepers
8 Eight crooked trenches
9 Nine waxed faces
10 The ten holy horrors
11 Eleven were brave
12 The twelve disguises
13 There are thirteen

Begbie, H.
1 Bundy in the greenwood
2 Bundy on the sea

Behaine, R.
HISTORY OF A SOCIETY:
1 The survivors
2 The conquest of life
3 The day of glory
*These are the only volumes published in
English of Behaine's great work. They
are nos. 2, 4 and 12 in the French
edition of 12 volumes. In the preface
to 'The day of glory' will be found
notes on all the volumes in the series as
follows:*
1 Les nouveaux Venus (Alfred Varambaud, Celine Armelle, Michel
Varambaud)
2 Les survivants
3 Se jeanesse savait
4 La conquête de la vie
5 L'enchantment du feu
6 Avec les yeux de 'l'esprit
7 Au prix même du bonheur
8 Dans la foule horrible des hommes
9 La solitude et le silence

10 Les signes dans le ciel
11 O peuple infortune
12 Le jour de gloire

Behan, B.
1 Borstal boy
2 The confessions of an Irish rebel 1965
N.F. Autobiography

Behrens, M.
PERCIVAL SOAMES SERIES:
1 In masquerade
2 Puck in petticoats

Bell, A.
1 Corduroy
2 Silver ley
3 The cherry tree
4 Apple acre
5 Sunrise to sunset
ROLAND PACE SERIES:
1 The balcony
2 Young man's fancy 1956
3 The mill house 1958

Bell, C. D.
1 Cousin Kate
2 Autumn at Carnford

Bell, J.
DR. DAVID WINTRINGHAM SERIES:
1 Murder in hospital
2 Fall over cliff
3 Death on the Borough Council
4 Death at half-term
5 From natural causes
6 All is vanity
7 Trouble at Wrekin farm
8 Death on the medical board
9 Death in clairvoyance
10 Summer school mystery
11 Bones in the barrow

Bell, J. J.
1 Wee Macgreegor
2 Wee Macgreegor again. *Same as* Later adventures of Macgreegor.
3 Wee Macgreegor enlists
☐
1 Oh, Christina!
2 Courtin' Christina
☐

1 Mr. Craw
2 Mr. and Mrs. Craw

Bell, V.
1 The Dodo
2 This way home
N.F. Autobiography
DR. BAYNES SERIES:
1 Death under the stars 1949
2 Two by day and one by night 1950
3 Death has two doors 1950
4 Death darkens council 1962
5 Death o' the night watches 1959
6 Death walks by the river 1959

Bellairs, G.
DET. INSPECTOR THOMAS LITTLEJOHN SERIES:
1 Littlejohn on leave
2 The four unfaithful servants
3 The dead shall be raised
4 Turmoil in Zion
5 Murder of a quack
6 Calamity at Harwood
7 Death of a busybody
8 He'd rather be dead
9 Death in High Provence
10 Bones in the wilderness
11 Toll the bell for murder 1959
12 Death in despair 1960
13 The body in the dumb river 1961
14 The tormentors 1962
15 Death in the fearful night 1962
16 Death in the wasteland 1963
17 Death spins the wheel 1965
18 Death of an intruder 1965
19 Intruder in the dark 1966
   Supt. Littlejohn in later volumes.

Bellamann, N. H.
1 King's Row
2 Parris Mitchell of King's Row, completed by Katherine Bellamann.

Bellamy, E.
1 Looking backward
2 Equality
Several rejoinders have been written on this series.

Belot, A.
1 The stranglers of Paris
2 Grand Florine

Bennett, E. A.

FIVE TOWNS SERIES:
Difference of opinion exists as to the reading order of this series. Hereunder is the author's own arrangement.

NOVELS:
1 A man from the north
2 Anna of the Five Towns
3 Leonora
4 A great man
5 Whom God hath joined
6 Sacred and profane love
7 The old wives' tale
8 Helen with the high hand
9 Clayhanger
10 The card
11 Hilda Lessways
12 The Regent
13 The price of love
14 These twain
15 The roll call

SEQUELS:
1 Clayhanger
2 Hilda Lessways
3 These twain
4 The roll call
   4 is about the son of Hilda Lessways by a previous marriage.
☐
1 The card
2 The Regent
☐
1 Riceyman Steps
2 Elsie and the child

SHORT STORIES:
1 Tales of the Five Towns
2 The grim smile of the Five Towns
3 The matador of the Five Towns

Bennett, R. A.
1 Into the primitive
2 Out of the primitive
☐
1 Branded wolf
2 Border wolf
3 Gold wolf
4 Hunted wolf

Bennett, R.
1 Adventures of Lieut. Lawless, R.N.
2 Commander Lawless, V.C.

Bennett, S.
1 Alscott experiment
2 Sea to Eden

Benson, A. C.
MOLLY DAVENANT SERIES:
1 The house of Menerdue
2 The Canon

Benson, B.
RALPH LINDSAY SERIES:
1 The girl in the cage 1954
2 The silver cobweb 1955
3 Broken shield 1955
4 The running man 1957
5 The end of violence 1959
6 Seven steps last 1959

Benson, B. K.
AMERICAN CIVIL WAR SERIES:
1 Who goes there?
2 A friend with the countersign

Benson, E. F.
DODO SERIES:
1 Dodo
2 Dodo the second. *Same as* Dodo's daughter.
GREEK WAR OF INDEPENDENCE SERIES:
1 The vintage
2 Capsina
SCHOOL LIFE SERIES:
1 David Blaize and the blue door
2 David Blaize
3 David of King's
☐
1 Colin
2 Colin the second
LUCIA SERIES:
1 Queen Lucia
2 Miss Mapp
3 Lucia in London
4 Mapp and Lucia
5 Lucia's progress. [Worshipful Lucia].
6 Trouble for Lucia
OLD LONDON SERIES:
1 Portrait of an English nobleman [Georgian]
2 Janet [Victorian]
3 Friend of the rich [Mid-Victorian]
4 The unwanted [Edwardian]

Benson, R. H.
1 Sentimentalists
2 Conventionalists

Bensusan, S. L.
1 Joan Winter
2 Maurice Dravidoff

Bentley, E. C.
1 Trent's last case
2 Trent's own case
3 Trent intervenes

Bentley, J.
SIR RICHARD HARRWELL SERIES:
1 The Berg case
2 The Lestrange case
3 The Opperman case
4 The Fairbairn case
5 The Landor case
6 The Griffith case
7 The Radcliffe case
8 The Whitelney case
9 Prelude to trouble
10 The Harland case
DICK MARLOW SERIES:
1 Dangerous waters
2 Front page murder
3 Rendezvous with death
4 Macedonian mix-up
5 Dead do talk
GLEN GIBSON SERIES:
1 Bullets make holes
2 Pattern for perfidy
3 Dead harvest
4 Call off the corpse
5 It was murder, they said
6 It never works out

Bentley, P.
WEST RIDING SERIES:
1 Panorama
2 Take courage. [Power and the glory]
3 Manhold
4 The house of Moreys
5 Inheritance
6 Carr
7 Life story
8 The spinner of the years
9 A modern tragedy
10 Sleep in peace
11 The rise of Henry Morcar

12 Quorum
13 Noble in reason
14 Love and money
15 Crescendo
16 Kith and kin 1960
17 A man of his times 1966
*This is the author's own arrangement.
Except for nos. 5, 11, and 17, which
form a trilogy, characters do not reappear,
but the series gives a picture of West
Riding life from the 17th century to the
present day. 'The partnership' and 'Trio'
are not part of the series, but serve to
contribute background material to the
West Riding picture.*

☐
1 Environment
2 Cat-in-the-manger

Benzoni, J.
1 One love is enough 1963
2 Catherine 1963
3 Belle Catherine 1966
*Historical novels about France in the
time of Joan of Arc.*

Beresford, J. D.
JACOB STAHL TRILOGY:
1 Early history of Jacob Stahl
2 A candidate for truth
3 The invisible event
THE HILLINGTONS TRILOGY:
1 The old people
2 The middle generation
3 The young people
*'There are various cross-references to
characters and places in other novels
of mine, but not sufficient inter-
dependence to make them "sequels."'
Author.*

Berger, J.
1 The foot of Clive 1963
2 Corker's freedom 1964

Berkeley, A.
ROGER SHERINGHAM SERIES:
1 The Wychford poisoning case
2 Roger Sheringham and the Vane
mystery
3 The silk stocking murders
4 The second shot

Berkeley, A. (*contd.*)
5 Murder in the basement
6 Top storey murder
7 Panic
8 Jumping Jenny
Roger Sheringham also appears in 'The Layton Court mystery,' first published anonymously.

Berkley, T.
1 We kept a pub
2 I go on the films
3 We cope with the kids
N.F. Autobiography

Berlin, I.
1 I am Lazarus
2 The dark monarch
N.F. Autobiography

Bernanos, G.
THE SPIRITUAL LIFE:
1 The star of Satan
2 Joy
3 Diary of a country priest
'L'Imposture', no. 2 in the French series, has not been translated.

Berners, G. H. T.–W., 4th Baron
1 First childhood
2 A distant prospect
N.F. Autobiography

Berrey, Mrs. M. E.
1 Crooked and straight
2 The crook straightened

Berstl, J.
LIFE OF ST. PAUL:
1 The tentmaker
2 The cross and the eagle

Best, R.
THE YARROW SERIES:
1 The house called Yarrow 1961
2 The honest rogue 1962
3 High tide 1964
4 Idle rainbow 1965

Betteridge, D.
'TIGER' LESTER SERIES:
1 Balkan spy

2 The escape of General Gerard
3 Dictator's destiny
4 The Potsdam murder plot
5 Spies left!
6 Not single spies
7 Spy-counter-spy
8 The case of the Berlin spy

Bevan, T.
1 The beggars of the sea
2 The Grey Fox of Holland

Beyle, H., *see* Stendhal, *pseud.*

Biggers, E. D.
CHARLIE CHAN SERIES:
1 House without a key
2 The Chinese parrot
3 Behind that curtain
4 The black camel
5 Charlie Chan carries on
6 Keeper of the keys

Binstead, A. M.
1 Gal's gossip
2 More gal's gossip

Birmingham, G. A.
pseud. [**J. O. Hannay**]
GORMAN, M.P. SERIES:
1 Gossamer
2 Island mystery
3 Lady bountiful
Contains three short stories in the series.
J. J. MELDRUM SERIES:
1 Spanish gold
2 The Simpkins plot
3 The Major's niece
4 The Major's candlesticks
5 A sea battle
'General John Regan' and 'The adventures of Dr. Whitty' include Major Kent as a character.

Bishop, M.
1 It's a dog's life
2 Love in the dog house

Bisset, Sir J.
1 Sail ho!
2 Tramps and ladies
3 Commodore's farewell
N.F. Autobiography

Bjarnhof, K.
1 The stars grow pale 1957
2 The good light 1959
The story of a blind boy growing up in Copenhagen in the early 1900's.

Bjorkman, E. A.
1 The soul of a child
2 Gates of life

Black, G.
PAUL HARRIS SERIES:
1 Suddenly at Singapore
2 Dead man calling 1961
3 A dragon for Christmas 1962

Black, L.
1 Mr. Preed investigates
2 Mr. Preed's gangster

Black, M.
RICK VANESS SERIES:
1 Dead on course
2 Sinister cargo
3 Shadow of evil
4 Steps in the dark

Black, W.
1 A princess of Thule
2 The maid of Kileena

Blackburn, J.
GENERAL KIRKE:
1 The gaunt woman 1962
2 Colonel Bogus 1963

Blackmore, R. D.
1 Lorna Doone
2 Tales from the telling-house
Containing:
(a) Slain by the Doones, (b) Frida, (c) George Bowring, (d) Crocker's Hole.

Blackwood, A.
1 The education of Uncle Paul
2 A prisoner in Fairyland
A sequel in the sense that this is the book 'Uncle Paul' is presumed to have written.
□
1 Julius Le Vallon
2 The bright messenger

Blair, T.
1 Belinda
2 Belinda engaged

Blake *pseud.* [**John Strachey**]
1 Readiness at dawn
2 Rendezvous at ten

Blake, F.
1 Johnny Christmas
2 Wilderness passage

Blake, G.
1 The constant Star
2 The westering Sun

Blake, Mrs. H. N. W. *see* Leslie, Mrs. M.

Blake, N. M.
1 The siege of Norwich Castle
2 The sorrow and the glory of Norwich

Blake, Nigel
NIGEL STRANGEWAYS SERIES:
1 A question of proof
2 Thou shell of death
3 There's trouble brewing
4 The beast must die
5 The Smiler with the knife
6 Malice in wonderland. [Summer camp mystery].
7 The case of the abominable snowman
8 Minute for murder
9 Head of a traveller
10 The dreadful hollow
11 The whisper in the gloom
12 End of a chapter 1958
13 Widow's cruise 1959
14 The worm of death 1960

Blaker, R.
1 Here lies a most beautiful lady
2 But beauty vanishes

Blamires, H.
TRILOGY ON HEAVEN AND HELL:
1 The devil's hunting ground 1954
2 Cold war in Hell 1955
3 Blessing unbounded 1956
□
1 Kirkbride conversations
2 Kirkbride and company

Blanc, S.

MIGUEL MERNANDES SERIES:
1 The green stone 1963
2 The yellow villa 1964

Blasco Ibanez, V.

1 The temptress
2 Queen Calafia

SPANISH HISTORY SERIES:
1 The pope of the sea
2 The Borgias
3 Unknown lands
4 The knight of the virgin
   '*A series conceived as an epic of Spanish heroes and deeds*' – Oxford dictionary of modern European literature.

VALENCIA SERIES:
1 The three roses (Arroy tartana)
2 The Mayflower
3 The cabin
4 The torrent (Entre naranjos)
5 Reeds and mud
   A series about different aspects of the same region.

CATHOLIC CHURCH IN SPAIN TRILOGY:
1 The shadow of the cathedral
2 The intruder
3 The fruit of the vine

Bleakley, H.

1 Tales of the stumps
2 More tales of the stumps

Bligh, E.

1 Tooting corner
2 Faintly smiling mouth
N.F. Autobiography

Blish, J.

CITIES IN FLIGHT:
1 They shall have stars
2 A life for the stars
3 Earthman come home
4 A clash of cymbals
Science Fiction
   Connected novels. Parts of these have been published in magazine form under other titles.

Bloom, U.

1 Time, tide and I
2 Trilogy 1954

3 Down to the sea in ships 1957
4 Youth at the gate 1959
5 War isn't wonderful 1961
N.F. Autobiography

NO LADY SERIES:
1 Log of no lady 1940
2 No lady buys a cot 1943
3 No lady in bed 1944
4 No lady with a pen 1947
5 No lady meets no gentleman 1947
6 No lady in the cart 1949
7 Mum's girl was no lady 1950
8 No lady on the spree 1954
9 No lady has a dogs day 1956
N.F. Autobiography

Blumenfeld, J.

1 Pin a rose on me
2 See me dance the polka 1962
N.F. Autobiography

Blyth, J.

1 Thrift
2 Respectability

Boardman, Mrs. M. M.

1 Haps and mishaps of the Brown family
2 Sister's triumph

Bodkin, M. M.

PAUL BECK SERIES:
1 Paul Beck
2 The quests of Paul Beck
3 The capture of Paul Beck
4 Young Beck
   Dora Angel appears in 'Dora Angel, lady detective', and in 3 and 4 above.

ANOTHER SERIES:
1 Lord Edward Fitzgerald
2 The rebels

Boileau, E.

1 Hippy Buchan
2 The arches of the years
   □
1 Turnip tops
2 Ballade in D minor

Bojer, J.

1 The great hunger
2 The new temple

Boland, J.
1 Counterpol 1963
2 Counterpol in Paris 1964
☐
1 League of gentlemen 1960
2 The gentlemen reform 1961
3 The gentlemen at large 1962

Bonavia-Hunt, D. *see*
Hunt, D. Bonavia-

Bone, E.
1 Thirty years hard 1964
2 Seven years solitary 1960
N.F. Autobiography
Order of events, not publication.

Bonney, J.
SIMON ROLFE SERIES:
1 Death by dynamite
2 No man's hand

Bonsels, W.
1 Maya, the Bee
2 Heaven folk

Boothby, G.
DR. NIKOLA SERIES:
1 A bid for fortune
2 Dr. Nikola
3 The lust of hate
4 Dr. Nikola's experiment
5 Farewell Nikola
In 'The Times' for 20th December,
1956, there is an article by 'Oliver
Edwardes' on the 'Dr. Nikola' series.

Boothroyd, D.
1 Value for money 1955
2 Shoddy kingdom 1957
Novels about the woollen industry in
the West Riding. Not otherwise sequels.

Borden, M.
1 Mary of Nazareth
2 King of the Jews

Borrow, G.
1 Lavengro
2 Romany Rye

Borton, E., *see* Porter, E. H.

Bosher, Mrs. K. L.
1 Mary Carey
2 Miss Gibie Gault

Bottome, P.
1 Search for a soul
2 Challenge
N.F. Autobiography

Bourne, L. R.
COPPERKNOB SERIES:
1 Copperknob Buckland
2 Copperknob second mate
3 Captain Copperknob
4 Copperknob: shipowner

Bourne, P.
1 Black saga
2 Ten thousand shall die
Henry Stewart, the hero of 2 is the son
of Duncan Stewart of 1.

Boussenard, L.
1 The crusoes of Guiana
2 The gold seekers

Bowen M. (Mrs. G. M. Long)
WILLIAM OF ORANGE SERIES:
1 Prince and heretic
2 William, by the grace of God
WILLIAM III OF ENGLAND SERIES:
1 I will maintain
2 Defender of the faith
3 God and the king
RENAISSANCE TRILOGY:
1 The golden roof
2 The triumphant beast
3 Trumpets at Rome
☐
1 God and the wedding dress
2 Mr. Tyler's saints
3 Circle on the water
☐
1 Exchange Royal
2 To-day is mine
FRENCH REVOLUTION SERIES:
Under the name of George Preedy
1 Laurell'd captains
2 Primula
Under the name of Marjorie Bowen
3 A giant in chains
Though not strictly sequels, these three
novels cover the period of the 1789
revolution.

Bower, B. M. (Mrs. B. M. Sinclair)
1 Casey Ryan
2 Tale of the white mule
☐
1 Meadowlark basin
2 White wolves
☐
1 Skyrider
2 The thunder bird
FLYING U SERIES:
1 Chip of the Flying U
2 The lonesome trail
3 Flying U ranch
4 Flying U's last stand
5 Heritage of the Sioux
6 The phantom herd
7 Dark horse
8 The Flying U strikes
9 Trouble rides the range
10 Whoop-up trail
11 Spirit of the range
Bower, U. G.
1 The Naga path
2 The hidden land
N.F. *Travel*

Bowers, D.
INSPECTOR PARDOE SERIES:
1 Postscript to poison
2 Shadows before
3 A deed without a name
4 Fear for Miss Betony

Box, E.
PETER CUTLER SERGEANT II SERIES:
1 Death in the fifth position
2 Death before bedtime
3 Death likes it hot

Boyd, J.
1 Drums
2 Marching on
James Fraser of 2 is a descendent of John Fraser of 1.

Boyd, M.
THE LANGTONS:
1 The cardboard crown
2 A difficult young man
3 Outbreak of love 1957
4 Much in evidence 1957
A series of novels about an Anglo-
Australian family. Characters change in all the novels.

Boyd, T. A.
1 Through the wheat
2 In time of peace

Bradby, G. F.
1 Dick
2 For this I had borne him

Braddon, M. E. (Mrs. J. Maxwell)
1 Birds of prey
2 Charlotte's inheritance

Braddon, R.
1 The naked island
2 End of a hate
N.F. *Autobiography*

Bradley, E.
1 The adventures of Mr. Verdant Green
2 Little Mr. Bouncer and his friend, Mr. Verdant Green

Bradley, Mrs. M. E. N.
PROVERB SERIES:
1 Birds of a feather
2 Handsome is that handsome does
3 A wrong confessed
OLD CHICAGO SERIES:
1 The fort
2 The duel
3 Debt of honor
4 Metropolis

Bradley, S.
1 The adventures of an A.D.C.
2 More adventures of an A.D.C.

Braine, J.
JOE LAMPTON:
1 Room at the top 1959
2 Life at the top 1962

Brainerd, E. C.
1 Concerning Belinda
2 The personal conduct of Belinda
☐
1 The misdemeanors of Nancy
2 Nancy's country Christmas

Braithwaite, E. R.

1 To sir, with love
2 Paid servant
N.F. Autobiography

Bramah, E.

KAI LUNG SERIES:

1 The wallet of Kai Lung
2 Kai Lung's golden hours
3 Kai Lung unrolls his mat
4 Kai Lung beneath the mulberry
tree
'*The celestial omnibus,*' *1963 is a selection from the above.*

MAX CARRADOS SERIES:

1 Max Carrados
2 The eyes of Max Carrados
3 Specimen case
4 Max Carrados mysteries
5 The bravo of London

Brand, C.

INSPECTOR COCKRILL SERIES:

1 Death in high heels
2 Heads you lose
3 Green for danger
4 Suddenly at his residence
5 Death of Jezebel
6 Cat and mouse
7 London particular
8 Tour de force 1955

Brand, M.

1 The untamed
2 The night horseman
3 The seventh man

DR. KILDARE SERIES:

1 The secret of Dr. Kildare
2 Calling Dr. Kildare
3 Young Dr. Kildare
4 Dr. Kildare takes charge
5 Dr. Kildare's crisis
6 Dr. Kildare's trial
7 Dr. Kildare's search

SILVERTIP SERIES:

1 Silvertip
2 Silvertip's strike
3 Silvertip's round-up
4 Silvertip's trap
5 The fighting four
6 Silvertip's chase
7 Silvertip's search

8 The stolen stallion
9 Mountain riders
10 Valley thieves
11 Valley of vanishing men
12 The false rider

Brandon, J. G.

INSPECTOR MCCARTHY SERIES:

1 The blue print murders
2 Candidate for a coffin
3 The crooked fire
4 The case of the withering hand
5 Death burns swiftly
6 Death in the quarry
7 Death in duplicate
8 Death on delivery
9 The dragnet
10 The espionage killings
11 The £50 marriage case
12 The frame up
13 Fingerprints never lie
14 The hand of Seeta
15 The mail van mystery
16 The mark of the fang
17 Murder at the Yard
18 Murder in Soho
19 Murder for a million
20 McCarthy, C.I.D.
21 The night club murder
22 The Regent St. raid
23 A scream in Soho
24 The transport murders 1955
25 Yellow Gods 1956
26 Bonus for murder 1957
27 The corpse from the city 1958

A. S. PENNINGTON SERIES:

1 The Cork St. crime
2 Death in the ditch
3 Mr. Pennington goes nap
4 Mr. Pennington comes through
5 Mr. Pennington barges in
6 Mr. Pennington sees red
7 The riverside mystery
8 Murder in Mayfair
9 One-minute murder
10 The pawnshop murder
11 The 'snatch' game
12 The Bond St. murders
13 Death in D division
14 Death in Downing St.
15 Death in Jermyn St.
16 Death foils the gang

Brandon, J. G. (*contd.*)
17 M for murder
18 Case of would-be widow
19 The coffin rode on
20 Murderers stand in
21 Death of a Greek
22 Murder comes smiling 1959
23 Death of a mermaid 1960

Branson, H. C.
JOHN BENT SERIES:
1 I'll eat you last
2 The pricking thumb
3 The case of the giant killer
4 The fearful passage
5 Last year's blood
6 The leaden bubble

Bratby, J.
PETER CARR:
1 Breakfast and elevenses 1960
2 Brake pedal down 1962

Brathwaite, E.
1 The flying fish 1963
2 The needle's eye 1965
First two volumes of a trilogy on the Maori wars in New Zealand.

Brebner, P. J.
1 Christopher Quarles
2 The master detective

Bremond D Ars, Y de
1 In the heart of Paris 1959
2 An antique dealer's tale 1961
3 The chest with a secret 1964
N.F. Anecdotes of antique dealing in Paris.

Brent, N.
BARNEY HYDE SERIES:
1 The scarlet lily
2 Motive for murder
3 Blood in the bank
4 Dig the grave deep
5 Murder swings high
6 The leopard died too 1957
7 The golden angel 1959
8 Badger in the dusk 1960
9 Spider in the web 1961

Brent of Bin Bin, *pseud.*
BERT POOLE SERIES:
1 Up the country
2 Ten creeks run
3 Ten creeks
4 Cockatoos
5 Gentlemen at Gyang Gyang
6 Back to Bool Bool

Bresler, F.
1 Within the law
2 Strictly legal
3 Strictly illegal

Brett, M.
HUGO BARON SERIES:
1 Diecast 1964
2 A plague of dragons 1965

Bridge, A.
JULIA PROBYN SERIES:
1 The lighthearted quest 1956
2 The Portuguese quest 1958
3 The numbered account 1960
4 The dangerous islands 1964
5 Emergency in the Pyrenees 1965
(*Miss Probyn becomes Julia Jamieson*)

Bridges, R.
AUSTRALIAN TRILOGY:
1 And all that beauty
2 Negrohead
3 Trinity

Briffault, R.
1 Europa
2 Europa in limbo

Bright, P.
1 Life in our hands 1955
2 Breakfast at night 1956
3 The day's end 1959
N.F. Autobiography

Brinig, M.
1 Singermann
2 Sons of Singermann [This man is my brother]

Brinton, H.
JOHN STRANG SERIES:
1 Death to windward
2 One down and two to slay
3 Now like to die 1955
4 Coppers and gold 1957
5 Drug on the market 1958

Bristow, G.
LOUISIANA TRILOGY:
1 Deep summer
2 The handsome road
3 This side of glory

Brittain, Sir H.
1 Pilgrims and pioneers
2 Happy pilgrimage
'Pilgrim partners' is also autobio-graphical, but mainly about the Pilgrims' Society.

Brittain, V.
1 Testament of youth
2 Testament of experience
N.F. Autobiography

Broch, H.
THE SLEEPWALKERS:
1 The romantic
2 The anarchist
3 The realist

Brock, L.
COLONEL GORE SERIES:
1 The deductions of Colonel Gore
2 Colonel Gore's second case
3 Colonel Gore's third case: the link
4 The slip-carriage mystery
5 The Dagwort Combe mystery
6 The Mendip mystery
7 Q.E.D. [Murder on the bridge]
8 The stoat
INSPECTOR MCIVER AND SERGEANT
BENN SERIES:
1 The silver sickle case
2 Four fingers
3 The riddle of the roost

Brockway, F.
1 Inside the left 1960
2 Outside the right 1962
N.F. Autobiography

Brode, A.
1 Picture of a country vicarage 1956
2 To bed on Thursday 1958
N.F. Autobiography

Broderick, A. H.
1 Little China
2 Little vehicle
N.F. Travel in Indo-China

Bromfield, L.
ESCAPE SERIES:
1 Green bay tree
2 Possession [Lilli Barr]
3 Early autumn
4 Good woman
FARMING SERIES:
1 Pleasant valley
2 Malabar farm
3 Out of the earth
4 Pleasures and miseries of life on a farm
A series of books about the author's experience as a farmer.

Brooke, C.
THE MARSHALL FAMILY:
1 As others see us
2 The changing tide
3 Bitter summer
4 The way of life 1956

Brooke, J.
1 The military orchid
2 A mine of serpents
3 The goose cathedral
Best described as a mixture of fiction and autobiography.

Brookes, E.
1 Proud waters
2 The glass years
1 is a war novel. Of 2 the author says, 'I have tried to follow the story of a few of the characters in 'Proud waters'.

Brooks, C.
RAEBURN STEEL SERIES:
1 Mr. X
2 The body snatcher
3 The ghost hunters
□
1 Tavern talk
2 More tavern talk
N.F. Essays

Brooks, J.
1 Jampot Smith 1962
2 Smith, as hero 1964
The diary of a young man, first in adolescence and then as a young naval officer in World War II

Brooks, V. W.
1 Scenes and portraits
2 Days of the phoenix
3 From the shadow of the mountain
N.F. Autobiography

Brophy, J.
1 Green glory
2 Green ladies

Broster, D. K.
'FORTY-FIVE' SERIES:
1 The flight of the heron
2 The gleam in the north
3 The dark mile
□
1 The sea without a haven
2 The captain's lady

Broun, D.
HARRY EGYPT, MASTER CRIMINAL:
1 The subject of Harry Egypt 1963
2 Egypt's choice 1964

Brown, A. J.
1 I bought a hotel
2 Farewell Highfell
Two books on hotel keeping.

Brown, C.
THE BUNYAN'S TALKS:
1 The wonderful journey
2 Children on the King's highway
3 The oldest city in the world

Brown, C. Rae-
1 Kissing-cup's race
2 Kissing-cup the second

Brown, E.
1 Knave of clubs
2 Out of the bag
N.F. Autobiography

Brown, F.
ED HUNTER SERIES:
1 The fabulous clipjoint 1947
2 The dead ringer 1948
3 The late lamented 1957

Brown, R. W.
EMERGENCE SERIES:
1 The firemakers
2 Toward romance
3 The Hillikin
4 As of the gods

Brown, W.
1 Duffers on the deep
2 No distress signals
3 Under six planets 1955
N.F. Autobiography

Browne, B.
1 The quest of the Golden Valley
2 The white blanket

Browne, D. G.
MR. HARVEY TUKE SERIES:
1 Too many cousins
2 What beckoning ghost
3 Rustling end
4 Death in perpetuity
5 Death in seven volumes 1958
6 Sergeant Death 1961

Browne, E. O.
1 The broken cup
2 When the saints slept

Browne, G. W.
1 The woodranger
2 The young gun-bearer
3 The hero of the hills

Bruce, H.
EURASIAN TRILOGY:
1 The residency 1914
2 The song of surrender 1915
3 The 'Wonder Mist' 1917
□
1 The temple girl 1919
2 The bride of Shiva 1920

Bruce, H. J.
1 Silken dalliance
2 Thirty dozen moons
N.F. Autobiography

Bruce, J.
SECRET AGENT OSS 17:
1 Deep freeze 1963
2 Short wave 1964
3 Double take 1964
4 Flash point 1965
5 Pole reaction 1965
6 Shock tactics 1965

Bruce, L.
CAROLUS DEANE SERIES:
1 Cold blood
2 At death's door
3 Death of cold
4 Dead for a ducat 1956
5 Dead man's shoes 1958
6 A louse for the hangman 1959
7 Our justice is death 1959
8 Jack or the gallows tree 1960
9 Nothing like blood 1961
10 Crack of doom 1962
11 Death at Hallows End 1965
12 Death on the black sands 1966
SERGEANT BEEF SERIES:
1 Case for three detectives
2 Case without a corpse
3 Case with no conclusion
4 Case with four clowns
5 Case with ropes and rings
6 Case for Sergeant Beef
7 Neck for neck
8 Furious old women 1960

Brun, V.
1 Alcibiades, beloved of gods and men
2 Alcibiades, forsaken by gods and men

Brunner, E.
1 Celia and her friends
2 The elopement
3 Celia once again
4 Celia's fantastic voyage

Brush, K.
1 Red-headed woman

2 Other women
2 gives more detailed stories of minor characters in 1.

Bruton, E.
1 The laughing policeman 1963
2 The Finsbury mob 1964
3 The wicked saint 1965
Novels about the City of London Police.

Bryan, J.
RICHARD SARET SERIES:
1 The difference to me 1956
2 The contessa came too 1957
3 The man who came back 1958

Bryant, Sir A.
1 The man in the making
2 The years of peril
3 The saviour of the navy
Biography of Samuel Pepys.
☐
1 The years of endurance (1793–1802)
2 The years of victory (1802–1812)
3 The age of elegance (1812–1822)
A history of England in the struggle against Napoleon.
THE ALANBROOKE DIARIES:
1 The turn of the tide
2 Triumph in the West
The war diaries of Lord Alanbrooke, C.I.G.S.
THE STORY OF ENGLAND:
1 Makers of the realm 1953
2 The age of chivalry 1963
N.F. History. In progress.

Bryant, M.
1 Christopher Hibbault, roadmaker
2 Anne Kempburn, truthseeker
3 The shadow on the stone

Bryher, W.
1 Development
2 Adventure

Buchan, J. [1st Viscount Tweedsmuir]
RICHARD HANNAY SERIES:
1 The thirty-nine steps
2 Greenmantle
3 Mr. Standfast
4 The three hostages

Buchan, J. [1st Viscount Tweedsmuir]
(contd.)
  5 The courts of the morning
  6 The island of sheep
  SIR EDWARD LEITHEN SERIES:
  1 The power house
  2 John Macnab
  3 The dancing floor
  4 Gap in the curtain
  5 The runagates club
  6 Sick heart river
  DICKSON MACCUNN SERIES:
  1 Huntingtower
  2 Castle gay
  3 House of the four winds
    Order as given in 'Memory hold the door'.

Buchan, S. C., Viscountess Tweedsmuir
  1 The lilac and the rose
  2 Winter bouquet
  N.F. Autobiography
  VICTORIAN TRILOGY:
  1 Cousin Harriet 1959
  2 Dashbury Park 1960
  3 A stone in the pool 1961

Buchholtz, J.
  1 Egholm and his God
  2 The miracles of Clara van Haag

Buchwald, A.
  1 I chose caviar
  2 More caviar

Buck, P. S.
  1 The good earth
  2 Sons
  3 A house divided
  □
  1 Exile
  2 Fighting angel
  □
  1 Dragon seed
  2 The promise
  □
  1 The long love 1949
  2 The townsman 1945
  3 Voices in the house 1953
    Facets of American life. Designed as a series, but characters do not recur.

  □
  1 My several worlds
  2 A bride for passing
  N.F. Autobiography

Buckingham, B.
  DON PANCHO SERIES:
  1 Three bad nights
  2 Boiled alive 1957

Buckley, E.
  1 For benefits received
  2 Fiorina 1961
  □
  1 Blue Danube
  2 Family from Vienna

Buckley, F. R.
  1 The blithe sheriff
  2 Re-enter the blithe sheriff

Buckley, H. B.
  1 Grandmother and I
  2 Grandfather and I 1962
  N.F. Autobiography

Bubb, L.
  CHRISTIANSSON FAMILY TRILOGY:
  1 April snow 1951
  2 Land of strangers 1953
  3 April harvest 1957

Bude, J.
  DET. INSPECTOR MEREDITH SERIES:
  1 The Cornish coast murder
  2 The Cheltenham Square murder
  3 Hand on the alibi
  4 Loss of a head
  5 Death on paper
  6 Death of a cad
  7 Death knows no calendar
  8 Death deals a double
  9 Slow vengeance
  10 Death in ambush
  11 Death in white pyjamas
  12 Trouble brewing
  13 Death makes a prophet
  14 Dangerous sunlight
  15 A glint of red herrings
  16 Death steals the show
  17 The constable and the lady
  18 Death on the Riviera

19 When the case was opened
20 Twice dead
21 So much is dark 1954
22 Two ends to the town 1955
23 Shift of guilt 1956
24 Telegram from Le Touquet 1956
25 Another man's shadow 1957
INSPECTOR SHERWOOD SERIES:
1 Night the fog came down 1958
2 A twist of the rope 1958

Bull, G. T.
1 When the iron gates yield
2 God holds the key

Bull, P.
1 To sea in a sieve
2 Bulls in the meadows
3 I know the face but . . .
N.F. Autobiography

Bullett, G.
1 Egg Pandervil
2 Nicky son of Egg
□
1 The daughters of Mrs. Peacock 1956
2 The Peacock brides 1958
GEORGE LYDNEY SERIES:
1 One man's poison 1960
2 Odd woman out 1961
*First published under the name of
S. Fox.*

Buncher, W.
1 A mother's secret
2 Donald O'Dare

Bunner, H. C.
1 Short sixes
2 More short sixes

Burgess, A.
MALAYAN TRILOGY:
1 Time for a tiger 1956
2 The enemy in the blanket 1957
3 Beds in the east 1958
Richard Ennis also appears in:
4 The worm and the ring 1964
5 A vision of battlements 1965

Burgin, G. B.
FOUR CORNERS SERIES:
No particular order of reading.
1 The dance at Four Corners

2 Old Man's marriage
3 The marble city
4 The King of Four Corners
5 A puller of strings
6 Dickie Silver
7 The judge of Four Corners
8 The land of silence
9 The Devil's due
10 The hut by the river
11 The Duke's twins
12 A game of hearts
13 The herb of healing
14 Manetta's marriage
15 Sally's sweetheart
16 Fleurette of Four Corners
17 The honour of Four Corners
MONASTERY OF MAHOTA SERIES:
1 The shutters of silence
2 Within the gates
□
1 The slaves of Allah
2 Diana of dreams

Burke, B. *and* **Skipp, C.**
1 With a feather on my nose
2 With powder on my nose
N.F. Autobiography

Burke, F. *pseud.* [**Mrs. O. Dargan**]
1 Call home the heart
2 A stone came rolling

Burke, J.
MIKE MERRIMAN SERIES:
1 Fear by instalments 1960
2 Deadly downbeat 1962

Burke, T.
1 Limehouse nights
2 More Limehouse nights
3 East of Mansion House
4 Pleasantries of Old Quong
*Although these volumes have the
same setting, they are not strictly
sequels.*

Burman, B. L.
1 Steamboat round the bend
2 Then there's Cripple Creek

Burnand, Sir F. C.
1 Happy thoughts
2 More happy thoughts
3 Happy Thought Hall

Burne, A. H.
1 The Crecy war
2 The Agincourt war
N.F. Military History of the 100 years war

Burnett, Mrs. F. H.
1 Good Wolf
2 Barty Crusoe and his man Saturday
☐
1 A lady of quality
2 His Grace of Osmonde
☐
1 The making of a marchioness
2 The methods of Lady Walderhurst
☐
1 The head of the house of Coombe
2 Robin

Burnett, W. R.
1 Adobe walls 1955
2 Pale moon 1957

Burnham, Mrs. C. L.
1 Jewel: a chapter of her life
2 Jewel's story book

Burns, Tex *pseud. see* Mulford, C. E.

Buron, Nicole de
1 Sahara-boom-de-ay
2 To the gondolas

Burr, S.
LISA LONGLAND:
1 Life with Lisa 1958
2 Leave it to Lisa 1959

Burrard, G.
1 The tiger of Tibet
2 The mystery of Mekong

Burress, J.
THE SINGLETON FAMILY:
1 Little mule
2 Apple on a pear tree

Burroughs, E. R.
MARTIAN SERIES:
1 A princess of Mars
2 The gods of Mars
3 The warlord of Mars
4 Thuvia, maid of Mars
5 Chessmen of Mars
6 A fighting man of Mars
7 Master mind of Mars
8 Synthetic men of Mars
9 Swords of Mars
10 Llana of Gathol
There is a reference to John Carter of Mars in 'The Moon Maid'. There is a 'phantom' 11th volume in the Martian series, known to have been published in magazine form. This has now been published by Canaveral Press as 'John Carter of Mars' (1964). It consists of two novelettes, 'The Giant of Mars' and 'Skeleton men of Jupiter'.

TARZAN SERIES:
1 Tarzan of the apes
2 The return of Tarzan
3 The beasts of Tarzan
4 The son of Tarzan
5 Tarzan and the jewels of Opar
6 Tarzan, the untamed
7 Jungle tales of Tarzan
8 Tarzan, the terrible
9 Tarzan and the Golden lion
10 Tarzan and the Ant-men
11 Tarzan and the lost Empire
12 Tarzan and the city of gold
13 Tarzan and the leopard men
14 Tarzan the invincible
15 Tarzan at the earth's core
16 Tarzan Lord of the jungle
17 Tarzan triumphant
18 Tarzan's quest
19 Tarzan the magnificent
20 Tarzan and the forbidden city
21 Tarzan and the lion man
22 Tarzan and the foreign legion
23 Tarzan and the Tarzan twins

PELLUCIDAR SERIES:
1 At the earth's core
2 Pellucidar
3 Tarzan at the earth's core
4 Tanar of Pellucidar
5 Back to the stone-age

Burt, M.

Burton, M.

Burton, M. (*contd.*)
61 A smell of smoke 1959
62 Death paints a picture 1960
63 Legacy of death 1961
Inspector Arnold does not appear in the first three.

Burton, T.
1 The great grab. [And so divided]
2 Bloodbird

Busch, N.
1 California Street 1959
2 The San Franciscans 1962

Bush, C.
LUDOVIC TRAVERS SERIES:
1 The perfect murder case
2 Dancing death
3 Dead man's music
4 Dead man twice
5 Murder at Fenwold
6 Cut-throat
7 Case of the green felt hat
8 Case of the unfortunate village
9 Case of the April fools
10 Case of the three strange faces
11 Case of the 100% alibis
12 Case of the dead shepherd
13 Case of the Chinese gong
14 Case of the Monday murders
15 Case of the bonfire body
16 Case of the missing minutes
17 Case of the hanging rope
18 Case of the Tudor queen
19 Case of the leaning man
20 Case of the flying ass
21 Case of the fighting soldier
22 Case of the climbing rat
23 Case of the kidnapped colonel
24 Case of the murdered major
25 Case of the magic mirror
26 Case of the running mouse
27 Case of the platinum blonde
28 Case of the corporal's leave
29 Case of the missing men
30 Case of the second chance
31 Case of the curious client
32 Case of the Haven hotel
33 Case of the housekeeper's hair
34 Case of the seven bells
35 Case of the purloined picture

36 Case of the happy warrior
37 Case of the corner cottage
38 Case of the fourth detective
39 Case of the happy medium
40 Case of the counterfeit colonel
41 Case of the burnt Bohemian
42 Case of the silken petticoat
43 Case of the red brunette
44 Case of the three lost letters
45 Case of the benevolent bookie
46 The case of the amateur actor 1955
47 The case of the extra man 1956
48 The case of the flowery corpse 1956
49 The case of the Russian cross 1957
50 The case of the treble twist 1958
51 The case of the running man 1958
52 The case of the careless thief 1959
53 The case of the sapphire brooch 1960
54 The case of the extra grave 1961
55 The case of the dead man gone 1961
56 Three ring puzzle 1962
57 Heavenly twin 1963
58 The case of the grand alliance 1964
59 The case of the Jumbo sandwich 1965
60 The case of the good employer 1966

Bussell, J.
1 Puppet and I
2 Puppet's progress
N.F. Autobiography

Butler, E. M.
1 The myth of the magus
2 Ritual magic
3 The fortunes of Faust
N.F. A treatise on the Faust myth.

Butler, G.
INSPECTOR WINTON SERIES:
1 Receipt for murder 1956
2 Dead in a row 1957
3 The dull dead (Insp. Winton and Sgt. Coffin)
INSPECTOR COFFIN SERIES:
1 The murdering kind 1958
2 The interloper 1959
3 Death lives next door 1960
4 Make me a murderer 1961
5 Coffin in Oxford 1962
6 Coffin for baby 1963
7 Coffin waiting 1964

8 Coffin in Malta 1964
9 A nameless Coffin 1966

Butler, M. M.
1 Waiting and serving
2 Daffodil

Butler, S.
1 Erewhon
2 Erewhon revisited twenty years
later

Byam, W.
1 The road to Harley St. 1963
2 Dr. Byam in Harley St. 1961
N.F. Autobiography

Cabell, J. B.
THE BIOGRAPHY OF DON MANUEL AND
HIS DESCENDANTS:
1 Beyond life
2 The lineage of Lichfield
3 Figures of earth
4 The silver stallion
5 The witch woman
   (*a*) The music from behind the
      moon
   (*b*) The white robe
   (*c*) The way of Ecben
6 Domnei
7 Chivalry
8 Jurgen
9 The line of love
10 The high place
11 Gallantry
12 Something about Eve
13 The certain hour
14 The cords of vanity
15 From the hidden way
16 The jewel merchants
17 The rivet in Grandfather's neck
18 The eagle's shadow
19 The cream of the jest
20 Straws and prayer-books
*This series was not originally planned
as such, and some of the books were
re-written later to fit the sequence.
Apart from Domnei, which was
originally published as 'The soul of
Mellicent', they were all re-published
under the original title.
'Figures of earth', 'The silver stallion'*

*and 'Jurgen' form a trilogy within the
sequence.*
□
1 Hamlet had an uncle
2 The king was in his counting house
3 The first gentleman of America
□
1 Smirt
2 Smith
3 Smire

Cadell, E.
WAYNES OF WOOD MOUNT SERIES:
1 Lark shall sing
2 Blue sky of spring

Caine, O. V.
1 Face to face with Napoleon
2 In the year of Waterloo

Caldwell, J.
1 Desperate voyage
2 Family at sea
N.F. Autobiography

Caldwell, T.
1 Dynasty of death
2 The eagles gather
3 The final hour

Calhoun, F. B. *and* **Sampson, E. S.**
see Sampson, E. S.

Calhoun, M.
1 Katie John
2 Depend on Katie John
3 Honestly, Katie John

Cameron, C.
1 Rangers is powerful hard to kill
2 It's hell to be a ranger
3 At the end of a Texas rope
4 Ghosts on the range to-night

Cameron, I.
1 The doctor
2 More about the doctor
3 The doctor calls again
4 The doctor and his friends
5 More friends of the doctor
□
1 The but and ben

Cameron, I. (*contd.*)
2 Tattered tartan
3 Heather mixture
4 Kirk of the Corrie 1956
Not strictly sequels, but characters re-appear in all novels.

Cameron, M. J. Locherbie-
1 Nicolette detects
2 Nicolette finds her

Cammell, C. R.
1 Castles in the air
2 Heart of Scotland
N.F. Autobiography

Camp, W. C.
1 Danny Fists
2 Captain Danny

Campbell, A.
INSPECTOR HEADCORN SERIES:
1 Death framed in silver
2 Flying blind
3 They hunted a fox
4 The cockroach sings
Other recurring characters –
TOMMY ROSTETTER:
1 The click of the gate
2 Desire to kill
3 Flying blind
COLIN LADBROKE:
1 Death framed in silver
2 A door closed softly
3 They hunted a fox
GEOFFREY MACADAM AND CATHERINE WEST:
1 Spiderweb
2 No light came on
ALISON YOUNG:
1 A door closed softly
2 They hunted a fox
HELEN RODERICK:
1 The click of the gate
2 Desire to kill

Campbell, D. R.
1 The fiddling lady
2 The proving of Virginia
3 The violin lady

Campbell, H.
SIMON BRAVE SERIES:
1 The moor fires mystery
2 The string glove mystery
3 The porcelain fish
4 Three names for murder

Campbell, I. H.
1 Wayward tendrils on the vine
2 Reminiscences of a vintner
N.F. Autobiography

Campbell, K.
MIKE BRETT SERIES:
1 Goodbye, gorgeous
2 Listen lovely
3 Born beautiful
4 Darling, don't
5 That was no lady
6 Pardon my gun

Campbell, R.
1 Broken record
2 Light on a dark horse
N.F. Autobiography

Campbell, R. W.
1 Private Spud-Tamson
2 Sergeant Spud-Tamson, v.c.
3 Spud-Tamson out West

Campion, S.
1 Mo Burdekin
2 Bonanza
3 The Pommy cow

Canfield, D.
1 Rough hewn
2 The brimming cup

Cannan, G.
THE LAURIE SAGA:
1 Little brother
2 Round the corner
3 The stucco house
4 Three pretty men. [Three sons and a mother]
5 Time and eternity
6 Annette and Bennett
NOVELS OF THE NEW TIME:
1 Pugs and peacocks
2 Sembal

3 The house of prophecy
This is the author's own classification of the novels as given in 'The house of prophecy', but there is also an internal trilogy formed by 'Round the corner', Sembal', and 'The house of prophecy'.

Cannan, J.
INSPECTOR NORTHCAST SERIES:
1 They rang up the police
2 Death at 'The Dog'

Canning, V.
1 Mr. Finchley discovers his England. [Mr. Finchley's holiday]
2 Mr. Finchley goes to Paris
3 Mr. Finchley takes the road

Capon, P.
ANTIGEOS TRILOGY:
1 The other side of the sun
2 The other half of the planet
3 Down to earth

Cardus, N.
1 Autobiography
2 Second innings
N.F. *Autobiography*

Carey, E. G., *see* Gilbreth, F. B. and Carey, E. G.

Carey, W.
1 Monsieur Martin
2 For the White Rose

Cargill, L.
MAJOR MOSSOM SERIES:
1 Murder in the procession
2 It might have been murder
3 Missing background
MORRISON SHARPE SERIES:
1 Death goes by bus
2 Heads you lose

Carmichael, H.
JOHN PIPER SERIES:
1 Death leaves a diary 1952
2 The vanishing trick 1952
3 Deadly nightcap 1953

4 School for murder 1953
5 Why kill Johnnie? 1954
6 Death counts three 1954
7 Noose for a lady 1955
8 Justice enough 1956
9 Emergency exit 1957
10 Put out that star 1957
11 James Knowland dec. 1958
12 Or he be dead 1959
13 Stranglehold 1959
14 The seeds of hate 1960
15 Requiem for Charles 1960
16 Alibi 1961
17 The link 1962
18 Of unsound mind 1962
19 Vendetta 1963
20 Flashback 1964
21 Post mortem 1965

Carmichael, M.
1 The solitaries of the Sambuca
2 Christopher and Cressida

Carnac, C.
JULIAN RIVERS SERIES:
1 A double for detection
2 The striped suitcase
3 When the devil was sick
4 Clue sinister
5 Over the garden wall
6 Upstairs downstairs
7 Copy for crime
8 It's her own funeral
9 Crossed skis
10 Murder among members 1957
11 Long shadows 1958
12 A policeman at the door 1959
INSPECTOR STRANG SERIES:
1 Double turn 1956
2 Death of a ladykiller 1958

Carnegie, S.
MAJOR GAIR MAINWARING SERIES:
1 Noble purpose
2 Sunset in the East

Carossa, H.
1 Childhood
2 Boyhood and youth
3 Year of sweet illusions

Carr, G.

Carr, J. B.

Carr, J. D.
'The men who explained miracles' (1964) has two Dr. Fell short stories and one about Sir Henry Merivale

(originally published under the name of Carter Dickson).
A trilogy of novels showing episodes in the history of the Metropolitan Police. 1 is Georgian, 2 Mid-Victorian, 3 Edwardian.
See also Dickson, Carter.

Carr, Mrs. S. P.
BILLY TOMORROW SERIES – 4 VOLUMES

Carrington, C.
N.F. Autobiography

Carroll, G. H.
2 is the story of some of the minor characters in 1.

Carson, R.
N.F. Two books on oceanography.

Carstairs, H.

Carstairs, J. P.

Cary, J.
1 Herself surprised
2 To be a pilgrim
3 The horse's mouth
□

THE LIFE OF CHESTER NIMMO:
1 Except the Lord
2 Prisoner of grace
3 Not honour more
1 and 2 published in reverse order.

Cary, L.
1 The Duke steps out
2 The Duke comes back

Casanova Di Seingalt, G.
MEMOIRS:
1 Venetian years
2 Paris and prison
3 The eternal quest
4 Adventures in the west
5 In London and Moscow
6 Spanish passions
These are the titles given to the series by the English publishers. The memoirs were not written as a series.

Case, F.
1 Tales of a wayward inn
2 Do not disturb

Cassel, M. *see* Feval, P. and M. Cassell

Cassells, J.
LUDOVIC SAXON (PICAROON) SERIES:
1 Enter the Picaroon
2 The avenging Picaroon
3 Beware the Picaroon
4 Meet the Picaroon
5 The engaging Picaroon 1958
6 The enterprising Picaroon 1960
7 Salute the Picaroon 1960
8 The Picaroon goes west 1962
9 Prey for the Picaroon 1962
10 Challenge for the Picaroon 1964
11 The benevolent Picaroon 1965
12 Plunder for the Picaroon 1966
CHIEF-INSPECTOR FLAGG SERIES:
1 Doctor deals with murder
2 Murder comes to Rothesay
3 Master in the dark
4 The castle of sin

5 League of nameless men
6 Clue of the purple asters
7 Waters of sadness
8 Exit Mr. Shane
9 The circle of dust
10 The grey ghost
11 The second Mrs. Locke
12 The rattler
13 Salute Inspector Flagg
14 Case for Inspector Flagg
15 Inspector Flagg and the scarlet skeleton
16 Again Inspector Flagg
17 Presenting Supt. Flagg 1959
18 Case 29 1959
19 Enter Supt. Flagg 1960
20 Score for Supt. Flagg 1960
21 Problem for Supt. Flagg 1961
22 The brothers of benevolence 1962
23 The Council of the Rat 1963
24 Blue mask 1964
25 Grey face 1965

Casserly, G.
1 The elephant god
2 The jungle girl
3 Ghost tiger

Castelhun, D.
1 Penelope's problems
2 Penelope and the golden orchard

Casteret, N.
1 Ten years under the earth
2 My caves
3 Cave men new and old
4 More years under the earth 1961
N.F. Accounts of cave exploration in France

Castle, A. and E.
BEAU NASH REGIME ROMANCES:
1 The Bath comedy
2 The incomparable Bellairs
3 French Nan
4 Love gilds the scene
5 The ways of Miss Barbara
'Pamela Pounce' and 'Kitty and others' contain stories where Kitty appears occasionally, together with her coterie, but, the authors say, they are not really part of the above series in the same sense in which the earlier five books are part of the series.

Cato, N.
AUSTRALIAN TRILOGY:
1 All the rivers run
2 Time, flow softly
3 But still the stream 1962

Catton, B.
1 The coming fury 1961
2 Terrible swift sword 1963
N.F. American Civil War.
1 Mr. Lincoln's army
2 Glory road
3 A stillness at Appomattox
N.F. History of the American Civil War.

Caudill, R.
1 Happy little family
2 Schoolhouse in the woods

Cecil Lord, D.
1 The furry Melbourne
2 'Lord M'
N.F. Biography

Cecil, H.
ROGER THURSBY:
1 Brothers in law 1955
2 Friends at court 1956
3 Sober as a judge 1957
Three novels about law. There is a gap of 12 years between 1 and 2.

Chaber, M. E.
NILO MARCH SERIES:
1 No grave for March
2 The man inside
3 The splintered man
4 A lonely walk
5 The gallows garden
6 A hearse of another colour
7 So dead the rose 1960
8 Jade for a lady 1961
9 Softly in the night 1962

Chakrabongse, Prince Chula of Thailand
1 The Twain have met
2 First-class ticket
N.F. Autobiography

Chambers, D.
JIM STEELE SERIES:
1 Some day I'll kill you
2 She'll be dead by morning
3 Too like the lightning
4 The blonde died first
5 Darling this is death
6 The last secret
7 Rope for an ape
8 Case of Caroline Animus
9 Death against Venus

Chambers, P.
MARK PRESTON SERIES:
1 This'll kill you 1963
2 Nobody lives forever 1964

Chambers, R. M.
NAPOLEON AND JOSEPHINE
1 Little Creole
2 The losing fight

Chambers, R. W.
AMERICAN REVOLUTION SERIES:
1 Cardigan
2 The Maid-at-arms
3 The reckoning
FRANCO-PRUSSIAN WAR SERIES:
1 Lorraine
2 Ashes of empire
3 Maids of paradise

Chamson, A.
1 Roux the bandit
2 The road
3 The crime of the just

Chance, J. N.
MR. DE HAVILLAND SERIES:
1 Wheels in the forest
2 Maiden possessed
3 Death of an innocent
4 The red knight
5 Knight and the castle
6 The black highway
7 Coven gibbett
8 The brandy pole
9 Night of the full moon
10 Alarm at Black Brake 1960
11 The forest affair 1962
12 Stormlight 1965
JASON SERIES:
1 The Jason affair
2 Jason and the sleep game

3 The Jason murders
4 Jason goes west 1955
CHANCE SERIES:
1 Screaming fog
2 The eye in darkness
3 The man in my shoes

Chancellor, J.
1 Frass
2 Return of Frass

Chandler, R.
PHILIP MARLOWE SERIES:
1 The big sleep 1939
2 Farewell my lovely 1940
3 The high window 1942
4 Lady in the lake 1944
5 Little sister 1949
6 Simple art of murder
Short stories, some of which feature Philip Marlowe.
7 The long good-bye 1953
8 Playback 1958
9 Marlowe takes on the syndicate
This is an abbreviated version published by the Daily Mail of a 12,000 word story originally called 'The pencil'. This story also appeared in the magazine Manhunt under the title 'Wrong pigeon', and in Ellery Queen's Mystery Magazine as 'Philip Marlowe's last case'. It now appears in 'The smell of fear' 1965, again as 'The pencil'. This volume also contains Marlowe stories from 'The simple art of murder'.

Chandos, D.
1 Village in the sun
2 House in the sun
N.F. Travel in Mexico.
☐
1 Abbie
2 Abbie and Arthur 1961

Channing, E. M. *see* Renton, *pseud.*

Chanslor, T.
THE BEAGLE DETECTIVE AGENCY:
1 Our first murder
2 Our second murder

Chapman, E.
1 The Eddie Chapman story told by Frank Owen.
2 Free agent 1956
N.F. Autobiography

Chapman, G.
1 The gentleman usher
2 Monsieur d'Olive

Chapman, M.
1 Happy mountain
2 Home place
3 The weather tree
4 Glen Hazard

Chapman, R.
REX BANNER SERIES:
1 One jump ahead
2 Crime on my hands
3 Winter wears a shroud
4 Murder for the million
5 Behind the headlines
6 The frozen cliff

Chapple, J. M.
1 Heart throbs
2 More heart throbs

Chardonne, J.
HOUSE OF BARNERY SERIES:
1 Wife of Jean Barnery 1955
2 Pauline 1956
Originally in French, 'Destinées Sentimentales'.
1 La Femme de Jean Barnery
2 Pauline
3 Porcelaine de Limoges
3 has not yet been translated.

Charles, Mrs. E.
1 The Draytons and the Davenants
2 On both sides of the shield
☐
1 Winifred Bertram
2 The Bertram family

Charles, R.
SIMON WARREN SERIES:
1 Nothing to lose
2 Dark vendetta
3 Mission of murder

Charlesworth, Mrs. M. L.
1 Ministering children
2 Ministering children, *continued*
☐
1 The old looking-glass
2 The broken looking-glass

Charques, D.
1 Time's harvest
2 The returning heart
3 Between the twilights

Charteris, L.
1 X esquire
2 The white rider
☐
SAINT SERIES:
1 Meet the tiger, *same as* The Saint meets the tiger
2 Enter the Saint
3 The last hero, *same as* The Saint closes the case
4 Knight Templar, *same as* The avenging Saint
5 Featuring the Saint
6 Alias the Saint
7 She was a lady, *same as* The Saint meets his match
8 The holy terror, *same as* The Saint versus Scotland Yard
9 Getaway, *same as* The Saint's getaway
10 Once more the Saint, *same as* The Saint and Mr. Teal
11 The brighter buccaneer
12 Misfortunes of Mr. Teal, *same as* The Saint in London
13 Boodle, *same as* The Saint intervenes
14 The Saint goes on
15 The Saint in New York
16 Saint overboard
17 The ace of knaves
18 Thieves' picnic, *same as* The Saint bids diamonds
19 Prelude for war, *same as* The Saint plays with fire
20 Follow the Saint
21 The happy highwayman
22 The Saint in Miami
23 The Saint goes west
24 The Saint steps in
25 The Saint on guard
26 The Saint sees it through

27 Call for the Saint
28 Saint errant. [Saint to the rescue]
29 The Saint in Europe 1954
30 The Saint on the Spanish Main 1955. [Senor Saint]
31 Saint around the world 1959
32 Thanks to the Saint 1961
33 Trust the Saint 1962
34 The Saint in the sun 1963
35 Vendetta for the Saint 1964

Chase, I.
1 Past imperfect
2 Free admission
N.F. *Autobiography*

Chase, J. H.
MARCH GARLAND:
1 This is for real 1965
2 You have yourself a deal 1960
MADDOX, INSURANCE INVESTIGATOR:
1 Shock treatment
2 The double shuffle
3 Tell it to the birds 1963

Chase, M. E.
1 The girl from the Big Horn Country
2 Virginia of Elk Creek Valley

Chateaubriand, Vicomte de
EPISODE IN THE 'LES NATCHES' POEM:
1 Atala
2 René

Chatrian, A. *see* Erckmann, E.

Chaudhuri, N. C.
1 The autobiography of an unknown Indian 1950
2 A passage to England 1963
N.F. *Autobiography*

Chauncy, N.
LOCENNY FAMILY:
1 Tiger in the bush 1959
2 Devil's hill 1960
3 The roaring 40 1963

Cheesman, E.
1 Things worthwhile
2 Time well spent
N.F. Autobiography

Cheesman, L.
1 Peter
2 Big Peter's Little Peter
3 That curly headed rogue

Cheever, J.
1 The Wapshott chronicle 1962
2 The Wapshott scandal 1964
Two novels on an eccentric New England family.

Cheney, Mrs. E. D.
'Nora's return' is a sequel to Ibsen's 'The doll's house'.

Chesney, M.
CALLAGHAN SERIES:
1 'Steel' Callaghan
2 Callaghan of Intelligence
3 Callaghan meets his fate

Chessman, C.
1 Cell 2455 death row
2 Trial by ordeal
3 The face of justice
N.F. Autobiography

Chester, G. R.
1 Get-rich-quick Wallingford
2 Young Wallingford
3 Wallingford in his prime
4 Wallingford and Blackie Daw

Chesterton, G. K.
FATHER BROWN SERIES:
1 The innocence of Father Brown
2 The wisdom of Father Brown
3 The incredulity of Father Brown
4 The secret of Father Brown
5 The scandal of Father Brown

Chesterton, R.
1 The *Phantom* battleship
2 The captain of the *Phantom*

Chetham-Strode, W.
see Strode, W. Chetham-

Chevallier, G.
1 Clochemerle
2 Clochemerle – Babylon 1959
3 Clochemerle-les Bains 1964
Trilogy of humorous novels on a small French provincial town.

Cheyney, E. G.
SCOTT BURTON SERIES – 5 VOLUMES

Cheyney, P.
LEMMY CAUTION SERIES:
1 This man is dangerous
2 Poison ivy
3 Dames don't care
4 Can ladies kill
5 Don't get me wrong
6 You'd be surprised
7 Mister Caution – Mr. Callaghan
8 Your deal, my lovely
9 Never a dull moment
10 You can always duck
11 I'll say she does
12 G2 man at the yard
SLIM CALLAGHAN SERIES:
1 The urgent hangman
2 Dangerous curves
3 You can't keep the change
4 Mister Caution – Mr. Callaghan
5 It couldn't matter less
6 Sorry you've been troubled
7 They never say when
8 Uneasy terms
SECRET SERVICE SERIES (KELLS IS A MAIN CHARACTER):
1 Dark duet
2 The stars are dark
3 The dark street
4 Sinister errand
5 Dark hero
6 Dark interlude
7 Dark wanton
8 But ladies won't wait
JOHNNY VALLON SERIES:
1 You can call it a day
2 Dark bahama

Chichester, J. J.
MAXWELL SANDERSON SERIES:
1 The silent cracksman
2 Rogues of fortune
3 Sanderson: master rogue
4 Sanderson's diamond loot

Chisholm, L.
1 In Fairyland
2 The enchanted land

Cholmondeley, M.
1 The Danvers jewels
2 Sir Charles Danvers

Chotzinoff, S.
1 A lost paradise
2 Days at the Mona

Christie, A.
POIROT SERIES:
1 The mysterious affair at Styles 1940
2 The murder on the links 1923
3 Poirot investigates 1924
4 The murder of Roger Ackroyd 1926
5 The mystery of the blue train 1928
6 The Seven Dials mystery 1929
7 Peril at End House 1932
8 Lord Edgeware dies. [Thirteen at dinner] 1933
9 Murder on the Orient Express 1934 [Murder in the Calais coach]
10 Three act tragedy. [Murder in three acts] 1935
11 Death in the clouds. [Death in the air] 1935
12 Murder in Mesopotamia 1936
13 Cards on the table 1936
14 Dumb witness 1937
15 Death on the Nile 1937
16 Appointment with death 1938
17 Murder in the mews 1938
18 Hercule Poirot's Christmas 1939
19 Sad cypress 1940
20 One two buckle my shoe 1940
21 Evil under the sun 1941
22 Five little pigs 1943
23 The hollow 1946
24 Labours of Hercules 1947
25 Taken at the flood. [There is a tide] 1948
26 After the funeral. [Funerals are fatal] 1951
27 Mrs. McGinty's dead 1952
28 Hickory dickory dock 1955
29 Dead man's folly 1956
30 Cat among the pigeons 1958
31 The adventure of the Christmas pudding 1959

32 The clocks 1963
MISS MARPLE SERIES:
1 Murder at the vicarage 1930
2 Body in the library 1942
3 The thirteen problems 1942
4 The moving finger 1943
5 A murder is announced 1950
6 They do it with mirrors. [Murder with mirrors] 1952
7 A pocket full of rye 1953
8 The 4.50 from Paddington 1957
9 The mirror crack'd from side to side 1962
10 A Caribbean mystery 1964
11 At Bertram's hotel 1965
TOMMY AND TUPPENCE SERIES:
1 Partners in crime
2 The secret adversary
3 N or M

Christie, K.
1 Smith 1954
2 Harold in London 1956

Christie, R. S.
THE BOOK OF SARAH:
1 Young experience
2 Gay application

Chuber, M. E.
MILO MARCH SERIES:
1 No grave for March
2 The man inside

Church, L. F.
1 The early Methodist people
2 More about the early Methodist people
N.F. *Methodist church in the 18th century*

Church, R.
JOHN QUICKSHOTT SERIES:
1 The porch 1955
2 The stronghold 1959
3 The room within 1961
□
1 Over the bridge
2 The golden sovereign
3 The voyage home 1964
N.F. *Autobiography*

Churchill, P.
1 Of their own choice
2 Duel of wits
3 The spirit in the cage
N.F. War memoirs

Churchill, W.
AMERICAN NATIONAL DEVELOPMENT
SERIES:
1 Richard Carvel
2 The crossing
3 The crisis
☐
1 Coniston
2 Mr. Crewe's career
3 A far country

Churchward, J.
1 Lost continent of Mu
2 The children of Mu 1959
N.F. Archaeology

Clandon, H.
MR. POWER SERIES:
1 Inquest
2 Ghost party
3 Rope by arrangement
4 This delicate murder
5 Power on the scent
6 Fog off Weymouth

Clark, S. R.
1 Yensie Walton
2 Yensie Walton's womanhood

Clarke, A.
1 Smilers
2 More smilers
3 Extra smilers
4 French smilers

Clason, C. B.
THEOCRITUS WESTBOROUGH SERIES:
1 Death angel
2 Fifth tumbler
3 Purple parrot
4 Camera clue
5 Man from Tibet
6 Whispering ear
7 Clue to the labyrinth. [Murder gone Minoan]
8 Dragon's cave
9 Green shiver

Clayton, J., *pseud. see* Webb, H. B. L.

Cleeve, L. (Mrs. H. Kingscote)
1 The Cardinal and Lady Susan
2 Lady Susan and not the Cardinal

Clemens, S. *see* Twain, M., *pseud.*

Clements, E. A.
1 Let him die
2 Bright intervals

Clements, E. H.
ALISTER WOODHEAD SERIES:
1 The other island 1956
2 Back in daylight 1956
3 Uncommon cold 1958
4 High tension 1959
5 Honey for the marshall 1960
6 A note of enchantments 1961

Cleugh, Mrs. S.
1 Matilda
2 Young Jonathan
There is a gap of ten years between the stories.

Cleveley, H.
1 The gang-smasher
2 Gang-smasher again
☐
1 Justin Kelly 1961
2 Garland of valour 1963
The Justin of 2 is the grandson of Justin Kelly.

Clifford, Sir H.
1 Sally
2 Saleh

Clive, Mrs. A.
1 Paul Ferroll
2 Why Paul Ferroll killed his wife

Cloete, S.
THE VANDER BERG FAMILY
1 The turning wheels
2 Watch for the dawn
3 The hill of doves
4 The Mask 1958
A series of novels on the early Boer settlements.

Closs, H.
THE ALBIGENSIAN CRUSADE:
1 High are the mountains
2 And sombre the valleys
3 The silent tarn

Clough, S.
1 Mathilda
2 Ernestine Sophie
3 Young Jonathan

Clouston, J. S.
MR. MANDELL-ESSINGTON SERIES:
1 The lunatic at large
2 Count Bunker
3 The lunatic at large again
5 The lunatic still at large
6 Mr. Essington in love
7 The best story ever
URSULA DOLLING SERIES:
1 Colonel Dam
2 The virtuous vamp

Coates, J. *see* Austin, J.

Cobb, B.
CHEVIOT BURMANN SERIES:
1 No alibi
2 The prisoner's mistake
3 Fatal dose
4 Quickly dead
5 Like a guilty thing
6 The fatal holiday
7 Inspector Burmann's busiest day
8 Death defies the doctor
9 Inspector Burmann's black-out
10 Double detection
11 Death in the 13th dose
12 No mercy for Margaret
13 Next door to death
14 Detective in distress
15 Corpse incognito
16 Need a body tell?
17 The willing witness
18 Corpse at Casablanca 1955
19 Drink alone and die 1955
20 Doubly dead 1956
21 Poisoner's base 1956
22 The missing scapegoat 1957
23 With intent to kill 1958
24 Like a guilty thing 1959
   No. 5 revised and re-issued.
25 Don't lie to the police 1959
26 Death with a difference 1960
27 Search for Sergeant Baxter 1961
28 Corpse in the cargo 1961
29 Murder: men only 1962
30 No shame for the devil 1963

31 Death of a peeping Tom 1964
32 Dead girl's shoes 1964
33 I never miss twice 1965
34 Last drop 1965
35 Some must watch 1966
   From No. 29, a new character, Kitty Armitage, is introduced.
SUPT. MANNING SERIES:
1 Early morning poison
2 Secret of Superintendent Manning
3 The framing of Carol Woan
4 No last words
5 Stolen strychnine
6 No charge for the poison
7 Seargeant Ross in disguise
8 Home Guard mystery
9 The lunatic, the lover

Cobb, I. S.
JUDGE PRIEST SERIES:
1 Back home
2 The escape of Mr. Trimm
3 Those times and these
4 From place to place
5 Sundry accounts
6 Snake doctor
7 Prose and cons
8 Down yonder with Judge Priest
9 Judge Priest turns detective
   Short stories. Each volume contains one or more Judge Priest stories.

Cobb, T.
DETECTIVE-INSPECTOR BEDISON SERIES:
1 Crime without a clue
2 Inspector Bedison and the Sunderland case
3 Inspector Bedison risks it
4 Who closed the casement

Cobban, J. M.
1 The White Kaid of the Atlas
2 The tyrants of Kool-Sim

Coccioli, Carlo
1 Heaven and earth 1958
2 The white stone 1961

Cockburn, C.
1 In time of trouble
2 Crossing the line
3 View from the west
N.F. Autobiography

Cockin, J.
CAM AND BEAVER SERIES:
1 Curiosity killed the cat
2 Villains at Vespers
3 Deadly earnest

Cody, S.
CACTUS CLANCY:
1 Trouble shooter 1964
2 The gunslick code 1965

Coffin, C. C.
1 Winning his way
2 My days and nights on the battlefield
3 Following the flag

Cohen, A.
THE GALLANTS SERIES:
1 Solal of the Solals
2 The Nailcruncher

Cohen, O. R.
JIM HARVEY SERIES:
1 The May day mystery
2 The backstage mystery
3 Star of earth
4 The Townsend murder mystery
☐
1 Polished ebony
2 Come seven
☐
1 Grey dusk
2 Six seconds of darkness

Cole, G. D. H. *and* **M.**
SUPERINTENDENT WILSON SERIES:
1 Brooklyn murders
2 Death of a millionaire
3 Blatchington tangle
4 The man from the river
5 Superintendent Wilson's holiday
6 Poison in the garden suburb
7 Burglar in Bucks
8 Corpse in canonicals
9 Great Southern mystery
10 Dead man's watch
11 A lesson in crime
12 End of an ancient mariner
13 Death in the quarry

14 Big business murder
15 Dr. Tancred begins
16 Scandal at school
17 Brothers Sackville
18 Missing aunt
19 Off with her head
20 Double blackmail
21 Wilson and some others
22 Murder at the munition works
23 Counterpoint murder
24 Toper's end
25 Birthday gifts

Cole, J. A.
1 Just back from Germany 1938
2 My host Michel 1955
N.F. Travel.
Although 20 years apart, these views of Germany are to be considered as a sequence.

Coles, M.
HAMBLEDON SERIES:
1 Drink to yesterday
2 Pray silence. [Toast to tomorrow]
3 They tell no tales
4 Without lawful authority
5 Green hazard
6 Fifth man
7 Brother for Hugh. [With intent to deceive]
8 Among those absent
9 Not negotiable
10 Let the tiger die
11 Diamonds to Amsterdam
12 Dangerous by nature
13 Now or never
14 Night train to Paris
15 Alias Uncle Hugo
16 Knife for a juggler
17 Not for export
18 Man in the green hat 1955
19 Basle Express 1956
20 The three beans 1957
21 Death of an ambassador 1958
22 No entry 1958
23 Crime in concrete 1960
24 Search for a sultan 1961
25 The house at Pluck's gutter 1962
1 and 2 are direct sequels.

Colette, *pseud.*

THE CLAUDINE SERIES:
The English translations of the Claudine series are a bibliographical puzzle. The original French titles are:
1 Claudine à l'école 1900
2 Claudine à Paris 1901
3 Claudine en ménage 1902
4 Claudine s'en va 1903
5 La retraite sentimentale 1907
   This is the original series, but in no. 4 Claudine is not the main character or narrator.
6 La maison de Claudine 1922
7 Sido 1929
   Though sometimes considered part of the series, these are not about Claudine, but Colette and her mother. Colette-Claudine are of course really the same person. The English edition published by Secker is:
1 Claudine at school
2 Claudine in Paris
3 Claudine married
4 Claudine and Annie
5 My mother's house
   These correspond to 1–4, and 6–7 of the original.
   The American, and an earlier British edition have:
3 The indulgent husband
4 The innocent wife
   Another title, 'The mother of Claudine', is apparently a partial translation of 6 and 7. There is apparently no translation of no. 5 'La retraite sentimentale'.
   □
1 Cheri
2 The last of Cheri
RENÉE NÉRÉ SERIES:
1 The vagabond (Renée la vagabonde)
2 Recaptured (L'entrave)
   2 also published as 'The Shackle'.

Collingwood, W. G.
NORSEMEN SERIES:
1 Thorsten of the mere
2 The bondwoman

Colson, J.
1 The Goose and I 1963

2 The Goose up the creek 1964
3 Goose at sea 1965

Connington, J. J.
SIR CLINTON DRIFFIELD SERIES:
1 Murder in the maze
2 Tragedy at Ravensthorpe
3 Mystery at Lynden Sands
4 The case with nine solutions
5 Nemesis at Raynham Parva
6 The boathouse riddle
7 The sweepstake murders
8 The Castleford conundrum
9 The Ha-ha case
10 In whose dim shadow
11 A minor operation
12 Truth comes limping
13 Murder will speak
14 The twenty-one clues
15 No past is dead
16 Jack in the box
17 Commonsense is all you need

Connor, R. *pseud.* **[Rev. C. W. Gordon]**
CROW'S NEST SERIES:
1 The prospector
2 The doctor of Crow's Nest
GLENGARRY SERIES:
1 Glengarry days, *same as* Glengarry school days
2 The man from Glengarry
NORTH WEST MOUNTED POLICE SERIES:
1 Corporal Cameron of the North West Mounted Police
2 The patrol of the Sun Dance trail
   □
1 Sky pilot
2 Sky pilot of no man's land

Conquest, J.
1 Desert love
2 The hawk of Egypt

Conrad, J.
1 Lord Jim
2 Youth
3 Chance
   □
1 An outcast of the islands
2 Almayer's folly
   'The rescue' is a story of the younger days of Captain Lingard, who is a

character in the above volumes.

Conrad, S. *pseud.* [**S. C. Stuntz**]
1 Second Mrs. Jim
2 Mrs. Jim and Mrs. Jimmie

Constanduros, M. *and* **D.**
1 Here come the Huggetts
2 Vote for Huggett
3 The Huggetts abroad

Constant, B.
1 Adolphe
2 Cecile
N.F. Autobiography

Conway, A. *and* **F.**
1 Enchanted Islands
2 Return to the island
N.F. Travel

Conyers, D.
1 Strayings of Sandy
2 Further strayings of Sandy
3 Sandy married
4 Sandy and others
　□
1 Meave
2 A meave must marry

Cooke, G. W.
PETER MITCHELL SERIES:
1 Death can wait
2 Death takes a dive
3 Death is the end 1965

Cooke, J. E.
EFFINGHAM SERIES:
1 The Virginia comedians
2 Henry St. John, gentleman
SOUTHERN ARMY CAMPAIGN SERIES:
1 Survey of Eagle's-nest
2 Hilt to hilt
3 Mohun

Cooke, R. Croft-
EARLY LIFE:
1 The gardens of Camelot 1957
2 The altar in the loft 1959
3 The drums of morning 1960
4 The glittering pastures 1962
5 The numbers came 1963

6 The last of spring 1964
7 The purple streak 1966
N.F. Autobiography
LATER LIFE:
1 The circus has no home
2 The man in Europe St.
3 The moon in my pocket
4 The blood red island
5 The life for me
6 The verdict of you all
7 The tangerine house
8 The quest for Quixote
The first series is a sequence still in progress. The second series consists of episodes written at various times, here arranged in chronological order. They are considered as a single series by the author, but are arranged in this way for convenience in reading.

Cookson, C.
MARY ANN SHAUGHNESSY:
1 A grand man
2 The Lord and Mary Ann
3 The devil and Mary Ann 1958
4 Love and Mary Ann 1961
5 Life and Mary Ann 1962
6 Marriage and Mary Ann 1964
7 Mary Ann's angels 1965
'Fanny McBride' (1959) is not in series but re-introduces some minor characters.

Cooper, Lady D.
1 The rainbow comes and goes 1957
2 The light of common day 1959
3 Trumpets from the steep 1960
N.F. Autobiography

Cooper, J. F.
LEATHER-STOCKING TALES:
1 The deerslayer
2 The last of the Mohicans
3 The pathfinder
4 The pioneers
5 The prairie
LITTLEPAGE MANUSCRIPT:
1 Satanstoe
2 The chain bearer
3 The Redskins
　□
1 Afloat and ashore

Cooper, J. F. (*contd.*)
2 Miles Wallingford, *same as* Lucy
  Hardinge
  ☐
1 Homeward bound
2 Home as found
  Cooper's novels may be classified as
  follows:
HISTORICAL NOVELS:
  Mercedes of Castile
  The Heidenmauer
  The bravo
NOVELS:
  The headsman
  Precaution
  The Monikins
  Oak openings
  Ways of the hour
SEA TALES:
  The pilot
  The red rover
  The water-witch
  The two admirals
  Wing-and-Wing, *same as* Jack
  O'Lantern
  Afloat and ashore
  Miles Wallingford
  The crater, *same as* Mark's Reef
  Jack Tier
  The sea lions
  Homeward bound
  Home as found
TALES OF THE INDIAN WARS AND OF
THE REVOLUTION:
  Wept of Wish-ton-Wish, *same as*
  The borderers
  Wyandotté
  Thy spy
  Lionel Lincoln
  A. Dumas' 'Le Capitaine Paul' [*Jones*]
  is a sequel to 'The Pilot'.

Cooper, W.
1 Scenes from provincial life
2 Scenes from married life 1960

Copping, A. E.
1 Gotty and the guv'n'r
2 Gotty in furrin parts

Copplestone, B.
1 The lost naval papers

2 The diversions of Dawson
3 Madam Gilbert's cannibal

Copus, J. E.
1 Saint Cuthbert's
2 Shadows lifted

Corbett, E. F.
1 The Graper girls
2 The Graper girls go to college
3 Growing up with the Grapers
4 Beth and Ernestine Graper
  ☐
1 She was Carrie Eaton
2 Mr. and Mrs. Meigs
3 The young Mrs. Meigs
4 A nice long evening
5 Mrs. Meigs and Mr. Cunningham
6 Excuse me, Mrs. Meigs
MOUNT ROYAL SERIES:
1 The Langworthy family
2 Light of other days
3 The far-down
  ☐
1 Faye's folly
2 Early summer

Corbett, J.
1 Man-eaters of Kumaon
2 Man-eating leopard of Rudraprayag
  1948
3 The temple tiger 1957
N.F. Autobiography
  Events run parallel in 1 and 2.

Cordell, A.
1 Rape of the fair country
2 The hosts of Rebecca
3 Race of the tiger
  A series of novels on emigrants to the
  U.S.A. in the 19th century. No other
  connection.

Corelli, M.
1 A romance of two worlds
2 Ardath

Corey, P.
1 Three miles square
2 The road returns
3 County seat

Corrigan, M.

CORRIGAN AND TUCKER SERIES:
1 Bullets and brown eyes
2 Sinner takes all
3 Lovely lady
4 Wayward blonde
5 Golden angel
6 Shanghai Jezebel
7 Madame Sly
8 Baby face
9 Lady of China St.
10 All brides are beautiful
11 Sweet and deadly
12 The naked lady
13 Madam and Eve
14 The big squeeze
15 Big boys don't cry
16 Sydney for sin
17 The cruel lady
18 Dumb as they come
19 Menace in Siam
20 Honolulu snatch 1958
21 Singapore downbeat 1959
22 Sin of Hongkong 1960
23 Lady from Tokyo 1960
24 Girl from Moscow 1961
25 Danger's green eyes 1961
26 Riddle of double island 1962
27 Why do women 1963
28 Riddle of the Spanish circus 1964

Corvo, Baron, *pseud, see* Rolfe, F. W.

Cory, Desmond

LINDY GRAY SERIES:
1 Begin, murderer
2 This is Jezebel
3 Lady lost
☐
JOHNNY FEDORA SERIES:
1 Secret ministry
2 This traitor death
3 Dead man falling
4 Intrigue
5 Height of day
6 High requiem 1955
7 Johnny goes north 1956
8 Johnny goes east 1959
9 Johnny goes west 1959
10 Johnny goes south 1959
11 The head 1960

12 Undertow. [Johnny goes under] 1961
13 Hammerhead 1962
M. PILGRIM SERIES:
1 Pilgrim at the gate
2 Pilgrim on the island
DEE SERIES:
1 Stranglehold 1962
2 The name of the game 1964

Coryn, M.

NAPOLEONIC TRILOGY:
1 Marriage of Josephine
2 Swarm of bees. [Goodbye my son]
3 Power instead. [Alone among men]

Cost, M.

1 The hour awaits
2 Invitation from Minerva

Cotes, Mrs. E.

1 An American girl in London
2 A voyage of consultation

Cottenham, M. Pepys, 6th Earl of,
see Pepys, M., 6th Earl of Cottenham

Couperus, L.

THE BOOK OF SMALL SOULS:
1 Small souls
2 The later life
3 The twilight of the soul
4 Dr. Adrian

Courlander, A.

1 Henry in search of a father
2 Henry in search of a wife

Cournos, J.

JOHN GOMBAROV SERIES:
1 The mask
2 The wall
3 Babel

Cousins, E. G.

STORY OF LARRY GRAIL:
1 Untimely frost
2 To comfort the Signora
3 Moab is my washpot
Not published in this order. Minor characters recur in many of this author's novels. Captain Moffat appears in 2 and in 'Come like a storm'. Brigadier Worriall' in 2 and in 'Any kind of danger'.

Coward, N.
1 Present indicative
2 Future indefinite
N.F. *Autobiography*

Cowdroy, J.
INSPECTOR GORHAM SERIES:
1 Watch Mr. Moh
2 Murder of Lydia

Cox, Sir E. C.
1 John Carruthers, Indian policeman
2 The achievement of John Carruthers
3 The exploits of Kesho Nait, Dacoit

Coxe, G. H.
KENT MURDOCK SERIES:
1 The camera clue
2 The frightened women. [Four frightened women]
3 The lady is afraid
4 Murder for the asking
5 The Jade Venus 1946
6 The fifth key 1950
7 The hollow needle 1951
8 Eye witness 1953
9 The widow had a gun 1954
10 Lady killer 1955
11 The crimson clue 1955
12 Focus on murder 1956
13 Murder on their minds 1958
14 The big gamble 1960
15 The last commandment 1961
16 The hidden key 1964

Cozzens, S. W.
1 The young trail hunters
2 Crossing the quicksands
3 The young silver seekers

Crabb, A. L.
SAGA OF NASHVILLE SERIES:
1 Dinner at Belmont
2 Supper at the Maxwell House
3 Breakfast at the Hermitage
4 Lodging at the St. Cloud
5 Home to the Hermitage
   This is a connected series of Nashville Tennessee after the civil war. 'Journey to Nashville' tells the story of the foundation of the city.

Craddock, M.
1 A north country maid
2 Return to Rainton
N.F. *Autobiography*

Cradock, P.
1 Gateway to remembrance
2 The eternal echo

Craigie, Mrs. P. M. T., *see* Hobbes, J.

Craik, D. M.
AVILLON AND OTHER TALES:
1 Domestic stories
2 Romantic tales

Crake, A. D.
THE CHRONICLES OF AESCENDUNE:
1 Edwy the fair
2 Alfgar the Dane
3 The rival heirs

Crane, F.
PAT ABBOTT SERIES:
1 The turquoise shop 1943
2 The golden box 1944
3 The yellow violet 1944
4 The pink umbrella 1944
5 The applegreen cat 1945
6 The amethyst spectacles 1946
7 The indigo necklace 1946
8 The shocking pink hat 1948
9 The cinnamon murder 1949
10 Murder on the purple water 1949
11 Black cypress 1950
12 Flying red horse 1951
13 The daffodil blonde 1951
14 The polkadot murder 1952
15 Death in the blue hour 1952
16 13 white tulips 1953
17 Murder in bright red 1954
18 The coral princess murders 1955
19 Death in lilac time 1955
20 Horror on the Ruby X 1956
21 The ultra-violet widow 1957
22 The grey stranger 1958
23 The buttercup case 1958
24 Death-wish green 1960
25 Amber eyes 1962
26 Body beneath a mandarin tree 1965

Crawford, F. M.

In 2 members of the Saracinesca family appear. The character Paul Griggs appears in 'Paul Patoff', 'The prima-donna', 'Casa Braccio', 'Katherine Lauderdale', 'Mr. Isaacs' and 'The Ralstons'.

Creasey, J.

Creasey, J. *(contd.)*

26 The department of death
27 Enemy within
28 Dead or alive
29 A kind of prisoner
30 The black spiders 1957

DR. PALFREY SERIES:

1 Traitor's doom
2 The valley of fear, *same as* The perilous country
3 The legion of the lost
4 Dangerous quest
5 The hounds of vengeance
6 Death in the rising sun
7 Shadow of doom
8 The house of the bears
9 Sons of Satan
10 Dark harvest
11 The wings of peace
12 The dawn of darkness
13 The league of light
14 Man who shook the world
15 The prophet of fire
16 The children of hate
17 The touch of death
18 The mists of fear 1957
19 The flood 1958
20 The plague of silence 1958
21 The draught 1959
22 The terror: the return of Dr. Palfrey 1962
23 The depths 1963
24 The sleep 1964
25 The inferno 1965

INSPECTOR WEST SERIES:

1 Inspector West takes charge
2 Inspector West leaves town
3 Inspector West at home
4 Inspector West regrets
5 Holiday for Inspector West
6 Triumph for Inspector West
7 Battle for Inspector West
8 Inspector West kicks off
9 Inspector West cries wolf
10 Inspector West alone
11 Puzzle for Inspector West
12 Case for Inspector West
13 Inspector West at bay
14 Send Inspector West
15 A gun for Inspector West
16 A beauty for Inspector West
17 Inspector West makes haste

18 Two for Inspector West 1955
19 A prince for Inspector West 1956
20 Parcels for Inspector West. [Death of a postman] 1956
21 Accident for Inspector West. [Hit and run] 1957
22 Find Inspector West. [Trouble at Saxby's] 1957
23 Strike for death 1958
24 Murder London–New York 1958
25 Death of a racehorse 1959
26 The case of the innocent victims 1959
27 Murder on the line 1960
28 The scene of the crime 1960
29 Death in cold print 1961
30 Policeman's dread 1962
31 Hang the little man 1963
32 Look three ways at murder 1964
33 Murder, London–Australia 1965
34 Murder London–South Africa 1966

☐

1 The mountain of the blind 1960
2 The foothills of fear 1961
Readers of this author may be interested to know that he has also written novels under the following pen names: J. J. Marric, Michael Halliday, Anthony Morton, Gordon Ashe, Jeremy York, Norman Deane, Peter Manton, Richard Martin, Tex Reilly, and W. C. Reilly. Where there are sequels they are entered under the pen-name.

Creighton, B.

1 The amorous cheat
2 The old Eve

Creswell, H. B.

1 The Honeywood file
2 The Honeywood settlement
3 Grig
4 Grig in retirement
The first two are sequels, but Grig as a minor character becomes the central character in 3 and 4, with many of the characters in 1 and 2 reappearing.

☐

1 Thomas
2 Thomas settles down

Cripps, A. S.
1 A martyr's servant
2 A martyr's heir
N.F. *Jesuit missions in South-East Africa.*

Crispin, E.
GERVASE FEN SERIES:
1 The case of the gilded fly
2 Holy disorders
3 The moving toyshop
4 Swan song
5 Love lies bleeding
6 Buried for pleasure
7 Frequent hearses
8 The long divorce
9 Beware of the trains

Crockett, S. R.
1 The Black Douglas
2 Maid Margaret of Galloway
□
1 Kit Kennedy
2 Bog-myrtle and peat
□
1 The raiders
2 The dark o' the moon
□
1 The red axe
2 Joan of the Sword-hand
□
1 Red Cap tales
2 Red Cap adventures
□
1 The Stickit Minister and some
common men
2 The Stickit Minister's wooing, etc.
□
1 Sweetheart travellers
2 Sweethearts at home
□
1 The men of the moss-hag
2 Lochinvar
□
1 Sir Toady Lion
2 Sir Toady Crusoe

Crofts, F. W.
INSPECTOR FRENCH SERIES:
1 Inspector French's greatest case
2 Inspector French and the Cheyne
mystery

3 Inspector French and the Starvel
tragedy
4 The sea mystery
5 The box office murders
6 Sir John Magill's last journey
7 Mystery in the Channel
8 Sudden death
9 Death on the way
10 Crime at Guildford
11 The Hog's Back mystery
12 12.30 from Croydon
13 Mystery on Southampton Water
14 The loss of the *Jane Vosper*
15 Man overboard
16 Found floating
17 The end of Andrew Harrison
18 Antidote to venom
19 Fatal venture
20 Golden ashes
21 James Tarrant, adventurer
22 The losing game
23 Fear comes to Chalfont
24 The affair at Little Wokeham
25 Enemy unseen
26 Death of a train
27 Murderers make mistakes
28 Silence for the murderer
29 French strikes oil
30 Many a slip
31 The mystery of the sleeping car
express
32 Anything to declare

Crompton, R.
THE WILDINGS SERIES:
1 The Wildings
2 David Wilding
3 The thorn bush

Cronin, A. J.
1 The green years
2 Shannon's way

Cronin, M.
MR. PILGRIM SERIES:
1 Paid in full 1956
2 Sweet water 1958
3 Begin with a gun 1959
4 Curtain call 1960

Cross, M.

Croy, K.

Cuddon, J. A.
Novels about a young English painter.

Cumberland, M.

Curling, H.

Curtain, M. T.

Curwood, J. O.
1 Kazan, the wolf-dog
2 The son of Kazan
3 The courage of Marge O'Doone
□
1 Wolf hunters
2 Gold hunters
□
1 The black hunter
2 The plains of Abraham

Cuthrell, F. B. *see* Baldwin F., *pseud.*

Cutting, M. S.
1 Little stories of courtship
2 Little stories of married life
3 More stories of married life
4 The suburban girls and other
stories of married life.

Dalgliesh, A. J.
1 The silver pencil
2 Along Janet's road

Dall, Mrs. C. W. H.
PATTY GRAY'S JOURNEY:
1 From Boston to Baltimore
2 From Baltimore to Washington
3 On the way: Patty at Mount Vernon

Dalton, Baron, [H. Dalton]
1 Call back yesterday 1953
2 The fateful years 1957
3 High tide and after 1962
N.F. Autobiography

Daly, E.
HENRY GAMADGE SERIES:
1 Unexpected night
2 Murders in vol. 2
3 House without the door
4 Nothing can rescue me
5 Evidence of things seen
6 Arrow pointing nowhere
7 Book of the dead
8 Deadly nightshade
9 Any shape or form
10 Somewhere in the house
11 Wrong way down
12 Night walk
13 The book of the lion 1951
14 And dangerous to know 1952
15 Death and letters 1953
16 The book of the crime 1954

Dane, C., *and* **H. Simpson**
1 Enter Sir John
2 Printer's devil. [Author unknown]
3 Re-enter Sir John

Daniel, R.
1 The Remover
2 The Remover returns
3 Again the Remover
□
1 Wu-Fang
2 Wu-Fang's return
3 Wu-Fang's revenge
4 Son of Wu-Fang

Daniels, N.
DR. KILDARE SERIES:
1 Dr. Kildare's secret romance 1964
2 Dr. Kildare's finest hour 1965

Daninos, P.
MAJOR THOMPSON SERIES:
1 Major Thompson lives in Paris.
[The notebooks of Major Thompson]
2 Major Thompson and I
*Later issued in one volume under title of
'Major Thompson'.*

Danoen, E.
JEANNET AND LYDIE:
1 Dust in the wind
2 The wind rises
*2 announced but not yet published in
English.*

Darbyshire, S.
MELBURY TRILOGY:
1 Journey to Melbury
2 The years at Melbury
3 High noon at Melbury
□
1 Young nurse Carter
2 Nurse Carter married
3 District nurse Carter, *by* L. Meynell.

Dargan, Mrs. O., *see* Burke, F., *pseud.*

Dark, E.
THE MANNION FAMILY:
1 The timeless land
2 Storm of time
3 No barrier
Novels on the history of Australia.

Dark, S.
1 Not such a bad life
2 I sit and I think and I wonder
3 On the outskirts
N.F. Autobiography

Darlington, W. A.
1 Alf's button
2 Alf's carpet
3 Alf's new button

Dasent, Sir G. W.
1 Popular tales from the north
2 Tales from the fjeld

Daudet, A.
MODERN DON QUIXOTE SERIES:
1 Tartarin of Tarascon
2 Tartarin on the Alps
3 Port Tarascon

Davey, J.
AMBROSE USHER SERIES:
1 The undoubted deed
2 The naked villainy
3 A touch of stage fright 1960
4 A killing in hats 1965

Davey, N.
1 The pilgrim of a smile
2 The penultimate adventure

Davies, A. C. Fox
1 The average man
2 The ultimate conclusion
☐
1 The Mauleverer millions
2 The Dangerville inheritance

Davis, A. H.
1 On our selection
2 Our new selection

Davis, A. J.
1 The magic staff
2 Beyond the valley
*N.F. Two books on spiritualism. Not
published in U.K.*

Davis, D. S.
JIMMIE JARVIS SERIES:
1 Death of an old sinner 1958

2 A gentleman called 1959
3 Old sinners never die 1960

Davis, J.
THE MACLEODS OF VIRGINIA:
1 Cloud on the land 1954
2 Bridle the wind 1955
3 Eagle on the sun 1957
*Novels about the development of the
Missouri country and the Shenandoah
valley in the 1820's.*

Davis, R. H.
1 Gallegher and other stories
2 Van Bibber and others
*There is one Van Bibber story in each
of the following: 'Stories for boys'
'Cinderella and other stories'.*

Davison, A.
1 Home was an island
2 Last voyage
3 Money no object 1957
*N.F. Autobiography
Not published in this order. 2 is an
expanded episode from 1.*

Davison, G.
TWISTED FACE SERIES:
1 The man with the twisted face
2 A prince of spies
3 A traitor unmasked
4 The devil's apprentice
5 Twisted Face, the avenger
6 Twisted Face strikes again
7 Twisted Face defends his title
☐
1 Mysterious Mr. Brent
2 Exit Mr. Brent

Dawe, C.
COL. 'LEATHERMOUTH' GANTIAN SERIES:
1 Leathermouth
2 Sign of the glove
3 Cumpled lilies
4 Fifteen keys
5 Missing treaty
6 Leathermouth's luck
7 Tough company

Dawson, A. J.
1 Finn, the wolfhound
2 Jan, the son of Finn
□
1 Joseph Khassan, half-caste
2 Hidden manna

Day, C.
1 Life with father
2 Life with mother

Deal, P.
1 Nurse! nurse! nurse!
2 Forward staff nurse
3 Nurse at Butlins
4 Surgery nurse
5 Village nurse 1960
6 Factory nurse 1962
N.F. Autobiography

Deane, N.
BRUCE MURDOCH SERIES:
1 Secret errand
2 Dangerous journey
3 Unknown mission
4 The withered man
5 I am the withered man
6 Where is the withered man?
4, 5 and 6 are sequels within the series,
LIBERATOR SERIES:
1 Return to adventure
2 Gateway to escape
. 3 Come home to crime

De Banke, C.
1 Hand over hand
2 Bright weft
3 American plaid
N.F. Autobiography

De Born, E.
THE DE KAILERN FAMILY:
1 Schloss Fielding. [Fielding Castle]
2 The house in Vienna
3 The flat in Paris
4 A question of age

Deeping, W.
1 Slade
. 2 Mr. Gurney and Mr. Slade

Defoe, D.
1 Robinson Crusoe
2 The return of Robinson Crusoe
1958, *by Henry Treece.*

Dehan, R. [Miss C. I. N. Graves]
1 The dop doctor, *same as* One braver thing
2 That which hath wings
□
1 The pipers of the market place
2 The lovers of the market place

Deighton, L.
1 The Ipcress file 1962
2 Horse under water 1963
3 Funeral in Berlin 1964
4 Billion dollar brain 1966

Dekobra, M.
THE LADY DIANA TRILOGY:
1 Wings of desire
2 The madonna of the sleeping cars
3 The phantom gondola

Delafield, E. M.
1 Diary of a provincial lady
2 A provincial lady goes farther
3 A provincial lady in America
4 Provincial lady in war-time

Deland, M.
1 Philip and his wife
2 Old Chester tales
3 Dr. Lavendar's people
4 Around old Chester
5 An old Chester secret
6 New friends in old Chester
□
1 The awakening of Helena Ritchie
2 The iron woman

De la Pasture, Mrs.
1 Catherine of Calais
2 Catherine's child

De la Roche, M.
WHITEOAKS SERIES:
1 The building of Jalna
2 Mary Wakefield
3 Morning at Jalna 1960
4 Young Renny

De la Roche, M. (*contd.*)
    5 Whiteoak heritage
    6 Whiteoak brothers
    7 Jalna
    8 Whiteoaks
    9 Finch's fortune
    10 Master of Jalna
    11 Whiteoak harvest
    12 Wakefield's course
    13 Return to Jalna
    14 Renny's daughter
    15 Variable winds at Jalna
    16 Centenary at Jalna 1958
    This is correct order of reading, not of publication.
    ☐
    1 Beside a Norman tower
    2 The very house

Delderfield, R. F.
    1 The dreaming suburb
    2 The avenue goes to war
    Republished (1964) in one volume as 'The avenue story'.
    ☐
    1 There was a fair maid dwelling 1960
    2 The unjust skies 1962
    The story of an adolescent love affair and a later reunion.

Dell, E. M.
    1 The way of an eagle
    2 The keeper of the door
    3 By request

Dell, F.
    1 Mooncalf
    2 The briary bush
    3 Souvenir

Delmer, S.
    1 Trail sinister
    2 Black boomerang
    N.F. Autobiography

De Mille, Agnes
    1 Dance to the piper
    2 And promenade back 1958
    N.F. Autobiography

Dennis, P.
    AUNTIE MAME SERIES:
    1 Auntie Mame

    2 Around the world with auntie Mame

Dennys, J.
    1 Mrs. Dose, the doctor's wife
    2 Repeated doses

De Polnay, P.
    1 Death and tomorrow
    2 Fools of choice
    3 A door ajar 1959
    4 Rough childhood 1960
    N.F. Autobiography
    ☐
    1 Out of the square 1950
    2 Mario 1961
    Mario and Giovanna are minor characters in 1, but principal in 2.

Derleth, A. W.
    SAC PRAIRIE, WISCONSIN SERIES:
    1 And day now
    2 Bright journey
    3 Restless is the river
    4 Wind over Wisconsin
    5 Shadow of night
    6 Still is the summer night
    7 Evening in spring
    8 Sweet Genevieve
    9 The shield of the valiant
    Each novel is complete in itself though some characters recur.

De Selincourt, H.
    CONSTANCE HOWARD SERIES:
    1 A daughter of the morning
    2 Realms of day
    3 Evening light
    GAUVINER SERIES:
    1 The cricket match
    2 Game of the season
    3 Gauviner takes to bowls

Desmond, H.
    ALAN FRASER SERIES:
    1 Death walks in scarlet
    2 Suicide pact

Deutscher, I.
    1 The prophet armed 1879–1921
    2 The prophet unarmed 1921–1929
    3 The prophet outcast 1929–1940
    N.F. Biography of Leon Trotsky

De Voto, B.
1 Westward the course of Empire
2 Across the wide Missouri
3 The year of decision, 1846
N.F. A trilogy on the settlement of the American West.

Dewes, S.
1 A Suffolk childhood
2 Essex schooldays
3 When all the world was young
N.F. Autobiography

Dewey, T. B.
SINGER BATTS SERIES:
1 Every bet's a sure thing
2 Mourning after
3 Handle with fear

De Wohl, L.
LIVES OF THE SAINTS:
1 Golden thread. (St. Ignatius of Loyola)
2 Restless flame (St. Augustine)
3 Set all afire (St. Francis Xavier) 1953
4 The quiet light (St. Thomas Aquinas)
5 The glorious folly (St. Paul) 1957
6 The joyful beggar (St. Francis) 1958
7 Citadel of God (St. Benedict) 1960
8 Lay siege to heaven (St. Catharine of Siena) 1960

Dexter, W.
1 World in eclipse
2 Children of the void

Dick, K.
ROBERT STAIREY SERIES:
1 By the lake
2 Young man
3 Told on a summer night

Dickens, C.
1 Pickwick papers
2 Pickwick abroad, *by G. W. M. Reynolds.*
3 Mr. Pickwick's second time on earth, *by C. G. Harper.*
'The mystery of Edwin Drood'. This unfinished story has been 'completed' by several authors. There is quite a literature
on Edwin Drood.
'The Gay Dombeys', and 'The Veneerings', by Sir H. Johnston, are sequels to 'Dombey and Son' and 'Our mutual friend' respectively.

Dickens, M.
1 One pair of hands
2 One pair of feet
3 My turn to make the tea
N.F. Autobiography

Dickson, C. *pseud.* [**John Dickson Carr**]
SIR HENRY MERIVALE SERIES:
1 Bowstring murders
2 The Plague Court murders
3 The White Priory murders
4 The Red widow murders
5 Unicorn murders
6 Magic lantern murders
7 Ten teacups
8 The Judas window
9 Death in five boxes
10 The reader is warned
11 Murder in the submarine zone
12 The department of queer complaints
13 And so to murder
14 Seeing is believing
15 The gilded man
16 She died a lady
17 He wouldn't kill patience
18 Lord of the sorcerers
19 My late wives
20 Skeleton in the clock
21 Graveyard to let
22 Night at the mocking widow
23 Behind the crimson blind
24 Cavalier's cup

Dickson, G.
SUPERINTENDENT MARLOW SERIES:
1 Knight's gambit
2 The seven screens

Dickson, L.
1 The ante-room
2 The house of words
N.F. Autobiography

Didelot, F.
COMMANDER BIGNON:
1 The tenth leper 1961
2 Death on the Champs Elysees 1965

Dillon, E.
PROFESSOR DALY SERIES:
1 Death at Crane's Court
2 Death in the quadrangle

Dimock, A. W.
1 Dick among the lumberjacks
2 Dick among the seminoles

Disraeli, B., 1st Earl of Beaconsfield
1 Coningsby
2 Sybil
3 Tancred
Not strictly sequels, but the same characters reappear

Diver, M.
DESMOND SERIES:
This is the author's own arrangement
1 Captain Desmond, v.c.
2 The great amulet
3 Candles in the wind
4 Desmond's daughter
5 A wild bird
6 Ships of youth
CHALLONERS SERIES:
1 Lonely furrow
2 But yesterday
3 A wild bird
4 Brave wings (later published with A wild bird]
5 Ships of youth
This series continues and overlaps the Desmond series.
THE ENGLISH SCENE:
1 Unconquered
2 Strange roads
3 Strong hours
4 Coombe St. Mary's
ELDRED POTTINGER SERIES:
1 The hero of Herat
2 The judgement of the sword
SINCLAIR SERIES:
1 Lilamani (Awakening]
2 Far to seek
3 The singer passes
4 The dream prevails
There is considerable overlapping of minor characters in all Maud Diver's novels.

Dixelius, F. H.
1 Minister's daughter
2 The son
3 The grandson

Dixon, T.
AMERICAN RECONSTRUCTION (1865–70) SERIES:
1 The leopard's spots
2 The clansman
3 The traitor

Dodd, C. I.
1 The farthing spinster
2 Queen Anne farthings
□
1 Lords of red lattice
2 Paul and Perdita

Dodge, D.
AL COLBY SERIES:
1 The long escape
2 Plunder of the sun
3 The red tassel
JAMES WHITNEY SERIES:
1 A drug on the market
2 Shear the black sheep
3 Bullets for the bridegroom
4 Death and taxes
□
1 How lost was my weekend
2 How green was my father
3 High life in the Andes
N.F. Autobiography

Dodge, H. I.
1 Skinner's dress suit
2 Skinner's baby
3 Skinner's idea
4 Skinner makes it fashionable

Dodge, L.
1 The sandman's forest
2 The sandman's mountain

Doell, E. W.
1 Doctor against witch doctor
2 Hospital in the bush
N.F. Autobiography

Doherty, L.
1 The good lion 1958
2 The good husband 1959

Doke, J. J.
1 The secret city
2 The queen of the secret city

Dolci, D.
1 To feed the hungry
2 The outlaws of Partinico
3 Waste 1962
N.F. A survey of poverty and crime in Sicily.

Donaldson, F.
1 Approach to farming
2 Four year's harvest
N.F. Autobiographical books on farming.

Dorling, T. *see* Taffrail, *pseud.*

Dos Passos, J.
U.S.A. TRILOGY:
1 The forty-second parallel
2 Nineteen nineteen
3 The big money
Later published in one volume as 'U.S.A.'
STORY OF THE SPOTSWOODS:
1 Adventures of a young man (Glenn Spotswood)
2 Number one (Tyler Spotswood)
These two volumes were published later in one volume as 'District of Columbia' with the inclusion of 'Grand Design'. Though the third volume is not a sequel the three together form a record of the period 1920–1936, and also a pendant to 'U.S.A.'

Douglas, E.
1 A family's affairs 1962
2 Black cloud, white cloud 1964

Douglas, G.
CAPTAIN SAMSON SERIES:
1 Obstinate captain Samson
2 Captain Samson, A.B.

Douglas, G. A. H.
1 Rab Hewison's adventures
2 Further adventures of Rab Hewison

Douglas, Ll. C.
1 Green light

2 Invitation to live
☐
1 Magnificent obsession
2 Dr. Hudson's secret journal
EARLY CHRISTIANITY SERIES:
1 The robe
2 The big fisherman

Douglass, D. McN.
BOLIVAR MANCHENIL SERIES:
1 Rebecca's pride
2 Many brave hearts 1959
3 Saba's treasure 1963

Douie, C.
1 The weary road
2 Beyond the sunset
3 So long to learn
N.F. Autobiography

Dowdall, Hon. Mrs.
1 The book of Martha
2 The second book of Martha

Dowdey, C.
STORY OF RICHMOND, VIRGINIA:
1 Gamble's hundred (1730)
2 Tidewater (1830's)
3 Bugles blow no more (Civil War)
4 Where my love sleeps (Civil War)
5 Sing for a penny (1880's)

Downe, P.
1 Dear doctor 1958
2 The doctor calls again 1959
3 Come in, doctor 1960
N.F. Autobiography

Downing, J. H.
1 Sioux city
2 Anthony Trant

Downing, T.
HUGH RENNERT SERIES:
1 Case of the unconquered sisters
2 Murder on the tropic
3 Vultures in the sky
4 The cat screams
5 The last trumpet
6 Night over Mexico

Doyle, Sir A. C.
ENGLISH BOWMEN SERIES:
1 Sir Nigel
2 The White Company
SHERLOCK HOLMES SERIES:
1 A study in scarlet
2 The sign of four
3 Adventures of Sherlock Holmes
4 The memoirs of Sherlock Holmes,
   same as Last adventures of Sherlock
   Holmes.
5 The hound of the Baskervilles
6 The return of Sherlock Holmes
7 The valley of fear
8 His last bow
9 The case-book of Sherlock Holmes
   *'The exploits of Sherlock Holmes', by
   Adrian Conan Doyle and J. D. Carr.
   Based on unrecorded exploits mentioned
   by Dr. Watson.
   'Misadventures of Sherlock Holmes',
   edited by Ellery Queen, is a collection
   of parodies of the Holmes stories by
   various writers, including Maurice
   Le Blanc, S. Leacock, Sir James
   Barrie, Agatha Christie and others.*
BRIGADIER GERARD SERIES:
1 The exploits of Brigadier Gerard
2 Adventures of Gerard
3 The crime of the Brigadier
   A story in 'The Green flag'
4 Marriage of the Brigadier
   A story in 'The last Galley'
PROFESSOR CHALLENGER SERIES:
1 The lost world
2 The poison belt
3 The land of mist
4 When the world screamed
5 The disintegration machine (*in 'The
   Maracot Deep' and other stories*).
   *All the above collected in one volume
   'The Professor Challenger stories'.*

Doyle, L.
1 Ballygullion
2 Dear Ducks

D'Oyley, E.
PRINCE RUPERT:
1 The English march
2 Prince Rupert's daughter

Draper, H.
1 Wiggery pokery
2 Wigged and gowned 1958

Dreiser, T.
FRANK COWPERWOOD TRILOGY:
1 The titan
2 The financier
3 The stoic

Drummond, H.
RELIGIOUS WARS IN FRANCE SERIES:
1 For the religion
2 A man of his age
3 A king's pawn

Druon, Maurice
THE ACCURSED KINGS, SERIES 1:
1 The Iron king 1956
2 The strangled queen 1956
3 The poisoned crown 1957
4 The royal succession 1958
THE ACCURSED KINGS, SERIES 2:
5 She-wolf of France 1960
6 The lily and the lion 1961
   *A series of novels about the long
   tragedy of France under the weak
   Capetan and Valois kings of the 14th
   century. The curse is the one supposed to
   have been uttered on the scaffold by the
   master of the Templars when executed
   by Philip the Fair.
   The scene changes often from France to
   Italy and England, and the story is
   immensely detailed with a huge cast of
   characters, but always following the
   main theme.*
THE CURTAIN FALLS:
1 The magnates
2 Feet of clay
3 Rendezvous in hell
   *Republished in one volume under title
   'The curtain falls' (1959). French title
   'Les grandes familles'. Prix Goncourt.*

Drury, A.
1 Advise and consent 1962
2 A shade of difference 1964
   *Two novels of American political
   life. Not strictly sequels, but characters
   reappear.*

Drury, W. P.
1 The Peradventures of Private Pagett
2 Pagett calling
□
1 The flag-lieutenant
2 The flag-lieutenant in China

Du Bois, M. C.
1 The lass of the silver sword
2 The League of the Signet-ring

Du Bois, W. J.
1 Otto at sea
2 Otto in Texas
3 Otto in Africa 1962

Du Boisgobey, F.
'The old age of Lecoq the detective'
is a sequel to Gaboriau's *Lecoq* series.

Ducat, E., *and* **Oliver, M. M.** *see*
Oliver, M. M.

Duche, S.
1 I said to my wife
2 Not at home

Dudley, E.
DR. MORELLE SERIES:
1 Meet Dr. Morelle
2 Dr. Morelle again
3 Menace for Dr. Morelle
4 Dr. Morelle and the drummer girl
5 Dr. Morelle takes a bow
6 Callers for Dr. Morelle 1957
7 The mind of Dr. Morelle 1958
8 Dr. Morelle and destiny 1958
9 Confess to Dr. Morelle 1958
10 Dr. Morelle at midnight 1959
11 Alibi for Dr. Morelle 1959
12 Nightmare for Dr. Morelle 1960
13 Dr. Morelle and the doll 1960

Dudley, O. F.
MASTERFUL MONK SERIES ?
1 Will men be like gods?
2 The shadow on the earth
3 The masterful monk
4 Pageant of life
5 The coming of the monster
6 The Tremaynes and the masterful
monk

7 Michael
8 The last crescendo

Dudley-Smith, T., *see* Smith, T. Dudley-

Duffield, E. M.
1 Lucille, the torch bearer
2 Lucille, bringer of joy
3 Lucille triumphant
4 Lucille on the heights

Dugmore, A. R.
1 Adventures in Beaver Stream
Camp
2 Two boys in Beaver Land

Duhamel, G.
1 News from Havre (*Le Notaire de
Havre*)
2 Young Pasquier (*Le jardin de
bêtes sauvages*)
3 In sight of the promised land (*Vue
de la terre promise*)
4 St. John's Eve (*Nuit de la Saint-Jean*)
5 The house in the desert (*Le desert de
bievres*)
All the above are collected in one
volume entitled, 'The Pasquier
Chronicles', no. 2 being re-titled
'Caged beasts'.
6 Pastors and masters (*Les maitres*)
7 Cécile (*Cécile parmi nous*)
8 The fight against the shadows (*Le
combat contre les ombres*)
These were later collected as a single
volume, 'Cécile among the Pasquiers'.
9 Suzanne and the young men
(*Suzanne et les jeunes hommes*)
10 The passion of Joseph Pasquier (*La
passion de Joseph Pasquier*)
Published in one volume as 'Suzanne
and Joseph Pasquier'.
Titles in parenthesis are the original
French titles.
'News from Havre' was published in
U.S. as 'Papa Pasquier', 'Caged beasts'
and 'In sight of the Promised Land' in
one volume as 'Fortunes of the
Pasquiers'.
SALAVIN:
1 Confession at midnight (*Confession
de minuit*)

Duhamel, G. (*contd.*)
2 Deux hommes
3 Salavin's journal (*Journal de Salavin*)
4 Lyonnais club (*Club de Lyonnais*)
5 End of illusion (*Tel qu'en lui-meme*)
No. 2 is omitted in both British and
American translations. Published in one
volume as 'Salavin'.

Duke, M.
THE SUNDMANS: A TRIPTYCH:
1 A city built to music 1960
2 Ride the brooding wind 1961
3 The Sovereign Lords 1963
*A trilogy of novels dealing with world
events from the 1840's to World War II.*

Duke, W.
HAROLD FIELDEND TETRALOGY:
1 Bastard verdict
2 The dark hill
3 The sown wind
4 Finale
5 These are they
6 Magpies' hoard
5 and 6 are pendant to the tetralogy.

Dumas, A.
THE EARLIER VALOIS ROMANCES (1540–60):
1 Ascanio, *same as* Francis I, *or* The
sculptor's apprentice and the
provost's daughter
2 The two Dianas
3 Page of the Duke of Savoy, *same
as* The Duke's Page. *Published also
in three parts as:*
(*a*) Leone-Leona
(*b*) St. Quentin
(*c*) Tourney, *or* The Rue St. Antoine
4 The horoscope. The brigand
VALOIS ROMANCES (1560–89):
1 Marguerite de Valois
2 Chicot, the Jester, *same as* La Dame
de Monsoreau, *same as* Diana of
Meridor. ·
3 The forty-five guardsmen, *same as*
The forty-five.
D'ARTAGNAN ROMANCES (1626–71):
1 The three musketeers, *same as* The
three guardsmen.
2 Twenty years after
3 The Vicomte de Bragelonne, *same*

as Ten years later.
*There is a good deal of confusion about
no. 3. The original French edition was
'Le Vicomte de Bragelonne, ou Dix ans
plus tard', in 26 volumes. English
editions are usually divided into four
parts, as follows:*
1 Vicomte de Bragelonne
2 Louise de la Valliére
3 The iron mask
4 Son of Porthos
*Volumes entitled 'Ten years later', are
usually the first part of the series to
Ch. 'Royal psychology', which is
halfway through 'Louise de La Valliere'.
The Routledge 2-volume edition, and
the 5-volume edition, and the Everyman
3-volume edition go to Ch. 'Death of
D'Artagnan', which is the end of 'Iron
mask'. The edition in print at time of
writing is the Collins 4-volume edition
subdivided as follows:*
*'Vicomte de Bragelonne, to ch. 'For
ever'. 'Louise de La Valliere' to ch.
'St. Aignan follows . . .'*
*'Man in the iron mask' to ch. 'Death of
D'Artagnan'.*
'Son of Porthos' to ch. 'Au revoir'.
*Other volumes by various publishers
entitled 'Son of Porthos', 'Death of
Aramis', are all a part of this last
section from ch. 'From father to son' to
'Au revoir'.*
*Readers are recommended to use one
edition only to avoid missing some
sections, the Collins being most complete.
In 1853 the publication was announced
of Le Maréchal Ferrant, in 4 volumes, a
sequel to the D'Artagnan cycle. The
work was not written.*
REGENCY ROMANCES (1717–29):
1 The conspirators, *same as* Chevalier
d'Harmental
2 The Regent's daughter
3 Olympe de Clèves
MARIE ANTOINETTE ROMANCES (1770–93):
1 Memoirs of a physician, *same as*
Joseph Balsamo
2 The queen's necklace
3 Taking the Bastile, *same as* Ange
Pitou, *same as* Six years later.
4 Countess de Charny

5 Chevalier de Maison Rouge, *same as* Andree de Taverney, Mesmerists victim, Reign of terror, *same as* The Chevalier
6 Monsieur de Chauvelin's will, *same as* The velvet necklace

NAPOLEON ROMANCES (1793–1844):
1 The Whites and the Blues, *two series. Same as* The First Republic
2 The companions of Jehu, *same as* Roland Montrevel
3 La Vendée, *same as* She wolves of Machecoul, *same as* Last Vendée
4 The Corsican brothers

THE NELSON AT NAPLES ROMANCES:
1 The Neapolitan lovers
2 Love and liberty
These two titles are translations by W. H. Garnett of 'La San-Felice' and its sequel 'Souvenirs d'une favourite'. Other versions of parts of this work have appeared under the titles 'The lovely Lady Hamilton'. 'Nelson at Naples'. Part of 'San-Felice' was re-issued as 'Emma Lyonna' and it appears that it is from this that most of the abridged versions are taken.

THE GERMAN ROMANCES (1810–30):
1 The mouth of hell, *same as* The Devil's hole.
2 Olympia ·
3 Samuel Gelb
The two latter form in the French one story entitled 'Dieu dispose'.

THE PARIS ROMANCES (1827–30):
1 The Mohicans of Paris
2 Salvator
☐
1 The prince of thieves
2 Robin Hood

OTHER HISTORICAL ROMANCES:
Agenor de Mauleon (1361)
Black, the story of a dog (1814)
The black tulip (1672–75)
The Count of Monte Cristo (1814).
At least two sequels have been written to this work.
Sylvandire (1708–16)
Tales of the Caucasus
The war of women (1650)
A number of Dumas' stories have not been translated into English. Hereunder

a list of the sequel stories available only in the French text.
1 La dame de Volupté
2 Les deux reines
☐
1 Le docteur Mystérieux
2 La fille du Marquis
'Le Capitaine Paul' [Jones] is a sequel to J. F. Cooper's 'The Pilot'.

Du Maurier, A.
1 Stage and I
2 These I have loved
3 Those twenties
4 It's only the sister
N.F. Autobiography

Dumitriu, P.
THE BOYARS TRILOGY:
1 Family jewels 1960
2 The prodigals 1962
Novels of modern Roumania.

Dunboyne, Lady
1 Elsie's summer at Malvern
2 A sunbeam's influence

Duncan, A.
1 It's a vet's life
2 The vet has nine lives
3 Vets in the belfrey 1963
N.F. Autobiography

Duncan, F.
M. E. TREMAINE SERIES:
1 Murderer's bluff
2 They'll never find out
3 So pretty a problem
4 In at the death
5 Behold a fair woman 1955
PETER JUSTICE SERIES:
1 Hand of justice
2 Sword of justice
3 The League of justice
4 Justice returns
5 Justice limited

Duncan, J.
REACHFAR SERIES:
1 My friends the Miss Boyds
2 My friend Miss Muriel 1959
3 My friend Monica 1960

Duncan, J. (*contd.*)
4 My friend Annie
5 My friend Sandy 1961
6 My friend Martha's aunt 1961
7 My friend Flora 1962
8 My friend Madame Zora 1963
9 My friend Rose 1964
10 My friend Emmie 1964
11 My friends the Mrs. Millers 1965
12 My friends from Cairnton 1966

Duncan, R.
1 Don Juan
2 Death of Satan
N.F. verse

Duncan, W. M.
SUPERINTENDENT RONALD REAMER SERIES:
1 Meet the dreamer 1963
2 Again the dreamer 1964
3 Presenting the dreamer 1966
GREENSLEEVES SERIES:
1 Mystery on the Clyde
2 Straight ahead for danger
3 Cult of queer people

Dunn, Detective
1 The beautiful devil
2 A queen of crooks

Dunn, B. A.
YOUNG KENTUCKIANS SERIES – 5 VOLS.
YOUNG MISSOURIANS SERIES – 5 VOLS.

Dunne, F. P.
1 Mr. Dooley in peace and war
2 Mr. Dooley in the hearts of his
   countrymen
3 Mr. Dooley's philosophy
4 Mr. Dooley's opinions
5 Observations by Mr. Dooley
6 Dissertations by Mr. Dooley
7 Mr. Dooley says
8 Mr. Dooley on making a will

Dunnett, D.
1 The game of kings
2 Queen's play

Dunsany, E. J. Plunkett, 18th Baron
1 The travel tales of Mr. Joseph
   Jorkens

2 Mr. Jorkens remembers Africa
3 Jorkens has a large whisky
4 The fourth book of Jorkens
5 Jorkens borrows another whisky

Dunton, T. Watts-
1 Aylwin
2 The coming of love (poetry)

Dupuy, E. A.
1 The dethroned heiress
2 Hidden sin

Durbridge, F.
1 Send for Paul Temple
2 Paul Temple and the front page
   men
3 Paul Temple intervenes
4 News of Paul Temple
5 Send for Paul Temple again

Durrell, L.
THE ALEXANDRIA QUARTET:
1 Justine 1957
2 Balthazar 1958
3 Mountolive 1958
4 Clea 1960
Now published in one volume (1962).
□
1 Prospero's cell
2 Reflections on a marine Venus
3 Bitter lemons of Cyprus
*Three connected travel books on Greek
islands – Rhodes, Capri and Cyprus.*
□
1 Esprit de corps
2 Stiff upper lip

Dutton, C. J.
TIMOTHY ROGAN SERIES:
1 Circle of death
2 Black fog

Dutton, G.
1 A long way south
2 Africa in black and white
N.F. Autobiography

Duun, O.
THE PEOPLE OF JUVIK SERIES:
1 The trough of the wave
2 Blind man

3 The big wedding
4 Odin in faery land
5 Odin grows up
6 The storm

Dyson, E.
REVILL–GORDON SERIES:
1 With swords in their lips
2 Proud suitor 1959

Eastwood, D.
1 River diary
2 Valleys of springs
N.F. Travel and autobiography in Wales.

Eaton, E.
1 Every month was May
2 North star is nearer
N.F. Autobiography

Eberhart, M. G.
SARAH KEATE SERIES:
1 The patient in room 18
2 While the patient sleeps
3 The mystery of Hunting s End
4 From this dark stairway
5 Murder of my patient
6 Wolf in man's clothing
7 Man missing

Edel, L.
HENRY JAMES:
1 The untried years
2 The conquest of London
3 The middle years, 1884–1894 1963
N.F. Biography

Edelman, M.
1 The minister 1963
2 The Prime Minister's daughter 1964

Eden, Hon. E.
1 The semi-attached couple
2 The semi-detached house

Eden, R. A., *see* Avon, 1st Earl of

Edmonds, H.
1 The clockmaker of Heidelberg
2 The rockets – operation Manhattan
3 The orphans of Brandenburg

Edmonds, W. D.
1 Erie water
2 Rome haul
3 The big barn
4 Mostly canallers
Chronicles of the building of the Erie canal.

Edmunds, B.
PETE MARVIN SERIES:
1 A gun in my back
2 Ride a dark horse
3 Beware the crimson cord 1956
4 Spiders in the night 1956

Edwards, H.
1 Under four flags
2 Their lawful occasions
N.F. Autobiography

Egan, L.
JESSE FALKENSTEIN AND VIC VARALLO:
1 A case for appeal (both) 1962
2 The borrowed alibi (Varallo] 1962
3 Against the evidence (Falkenstein) 1963
4 Run to evil (Varallo) 1963
5 My name is death (Falkenstein) 1965
6 Detective's due (Varallo) 1965

Egan, P.
1 Life in London
2 Finish to the adventures of Tom, Jerry and Logic

Eggleston, G. C.
INDIAN WAR OF 1812 SERIES:
1 The big brother
2 Captain Sam
3 The signal boys
□
1 Dorothy South
2 Master of Warlock
3 Evelyn Byrd

Ehrenburg, I.
1 The thaw
2 The spring

Ehrenburg, I. (*contd.*)

☐
1 The storm
2 The ninth wave
MEN, YEARS, AND LIFE:
1 Childhood and youth (1891–1917)
2 First years of revolution (1918–1921)
3 Truce (1921–1933)
4 Eve of war (1933–1941)
5 The war (1941–1945)
6 The post-war years
N.F. Autobiography

Eichler, A.
MARTIN AMES SERIES:
1 Death at the mike
2 Death of an artist

Elias, F.
1 Cricket on the brain
2 Cricket at the breakfast table

Eliot, George *pseud.* [**M. Evans,**
afterwards **Mrs. Cross**]
'Gwendolen' (anonymous author) was
written as a sequel to 'Daniel Deronda'.

Elliot, J., *joint author, see* Hoyle, F. *and*
J. Elliot

Ellis, W. D.
THE OHIO FRONTIER:
1 The Bounty lands 1952
2 Jonathan Blair 1954
3 The Brooks legend 1958
*Although characters re-appear, the real
connection is the story of the settlement
of Ohio.*

Elsna, H.
1 A house called Pleasance 1962
2 Too well beloved 1964
3 The undying past 1964
*Novels on the history of a country house,
from Tudor times to Victorian.*

Emerson, D.
1 Pride of Parson Carnaby
2 The trouble at Shaplinck 1959
☐
1 The surgeon of Sedbridge
2 The warden of Greys 1957

Enright, D. J.
1 Academic year 1955
2 Heaven knows where 1956
*Adventures of a schoolmaster in foreign
countries. Not sequels but main character
is the same.*

Erckmann, E., *and* **Chatrian, A.**
FRENCH CAMPAIGN SERIES:
1 The conscript
2 Waterloo
STORY OF A PEASANT SERIES:
1 The States General
2 The country in danger
3 Year one of the republic
4 Citizen Bonaparte

Erdman, L. G.
PIERCE FAMILY SERIES:
1 The wind blows free
2 The wide horizon
3 The good land 1960
Novels about pioneer farming in Texas.

Erskine, L. Y.
1 Renfrew of the Royal Mounted
2 Renfrew rides again
3 Renfrew rides the sky
4 Renfrew rides north
5 Renfrew's long trail
6 Renfrew rides the range
7 Renfrew in the valley of vanished
men
8 Renfrew flies again

Erskine, M.
SEPTIMUS FINCH SERIES:
1 Give up the ghost
2 I knew Macbean
3 Whispering house
4 Dead by now
5 And being dead
6 The disappearing bridegroom
7 Fatal relations
8 The voice of murder 1956
9 Death of our dear one 1957
10 Sleep no more 1958
11 The house of the enchantress 1959
12 The woman at Belguardo 1961
13 The house on Belmont Square 1963
14 Take a dark journey 1965

Erskine, R.
1 The passion-flower hotel 1962
2 Passion flowers in Italy 1963
3 Passion flowers in business 1965

Essex, J. R. *see* Gaunt, M. *and* Essex, J. R.

Essex, R.
SLADE OF THE YARD SERIES:
1 Slade of the Yard
2 Slade scores again
LESSINGER SERIES:
1 Lessinger comes back
2 Murder in the bank
3 Lessinger laughs last
4 Marinova of the secret service
5 Assisted by Lessinger

Ethel, *pseud.*
1 Wreck
2 Lufness

Evans, B.
1 Natural history of nonsense
2 The spoor of Sparks
N.F. Exposure of popular fallacies.

Evans, B. Ifor
1 The shop in the King's High Rd.
2 The church in the markets

Evans, C.
1 Love from Belinda 1961
2 Lalage in love 1962

Evans, E.
THE MONTANA KID:
1 The song of the whip
2 Montana rides!

Evans, M.
1 Autobiography
2 Ray of darkness
N.F. Autobiography

Eyre, D. C.
CAPTAIN O'DONNELL SERIES:
1 Foxes have holes
2 Drum beat

Eyton, J.
1 Kulla of the carts
2 Bulbulla, a novel of India

Fabian, W.
1 Flaming youth
2 Sailors' wives

Fair, A. A. *pseud.* [**E. S. Gardner**]
BERTHA COOL–DONALD LAM SERIES:
1 Lam to the slaughter
2 Turn on the heat
3 Gold comes in bricks
4 Spill the jackpot
5 Axe to grind
6 Crows can't count
7 Owls don't blink
8 Cats prowl at night
9 Bats fly at dusk
10 Double or quits
11 Fools die on Friday 1955
12 Bedrooms have windows 1956
13 Top of the heap 1957
14 Some women won't wait 1957
15 Beware of the curves 1958
16 You can die laughing 1958
17 Some slips don't show 1959
18 The count of nine 1959
19 Pass the gravy 1959
20 Kept women can't quit 1960
21 Bachelors get lonely 1961
22 Stop at the red 1962
23 Try anything once 1963
24 Fish or cut bait 1964
25 Up for grabs 1965
26 Cut thin to win 1966

Fairbank, Mrs. J. A.
1 The Costlandts of Washington Square
2 The Smiths
3 Rich man, poor man

Fairbrother, N.
1 Children in the house
2 The cheerful day
N.F. Autobiography

Fairlie, G.
MR. MALCOLM SERIES:
1 A shot in the dark
2 Mr. Malcolm presents
3 Men for counters
CARYLL SERIES:
1 Scissors cut paper
2 Man who laughed

Fairlie, G. (*contd.*)
   3 Stone blunts scissors
JOHN MACALL SERIES:
   1 Winner take all
   2 No sleep for Macall
   3 Deadline for Macall 1956
   4 Double the bluff 1957
   5 Macall gets curious 1959
   6 Murder most discreet 1960
   7 Please kill my cousin 1961
See also Sapper

Falla, R.
   1 Life in Emergency Ward 10 1959
   2 Love in Emergency Ward 10 1960
   3 The sisters of Emergency Ward 10
     1961
   4 Case for Emergency Ward 10 1962
   5 The boy in Emergency Ward 10
     1963

Faralla, D.
   1 The magnificent barb 1947
   2 Black renegade 1954
   *Horse breeding and plantation life in
   Georgia at the turn of the 19th century.*

Farewell, N.
   1 The unfair sex
   2 Someone to love

Farjeon, J. J.
BEN SERIES:
   1 No. 17
   2 The house opposite
   3 Riverside mystery
   4 The crook's shadow
   5 Ben sees it through
   6 Murderer's trail
   7 Little God Ben
   8 Detective Ben
   9 Number nineteen
  10 Ben on the job
Z SERIES:
   1 Person called 'Z'
   2 The Z murders

Farmer, B. J.
SERGEANT WIGAN SERIES:
   1 Death at the cascades 1955
   2 Death of a bookseller 1956

   3 Once and then the funeral 1957
   4 Murder next year 1959

Farnol, J.
   1 Black Bartelmy's treasure
   2 Martin Conisby's vengeance
   ☐
   1 The crooked furrow
   2 The happy harvest
   ☐
   1 The broad highway
   2 Charmian Lady Vibart
   3 The way beyond
   *Minor characters of the first book appear
   in 'Peregrine's progress'.
   Mr. Shrig of Bow St. appears in
   'Amateur Gentleman' and again in
   'Ninth Earl', 'The Loring mystery' and
   'Peregrine's progress'.*

Farran, R.
   1 Winged dagger
   2 Operation Tombola 1960
   *N.F. Wartime experiences with Special
   Air Service.*

Farrar, C. A. J.
   1 Eastward ho!
   2 Wild woods life
   3 Down the west branch
   4 Up the north branch

Farrar, S.
   1 The snake on 99 1962
   2 Zero in the gate 1963
   3 Death in the wrong bed 1964

Farre, R.
   1 Seal morning 1957
   2 A time from the world 1962
   N.F. Autobiography

Farrell, J. T.
DANNY O'NEILL SERIES:
   1 Face of time
   2 A world I never made
   3 No star is lost
   4 A father and his son
   5 My days of anger
   ☐
STUDS LONIGAN SERIES:
   1 Young Lonigan

2 Young manhood of Studs Lonigan
3 Judgement day
Minor characters reappear in both series.
□
1 Bernard Clayre
2 The road between
Hero is named Bernard Carr in 2.

Farrer, K.
DET.-INSP. RINGWOOD SERIES:
1 The missing link
2 The Cretan counterfeit 1954
3 Gownsman's gallows 1957

Farson, N.
1 Way of a transgressor
2 A mirror for Narcissus
N.F. Autobiography

Faulkner, W.
1 Sartoris
2 Sound and the fury
3 As I lay dying
4 Sanctuary
5 Light in August
6 Absalom, Absalom
7 The hamlet
8 Requiem for a nun
9 The town 1957
10 The mansion 1957
Of these, 4 and 8 are direct sequels, and other minor characters re-appear. Gavin Stephens appears in 8 and also in 'Knight's gambit' and 'Intruder in the dust'. 7, 9 and 10 form a trilogy on the Snopes family, but they are also part of the series.
The main body of Mr. Faulkner's work is in the nature of a continuous 'Roman Fleuve', each volume of which is complete in itself, although the novels exist in the mind of the author as interdependent and inseparable one from the other. Thus Narcissa in 'Sanctuary' is a main figure in 'Sartoris' and the Quentin who commits suicide in the 'Sound and the Fury' reappears as the Listener in 'Absalom'. These additions and developments never appear to have been looked on as afterthoughts, but seem to have been held in reserve until the time was ripe for telling.

Fausset, H. I'A.
1 Modern prelude
2 Towards fidelity
N.F. Autobiography

Fearon, D.
MISS ARABELLA FRANT SERIES:
1 Death before breakfast 1959
2 Murder-on-Thames 1960

Fedorova, Nina
1 The family
2 The children

Ferber, E.
1 Roast beef, medium
2 Personality plus
3 Emma McChesney and Co.
4 Fanny herself

Ferguson, Rachel
1 Passionate Kensington
2 Royal Borough
N.F. Partly a sequel and partly in answer to the many correspondents who wrote about 'Passionate Kensington' – Author's note.

Ferguson, W. B. M.
CALVERT SERIES:
1 Lightnin' Calvert
2 The reckoning

Fergusson, B.
1 Beyond the Chindwin
2 The wild green earth
Account of the Burma campaign.

Fergusson, H.
FOLLOWERS OF THE SUN; A TRILOGY
OF THE SOUTH-WEST:
1 Wolf song
2 In those days
3 Blood of the conquerors

Fermor, P. L.
1 Mani 1963
2 Roumeli 1965
N.F. Travel in Greece.

Fetterless, A.
1 Gog
2 Battle days

Fetzer, H.
1 Jacoby's corners
2 The big snow
3 Come back to Wayne County

Feuchtwanger, L.
1 Success
2 The Oppermans
　□
1 Josephus
2 The Jew of Rome
3 The day will come

Feval, P. *and* **Cassez, M.**
THE YEARS BETWEEN SERIES:
1 The mysterious cavalier
2 Martyr to the queen
3 Secret of the Bastille
4 Heir of Buckingham
5 Comrades at arms
6 Salute to Cyrano
Note: these are sequels to 'Three Musketeers', by Dumas.

Field, P.
POWDER VALLEY SERIES:
1 Law man of Powder Valley
2 Trail south from Powder Valley
3 Fight for Powder Valley
4 Death rides the night
5 Smoking iron
6 Guns from Powder Valley
7 Powder Valley vengeance
8 Canyon hideout
9 Road to Laramie
10 End of the trail
11 Powder Valley showdown
12 Ravaged Range
13 Sheriff wanted
14 Gamblers gold
15 Trail from Needle rock
16 Outlaw valley
17 Sheriff on the spot
18 Return to Powder Valley
19 Blacksnake trail
20 Powder Valley ambush
21 Back trail to danger 1951
22 Three guns from Colorado
23 Guns in the saddle 1952
24 Powder Valley holdup 1952
25 Mustang mesa 1952

26 Putlaw of Eagle's Nest 1952
27 Riders of the outlaw trail 1952
28 Powder Valley stampede 1954
29 Powder Valley deadlock 1954
30 War in the painted buttes 1954
31 Outlaw of Cattle Canyon 1955
32 Breakneck Pass 1955
33 Rawhide rider 1955

Fielding, A.
INSPECTOR POINTER SERIES:
1 The Charteris mystery
2 The Eames-Erskine case
3 Deep currents
4 The footsteps that stopped
5 The Clifford affair
6 The net around Joan Ingleby
7 The cluny problem
8 The mysterious partner
9 Murder at the nook
10 The Craig poisoning mystery
11 The wedding chest mystery
12 The Upfold farm mystery
13 Death of John Tait
14 The Westwood mystery
15 The Tall house mystery
16 The Cautley conundrum
17 The paper chase
18 Tragedy at Beechcroft
19 The case of the missing diary
20 The case of the two pearl necklaces
21 Mystery at the rectory
22 Black cats are lucky
23 Murder in Suffolk
24 Pointer to a crime

Fielding, G.
1 Brotherly love
2 In the time of Greenbloom

Finch, M.
1 Dentist in the chair
2 Teething troubles
N.F. Autobiography
　□
1 Five are the symbols
2 Jones is a rainbow 1965
3 The beauty farm 1965

Findley, D.
JOHNNY MALONE SERIES:
1 My old man's badge
2 Remember that face

Finn, Mrs. E. A. M.
1 Home in the Holy Land
2 A third year in Jerusalem

Finnegan, R.
DAN BANION SERIES:
1 The lying ladies
2 The bandaged nude
3 Many a monster

Firbank, T.
1 I bought a mountain
2 From mountain so rocky
3 I bought a star
4 Country of memorable honour
5 Log hut
6 I am a traveller
N.F. Autobiography

Fish, A. H.
1 The Eve book
2 The new Eve
3 The third Eve book

Fisher, D.
JEFF TELFORD SERIES:
1 What's wrong at Pyford
2 Poison pen at Pyford
3 Death at Pyford Hall

Fisher, D. C.
1 Rough-hewn
2 The brimming cup

Fisher, J. A., 1st Baron. Edited by
A. J. Mander
FEAR GOD AND DREAD NOUGHT:
1 The making of an admiral
(1854–1904)
2 Years of power (1904–1915)
3 Restoration, abdication and last
years (1914–1920)
N.F. Autobiography

Fisher, V.
1 I see no sin. [In tragic life]
2 Passions spin the plot
3 We are betrayed
4 No villain need be
TESTAMENT OF MAN SERIES:
1 Darkness and the deep
2 Golden rooms

3 Intimations of Eve
4 Adam and the serpent
5 The divine passion
6 Valley of vision
7 The island of the innocent

Fitch, G. H.
1 At good old Siwash
2 Petey Simmons at Siwash

Fitt, M.
SUPERINTENDENT MALLETT SERIES:
1 Expected death
2 Sky rocket
3 Death at dancing stones
4 Murder of a mouse
5 Death starts a rumour
6 Death and Mary Dazill
7 Death on Heron's mere
8 Requiem for Robert
9 Death and the pleasant voices
10 Clues re Christabel
11 Death and the bright day
12 The banquet ceases
13 Death and the shortest day
14 An ill wind
15 The man who shot birds
16 Love from Elizabeth
17 Mizmaze 1959

Fitzgerald, J. D.
1 Papa married a Mormon
2 Mamma's boarding house
3 Uncle Will and the Fitzgerald curse
N.F. Autobiography

Fitzgerald, N.
SUPERINTENDENT DUFFY SERIES:
1 Midsummer malice
2 The rosy pastor
3 Imagine a man 1956
4 The house is falling 1958
5 Suffer a witch 1958

Fitzgerald, P.
1 Bella Donna
2 Jenny Bell
3 Seventy-five Brooke Street

Fleming, I.
JAMES BOND SERIES:
1 Casino Royale 1953
2 Live and let die 1954
3 Moonraker 1955
4 Diamonds are forever 1956
5 From Russia with love 1957
6 Dr. No 1958
7 Goldfinger 1959
8 For your eyes only 1960
9 Thunderball 1961
10 The spy who loved me 1961
11 On His Majesty's Secret Service 1963
12 You only live twice 1964
13 The man with the golden gun 1965
14 Octopussy and the living daylights 1966
For an analysis of the stories see 'The James Bond dossier', by Kingsley Amis, 1965. 'The book of Bond', by William Tanner is a guide to 007ship.

Fleming, J.
NURI BEY SERIES:
1 When I grow rich 1964
2 Nothing is the number when you die 1965

Fletcher, G. N.
1 In my father's house
2 Preacher's kids
N.F. Autobiography

Fletcher, I.
HISTORY OF VIRGINIA SERIES:
1 Roanoke hundred (Elizabethan) 1948
2 Bennett's welcome (Cromwellian) 1950
3 Men of Albemarle (1710–1712) 1945
4 Cormorant's brood (1712–1718) 1959
5 Lusty wind for Carolina (1718–1725) 1944
6 Raleigh's Eden (1765–1782) 1940
7 The wind in the forest (1771) 1957
8 Toil of the brave (1779–1780) 1946
9 Queen's gift (1788) 1952
This is the suggested order of reading, not order of publication.

Fletcher, J. S.
1 Owd Poskitt

2 Mr. Poskitt
3 Mr. Poskitt's nightcaps
RONALD CAMBERWELL SERIES:
1 Murder at Wrides Park
2 Murder in four degrees
3 Murder in the Squire's pew
4 Murder of the 9th baronet
5 Who killed Alfred Crowe
6 Murder of the only witness
7 Mystery of the London banker
8 Murder of the secret agent
9 The ebony box
10 The eleventh hour

Flint, E.
1 Hot bread and chips 1963
2 Kipper stew 1964
N.F. Autobiography

Flower, P.
INSPECTOR SWINTON SERIES:
1 Goodby Sweet William
2 Wax flowers for Gloria
3 A wreath of water lilies 1959
4 One rose less 1960

Flynn, B.
ANTHONY BATHURST SERIES:
1 The billiard room mystery
2 The case of the black twenty-two
3 Mystery of the peacock's eye
4 The murders near Mapleton
5 Invisible death
6 The five red fingers
7 The creeping Jenny mystery
8 Murder en route
9 The orange axe
10 The triple bite
11 The padded door
12 The edge of terror
13 The spiked lion
14 The League of Matthias
15 The horn
16 The case of the purple calf
17 The Sussex cuckoo
18 The Fortescue candle
19 Fear and trembling
20 Cold evil
21 Tread softly
22 The ebony stag
23 Black edged
24 The case of the faithful heart

25 The case of the painted ladies
26 They never came back
27 Such bright disguises
28 Glittering prizes
29 Reverse the charge
30 The grim maiden
31 The case of Elymas the sorcerer
32 Conspiracy at Angel
33 The sharp quillet
34 Exit Sir John
35 The swinging death
36 Men for pieces
37 Black agent
38 Where there was smoke
39 And cauldron bubble
40 The ring of Innocent
41 The seventh sign
42 The running nun
43 Out of the dusk
44 The feet of death
45 The doll's done dancing
46 The shaking spear 1954
47 Conspiracy at Angel
48 The dice are dark 1955
49 The toy lamb 1955
50 The murder collection 1956
51 The wife who disappeared 1956
52 The hands of justice 1956
53 The nine cuts 1957
54 The saints are sinister 1958

Fogazzaro, A.
TRILOGY OF ROME:
1 The patriot
2 The sinner, *same as* The man of the world.
3 The saint
'Leila' *is a companion volume to* 'The Saint'.

Foley, R.
HIRAM POTTER SERIES:
1 Dangerous to me 1960
2 The deadly noose 1962
3 It's murder, Mr. Potter 1963
4 Back door to death 1964

Foote, J. T.
1 Fatal gesture
2 Daughter of Delilah

Footner, H.
MADAME STOREY SERIES:
1 Madame Storey
2 The velvet hand
3 The doctor who held hands
4 The casual murderer
5 The Deaves mystery
6 Easy to kill
7 Almost perfect murder
8 The viper
9 Kidnapping of Madame Storey
LEE MAPPIN SERIES:
1 Death of a saboteur
2 Murder that had everything
3 Unneutral murder
4 House with the blue door
5 Orchids to murder

Ford, D.
GWYNETH SERIES:
1 The following seasons
2 The catch of time 1960
3 No further elegy 1961
☐
1 The deprived child and the community 1955
2 The delinquent child and the community 1956
N.F. Sociology

Ford, E.
THE TYLDENS:
1 Meeting in spring
2 One fine day

Ford, F. M. [F. M. Hueffer]
PARADE'S END:
1 Some do not
2 No more parades
3 A man could stand up
4 The last post
Republished in two volumes, 1963.
☐
1 The fifth queen
2 Privy seal
3 The fifth queen crowned

Ford, H.
FELIX SERIES:
1 Felix walking
2 Felix running

Ford, J. A.
1 The brave white flag
2 Season of escape

Ford, L.
COLONEL PRIMROSE SERIES:
1 The strangled witness
2 Ill met by moonlight
3 The simple way of poison
4 Mr. Cromwell is dead. [Reno Rendezvous]
5 Snow-white murder. [False to any man]
6 Old lover's ghost
7 A capital crime. [The murder of the fifth columnist]
8 Priority murder [Murder in the O.P.M.]
9 Siren in the night
10 Crack of dawn [All for the love of a lady]
11 The Philadelphia murder story
12 Honolulu murder story
13 Woman in black
14 The Devil's stronghold
15 Shot in the dark
16 Murder is the payoff
17 The lying jade [Washington whispers murder]
18 Road to folly
19 Three bright pebbles
20 The town cried murder
21 Date with death
22 Bahamas murder case
23 Invitation to murder
24 Murder comes to Eden 1956

Ford, S.
SHORTY MCCABE SERIES:
1 Shorty McCabe
2 Shorty McCabe on the job
3 Odd numbers
4 Meet 'em with Shorty McCabe
TORCHY SERIES:
1 Torchy
2 Trying out Torchy
3 On with Torchy
4 Torchy, private sec.
5 Wilt thou, Torchy
6 The house of Torchy
7 Torchy as a pa
8 Torchy and Vee

Foreman, R.
1 Long pig
2 Sandalwood Island

Fores, J.
1 Forgotten place
2 The springboard 1956
Novels about London airport.

Forester, C. S.
CAPTAIN HORNBLOWER SERIES:
1 Mr. Midshipman Hornblower
2 Lieutenant Hornblower
3 Hornblower and the Atropos
4 Hornblower and the Hotspur
5 The happy return [Beat to quarters]
6 Ship of the line
7 Flying colours
8 The Commodore
9 Lord Hornblower
10 Hornblower in the West Indies
Nos. 5, 6 and 7 published in one volume as 'Captain Hornblower, R.N.' Nos. 8 and 9 published as 'Horatio Hornblower'. Nos. 1, 2 and 3 published as 'The young Hornblower'. 'Hornblower's triumph' and 'Hornblower in captivity' are abridgements of 8 and 9 and 6 and 7 for junior reading. 'The Hornblower companion', 1964 is Forester's own description of the background of the series.
☐
1 The voyage of the Annie Marble
2 The Annie Marble in Germany
N.F. Travel

Forsyte, C.
DETECTIVE INSPECTOR LEFT:
1 Diplomatic death 1961
2 Diving death 1962
3 Double death 1965

Forsythe, R.
INSPECTOR HEATHER AND ANTHONY VEREKER SERIES:
1 Missing or murdered
2 The hounds of justice
3 The polo ground mystery
4 Pleasure cruise mystery
5 Ginger cat mystery
6 Spirit murder mystery

Fortescue, Lady
1 Perfume from Provence
2 Sunset house
3 There's Rosemary, there's rue
4 Trampled lilies
5 Mountain madness
6 Beauty for ashes
7 Laughter in Provence
N.F. Autobiography

Foster, E. A.
1 Hortense
2 Cordelia's pathway out

Fothergill, J.
1 An innkeeper's diary
2 Confessions of an innkeeper
3 My three inns
   Contains parts 1 and 2 with some new matter.
N.F. Autobiography

Fowler, Hon. E. T. [Mrs. A. L. Felkin]
1 Concerning Isabel Carnaby
2 In subjection
3 Ten degrees backward

Fowler, S. (S. F. Wright *pseud.***)**
1 A bout with the Mildew gang
2 A second bout with the Mildew gang
3 The end of the Mildew gang
MR. JELLIPOT SERIES:
1 The murder in Bethnal Square
2 Four callers in Razor St.
3 The Jordans murder
4 The wills of Jane Kanwhistle
5 Too close to crime
6 Too much for Mr. Jellipot
7 With cause enough
GREAT WAR OF 1938 SERIES:
1 Prelude in Prague
2 Four days' war
3 Megiddo's ridge
   □
1 Deluge
2 Dawn
THE SIEGE OF MALTA:
1 St. Elmo
2 St. Angelo
   Based on an unfinished novel by Sir Walter Scott.

Fox, J. M.
JOHN AND SUZY MARSHALL SERIES:
1 Death commits bigamy
2 The inconvenient bride
3 Gentle hangman
4 Aleutian blue mink
5 The wheel is fixed

Fox, S. *pseud. see* Bullett, G.

Foxall, R.
1 The devil's smile 1963
2 The devil's spawn 1965
   Historical novels of the Stuart period. Not strictly sequels, but characters recur.

Foyle, K.
AUGHERIM SERIES:
1 The doctor's lady
2 Whither thou goest
3 Other people's shoes

France, A. *pseud.* **[J. A. Thibault]**
ABBE COIGNARD SERIES:
1 At the sign of the Reine Pédauque
2 The opinions of Jerome Coignard
3 The merrie tales of Jacques Tournebroche
CONTEMPORARY HISTORY SERIES:
1 The wicker-work woman
2 The elm tree on the Mall
3 The amethyst ring
4 M. Bergeret in Paris
PIERRE NOZIERE SERIES:
1 My friend's book
2 Pierre Noziere
3 Little Pierre
4 Bloom of life

France, V.
HUGO TOWER SERIES:
1 The carved emerald
2 The naked fire
3 Somebody in the audience

Frank, L.
1 Carl and Anna
2 Brother and sister

Frank, W. D.
1 The death and birth of David Markand
2 The bridegroom cometh

Frankau, G.

PETER JACKSON SERIES:
1 Men, maids and mustard-pot
2 Peter Jackson, cigar merchant
3 Woman of the horizon
4 Concerning Peter Jackson and others
5 Wine, women and waiters
Contains story of P.J.
The first contains a story – 'Patricia Jackson's pearl necklace' – dealing with Peter Jackson at a period prior to that of the second.
1 One of us
2 More of us
Verse

Frankau, P.

CLOTHES FOR A KING'S SON:
1 Sing for your supper 1963
2 Slaves of the lamp 1965
First two volumes of a family trilogy.

Franken, R.

1 Claudia
2 Claudia and David
3 Another Claudia
4 Young Claudia
5 The marriage of Claudia
6 From Claudia to David
7 The fragile years
8 Return of Claudia
Later published in one volume as 'The Book of Claudia'.

Frankland, E.

1 The Retreat
2 Reform

Franklin, C.

ANNABEL SERIES:
1 Adventures of Annabel
2 Face the music
GRANT GARFIELD SERIES:
1 Exit without permit 1946
2 Cocktails with a stranger 1947
3 Rope of sand 1948
4 Storm in an inkpot 1949
5 The mask of Kane 1949
6 She'll love you dead 1950
7 One night to kill 1950
8 Maid for murder 1951

9 Escape to death 1951
10 No other victim 1952
11 Gallows for a fool 1952
12 The stranger came back 1953
13 Stop that man 1954
14 Girl in shadow 1955
15 Out of time 1956
16 Death on my shoulder 1958
17 Gently you must be 1959
18 Breathe no more 1959
19 Handful of sinners 1959
20 Fear runs softly 1961
JIM BURGESS SERIES:
1 Guilt for innocence 1960
2 Kill me and live 1961
3 The bath of acid
4 Murder before dinner 1963
MRS. MAXINE DANGERFIELD:
1 The dangerous ones 1964
2 On the day of the shooting 1965

Franklin, G.

1 A naval digression
2 Another naval digression

Franzero, C. M.

1 The house of Mrs. Caroline
2 Appassionata

Fraser, R.

1 A visit to Venus 1957
2 Jupiter in the chair 1958
3 Trout's Testament 1959
4 City of the sun 1961

Frazer, R. C.

MARK KILBY SERIES:
1 Secret syndicate 1963
2 The Hollywood hoax 1964
3 The Miami mob *and* Mark Kilby stands alone 1965

Frederic, H.

1 Seth's brother's wife
2 The Lawton girl

Freeling, N.

VAN DER VALK SERIES:
1 Love in Amsterdam 1962
2 Because of the cats 1963
3 Gun before butter 1963
4 Double-barrel 1964

5 Criminal conversations 1965
6 The king of the rainy country 1966
7 The Dresden green 1966

Freeman, H. W.
1 Fathers of their people
2 Pond Hall's progress

Freeman, R. A.
DR. THORNDYKE SERIES:
1 The red thumb mark
2 John Thorndyke's cases
3 The eye of Osiris
4 The mystery of 31 New Inn
5 A silent witness
6 The cat's eye
7 Mystery of Angelina Froud
8 The shadow of the wolf
9 The D'Arblay mystery
10 A certain Dr. Thorndyke
11 As a thief in the night
12 Mr. Pottermack's oversight
13 Pontifex son and Thorndyke
14 When rogues fall out
15 Dr. Thorndyke intervenes
16 For the defence: Dr. Thorndyke
17 The Penrose mystery
18 Felo-de-se
19 The stoneware monkey
20 John Thorndyke's case book
21 M. Polton explains
22 The Jacob St. mystery

French, Mrs. A.
1 Susan Clegg and her friend Mrs. Lathrop
2 Susan Clegg and her neighbour's affairs

Freund, P.
THE VOLCANO GOD TRILOGY:
1 Saturnalia and the nomads
2 Eurasia and the rooftops
3 How the world began

Frome, D.
MR. PINKERTON SERIES:
1 The Hammersmith murders
2 The by-pass murder [Two against Scotland yard]
3 Mr. Simpson finds a body [The man from Scotland Yard]

4 The eel pie mystery [The eel pie murders]
5 Arsenic in Richmond [Mr. Pinkerton goes to Scotland yard]
6 The body in the Turl [Mr. Pinkerton finds a body]
7 The body in Bedford Square [Mr. Pinkerton grows a beard]
8 Mr. Pinkerton has the clue
9 The guilt is plain [The black envelope]
10 Mr. Pinkerton at the Old Angel
11 Murder on the square [Homicide House]
Three shorter Pinkerton pieces are in 'The mystery book', 'The second mystery book', and 'The third mystery book'.

Frye, P.
LIFE OF LORD NELSON:
1 Game for empires
2 Sleeping sword

Fuller, A.
1 Pratt portraits
2 Later Pratt portraits

Fuller, T.
JUPITER JONES SERIES:
1 Harvard has a homicide
2 This is murder Mr. Jones
3 Three thirds of a ghost
4 Keep cool, Mr. Jones

Fullerton, H. S.
JIMMY KIRKLAND SERIES – 3 VOLS.

Furman, L.
1 The quare women
2 The glass window
3 Lonesome road

Futrelle, J.
THE THINKING MACHINE:
1 The chase of the golden plate 1906
2 The thinking machine 1907
3 The thinking machine on the case 1908

G. G. *pseud.* [H. G. Harper]
1 Sporting stories and sketches
2 New sporting stories

Gaboriau, E.
LECOQ SERIES:
1 Monsieur Lecoq, *same as* Lecoq, the detective, *same as* The Widow Lerouge
2 The honour of the name
3 Crime at Orcival
4 File 113
5 The old age of Lecoq, the detective; by F. du Boisgobey
□
1 The Count's millions
2 Baron Trigault's vengeance

Gair, M.
MARK RAEBURN SERIES:
1 Sapphires on Wednesday
2 A long hard look 1958
3 The burning of Troy 1959

Gaite, F.
JAMES AND CHARLES LATIMER (DIED 1870):
1 Brief candles
2 A family matter 1955
3 Come and go 1958
Adventures of two ghosts.

Gale, Z.
1 Friendship village
2 Friendship village love stories
3 Mothers to men
4 Neighborhood love stories
5 Peace in Friendship village

Gallico, P.
1 Adventures of Hiram Holliday
2 The secret front
MRS. HARRIS SERIES:
1 Flowers for Mrs. Harris
2 Mrs. Harris goes to New York
3 Mrs. Harris, M.P. 1965
ALEXANDER HERO:
1 Too many ghosts 1961
2 The hand of Mary Constable 1964
Two novels about psychical research.

Galsworthy, J.
THE FORSYTE SAGA:
1 The man of property
2 Indian summer of a Forsyte
In the volume entitled 'Five tales'.
3 In chancery

4 Awakening
5 To let
6 The salvation of a Forsyte
In the volume entitled 'Villa Rubein and other stories'.
A MODERN COMEDY:
1 The white monkey
2 Silent wooing
3 The silver spoon
4 Passers-by
5 Swan song
2 and 4 are short interludes linking the novels published separately as 'Two Forsyte Interludes. Other Forsyte stories in 'On Forsyte change'.
THE END OF THE CHAPTER:
1 Maid in waiting
2 Flowering wilderness
3 Over the river
Continues the series, but with a different setting, the main family being the Cherwells.
□
1 The country house
2 Fraternity
3 The Patrician
□
1 The dark flower
2 Beyond
3 Saint's progress

Galway, R. C.
JAMES PACKARD:
1 Assignment New York
2 Assignment London 1963

Ganpat, *pseud.* [**M. L. A. Gompertz**]
1 Harilek
2 Wrexham's revenge

Gardner, A.
DAVIS TROY SERIES:
1 The escalator 1963
2 Assignment Tahiti 1964

Gardner, E. S.
PERRY MASON SERIES:
1 The case of the velvet claws
2 The case of the sulky girl
3 The case of the lucky legs
4 The case of the howling dog
5 The case of the curious bride

6 The case of the counterfeit eye
7 The case of the caretaker's cat
8 The case of the sleepwalker's niece
9 The case of the silent partner
10 The case of the empty tin
11 The case of the stuttering bishop
12 The case of the dangerous dowager
13 The case of the lame canary
14 The case of the substitute face
15 The case of the shop lifter's shoe
16 The case of the perjured parrot
17 The case of the rolling bones
18 The case of the baited hook
19 The case of the haunted husband
20 The case of the turning tide
21 The case of the drowning duck
22 The case of the careless kitten
23 The case of the buried clock
24 The case of the drowsy mosquito
25 The case of the crooked candle
26 The case of the golddigger's purse
27 The case of the half-wakened wife
28 The case of the borrowed brunette
29 The case of the fan-dancer's horse
30 The case of the vagabond virgin
31 The case of the lonely heiress
32 The case of the lazy lover
33 The case of the dubious bridegroom
34 The case of the backward mule
35 The case of the cautious coquette
36 The case of the negligent nymph
37 The case of the one-eyed witness 1956
38 The case of the musical cow 1956
39 The case of the angry mourner 1957
40 The case of the fiery fingers 1957
41 The case of the grinning gorilla 1958
42 The case of the moth-eaten mink 1958
43 The case of the green eyed sister 1959
44 The case of the hesitant hostess 1959
45 The case of the fugitive nurse 1959
46 The case of the runaway corpse 1960
47 The case of the restless redhead 1960
48 The case of the glamorous ghost 1960
49 The case of the sunbather's diary 1961
50 The case of the nervous accomplice 1961
51 The case of the terrified typist 1961
52 The case of the gilded lily 1962

53 The case of the demure defendent 1962
54 The case of the lucky loser 1962
55 The case of the screaming woman 1963
56 The case of the daring decoy 1963
57 Case of the long-legged models 1963
58 Case of the foot-loose doll 1964
59 Case of the calendar girl 1964
60 Case of the deadly toy 1964
61 Case of the mythical monkeys 1965
62 Case of the singing skirt 1965
63 Case of the waylaid wolf 1965
64 The case of the duplicate daughter 1966

DISTRICT ATTORNEY SERIES:
1 The District Attorney cooks a goose
2 The District Attorney calls it murder
3 The District Attorney holds a candle
4 The District Attorney draws a circle
5 The District Attorney goes to trial
6 District Attorney calls a tune
7 District Attorney breaks a seal
8 District Attorney takes a chance 1956
9 The District Attorney breaks an egg 1957
See also A. A. Fair, *pseud.*

Gardner, J.
BOYSIE L. OAKES SERIES:
1 The liquidator 1964
2 The understrike 1965

Garland, H.
MIDDLE BORDER SERIES:
1 Son of the Middle Border
2 Daughter of the Middle Border
3 Trail makers of the Middle Border
4 Back trailers of the Middle Border

Garnett, D.
1 Golden echo
2 Flowers of the forest
3 The familiar faces
N.F. *Autobiography*

Garstin, C.
1 The mud larks
2 The mud larks again

Garstin, C. (*contd.*)
THE PENHALES TRILOGY:
1 The owl's house
2 High noon
3 West wind

Garvice, C.
1 Staunch as a woman
2 Led by love

Gask, A.
GILBERT LAROSE SERIES:
1 Dark highway
2 Lonely house
3 Shadow of Larose
4 House on the island
5 Secret of the Sandhills
6 Gentlemen of crime
7 Judgment of Larose
8 Hidden door
9 Poisoned goblet
10 Hangman's knot
11 Cloud the smiter
12 The jest of life
14 Master spy
15 Night of the storm
16 Gravedigger of Monk's Arden
17 Fall of a dictator
18 Vengeance of Larose
19 House of the fens
20 Tragedy of the silver moon
21 Beachy head murder
22 His prey was man
23 Mystery of Fell Castle
24 Man of death
25 The dark mill stream
26 The unfolding years
27 Vaults of Blackarden Castle
28 Silent dead
29 Storm breaks
30 House with the high walls
31 Marauders by night
32 Night and fog
33 Crime upon crime

Gaskell, J.
1 The serpent 1963
2 Atlan 1965
*Two novels about an imaginary,
semi-primitive world.*

Gaulle, C. de
WAR MEMOIRS:
1 The call to honour (1940–1942)
2 Unity (1942–1944)
3 Salvation (1944–1946)

Gaunt, M., *and* **Essex, J. R.**
DR. CRAVEN SERIES:
1 The arm of the leopard
2 The silent ones

Gaunt, W.
1 The Pre-Raphaelite tragedy
2 The aesthetic adventure
3 March of the moderns
N.F. *A narrative of modern painting.*

Gavin, C.
1 Clyde valley
2 The hostile shore

Gaye, C.
1 Jane Scott 1963
2 Jane Scott again 1964
3 Jane Scott meets the doctor 1965
4 Jane Scott married 1965

Gaye, P. F.
THE VANDERWOOD TRILOGY:
1 The French prisoner
2 Louisa Vanderwood
3 On a darkling plain

Gee, H. L.
1 Do you agree?
2 It seems to me

Gee, J.
1 Isaacs
2 Isaacs reappears

Gerard, F.
1 The flail and the fish
2 The envoy of the emperor
*The Marquess de Brussac of 1 is a
minor character in 2.*
SIR JOHN MEREDITH SERIES:
1 Concrete castle
2 Number 1–2–3
3 The black emperor
4 The dictatorship of the dove
5 Red rope

6 Golden guilt
7 The prince of paradise
8 Secret sceptre
9 Wotan's wedge
10 Emerald embassy
11 The secret of the sapphire
12 The mind of John Meredith
13 Sorcerer's shaft
14 Transparent traitor
15 The prisoner of the pyramid
16 Flight into fear
17 The promise of the phoenix
See also Wallace, E.

Gerhardi, W.
1 Jazz and Jasper
2 Eve's apples

Ghose, S. N.
1 And gazelles leaping
2 Cradle of the clouds
☐
1 The vermilion boat
2 The flame of the forest
N.F. Autobiography

Gibb, L.
1 The Joneses: how to keep up with
them 1959
2 The higher Jones 1960
N.F. Humour

Gibbings, R.
1 Sweet Thames run softly
2 Till I end my song
N.F. Travel

Gibbon, L. G., *pseud.* [**I. L. Mitchell**]
A SCOTS QUAIR:
1 Sunset song
2 Cloud Howe
3 Grey granite

Gibbons, M. S.
1 'We donkeys' in Devon
2 'We donkeys' on Dartmoor

Gibbons, S.
1 Cold Comfort Farm
2 Christmas at Cold Comfort Farm
3 Conference at Cold Comfort Farm

Gibbs, A.
1 Here lies tomorrow
2 Daybreak

Gibbs, G.
OLD PHILADELPHIA SERIES:
1 The loyal rebel (the 1770's)
2 Supercargo (the 1790's)
3 Autumn (the 1830's)
4 The North Star (the 1850's)

Gibbs, H.
THE PRIOR REPORT:
1 Not to the swift
2 Blue days and fair
3 Withered garland
A trilogy of modern marriage.
SOUTH AFRICAN HISTORY SERIES:
1 The splendour and the dust 1955
2 The winds of time 1956
3 Thunder at dawn 1957
4 The tumult and the shouting 1959

Gibbs, L.
1 Kitty Villiers
2 The good beauties
*Complementary. 2 concerns the life of
Kitty's maid Elizabeth Spencer.*

Gibbs, Sir P.
1 Street of adventure
2 Oliver's kind women
☐
1 This nettle danger
2 Broken pledges
3 The interpreter
*The above are sequels. The following
may be considered to continue the series
in their background of current history
but have different plots and characters.*
4 Sons of the others
5 The amazing summer
6 The long alert
7 The battle within
8 Through the storm
9 The hopeful heart
10 Behind the curtain
11 Both your houses

Gibbs- Smith C., *see* Smith, C. Gibbs-

Gide, A.
1 Fruits of the earth
2 Later fruits of the earth
    □
1 Journals
2 So be it, or the chips are down 1960
N.F. Autobiography

Gilbert, A.
SCOTT EGERTON SERIES:
1 The tragedy at Freyne
2 The murder of Mrs. Davenport
3 Death at Four Corners
4 Mystery of the open window
5 The night of the fog
6 The body on the beam
7 The long shadow
8 The musical comedy crime
9 An old lady dies
10 The man who was too clever
M. DUPUY SERIES:
1 The man in button boots
2 Courtier to death
ARTHUR CROOK SERIES:
1 Murder by experts
2 The man who wasn't there
3 Murder has no tongue
4 Treason in my breast
5 The clock in the hat-box
6 The bell of death
7 Dear dead woman
8 The vanishing corpse
9 The woman in red
10 Something nasty in the wood shed
11 The case of the tea-cosy's aunt
12 The mouse who wouldn't play ball
13 He came by night
14 The scarlet button
15 Don't open the door
16 The black stage
17 The spinster's secret
18 Death in the wrong room
19 Spy for Mr. Crook
20 Die in the dark
21 Lift up the lid
22 Death knocks three times
23 Murder comes home
24 A nice cup of tea
25 Lady killer
26 Miss Pinnegar disappears
27 Footsteps behind me
28 Snake in the grass

29 Give death a name 1957
30 Death against the clock 1959
31 Third time lucky 1959
32 Death takes a wife 1959
33 Out for the kill 1960
34 Uncertain death 1962
35 Ring for a noose 1963
36 Knock knock who's there 1964
37 Passenger to nowhere 1965

Gilbert, B.
OLD ENGLISH SERIES:
1 Tyler of Barnet
2 The rural scene
    *The above follow 'Old England' and
    'King Lear at Hordle', which are not
    novels.*

Gilbreth, F. B., *and* Carey, E. G.
1 Cheaper by the dozen
2 Belles on their toes
3 Inside Nantucket 1955
N.F. Autobiography of a family.

Giles, J. H.
THE FOWLER FAMILY:
1 Hannah Fowler
2 The believers
3 Johnny Osage
    *Mother, son and daughter in three
    novels of the settlement of the West.*
KENTUCKY SERIES:
1 Enduring hills
2 Miss Willie
3 Tara's healing

Gill, E.
BENVENUTO BROWN SERIES:
1 Strange holiday
2 What dread hand
3 Crime de luxe

Gillespie, S.
LONGDEN–LORRISTONE FAMILY SERIES:
1 The martyr 1955
2 The grandson 1957
3 The visitors 1959
4 The neighbour 1960
5 A summer at home 1961
6 The young green blade 1963

Gilliat, E.
1 In Lincoln Green
2 Wolf's Head

Gillmore, I. H. [I. H. G. Irwin]
1 Phœbe and Ernest
2 Phœbe, Ernest and Cupid
3 The happy years

Gilmour, O. W.
1 Singapore to freedom
2 With freedom to Singapore
N.F. *War Memoirs.*

Gilpatric, G.
MUSTER GLENCANNON SERIES:
1 Scotch and water
2 Half seas over
3 Three sheets in the wind
4 Mr. Clencannon
5 The gentleman with the walrus moustache
6 Glencannon afloat
7 Canny Mr. Glencannon
8 Mr. Glencannon ignores the war
Short stories. Later published in three omnibus volumes.

Gilruth, S.
INSPECTOR HUGH GORDON:
1 Dawn her remembrance 1961
2 The snake is living yet 1963

Giono, J.
1 The hussar on the roof
2 L'âne rouge (not trans.)
3 Man of straw (L'artificier)
'Angelo' is 'the opening of the original draft of 'The hussar on the roof'—Author.
TRILOGY OF EARTH:
1 Hill of destiny (Colline)
2 Lovers are never losers (Un de Beaumunges)
3 Harvest (Regain)
□
1 Song of the world
2 Batailles dans le montagne (not trans.)
3 Joy of man's desiring (Ne ma Joie demeure)

Gipson, F.
1 Old yeller 1961
2 Savage Sam 1962

Girtin, T.
1 Come landlord!
2 Not entirely serious
N.F. *Autobiography*

Gittings, R.
1 John Keats: the living year
2 The mask of Keats
N.F. *Literary criticism.*

Glass, M.
1 Potash and Perlmutter
2 Abe and Mawruss
3 Y'understand
4 Lucky numbers

Glemser, B.
ROBERT CRANE SERIES:
1 High noon
2 Strangers in Florida
3 The dove on his shoulder

Glover, H.
1 Both sides of the blanket
2 Louise and Mr. Tudor
3 Louise in London

Glubb, Sir J.
1 A soldier with the Arabs 1957
2 War in the desert 1960
N.F. *Autobiography*
HISTORY OF ARABIA:
1 The great Arab conquests, A.D. 630–680 1961
2 The empire of the Arabs, A.D. 680–860 1963
3 The course of empire, A.D. 860–1150 1964

Glyn, C.
1 Don't knock the corners off 1964
2 Love and joy in the Mabillon 1965

Glyn, E. [Mrs. Clayton Glyn]
ELIZABETH SERIES:
1 The visits of Elizabeth
2 Elizabeth visits America

Glynne-Jones, W., *see* Jones, W. Glynne-

Godden, R.
DOLL SERIES:
1 Miss Happiness and Miss Flower
2 Little Plum

Godwin, F.
CAPTAIN JOHN HUNTER:
1 Mission to Samarkand 1964
2 The towers of pain 1965

Goethe, J. W. von
1 Wilhelm Meister's apprenticeship
2 Wilhelm Meister's travels

Gogarty, O. St. J.
1 As I was going down Sackville St.
2 Tumbling in the hay
3 Rolling down the Lea
N.F. *Autobiography*

Golding, L.
1 Forward from Babylon
2 Give up your lovers
□
ELSIE SILVER:
1 Five Silver daughters
2 Mr. Emmanuel
3 The glory of Elsie Silver
4 Dangerous places
5 To the quayside
□
1 In the steps of Moses
2 In the steps of Moses the lawgiver
3 In the steps of Moses the conqueror
N.F. *Biblical history.*

Goldthorpe, J.
1 The same scourge
2 No crown of glory
3 The hidden splendour

Goldring, D.
LOVE AMONG THE ARTISTS TRILOGY:
1 Nobody knows
2 The cuckoo
3 The façade

Gollancz, V.
1 My dear Timothy
2 More for Timothy

3 Last words for Timothy
N.F. *Autobiographical letters.*

Golon, A., *and* **Golon, S.** ('Sergeanne Golon')
1 Angelique 1958
2 Angelique and the king 1960
3 Angelique and the Sultan 1961
4 Angelique in revolt 1962
5 Angelique in love 1963

Gompertz, M. L. A., *see* Ganpat, *pseud.*

Goodchild, G.
1 Colorado Jim
2 Jim goes north
MACLEAN SERIES:
1 Maclean of Scotland Yard
2 Maclean investigates
3 Maclean at the Golden Owl
4 How now, Maclean
5 Chief Inspector Maclean
6 The triumph of Maclean
7 Yes, Inspector Maclean
8 Death on the centre court
9 Lead on, Maclean
10 Maclean remembers
11 Maclean finds a way
12 Maclean takes charge
13 Call Maclean
14 Maclean plays a hand
15 Maclean prevails
16 Maclean knows best
17 Maclean sees it through
18 Again Maclean
19 Up Maclean
20 Maclean intervenes
21 Maclean excels
22 Having no hearts
23 Maclean incomparable
24 Maclean deduces
25 Maclean the magnificent
26 Maclean non-stop
27 Maclean keeps going
28 Maclean takes a holiday
29 Uncle Oscar's niece
30 Hail Maclean
31 Companion to Sirius
32 Inspector Maclean's casebook
33 The Efford triangle
34 Maclean carries on
35 Maclean predominant

Goyne, R. (*contd.*)
8 Who killed my wife
9 Seven were suspect
10 Five roads Inn
11 Murder made easy
12 Fear haunts the fells
13 Murderer's moon
THE SUPER SERIES:
1 Introducing the Super
2 The missing minx
THE PADRE SERIES:
1 The crime philosopher
2 Savarin's shadow
3 Traitor's tide
4 The dark mind
5 The Courtway case

Graaf, P.
JOE DUST:
1 Dust and the curious boy 1958
2 Daughter fair 1958
3 The Sapphire conference 1959

Graeme, B.
1 Blackshirt
2 The return of Blackshirt
3 Blackshirt again
4 Alias Blackshirt
5 Blackshirt the audacious
6 Blackshirt the adventurer
7 Blackshirt takes a hand
8 Blackshirt counter-spy
9 Blackshirt interferes
10 Blackshirt strikes back
11 Son of Blackshirt
12 Lord Blackshirt
13 Calling Lord Blackshirt
continued by R. Graeme
14 Concerning Blackshirt
15 Blackshirt wins the trick
16 Blackshirt passes by
17 Salute to Blackshirt
18 Amazing Mr. Blackshirt 1955
19 Blackshirt meets the lady 1956
20 Paging Blackshirt 1957
21 Blackshirt helps himself 1957
22 Double for Blackshirt 1958
23 Blackshirt sets the pace 1959
24 Blackshirt sees it through 1959
25 Blackshirt finds trouble 1961
26 Blackshirt takes the trail 1962
27 Call for Blackshirt 1962

28 Blackshirt on the spot 1963
29 Blackshirt saves the day 1964
30 Danger for Blackshirt 1965
THEODORE I. TERHUNE SERIES:
1 Seven clues in search of a crime
2 House with crooked walls
3 A case for Solomon
4 Work for the hangman
5 Ten trails to Tyburn
6 A case of books
7 And a bottle of rum
8 Dead pigs at hungry farm
INSPECTOR ALLAIN SERIES:
1 Murder of some importance
2 Epilogue
3 Imperfect crime
4 International affair
5 Satan's mistress
6 Not proven
7 Mystery on the *Queen Mary*
8 The man from Michigan
9 Body unknown
10 Poisoned sleep
11 The corporal died in bed
12 Encore Allain
13 News travels by night
AUGUSTE JANTRY SERIES:
1 Cherchez la femme
2 Lady in black

Graeme, D.
1 Monsieur Blackshirt
2 Vengeance of Monsieur Blackshirt

Grafton, C. W.
1 The rat began to gnaw the rope
2 The rope began to hang the butcher

Graham, H.
1 The bolster book
2 The perfect gentleman
3 The complete sportsman
4 Biffin and his circle
5 The last of the Biffins
6 The Biffin papers

Graham, N.
SUPERINTENDENT SANDYMAN:
1 Passport to murder
2 Murder walks on tiptoe
3 The quest of Mr. Sandyman
4 Again Mr. Sandyman

5 Amazing Mr. Sandyman
6 Salute Mr. Sandyman
SOLO MALCOLM SERIES:
1 Murder makes a date 1955
2 Play it solo
3 Say it with murder
4 You can't call it murder
5 Hit me hard
6 Salute to murder
7 Murder rings the bell 1959
8 Killers are on velvet 1960
9 Murder is my weakness 1961
10 Murder on the Duchess 1962
11 Make mine murder 1962
12 Murder makes it certain 1962
13 Graft town 1963
14 Label it murder 1963
15 Murder made easy 1964
16 Murder of a black cat 1964
17 Murder on my hands 1965
18 Murder's always final 1965

Graham, W.
1 That reminds me
2 Observations
3 I introduce
N.F. Autobiography
POLDARK SERIES:
1 Ross Poldark
2 Demelza
3 Jeremy Poldark [Venture once more]
4 Warleggan [Last gamble]
Cornwall in the 18th century.

Grahame, K.
1 The golden age
2 Dream days

Grand, S. [Mrs. F. (Clarke) MacFall]
ADNAM PRATT SERIES:
1 Adnam's orchard
2 The winged victory
HEAVENLY TWINS SERIES:
1 Ideala
2 The heavenly twins

Grant, Jane
1 Come hither, nurse
2 Come again, nurse
N.F. Autobiography

Grant, Joan
1 Eyes of Horus
2 Lord of the horizon

Grant, R.
1 Jack Hall
2 Jack in the bush

Gras, F.
FRENCH REVOLUTION SERIES:
1 The Reds of the Midi
2 The Terror
3 The White Terror

Graves, C.
1 The thin blue line
2 The avengers
3 Seven pilots
Semi-fictional account of the R.A.F.

Graves, R.
1 Goodbye to all that
2 But it still goes on
N.F. Autobiography

Graves, R.
1 I Claudius
2 Claudius the god
□
1 Sergeant Lamb of the ninth
2 Proceed, Sergeant Lamb

Graves, R., *and* **Podro**
1 The Nazarene Gospel restored
2 Jesus in Rome 1957
*N.F. Two essays in theology, with an
unusual interpretation of the Gospels.*

Gray, B.
NORMAN CONQUEST SERIES:
1 Mr. Mortimer gets the jitters
2 Vultures, Ltd.
3 Miss Dynamite
4 Conquest marches on
5 Leave it to Conquest
6 Conquest takes all
7 Meet the Don
8 Six to kill
9 Convict 1066
10 Thank you, Mr. Conquest
11 Six feet of dynamite
12 Blonde for danger

Gray, B. (*contd.*)
13 The gay desperado
14 Cavalier Conquest
15 Alias Norman Conquest
16 Mr. Ball of fire
17 Killer Conquest
18 The Conquest touch
19 The spot marked X
20 Duel murder
21 Dare devil Conquest
21 Dare devil Conquest
22 Operation Conquest
23 Seven dawns to death
24 Conquest in Scotland
25 The lady is poison
26 The half-open door
27 Target for Conquest
28 Follow the lady
29 Conquest goes west
30 Turn left for danger
31 House of the lost 1956
32 Conquest at midnight 1957
33 Conquest goes home 1957
34 Conquest in command 1958
35 Conquest in California 1958
36 Death on the Hit Parade 1958
37 Conquest in command 1958
38 The big brain 1959
39 Conquest on the run 1960
40 Get ready to die 1960
41 Call Conquest for danger 1961
42 Conquest in the underworld 1962
43 Count down for Conquest 1963
44 Conquest overboard 1964
45 Calamity Conquest 1965
46 Conquest likes it hot 1965

Gray, H.
1 Gold for the gay masters
2 Bride of doom
3 The flame and the forest

Grayland, V. M.
HOANI MATA SERIES:
1 Night of the reaper 1963
2 The grave-digger's apprentice 1964

Grayson, D. *pseud.* [**R. S. Baker**]
1 Adventures in contentment
2 Adventures in friendship
3 The friendly road
4 Hempfield

5 Great possessions
6 Adventures in understanding
7 Adventures in solitude
8 A countryman's year

Grayson, R.
1 Guncotton
2 Guncotton goes to Russia
3 Guncotton in Hollywood
4 Guncotton murder at the bank
5 Guncotton outside the law
6 Guncotton secret airman
7 Guncotton in Mexico
8 Guncotton ace high
9 Guncotton adventure nine
10 Guncotton at blind man's hood
11 Escape with Guncotton
12 Guncotton – adventurer
13 Guncotton – secret agent

Green, C.
INSPECTOR WIELD SERIES:
1 Beauty a snare
2 Devil spider
3 Poison death

Green, J.
1 Memories of happy days
2 Personal record
N.F. Autobiography

Green, R.
1 Prophet without honour
2 Wilderness blossoms

Greene, L. P.
MAJOR SERIES:
1 Major adventures
2 Devil's Kloof
3 Red idol
4 Major developments
5 Major occasions
6 Major – diamond buyer
7 Major hazards
8 Major exploits
9 Major – knight errant
10 Vengeance
11 Lake of the dead
12 Forbidden valley
SERGEANT LANCEY SERIES:
1 Sergeant Lancey reports
2 Sergeant Lancey carries on

3 Sergeant Lancey tells his tale
DYNAMITE DRURY SERIES:
1 Dynamite Drury
2 Dynamite Drury again
3 Dynamite Drury patrols

Greenwell, D.
1 Two friends
2 Colloquia Crucis

Greenwood, R.
1 Mr. Bunting
2 Mr. Bunting at war
3 Mr. Bunting in the promised land
STORY OF ROSIE DAWES:
1 Good angel slept
2 O mistress mine

Greenwood, W.
TRELOOE SERIES:
1 So brief the spring
2 What everybody wants
3 Down by the sea 1956
Not sequels, but setting is the same for all books and some characters recur.

Gregg, C. F.
INSPECTOR HIGGINS SERIES:
1 The murdered manservant
2 The three daggers
3 The murder on the bus
4 The brazen confession
5 The Rutland mystery
6 The double solution
7 Inspector Higgins hurries
8 The body behind the bar
9 The duke's last trick
10 Inspector Higgins sees it through
11 The execution of Diamond Deutsch
12 The ten black pearls
13 Danger at Cliff House
14 Tragedy at Wembley
15 The wrong house
16 Mystery at Moor St.
17 Who dialled 999?
18 Danger in the dark
19 The fatal error
20 Justice!
21 The Vandor mystery
22 Two died at three
23 Melander's millions
24 The old manor

25 Exit Harlequin
26 Murder at midnight
27 Man with a monocle
28 The ugly customer
29 From information received
30 Inspector Higgins goes fishing
31 Accidental murder
32 Sufficient rope
33 Night flight to Zurich
34 The chief constable
35 Dead on time 1955
36 The obvious solution 1958
37 Professional jealousy 1959
HENRY PRINCE SERIES:
1 Henry Prince in action
2 The return of Henry Prince

Gregg, Miss H., *see* Grier, S. C., *pseud.*

Gregoire, J. A.
1 24 hours at Le Mans
2 The money masters

Gregory, J.
1 First case of Mr. Paul Savoy
2 Second case of Mr. Paul Savoy
3 Third case of Mr. Paul Savoy

Grenfell, W. T.
1 Down north on the Labrador
2 Tales of the Labrador
3 Labrador days

Grex, L.
PAUL IRVING SERIES:
1 The tragedy at Draythorpe
2 The Madison murder
3 The Lonely Inn mystery
4 Stolen death
5 The Carlent Manor crime

Grey, Z.
BORDER SERIES:
1 The last trail
2 The spirit of the border
KEN WARD SERIES:
1 The young forester
2 The young pitcher
3 The young lion hunter
4 Ken Ward in the jungle

Grey, Z. (*contd.*)
1 Riders of the purple sage
2 The Rainbow Trail
   □
1 Drift fence
2 Hash knife outfit
   □
1 Forlorn river
2 Nevada

Gribble, L. R.
ANTHONY SLADE SERIES:
1 Gillespie suicide mystery
2 Case of the Marsden rubies
3 Grand Modena murder
4 The stolen Home Secretary
5 Is this revenge
6 The yellow bungalow mystery
7 The secret of Tangles
8 The riddle of the ravens
9 The death chime
10 Mystery at Tudor Arches
11 Riley of the special branch
12 The case of the Malvern diamonds
13 Who killed Oliver Cromwell
14 Tragedy in E flat
15 Atomic murder
16 Hangman's moon
17 The Arsenal Stadium mystery
18 They kidnapped Stanley Matthews
19 The frightened chameleon
20 The glass alibi
21 Murder out of season
22 She died laughing
23 The inverted crime
24 Death pays the piper 1956
25 Supt. Slade investigates 1957
26 Stand in for murder 1957
27 Don't argue with death 1958
28 Wantons die hard 1961
29 Heads you die 1964
30 The violent dark 1965

Grieg, I.
INSPECTOR SWINTON SERIES:
1 Murder at Lintercombe
2 Baxter's second death

Grier, S. C. *pseud.* [**Miss H. Gregg**]
BALKAN BOOKS. FIRST SERIES:
1 An uncrowned king
2 A crowned queen

3 The kings of the east
4 The prince of the captivity
BALKAN BOOKS. SECOND SERIES:
1 The heir
2 The heritage
3 The prize
CENTURY SERIES:
1 A young man married
2 The path to honour
3 The keepers of the gate
4 Writ in water
5 England hath need of thee
6 The power of the keys
INDIAN HISTORICAL SERIES:
1 In furthest Ind
2 Like another Helen
3 The great proconsul
ISLAND SERIES:
1 The rearguard
2 The kingdom of waste lands
MODERN EAST SERIES:
1 The advanced-guard
2 His Excellency's English governess
3 Peace with honour
4 The Warden of the Marshes
PRINCESS SERIES:
1 A royal marriage
2 The princess's tragedy
3 The strong hand
4 Out of prison
   ' "*A brother of girls*", *which introduces*
   some of the characters of the series, runs
   parallel with nos. 3 and 4.' – *Author.*

Grierson, F. D.
SUPERINTENDENT ASH:
1 The blind frog 1955
2 The sign of the nine 1956
3 Green evil 1958
4 The red cobra 1960

SUPERINTENDENT MUIR SERIES:
1 Mad hatter murder
2 Thrice Judas
3 Entertaining murder
4 Out of the ashes
5 He had it coming to him

Griffith, G.
1 The angel of the revolution
2 Olga Romanoff

Grimble, Sir A.
1 A pattern of islands 1955
2 Return to the islands 1957
N.F. Travel

Griswold, G.
GROODE SERIES:
1 A gambit for Mr. Groode
2 A checkmate by the colonel
3 Red pawns 1955
4 Pinned man 1956

Griswold, L.
1 Deering of Deal
2 The winds of Deal
3 Deal Woods
4 Deering at Princeton

Gruber, F.
JOHNNY FLETCHER SERIES:
1 The navy colt
2 The laughing fox
3 The talking clock
4 The gift horse
5 The French key
6 The hungry dog
SIMON LASH SERIES:
1 Simon Lash, detective
2 The buffalo box

Guareschi, G.
1 Little world of Don Camillo
2 Don Camillo and the prodigal son
[Don Camillo and his flock]
3 Don Camillo's dilemma
4 Don Camillo and the devil 1959
5 Comrade Don Camillo 1960

Gubranssen, T.
1 Beyond sing the woods
2 The wind from the mountains
Chronicle of a Norwegian family.

Gunn, N. M.
1 Young Art and old Hector
2 The green Isle of the great deep

Gunn, V.
CHIEF INSPECTOR BILL CROMWELL SERIES:
1 Footsteps of death
2 Ironsides of the Yard
3 Ironsides smashes through

4 Ironsides lone hand
5 Death's doorway
6 Mad Hatter's rock
7 Ironsides sees red
8 The dead man laughs
9 Nice day for a murder
10 Ironsides smells blood
11 Death in shivering sand
12 Three dates with death
13 Ironsides on the spot 1948
14 Road to murder 1949
15 Dead man's morning 1949
16 Alias the hangman 1950
17 Murder on ice 1951
18 The Borgia head mystery 1951
19 The body vanishes 1952
20 Death comes laughing 1952
21 The whistling key 1953
22 The crooked staircase 1953
23 The crippled canary 1954
24 Laughing grave 1954
25 Castle dangerous 1955
26 The 64 thousand murder 1956
27 The painted dog 1956
28 Dead men's bells 1957
29 The treble chance murder 1958
30 Dead in a ditch 1959
32 Death on Bodmin Moor 1960
33 Devil in the maze 1960
34 Death at traitor's gate 1960
35 Sweet smelling death 1961
36 All change for murder 1962
37 The body in the boot 1962
38 Murder with a kiss 1963
39 The black cap murder 1965
40 Murder on Whispering Sands 1965
SUPERINTENDENT CROMWELL:
41 The Petticoat Lane murders 1966

Gunnarson, G.
1 Ships in the sky
2 The night and the dream

Gunter, A. C.
1 Dr. Burton
2 Dr. Burton's success
☐
1 Mr. Barnes of New York
2 Mr. Barnes, American, *same as*
The shadow of a vendetta
☐
1 A princess of Paris

Gunter, A. C. (*contd.*)
2 The King's stockbroker
☐
1 Susan Turnbull
2 Ballyho Bey

Guth, P.
1 Mémoirs d'un naïf
2 Le naïf sous les drapeaux
3 Le naïf aux quarantes enfants
4 Le naïf locataire
5 Le marriage du naïf
6 Le naïf amoureux
No. 4 has been translated as 'The innocent tenant' 1957. No other translations traced.

Guthrie, T. A., *see* Anstey, F., *pseud.*

Habberton, J.
1 Helen's babies
2 Other people's children

Habe, H.
1 Aftermath
2 Walk in darkness

Hackforth-Jones, G., *see*
Jones, G. Hackforth

Hackney, A.
1 Private's progress 1955
2 Private life 1957

Haggard, Sir H. R.
NADA THE LILY GROUP:
1 Nada the Lily
2 Marie
3 Child of storm
4 Finished
2, 3 and 4 form a trilogy about Allan Quatermain.
HOLY FLOWER GROUP:
1 The holy flower
2 The ivory child
3 The ancient Allan
KING SOLOMON'S MINES GROUP:
1 King Solomon's mines
2 Allan Quatermain
3 Allan's wife; and other tales
4 Maiwa's revenge

SHE GROUP:
1 She and Allan
2 She
3 Ayesha
4 Wisdom's daughter
5 Allan and the ice gods
2, 3 and 4 form a trilogy about 'She'. The stories in which Allan Quatermain appears are as follows in chronological order.
1 Marie
2 Allan's wife
3 Maiwa's revenge
4 Child of storm
5 The holy flower
6 She and Allan
7 The ivory child
8 Finished
9 King Solomon's mines
10 The ancient Allan
12 Allan Quatermain
13 Heu-Heu
14 Allan and the ice gods
☐
1 Morning star
2 Queen of the dawn
3 The way of the spirit

Haggard, L. K.
1 Norfolk life
2 A Norfolk notebook
3 A country scrapbook
N.F. Country Life.

Haggard, W.
COL. CHARLES RUSSELL:
1 The high wire 1963
2 The antagonists 1964
3 The powder barrel 1965
4 The hardsell 1965

Haig-Brown, R., *see* Brown, R. Haig-

Haines, A. C.
According to grandma. Also published in two parts as:
1 When grandma was little
2 What grandma says
☐
1 Luck of the Dudley Grahams
2 Cock-a-doodle hill

Hale, E.
MICKY REGAN SERIES:
1 Devil's traps
2 Death dealt the cards
3 Never shoot a lady
4 Death came back
MONTAGUE MICHLEWAITE SERIES:
1 Blue murder
2 Coffee for one

Hales, A. G.
MCGLUSKY SERIES:
1 McGlusky
2 McGlusky, the reformer
3 The career of McGlusky
4 McGlusky, the goldseeker
5 Ginger and McGlusky
6 McGlusky's great adventure
7 President McGlusky
8 The adventures of Signor McGlusky
9 McGlusky, the peacemaker
10 McGlusky, the sea rover
11 McGlusky, the trail blazer
12 McGlusky, the Mormon
13 McGlusky o' the Legion
14 McGlusky in prison
15 McGlusky the filibuster
16 McGlusky in India
17 Snowey and McGlusky
18 McGlusky, M.P.
19 McGlusky the seal poacher
20 McGlusky abroad
21 McGlusky, empire builder

Haliburton, T. C.
1 Sam Slick, the clockmaker
2 Sam Slick's wise saws

Hall, E. C. [Mrs. E. C. Obenchain]
1 Aunt Jane of Kentucky
2 The land of long ago
3 Clover and blue grass

Hall, J. C., *and* **Nordhoff, C.,** *see*
Nordhoff, C. and Hall, J. C.

Halliday, B.
MICHAEL SHAYNE SERIES:
1 Divided on death
2 Private practice of Michael Shayne
3 The uncomplaining corpses
4 Tickets for death

5 Michael Shayne investigates
6 Michael Shayne takes a hand
7 Michael Shayne's long chance
8 Murder is my business
9 Murder and the married virgin
10 Marked for murder
11 Blood on Biscayne Bay
12 Counterfeit wife
13 Murder is a habit
14 Call for Michael Shayne
15 A taste for violence
16 This is it Michael Shayne
17 Framed in blood
18 When Dorinda dances
19 What really happened
20 Lady came by night
21 She woke to darkness 1955
22 Death has three lives 1955
23 Stranger in town 1956
24 Blonde cried murder 1956
25 Weep for a blonde 1956
26 Shoot the works 1957
27 Murder of the wanton bride 1957
28 Death of a stranger 1957
29 Missing from home 1958
30 Fit to kill 1959
31 Date with a dead man 1960
32 Target: Mike Shayne 1960
33 Die like a dog 1961

Hambleden, P.
DET.-INSPECTOR 'TUBBY' MARTIN
1 Lucinder 1953
2 Keys for the criminal 1958

Hamilton, C.
1 Brummell
2 Brummell again
☐
1 Scandal
2 Another scandal

Hamilton, Elizabeth
1 The river full of stars 1954
2 An Irish childhood 1963
N.F. Autobiography

Hamilton, Lord F.
1 The holiday adventures of
  Mr. P. J. Davenant
2 Some further adventures of
  Mr. P. J. Davenant

Hamilton, Lord F. (*contd.*)
3 The education of Mr. P. J. Davenant
4 The beginnings of Mr. P. J. Davenant
5 P. J., the secret service boy
6 More about P.J., the secret service boy
VANISHED POMPS OF YESTERDAY:
1 Days before yesterday
2 Vanished pomps of yesterday
3 Here, there and everywhere
N.F. Autobiography

Hamilton, H.
JOHN AND SALLY HELDAR SERIES:
1 The two hundred ghost 1956
2 Death at one blow 1957
3 At night to die 1958
4 Answer in the negative 1959

Hamilton, M.
1 Green and gold
2 Silver road
N.F. Autobiography

Hamilton, P.
20,000 STREETS UNDER THE SKY:
1 The midnight bell
2 The siege of pleasure
3 Plains of cement
ERNEST RALPH GORSE:
1 The west pier
2 Mr. Stimpson and Mr. Gorse
3 Unknown assailant
  A series of novels on the life of a criminal, supposed to be based on the career of Neville Heath. Still unfinished at the author's death.

Hammet, D.
SAM SPADE:
1 The Dain curse
2 The Maltese falcon

Hammond, G.
BEAU PEPYS:
1 Fred in situ 1965
2 The loose screw 1966

Hammond, W. A.
1 Lal
2 A strong-minded woman

Hamnett, N.
1 Laughing torso
2 Is she a lady?
N.F. Autobiography

Hamsun, K.
SEGELFOSS ESTATE SERIES:
1 Children of the age
2 Segelfoss-Town
  □
1 Vagabonds
2 August
3 The road leads on
  □
1 Benoni
2 Rosa

Hanley, J.
THE FURIES CHRONICLE:
1 The furies
2 The secret journey
3 Our time is gone
4 Winter song
5 An end and a beginning 1958

Hannay, J. O., *see*
Birmingham, G. A., *pseud.*

Hannum, A.
1 Spin a silver coin
2 A shop in the desert
3 Paint the wind
N.F. description of an Indian trading post in S. West U.S.A.

Hanshew, T.
1 Cleek, the man of forty faces
2 Cleek of Scotland Yard
3 Cleek, the master detective
4 Cleek's greatest riddles, *same as* Cleek's government cases
5 The riddle of the night
6 The riddle of the Purple Emperor; *by T. and M. E. Hanshew.*
7 The frozen flames; *by T. and M. E. Hanshew.*
8 The mysterious light, *same as* The riddle of the mysterious light; *by T. and M. E. Hanshew.*
9 The house of discord
10 The house of seven keys
11 The amber junk

Hanson, L.
1 Shining morning face
2 Boy and man
N.F. Autobiography

Harben, W. N.
1 Abner Daniel
2 Gilbert Neal
3 The Georgians

Harbinson, R.
1 No surrender
2 Song of Erne
3 Up spake the cabin boy
4 The protege
N.F. Autobiography of an Ulsterman.

Hardie, D. M. F.
INSPECTOR HUGHES SERIES:
1 Riddle of the Cambrian Venus
2 The case of the praying evangelist
3 A grave for Miss Carling

Harding, D. C. F.
1 The Pendleton fortune
2 Pendleton harvest

Harding, G.
1 Along my line
2 Master of none
N.F. Autobiography

Hardy, T.
The Wessex novels may be classified as
    follows:
NOVELS OF CHARACTER AND
ENVIRONMENT:
1 Tess of the D'Urbervilles
2 Far from the madding crowd
3 Jude, the obscure
4 The return of the native
5 The Mayor of Casterbridge
6 The Woodlanders
7 Under the greenwood tree
8 Life's little ironies
9 Wessex tales
ROMANCES AND FANTASIES:
1 A pair of blue eyes
2 The trumpet-major
3 Two on a tower
4 The well beloved
5 A group of noble dames

NOVELS OF INGENUITY:
1 Desperate remedies
2 The hand of Ethelberta
3 A Laodicean

Hare, C.
SUPT. MALLETT AND M. PETTIGREW
1 Tenant for death
2 Death is no sportsman
3 Suicide excepted
4 With a bare bodkin
5 When the wind blows
6 The Yew tree's shade
7 He should have died hereafter 1958
    [Untimely death]

Hargreaves, E. A. I. Stewart-
1 Cotswold cider
2 The Hargreaves story
3 Man on the run
N.F. Autobiography

Harker, Mrs. L. A.
MR. WYCHERLEY SERIES:
1 Miss Esperance and Mr. Wycherley
2 Mr. Wycherley's wards
3 Montagu Wycherley, *same as* His
    first leave
4 Allegra
ANOTHER SERIES:
1 A romance of the nursery
2 Concerning Paul and Fiammetta

Harling, R.
1 Amateur sailor
2 Deep Atlantic stream
N.F. Autobiography

Harlow, R.
1 Royal Murdoch 1963
2 A gift of echoes 1966
    *Not sequels, but some characters recur
    and the background is the same.*

Harman, N.
PROTECTION LTD., SERIES:
1 Case of the wounded mastiff
2 Death and the Archdeacon

Harraden, B.
PATUFFA SERIES:
1 Spring shall plant
2 Patuffa

Harrar, H.
1 Seven years in Tibet
2 Tibet is my country 1960
N.F. Travel

Harriman, K. E.
1 The girl out there
2 The girl and the deal

Harris, B.
1 Purslane
2 Portulaca

Harris, C.
1 A circus rider's wife
2 A circus rider's widow
3 My son

Harris, W.
THE GUIANA QUARTET:
1 The palace of the peacock
2 The far journey of Oudin
3 The whole armour
4 The secret ladder 1962
Novels of the Caribbean.

Harrison, M.
1 All the trees were green
2 Vernal equinox

Harrison, R.
CHIEF INSPECTOR BASTION SERIES:
1 Brickbats for Bastion
2 Bootlaces for Bastion
3 Murder-on-sea
4 Rope over Jezebel
N.F. Autobiography

Harry, M.
1 The conquest of Jerusalem
2 The little daughter of Jerusalem

Hart, S.
1 Discharged dead
2 'Pommie' migrant

Harte, B.
There are no sequels, but several characters recur in the short stories. The following are the principal characters, with the stories they appear in:
JACK HAMLIN:

'The idyll of Red Gulch'; 'Brown of Calavaras'; 'The Iliad of Sandy Bar'; 'A passage in the life of Mr. John Oakhurst'; 'An heiress of Red Dog'; 'The fool of Five Forks'; 'Found at Blazing Star'; 'An apostle of the Tules'; 'A knight-errant of the foothills'; 'A Sappho of Green Springs'; 'A first family of Tasajaera'; 'The bell-ringer of Angel's'; 'A protege of Jack Hamlin's'; 'Three partners'; 'Mr. Jack Hamlin's mediation'; 'A Mercury of the foothills'; 'A ward of Colonel Starbottle'; 'The convalescence of Jack Hamlin'; 'Gabriel Conroy.'

YUBA BILL:
'Miggles'; 'Brown of Calavaras'; 'M'lias'; 'The Port of Sierra Flat'; 'Mrs. Skagg's husband'; 'The story of a mine'; 'Jeff Brigg's love story'; 'In the Carquinez woods'; 'Snow-bound at Eagle's'; 'Captain Jim's friend'; 'Cressy'; 'An ingenue of the Sierras'; 'Dick Spindler's family Christmas'; 'An Esmeralda of Rocky Canon'; 'A niece of snapshot Harry'; 'Gabriel Conroy'.

DR. DUCHESNE:
'M'lias'; 'The man on the beach'; 'The twins of Table Mountain'; 'A millionaire of Rough-and-Ready'; 'Cressy'; 'The chatelaine of Burnt Ridge'; 'The transformation of Buckeye camp'; 'A convert of the mission'; 'In the Tules'; 'See Yup'; 'The youngest prospector in Calavaras'; 'Mr. Bilson's housekeeper'; 'The convalescence of Jack Hamlin'; 'Gabriel Conroy'.

COLONEL STARBOTTLE:
'Brown of Calavaras'; 'The Iliad of Sandy Bar'; 'The romance of Madrone Hollow'; 'The poet of Sierra Flat'; 'A ward of Colonel Starbottle'; 'An episode of Fiddletown'; 'A passage in the life of Mr. John Oakhurst'; 'Wan Lee the pagan'; 'Jimmy'; 'The fool of Five Forks'; 'Captain Jim's friend'; 'Colonel Starbottle's client'; 'A first family of Tasajara'; 'The bellringer of Angel's'; 'Clarence'; 'Gabriel Conroy'; 'An Esmeralda of Rocky Canon'; 'What happened at the Fonda'; 'Colonel

Starbottle for the plaintiff'; 'Mr. MacGlowrie's widow'.

Harthern, E.
1 Going home
2 Home at last

Hartley, L. P.
THE LIFE OF EUSTACE CHERRINGTON:
1 The shrimp and the anemone
[The west window]
2 The sixth heaven
3 Eustace and Hilda
'The white wand' contains a Eustace and Hilda story, 'Hilda's letter'. Later published in one volume under the title 'Eustace and Hilda' (1958).
☐
1 The brickfield 1963
2 The betrayal 1965

Hartog, J. de
1 Stella
2 Distant shore

Harvester, S.
DORIAN SILK:
1 Unsung road
2 Silk road 1962
3 Red road 1963
M. MALCOLM KENTON:
1 The bamboo screen 1955
2 Dragon road 1955
BLUNDEN SERIES:
1 A breastplate for Aaron
2 Sheep may safely graze
3 Obols for Charon
HERON MARMORIN:
1 The Chinese hammer
2 Troika 1962

Hassett, M.
1 Educating Elizabeth
2 Beezer's End
MONTAGUE CORK SERIES:
1 Cork on the water 1953
2 Cork in bottle 1954
3 Cork and the serpent 1955
4 Cork in the doghouse 1957
6 Cork on the telly 1965

Hatch, R. W.
THE BRADFORDS:
1 Into the wind
2 Leave the salt earth

Havard, A.
1 Fighting westward
2 Where the trail divides

Haverfield, E. L.
1 Our vow
2 Blind loyalty

Hawk, J.
MORTIMER SARK SERIES:
1 Lone Lodge mystery
2 The serpent-headed stick

Hawkins, A. H., *see* Hope, A., *pseud.*

Hawkins, C. J.
1 Ned Brewster's year in the big woods
2 Ned Brewster's bear hunt

Hawton, H.
ASMUN HILL SERIES:
1 Murder most foul
2 Murder at H.Q.
3 Unnatural causes
4 Murder by mathematics
5 Deadly nightcap
6 Nine singing apes
7 Rope for a judge

Hay, I.
1 The first hundred thousand
2 Carrying on
Sketches of the first World War.

Hayes, F. W.
THE GWYNETT TRILOGY:
1 A Kent squire
2 Gwynett of Thornhaugh
3 The shadow of a throne

Hayter, A.
1 Sheila in the wind 1959
2 The second step 1962
N.F. Autobiography

Heberden, M. V.
SHANNON SERIES:
1 Murder follows Desmond Shannon
2 Vicious pattern
3 Murder unlimited
4 Exit this way
5 Murder goes astray
6 Tragic target

Hecht, B.
1 The journal of Fantazius Mallare
2 The kingdom of evil

Heckstall-Smith, A., *see*
Smith, A. Heckstall-

Heidenstam, V. von
1 Folk Fillyter
2 The Bilbo heritage

Heilgers, L.
1 Tabloid tales
2 More tabloid tales

Heimler, E.
1 Night of the mist 1959
2 A link in the chain 1962
N.F. Autobiography

Heinlein, R.
HISTORY OF THE FUTURE:
1 Universe
2 Common sense
These two were first published as a two part magazine serial. Universe was republished in U.S. as a paperback. They are now in one volume as 'Orphans of the sky', 1963.
3 Methuselah's children 1963
4 Revolt in 2100 1964
To be completed in five volumes.
RHYSLING SERIES:
1 Man who sold the moon
2 The green hills of earth

Henderson, C.
LONE RIDER SERIES:
1 Lone rider
2 Lone rider's guns
3 Lone rider's justice 1955
4 Lone rider's trail 1965
5 Lone rider's ranch 1957

6 Lone rider's quest 1957
7 Lone rider's war 1958

Hendryx, J. B.
1 Saga of Halfaday Creek
2 Justice on Halfaday Creek
3 Badmen on Halfaday Creek
□
1 Connie Morgan in Alaska:
2 Connie Morgan with the mounted
3 Connie Morgan in the lumber camps
4 Connie Morgan in the fur country
5 Connie Morgan in the cattle country
6 Connie Morgan with the Forest Rangers
7 Connie Morgan, prospector

Hennessy, J. Pope-
1 London fabric
2 Return visit
N.F. Topography

Henrey, Mrs. R.
1 Farm in Normandy
2 Return to the farm
3 Matilda and the chickens
□
1 Village in Piccadilly
2 The incredible city
3 The siege of London
An eyewitness account of London during the war.
□
1 The little Madeleine (girlhood)
2 Exile in Soho (adolescence)
3 Madeleine grows up (marriage)
4 A farm in Normandy and the return (birth of the child)
5 London (city of her adoption)
6 Madeleine's journal (Coronation year)
7 Month in Paris
8 Milou's daughter
9 A daughter for a fortnight
10 Mistress of myself
11 Madeleine young wife
12 Spring in a Soho street
13 Her April days
14 Wednesday four
N.F. Autobiography

Henry, M.
BOB AND HILARY DEAN:
1 Unlucky dip 1963
2 The householders 1964
The story of a young married couple in Australia.

Henry, O. *pseud.* [S. Porter]
In 'Waifs and strays' is a complete index to the author's stories giving the volumes in which they are to be found.

Hentz, Mrs. C. L. W.
1 Linda
2 Robert Graham

Hepburn, T. N., *see* Setoun, G., *pseud.*

Heppenstall, R.
1 The connecting door 1962
2 The woodshed 1962

Hepple, A.
1 The house of Gow
2 Jane of Gowlands

Hepworth, G. H.
1 Hiram Golf's religion
2 They met in heaven

Herbert, Sir A. P.
1 Trials of Topsy
2 Topsy, M.P.
3 Topsy turvy
Later collected in 'The Topsy omnibus'.
MISLEADING CASES:
1 Misleading cases
2 More misleading cases
3 Still more misleading cases
4 Codd's last case
'Uncommon law' is a omnibus volume of 1, 2 and 3.
ADMIRAL OF THE FLEET, EARL OF CARAWAY:
1 Number Nine
2 Made for man

Herbst, J.
TRILOGY COVERING THE DECAY OF CAPITALISM:
1 Pity is not enough

2 The executioner waits
3 Rope of gold

Hewitt, A.
1 Piccolo 1961
2 Piccolo and Maria 1962

Hewlett, M.
SAGAS RETOLD SERIES:
1 A lover's tale
2 Frey and his wife
3 Thorgils of Treadholt
4 Gudrid the Fair
5 The outlaw
6 The light heart
SANCHIA AND SENHOUSE SERIES:
1 Open country
2 Halfway House
3 Rest harrow
☐
1 Mrs. Lancelot
2 Bendish

Hichens, R. S.
1 The call of the blood
2 A spirit in prison

Hicks, Mrs. P., *see* Whitby, M.

Higgins, A.
1 Killochter meadow (in) Felo de se
2 Langrishe go down 1966
2 is an extension of 1, a short story.

Hilton, Jack
1 English ways
2 English ribbon
N.F. Record of two foot journeys through England in 1939 and 1938

Hilton, James
1 Goodbye Mr. Chips
2 To you, Mr. Chips

Himmel, R.
1 The name's Maguire
2 It's murder Maguire

Hine, M. [Mrs. Coxon]
1 Wild rye
2 Jenny Rorke
☐
1 Half in earnest
2 April Panhasard
☐
1 The flight
2 The spell of Siris

Hiscock, E. C.
1 Cruising under sail
2 Around the world in 'Wanderer III'
3 Voyaging under sail
N.F. Autobiography

Hislop, J.
1 Far from an gentleman 1963
2 Anything but a soldier 1965

Hobart, A. T.
1 River supreme [First published as Pidgin Cargo]
2 Oil for the lamps of China
3 Yang and Yin
4 Their own country
2 and 4 are direct sequels.
'Written ... with a series of four novels in mind. Each of these I hoped would make some contribution to the understanding of that interesting but baffling phase of Occidental life – its contact with the Far East.' – Preface to River Supreme.

Hobbes, J. O. [Mrs. P. M. T. Craigie]
1 The school for saints
2 Robert Orange

Hobson, H.
BRAD FORD SERIES:
1 The gallant affair
2 Death makes a claim 1958
3 The big twist 1959
4 Mission house murder 1959
5 Beyond tolerance 1960

Hobson, R. B.
1 Grass beyond the mountains
2 Nothing too good for a cowboy

3 The rancher takes a wife
N.F. Autobiography

Hocking, A.
DET. CHIEF SUPT. WILLIAM AUSTEN:
1 Poison in paradise 1955
2 Murder at midday 1956
3 Relative murder 1957
4 Epitaph for a nurse 1958
5 To cease upon the midnight 1959
6 Poisoned chalice 1959
7 The thin-spun life 1960
8 Candidate for murder 1961
9 He had to die 1962
10 Spies have no friends 1962

Hocking, J.
THE GREAT WAR (FRENCH FRONT) SERIES:
1 All for a scrap of paper
2 Dearer than life
3 The curtain of fire
THE GREAT WAR (GREEK FRONT] SERIES:
1 Tommy
2 Tommy and the Maid of Athens
3 The price of a throne
HISTORICAL NOVELS ON RELIGIOUS MOVEMENTS:
1 The sword of the Lord
2 A flame of fire
3 Lest we forget
4 Follow the gleam
5 The coming of the King
6 The chariots of the Lord
RELIGIOUS QUESTIONS SERIES:
1 The scarlet woman
2 The purple robe
3 The woman of Babylon
4 The soul of Dominic Wildthorne

Hodges, A.
THE BLAKE FAMILY:
1 The man of substance
2 The glittering hour

Hodgins, E.
1 Mr. Blandings builds his dream house
2 Blandings way
N.F. Humour

Hodson, J. L.
1 Harvest in the north
2 God's in his heaven

Hoff, H. S.
1 Trina
2 Rhéa

Hogue, O.
1 Love letters of an Anzac
2 Trooper Bluegum at the Dardanelles
3 The Cameliers

Holland, C.
1 My Japanese wife
2 Mousmé

Holland, E.
1 The house in the north
2 The house by the sea

Holland, J.
1 Spurs 1955
2 Spurs the double 1961
*N.F. History of Tottenham Hotspur
Football Club.*

Hollis, C.
1 Death of a gentleman
2 Fossett's memory
3 Letters to a sister

Holly, M.
1 Samantha among the brethren
2 Samantha among the coloured folk
3 Samantha at Saratoga
4 Samantha at the World's Fair
5 Samantha at the St. Louis Exposition
6 Samantha in Europe
7 Samantha at Coney Island
8 Samantha on the woman question
9 Josiah Allen's wife as a P.A. and P.I.,
  same as Samantha at the Centennial
10 Josiah's alarm and Abel Perry's
  funeral
11 Josiah Allen's wife
12 Around the world with Josiah
  Allen's wife

Holmes, M. J.
1 Mildred
2 Mildred's ambition

Holmes, O. W.
1 Elsie Venner
2 The guardian angel

Holmes, R.
1 Walter Greenway, spy
2 Walter Greenway, spy and hero

Holt, E. S. [Mrs. Avery]
MARGERY SERIES:
1 Mistress Margery
2 Margery's son
□
1 In all times of our tribulation
2 In convent walls

Holt, G.
PROFESSOR BASTION SERIES:
1 Six minutes past twelve
2 The white faced man
3 Green talons
4 Murder at Marble Arch
6 The garden of silent beasts
7 Red eagle
8 Drums beat at night
9 Mark of the paw
10 The golden witch
11 Dark lady
12 Death takes the stage
13 Trafalgar Square
14 Black bullets
15 The emerald spider
16 Steel shutters
SHERRETT YORK SERIES:
1 Murder train
2 Ivory ladies
RITZY TYLER SERIES:
1 The theme is murder
2 Green for danger
3 Swing it, death
4 Give a man a rope
5 Begonia Walk
6 Ladies in ermine

Holt, I.
THE RAMPOLE FAMILY:
1 Rampole Place
2 Mudpoint

Holt, W.
1 I haven't unpacked
2 I haven't unpacked yet
3 I still haven't unpacked
N.F. Autobiography

Holton, L.
FATHER BREDDER SERIES:
1 The saint maker 1960
2 A pact with Satan 1961

Home, M.
1 The place of little birds
2 House of shade
3 City of the soul
BRECKLAND SERIES:
1 God and the rabbit
2 In this valley
3 This string first
4 The questing man
5 The harvest is past
6 July at Fritham
7 No snow in Latching
8 Grain of the wood
9 The soundless years
10 Brackenford story
Not strict series, but connected.
JOHN BENHAM SERIES:
1 The strange prisoner
2 The Auber file

Homer
1 The Iliad
2 The Odyssey
'*The Odyssey': a modern sequel, 1959,
by Nikos Kazantzas, has been called
'a work of art in its own right'.*

Hook, T.
1 Gilbert Gurney
2 Gurney married

Hooke, N. W.
1 Striplings
2 Close of play
3 Own wilderness

Hoover, B. R.
1 Pa Flickinger's folks
2 Opal

Hope, A. *pseud.* [**A. H. Hawkins**]
1 The prisoner of Zenda
2 Rupert of Hentzau
3 Sophy of Kravonia

Hope, A. J. B.
1 Strictly tied up

2 The Brandreths

Hope, J.
1 Don't do it!
2 All this and Burnham too
3 One term at Utopia
4 The Inspector suggests
N.F. Humours of teaching.
□
1 Call me Florence
2 Leave it to Florence
*Humorous sketches of the nursing
profession.*

Hopkins, K.
DR. BLOW–PROFESSOR MANCIPLE SERIES:
1 She died because 1958
2 Dead against my principles 1959
3 Body blow 1961
GERRY LEE SERIES:
1 The girl who dies
2 The forty-first passenger
3 Pierce with a pin
4 Camper's corpse

Horgan, P.
1 Main line west
2 A lamp on the plain

Horler, S.
PAUL VIVANTI SERIES:
1 Mystery of No. 1
2 Vivanti
3 Vivanti returns
4 Lord of terror
ANOTHER SERIES:
1 False face
2 Miss Mystery
TIGER STANDISH SERIES:
1 Tiger Standish
2 Tiger Standish comes back
3 Tiger Standish steps on it
4 The grim game
5 Mystery of the seven cafés
6 Tiger Standish takes the field
7 Tiger Standish does his stuff
8 Lady with the lamp
9 Exit the disguiser
10 They thought he was dead
11 The house of Jackals

NIGHTHAWK SERIES:
1 They called him Nighthawk
2 The return of Nighthawk
3 Nighthawk strikes to kill
4 Nighthawk mops up
5 Ring up Nighthawk
6 Nap on Nighthawk
7 Nighthawk swears vengeance

Hornung, E. W.
1 Raffles, the amateur cracksman
2 A thief in the night
3 Mr. Justice Raffles
1 was originally published as two separate collections of short stories, 'The amateur cracksman', and 'The black mask'. See note on bibliography of this work T.L.S. 18 8 50.

Hossent, H.
MAX HEALD SERIES:
1 Spies die at dawn 1960
2 No end to fear 1961
3 Memory of treason 1962
4 Spies have no friends 1963
5 Run for your death 1965

Hougron, J.
M. LASTIN SERIES:
1 Blaze of the sun 1957
2 Reap the whirlwind 1958
Last years of French rule in Indo-China.

Hoult, N.
MONTY MALLORY SERIES:
1 Father and daughter 1957
2 Husband and wife 1959
□
1 Holy Ireland
2 Coming from the fair
□
1 Smilin' on the vine
2 Augusta steps out

Household, G.
ROGER TAINE SERIES:
1 Rough shoot
2 Time to kill

Housman, L.
1 John of Jingalo
2 The royal runaway and Jingalo in revolution

Howard, F. M.
1 Happy rascals
2 The little shop in Fore Street
3 'Orace and Co.
4 Cakes and ale

Howard, H.
GLENN BOWMAN SERIES:
1 Last appointment
2 Last deception
3 Last vanity
4 Death of Cecilia
5 The other side of the door
6 Bowman strikes again
7 Bowman on Broadway
8 Bowman at a venture
9 No target for Bowman
10 Sleep for the wicked 1955
11 A hearse for Cinderella 1956
12 The Bowman touch 1956
13 Key to the morgue 1957
14 Sleep my pretty one 1957
15 The long night 1957
16 The big snatch 1958
17 The Armitage secret 1958
18 Deadline 1959
19 Extortion 1960
20 Time bomb 1960
21 Fall guy 1960
22 I'm no hero 1961
23 Count-down 1962
24 The Stetton case 1963
25 Out of the fire 1965
26 Portrait of a beautiful harlot 1966

Howard, K. [J. K. Bell]
1 The Smiths of Surbiton
2 The Smiths of Valley View
3 The Smiths in war-time
□
1 The fast lady
2 The fast gentleman

Howe, B.
1 A galaxy of governesses
2 Child in Chile 1957
N.F. Autobiography

Howell, W.
1 The voyage of *Wanderer II* 1957
2 *Wanderer III* 1956
N.F. Travel

Howells, W. D.
1 Annie Kilburn
2 The quality of mercy
☐
1 A traveller from Alturial
2 Through the eye of the needle
☐
1 Their wedding journey
2 A hazard of new fortunes
3 An open-eyed conspiracy
4 Their silver wedding journey
5 A pair of patient lovers

Hoyle, F., *and* Elliot, J.
1 A for Andromeda 1963
2 Andromeda breakthrough 1964

Hsiung, S. I.
1 The bridge of heaven
2 The gate of peace

Hubbard, K.
1 Abe Martin
2 The Abe Martin almanac

Huch, R. O.
GARIBALDI AND THE NEW ITALY:
1 Defeat
2 Victory

Hudson, J. W.
1 Abbé Pierre
2 Abbé Pierre's people

Hudson, S.
CHRONICLES OF THE HOUSE OF KURT:
1 Richard Kurt
2 Elinor Colhouse
3 Prince Hempseed
4 Tony
5 Myrtle
6 Richard, Myrtle and I
*Nos. 1. 2 , 3 and the section 'Kurt', in
no. 5, were revised and issued in one
volume under the title 'A true story'
(1930). In 1948 a further revision
included parts of 4 and 6, with a new
epilogue. A new edition was published
in 1965, with an introduction by Lord
David Cecil.*

Hueffer, F. M., *see* Ford, F. M.

Hueston, E.
1 Prudence of the parsonage
2 Prudence says so
3 Sunny slope
4 Prudence's daughter
5 Prudence's sister
☐
1 Ginger Ella
2 Ginger and speed
3 For Ginger's sake

Hughes, L.
1 Simple speaks his mind 1950
2 Simple takes a wife 1953
3 Simple stakes a claim 1957
*Stories and anecdotes by, and about, a
Harlem negro.*

Hughes, P. C. ("Spike")
1 Opening bars
2 Second movement
N.F. Autobiography

Hughes, R.
1 The dozen from Lakerim
2 The Lakerim Athletic Club
☐
1 Miss 318
2 Miss 318 and Mr. 37

Hughes, Vivian
A LONDON FAMILY, 1870–1900:
1 London child of the seventies
2 London girl of the eighties
3 London home in the nineties
N.F. Autobiography

Hugo, V.
LES MISÉRABLES
Also published separately as:
1 Fantine
2 Cosette and Marius
3 Rue Plumet
4 Jean Valjean
*'Les misérables,' 'Toilers of the sea'.
and 'Notre Dame' are said to form a
trilogy.*

Huie, W. B.
1 The revolt of Mamie Stover
2 The Americanisation of Emily
3 Hotel Mamie Stover

Hull, E. M.
1 The Sheik
2 The sons of the Sheik

Hume, D.
MICK CARDBY SERIES:
1 Goodbye to life
2 They call him death
3 The return of Mick Cardby
4 Mick Cardby works overtime
5 Come back for the body
6 Heading for a wreath

Hume, F.
1 Madam Midas
2 Miss Mephistopheles

Hummel, G. F.
1 Heritage
2 Tradition

Huna, L.
BORGIA TRILOGY:
1 The Borgian bull [The bulls of Rome]
2 The star of the Orsini
3 The maid of the Nettuno

Hunt, D. Bonavia-, *see* Austen, J.

Hunt, Sir J.
1 Ascent of Everest
2 Our Everest adventure
N.F. Mountaineering

Hunt, V.
1 Their lives
2 Their hearts
☐
1 Tales of the uneasy
2 More tales of the uneasy

Hunter, A.
CHIEF INSPECTOR GENTLY:
1 Gently does it 1955
2 Gently by the shore 1956
3 Gently down the stream 1957
4 Landed Gently 1957
5 Gently through the mill 1958
6 Gently in the sun 1959
7 Gently with the painters 1960
8 Gently to the summit 1960

9 Gently go man 1961
10 Gently where the roads go 1962
11 Gently floating 1963
12 Gently sahib 1964
13 Gently with the ladies 1965

Hurt, F. M.
INSPECTOR BROOM:
1 The body at Bowman's hollow
2 Death by request
3 Sweet death 1961
4 Acquainted with murder 1962

Hutchings, M. M.
1 Chronicles of Church Farm
2 Romany Cottage, Silverlake
3 Rural reflections
4 Hundredfold
N.F. Rural Life.

Hutchinson, G. S., *see* Seton, G., *pseud.*

Hutten, Baroness von
1 Pam
2 What became of Pam? *same as* Pam decides
3 Pam at fifty
4 Pam's own story
☐
1 The halo
2 Kingsmead

Huxley, A.
1 Brave new world
2 Brave new world revisited

Huxley, E.
1 The flame trees of Thika
2 The mottled lizard
N.F. Autobiography of a Kenya childhood.

Huysmans, J. K.
1 Down there
2 En route
3 The cathedral
4 The oblate
5 The crowds of Lourdes

Hyne, C. J. C.
1 The marriage of Kettle
2 The little red captain, *same as* Honour of thieves

Hyne, C. J. C. (*contd.*)
3 The paradise coal-boat
4 Adventures of Captain Kettle
5 Further adventures of Captain Kettle
6 Mr. Horrocks, purser
7 Captain Kettle, K.C.B.
8 McTodd
9 Kate Meredith
10 The escape agents
11 Red herrings
12 Firemen hot
13 Captain Kettle on the warpath
14 Captain Kettle's bit
15 The Reverend Captain Kettle
16 Before Kettle was captain
17 Mr. Kettle third mate
18 Captain Kettle ambassador
19 President Kettle

Ibsen, H.
Mrs. E. D. Cheney's 'Nora's return' is a
sequel to Ibsen's 'The doll's house'.

Idell, A. E.
ROGERS FAMILY:
1 Roger's folly 1957
2 Centennial summer 1943
3 Bridge to Brooklyn 1944
4 Great blizzard 1948
*1 was the last written, but concerns a
period 40 years earlier than the others.*

Inchbald, R.
COL. PATERNOSTER SERIES:
1 Col. Paternoster
2 The five inns
3 September story 1955

Ingelow, J.
1 Off the Skelligs
2 Fated to be free

Ingram, S.
1 I found adventure
2 Land of mudcastles
N.F. Autobiography

Innes, M.
APPLEBY SERIES:
1 Death at the president's lodging
[Seven suspects]
2 Hamlet revenge

3 Lament for a maker
4 Stop Press
5 There came both mist and snow
6 The secret vanguard
7 Appleby on Ararat
8 The Daffodil affair
9 The weight of the evidence
10 Appleby's end
11 A night of errors
12 Private view [One man show]
13 Appleby talking
14 Appleby talks again 1956
15 Appleby plays chicken 1956
16 The long farewell 1957
17 Hare sitting up 1959
18 Silence observed 1961
19 A connoisseur's case 1962
20 The bloody wood 1965

Insight, J.
1 I turned my collar round
2 I am the vicar 1956
3 County purser 1961
4 I am a guinea pig 1964
N.F. Autobiography

Irvine, A.
1 My lady of the chimney corner
2 The souls of the poor folk

Irwin, G.
1 Least of all saints 1957
2 Andrew Connington 1958

Irwin, M.
1 Royal flush: the story of Minette
2 The proud servant: the story of
Montrose
3 The stranger prince: the story of
Rupert of the Rhine
4 The bride: the story of Louise and
Montrose
*'Four books about certain people in the
17th century whose lives were linked
together.'*
1 Young Bess
2 Elizabeth, captive princess
3 Elizabeth and the Prince of Spain
Fictionalized biography of Elizabeth I.

Irwin, R.
1 The origins of the English library
1958

2 The heritage of the English
library 1964
N.F. Bibliography

Isherwood, C.
1 Mr. Norris changes trains [Last of
Mr. Norris]
2 Goodbye to Berlin 1939
*From the preface to 2. 'Readers of
'Mr. Norris' may notice that certain
characters and situations overlap and
contradict what I have written here . . .
The explanation is simple. These six
pieces are the only existing fragments of
what was originally planned as a large
episodic novel. I had intended to call it
'The lost'. The adventures of Mr.
Norris once formed part of 'The lost'.
'Sally Bowles' in 2 was first published
separately.'*

Istrati, P.
1 Kyra Kyralina
2 Uncle Anghel
3 The bandits

Jacks, L. P.
1 The legends of Smokeover
2 The heroes of Smokeover
3 The last legend of Smokeover

Jackson, C.
1 The sunnier side
2 The lost weekend
*These were not written as sequels. 'The
lost weekend' was written first and is an
episode. 'The sunnier side' is a story of
the youth of the same person.*

Jackson, S.
1 Life among the savages 1953
2 Raising demons 1956
N.F. Autobiography

Jacob, N.
THE GOLLANTZ SAGA:
1 The founder of the house
2 That wild lie
3 Young Emmanuel
4 Four generations
5 Private Gollancz
6 Gollantz

7 London, Paris, Milan
8 Gollantz and partners 1957
*1–6 reissued in two volumes as 'The
Gollantz saga'.*
☐
1 Time piece
2 Fadeout
☐
1 Susan Crowther
2 Honour's a mistress
*The action in 1 takes place in World
War I. In 2 in World War II.*
☐
1 Me
2 Me again
3 More about me
4 Me in wartime
5 Me in the Mediterranean
6 Me over there
7 Me and mine
8 Me – looking back
9 Robert, Nana and me
10 Me – likes and dislikes
11 Me – yesterday and today 1957
12 Me – and the swans 1961
13 Me – and the stags 1963
14 Me – thinking things over 1964
N.F. Biography

Jacobs, T. C. H.
TEMPLE FORTUNE SERIES:
1 Red eyes of Kali
2 Good night sailor
3 Death in the mews 1957

Jacobs, W. W.
1 Many cargoes
2 Sea urchins [More cargoes]
3 Light freights
4 The lady of the barge
5 Odd craft
6 Captains all
7 Short cruises
8 Sailor's knots
9 Ship's company
10 Night watches
11 Deep waters
12 Sea whispers
*All the above contain stories told by the
Night Watchman.*

Jahvda, G.
1 The loving maid 1961
2 Delilah's mountain 1964
Connected but not sequels. 1 deals with the Bickley family in East Anglia. 2 with a member of the family in W. Virginia in the 18th century.

James, C. T. C.
1 Holy wedlock
2 Mrs. Grundy at home

James, G. P. R.
1 Henry Masterton
2 John Marston Hall

James, H.
1 Roderick Hudson
2 The Princess Casamassima

James, M. R.
1 Ghost stories of an antiquary
2 More ghost stories of an antiquary
3 A thin ghost and others
Later published in one volume as 'Collected ghost stories'.

Jameson, S.
1 Cousin Honoré
2 Cloudless May
THE TRIUMPH OF TIME:
1 The lovely ship
2 The voyage home
3 A richer dust
The above form a trilogy, the story of Mary Russell. The sequence is continued in
4 Farewell night, welcome day [The captain's wife] *which is the story of Sylvia Russell, daughter of the above.*
5 That was yesterday
6 The journal of Mary Hervey Russell
These continue the story with the granddaughter of Mary Russell, and serve as a link with the next sequence.
THE MIRROR IN DARKNESS:
7 Company parade
8 Love in winter
9 None turn back
'Before the crossing' and 'Black laurel' carry on the story of some of the main characters, but only incidentally mention Mary Russell. 'A cup of tea for Mr. Thorgill', is concerned with Nevil Rigden, a child of two of the characters in 'Mirror in darkness'.

Jefferies, I.
SERGEANT CRAIG SERIES:
1 Thirteen days 1959
2 Dignity and purity 1960
3 It wasn't me 1961

Jenkins, H.
BINDLE SERIES:
1 Bindle
2 The night club
3 The adventures of Bindle
4 Mrs. Bindle
5 The Bindles on the rocks
JOHN DENE AND MALCOLM SAGE SERIES:
1 John Dene of Toronto
2 Malcolm Sage, detective
3 The Stiffsons and other stories

Jennings, P.
1 Oddly enough
2 Even oddlier
Not sequels except for sequel in 2 to article on Resistentialism ('Things are against us').

Jensen, J. V.
THE LONG JOURNEY SERIES:
1 Fire and ice
2 The Cimbrians
3 Christopher Columbus

Jepson, E.
LADY NOGGS SERIES:
1 The Lady Noggs, peeress
2 Lady Noggs intervenes
3 Lady Noggs assists
POLLYOOLY SERIES:
1 Pollyooly
2 The second Pollyooly book
3 Pollyooly dances
TINKER SERIES:
1 The admirable Tinker
2 The triumph of Tinker
☐
1 The passion for romance

2 The keepers of the people
See also Leblanc, M.

☐

1 Memories of a Victorian
2 Memories of an Edwardian and
Neo-Georgian
N.F. Autobiography

Jepson, S.

1 The qualified adventurer
2 That fellow MacArthur
EVE GILL SERIES:
1 Man running
2 The golden dart
3 The hungry spider
4 Man dead
5 The black Italian
6 The laughing fish 1960

Jerome, J. K.

1 Three men in a boat
2 Three men on the bummel

Jewett, J. H.

1 Bunny stories
2 More bunny stories

Jewitt, S. O.

1 Betty Leicester
2 Betty Leicester's Christmas

John, A.

1 Chiaroscuro
2 Finishing touches
N.F. Autobiography

Johnson, D. McI.

1 A doctor regrets
2 Bars and barricades
3 A doctor returns
4 A doctor in Parliament
5 The hanging tree
N.F. Autobiography

Johnson, I. *and* E.

1 Westward bound in the schooner
Yankee
2 Sailing to see
3 Yankee's wander world
4 Yankee's people and places
N.F Travel and autobiography.

Johnson, P. H.

1 Too dear for my possessing
2 Avenue of stone
3 A summer to decide

☐

1 The unspeakable Skipton 1960
2 Night and silence, who is here 1963
*1 is a fictional version of part of the
life of Frederick Rolfe, but one character,
Matthew Pryar is the hero of 2.*
3 Cork St., next the hatters 1965
Reintroduces characters from 1 and 2.

Johnson, S.

*E. C. Knight's 'Dinarbas' is a con-
tinuation of Johnson's 'Rasselas'.*

Johnson, W. H.

1 The King's henchman
2 Under the spell of the fleur-de-lys,
same as King or knave

Johnston, G.

SILBER SERIES:
1 The claws of the scorpion
2 The two kings

Johnston, Sir H.

'The Gay-Dombeys' is a sequel to
Dickens' 'Dombey and Son'.
'Mrs. Warren's daughter' is a sequel to
G. B. Shaw's 'Mrs. Warren's profession.'
'The Veneerings' is a sequel to Dickens'
'Our mutual friend.'

Johnston, Mrs. H. K.

1 Roddy's ideal
2 Roddy's reality
3 Roddy's romance

Johnston, M.

1 By order of the company
2 Old dominion
3 Audrey
*Episodes in the history of Virginia, not
otherwise connected.*
AMERICAN CIVIL WAR TRILOGY:
1 The long roll
2 Cease firing
3 Michael Forth

Johnstone, N.
1 Hotel in Spain
2 Hotel in flight
N.F. Autobiography

Jokai, M.
1 'Midst the wild Carpathians
2 Slaves of the Padishah

Jones, B.
JAMES KEEN SERIES:
1 The Hamlet problem 1961
2 The crowded phoenix 1962
3 Tiger from the shadows 1963

Jones, E. B.
1 In Burleigh's days
2 The second Cecil
Connected novels, though not strictly sequels.

Jones, G. Hackforth-
EARL OF MILLINGTON:
1 Submarine flotilla
2 Rough passage
3 The price was high
4 The questing hound
5 Sixteen bells
JOE GARTON SERIES:
1 Danger below 1962
2 I am the captain 1963·

Jones, Jack
1 Unfinished journey
2 Me and mine
3 Give me back my heart
N.F. Autobiography

Jones, Joanna
NURSE JONES SERIES:
1 Nurse is a neighbour
2 Nurse on the district 1958
N.F. Autobiography

Jones, Sir L. E.
1 A Victorian boyhood
2 An Edwardian youth
3 Georgian afternoon
4 I forgot to tell you
N.F. Autobiography
FATHER LASCAUT:
1 Trepidation in Downing St. 1962

2 Father Lascaut hits back 1964
Collections of short stories, each containing some stories about this character.

Jones, W. Glynne-
1 Farewell innocence
2 Ride the white stallion

Joris, F. Mallet-
1 Into the labyrinth [The illusionist]
2 The red room
Two episodes in the life of Helene, the main character, that are unrelated except as they depict two episodes in the development of her 'vie sensuale'.

Joyce, J.
1 Portrait of the artist as a young man
2 Ulysses
Connected by the character Stephen Dedalus.

Joyce, S.
1 My brother's keeper
2 The Dublin diary of Stanislaus Joyce
N.F. Autobiography

Joynson, C.
1 In spite of Henry
2 In search of Henry
3 Yes, Henry 1964
N.F. Autobiography

Kafka, F.
1 The castle
2 The trial

Kane, H.
PETER CHAMBERS SERIES:
1 A halo for nobody
2 Armchair in hell
3 Hang by your neck
4 Report for a corpse
5 A corpse for Christmas
6 Trinity in violence
7 Trilogy in jeopardy
8 Death on the double
9 The narrowing lust
10 Sweet Charlie
11 Triple terror
12 The dangling dean
13 Nirvana can also mean death

14 Death of a flack
15 Death of a hooker
16 Death of a dastard
17 Killer's kiss
18 Dead in bed
19 Snatch an eye

Katz, H. W.
1 The Fishmans
2 No. 21 Castle Street

Kaye, B.
DUCKETTS GREEN SERIES:
1 Black market green
2 Rebellion on the green

Kaye, M. M.
1 Later than you think 1957
2 House of shade 1959

Kaye-Smith, *see* Smith, S. Kaye-

Kazantzas, N., *see* Homer

Keable, R.
1 Simon called Peter
2 Recompense
3 Lighten our darkness

Keeler, H. S.
1 The Marceau case
2 X Jones
The same story told from two angles.

Keating, H. R. F.
INSPECTOR GHOTE:
1 The perfect murder 1965
2 Inspector Ghote's good crusade 1966

Keevil, J. J.
1 Harvey the stranger
2 Stranger's son
N.F. Biography

Keith, A.
1 Land below the wind
2 Three came home
3 White man returns
4 Bare feet in the palace 1956
Autobiographical account of life in Borneo, including experiences as a prisoner during Japanese occupation.

Kelland, C. B.
SCATTERGOOD BAINES SERIES:
1 Scattergood Baines
2 Scattergood Baines pulls the strings
3 Scattergood Baines returns

Kelly, E.
THE URRUTY FAMILY:
1 Basquerie
2 The book of Bette
3 Nacio, his affairs

Kelly, M.
1 Little aliens
2 Wards of liberty
3 Little citizens

Kelly, Mary
DET.-INSPECTOR NIGHTINGALE SERIES:
1 A cold coming
2 Dead man's riddle
3 The Christmas egg

Kemp, P.
1 Mine were of trouble 1958
2 No colours or crest 1960
3 Alms for oblivion 1961
N.F. Autobiography

Kendrick, B.
DUNCAN MACLAIN SERIES:
1 Blind man's buff
2 Death knell
3 Out of control
4 You die today
5 Reservations for death
6 Clear and present danger 1958
7 The whistling hangman 1959

Kennedy, M.
THE WANGER FAMILY:
1 The constant nymph
2 Escape me never
3 The fool of the family

Kennelly, A.
1 The peaceable kingdom 1949
2 Up home Houghton 1955
A chronicle of Mormon life in the 19th century.

Kenneth, C.
1 The love riddle 1963
2 May in Manhattan 1963

Kent, L. A.
1 Mrs. Appleyard's year 1941
2 With kitchen privileges 1953

Kenyon, F. W.
JOHN CHURCHILL, DUKE OF
MARLBOROUGH:
1 The seeds of time
2 Glory o' the dream

Kenyon, T.
THE STACEYS OF FEATHERGRANT:
1 The golden feather
2 Dark root

Kerin, D.
1 The living touch
2 Fulfilling

Kernahan, Mrs. C.
1 Devastation
2 The fate of Felix

Kerner, A.
1 Woman detective
2 Further adventures of a woman
detective
N.F. Autobiography

Kerouac, J.
THE STORY OF JACK DULUOZ:
1 On the road
2 The Dharma bums
3 The subterraneans
4 The lonesome traveller
5 Big Sur 1963

Kersh, G.
1 They die with their boots clean
2 Nine lives of Bill Nelson
Stories of the Brigade of Guards.
□
1 Night and the city
2 Song of the flea
*Harry Fabian, who is the main character
of 1 appears as a minor character in 2.*

Kesey, K.
1 One flew over the cuckoo's nest
2 Sometimes a great notion

Keverne, R.
DETECTIVES PARRY AND HARRIS SERIES:
1 William Cook – antique dealer
2 Menace

Key, V.
1 The broken fang
2 Yellow death

Keyes, F. P.
1 Christian Marlowe's daughter
2 The great tradition
□
1 The river road
2 Vail D'Alvery
□
1 Steamboat Gothic
2 Larry Vincent
*2 deals with descendents of Clyde
Batchelor of 1.*
□
1 Dinner at Antoine's
2 Royal box
*Joe Racina reporter, and his wife
Judith are in both novels.*
CAROLINA TRILOGY:
1 Honour bright
2 Blue camellia 1957
3 The gold slippers 1958

Keyte, J. C.
1 A daughter of Cathay
2 Minsan

Kiddy, M. G.
STONEWALL STEVENS SERIES:
1 Stonewall Stevens investigates
2 Killing no murder
3 The jade hatpin

Kielland, A. L.
1 Garman and Worse
2 Skipper Worse

Kilbourne, F.
1 A corner in William
2 Mrs. William Norton speaking

3 The Norton twins
4 Dot and Will
5 Dot and Will at home

Killilea, M.
1 Karen – the story of a family 1963
2 With love from Karen 1964
N.F. Autobiography

Kilpatrick, F. A.
1 Our Elizabeth
2 Our Elizabeth again
3 Elizabeth to the rescue
4 Elizabeth in wartime
☐
1 Wild cat Hetty
2 Hetty married
3 Hetty's son

Kilroy, M.
1 Little torment
2 Study number eleven

King, A.
1 Mine enemy grows older 1958
2 May this house be safe from tigers 1960
3 I should have kissed her more 1961
4 Is there a life after birth 1962
N.F. Autobiography

King, C.
1 The Colonel's daughter
2 Marion's faith
3 A garrison tangle
4 Ray's recruit
5 Ray's daughter
6 Captain Blake
7 Captured, the story of Sandy Ray
8 Lieutenant Sandy Ray
9 The further story of Sandy Ray
☐
1 Cadet days
2 To the front

King, C. D.
1 Obelists at sea
2 Obelists en route
3 Obelists fly high

King, F.
INSPECTOR GLOOM SERIES:
1 The case of the painted girl
2 Green gold
DORMOUSE SERIES:
1 Enter the dormouse
2 The dormouse-undertaker
3 The dormouse has nine lives
4 The dormouse peacemaker
5 Dough for the dormouse
6 This doll is dangerous
7 They vanished at night
8 What price doubloons
9 Crook's cross
10 Gestapo dormouse
11 Sinister light
12 Catastrophe Club
13 Operation halter
14 Operation honeymoon
15 Big blackmail
16 Crook's caravan 1955
17 The case of strange beauties
Continued as 'The Conrad detective agency' (also 'the Dormouse').
18 That charming crook 1958
19 The two who talked 1958
20 The case of the frightened brother 1959

King, L. W.
1 The day we were mostly butterflies 1963
2 The velocipede handicap 1965
Characters in 2 reappear from 1. A collection of stories.

King, R.
COTTON MOON SERIES:
1 The case of the constant god
2 Crime of violence
3 Murder masks Miami
4 Holiday homicide
5 Diagnosis murder
6 Case of the dowager's etchings

King, Robin
1 No paradise
2 Sailor in the east
3 The angry sun
N.F. Autobiography

Kingsley, Mrs. F. M.
1 The transfiguration of Miss Philura
2 Miss Philura's wedding gown
3 The heart of Miss Philura

Kipling, R.
1 The jungle book
2 The second jungle book
   ☐
1 Puck of Pook's Hill
2 Rewards and fairies
STALKY AND CO.:
1 Stalky in 'Land and Sea Tales'
2 Stalky and Co.
3 A deal in cotton (short story)
4 Conference of the powers (short story)
   'Soldiers three' appear in the following stories: 'The big drunk Draf'; 'Black Jack'; 'The courting of Dinah Shaff'; 'The daughter of the regiment'; 'Garm-a-hostage'; 'The god from the machine'; 'His private honour'; 'Love o' women'; 'The madness of Private Ortheris'; 'My lord the elephant'; 'Private Learoyd's story'; 'The solid Muldoon'; 'The taking of Lungtungpen'; 'The three musketeers'; 'With the main guard'; 'On Greenhow Hill'; 'The incarnation of Private Mulvaney'.
   Other notes on recurring characters in Kipling's short stories may be found in Young, W. A. A dictionary of the characters and scenes in the stories and poems of Rudyard Kipling. Dutton. 1911.

Kirkbride, R.
1 Winds blow gently
2 Spring is not gentle

Kirkup, J.
1 The only child
2 Sorrows, passions, and alarms 1959
N.F. Autobiography

Kirst, A. H.
ZERO EIGHT-FIFTEEN: A TRILOGY OF GERMAN ARMY LIFE:
1 The strange mutiny of Gunner Asch 1955
2 Gunner Asch goes to war 1956

3 The return of Gunner Asch 1958
4 What became of Gunner Asch? 1964
   A pendant to the trilogy.

Kitchin, C. H. B.
MALCOLM WARREN SERIES:
1 Death of my aunt
2 Crime at christmas
3 Death of his uncle
4 The Cornish fox

Kneale, N.
1 The Quatermass experiment
2 Quatermass II

Knight, A. L.
1 Royal of Monkey Island
2 The cruise of the *Cormorant*

Knight, B.
1 Walking the whirlwind
2 The piping on the wind
   ☐
1 Old Amsterdam
2 I shall maintain
   The story of a Dutch financier in the 16th century, Peter Van Breda. 2 continues the story in the person of his daughter Helene.
   ☐
1 The house of the swan 1961
2 The house of the bird of Paradise 1962

Knight, C.
HUNTOON ROGERS SERIES:
1 Affair of the scarlet crab
2 Affair of the heavenly voice
3 Affair at Palm Springs
4 Affair of the crimson gull
5 Affair in death valley
6 Affair of the jade monkey
7 Affair of the fainting butler
8 Affair of the dead stranger
9 Affair of the golden buzzard
10 Affair of the corpse escort
11 Affair of the sixth button

Knight, E.
1 The flying Yorkshireman
2 Sam Small flies again

Knight, E. C.
Dinarbas is a sequel to S. Johnson's 'Rasselas'.

Knight, K. M.
ELISHA MACOMBER SERIES:
1 The poor man's shilling
2 Trouble at Turkey Hill
3 Footbridge to death
4 Bait for murder
5 Bass Derby murder
6 Death goes to a reunion
7 Valse Macabre

Knight, L. A.
JERRY SCANT SERIES:
1 Deadman's Bay
2 The creaking tree mystery
3 The creaking death
4 Murder by experiment
5 The Solander box mystery
6 The dancing stones

Knipe, Mrs. E. B., *and* **A. A.**
BENEDICT ARNOLD SERIES:
1 A continental dollar
2 Powder, patches and Patty
DENEWOOD SERIES:
1 The lucky sixpence
2 Beatrice of Denewood
3 Peg o' the Ring
LITTLE MISS FALES SERIES:
1 Little Miss Fales
2 The missing pearls

Knott, T. S.
1 Fools rush in
2 Keep it clean
N.F. Autobiography

Knox, B.
CHIEF INSP. THANE AND INSP. MOSS:
1 Deadline for a dream 1957
2 Death department 1958
3 Leave it to the hangman 1959
4 Little drops of blood 1960
5 Santuary Isle 1961
6 The man in the bottle 1962
7 Die for Big Betsy 1963
8 The scavengers 1964
9 The taste of proof 1964

10 Devilweed 1965
Novels about the Fishery Protection Service, setting is in the Outer Hebrides.

Knox, R. A.
1 The three taps
2 The footsteps at the lock
3 The body in the silo
See also Trollope, A.

Koestler, A.
1 Arrow in the blue
2 The invisible writing
N.F. Autobiography

Krasney, J.
LIEUT. ABE LASSEN SERIES:
1 Homicide west
2 Homicide call 1963

Kravchenko, V.
1 I chose freedom
2 I chose justice
N.F. Autobiography

Kuller, J. van Ammers-
1 The rebel generation
2 No surrender
☐
1 The house of joy
2 Jenny Heysten's career

Kyne, P. B.
1 Cappy Ricks
2 You can't cap Cappy
3 Cappy Ricks retires
4 The green pea pirates
5 Cappy Ricks comes back
6 The Cappy Ricks special

Lacon-Watson, E., *see* Watson, E. Lacon-

Lacy, Ed.
TOUSSAINT MOORE SERIES:
1 Room to swing 1964
2 Moment of truth 1965

Ladline, R.
REMINGTON SERIES:
1 The shoe fits
2 The devil in Downing St.
3 The sky's the limit
4 When fools endanger us
5 Stop that man

Lagerkvist, P.
TOBIAS TRILOGY:
1 Death of Ahasueras 1963
2 Pilgrim at sea 1964
3 The holy land 1965
The theme of another novel 'The Sybil' is linked to this series, but is not part of it.

Lagerlöf, S.
1 Jerusalem
2 The Holy City
□ .
1 Wonderful adventures of Nils
2 Further adventures of Nils
RING OF THE LÖWENSKOLDS:
1 The General's ring
2 Charlotte Löwenskold
3 Anna Svard

Laing, K.
ROLLING STONE SERIES:
1 Malignant snowman
2 No man's laughter

Lambert, D.
1 He must so live
2 No time for sleeping

Lambert, F.
1 The 20,000 thieves
2 The veterans
The Australian army in World War II.

Lambert, M.
1 The relentless marriage
2 Thaxford's wife
Characters reappear, but not otherwise sequels.

Lambourne, J.
1 The kingdom that was
2 The second leopard

Lamming, G.
1 Castle of my skin
2 The emigrants
Two novels of a West Indian village Characters are not the same.

Lancing, G. *pseud.* [**Lan Tso Chi**]
TZU HSI, EMPRESS OF CHINA:
1 Imperial motherhood
2 The mating of the dragon
3 Dragon in chains
4 Phoenix triumphant

Landon, H.
1 The grey phantom
2 The grey phantom's return
3 The grey terror
4 The grey phantom's triumph
PICAROON SERIES:
1 The elusive Picaroon
2 The green shadow
3 The Picaroon does justice
4 Buy my silence
5 The Picaroon resumes practice
6 Picaroon in pursuit
7 Picaroon: knight errant
8 The trailing of the Picaroon

Lane, G.
KATE AND TONY MARSH SERIES:
1 Curlew Coombe mystery
2 Lantern House affair
3 Hotel Cremona mystery
4 Unknown enemy
5 Three died that night
6 Red mirror mystery
7 Death visits the summer house
8 Death in Mermaid Lane
9 Death prowls the cove
10 Guest with the scythe

Lane, J.
1 King's critic
2 England for sale
3 Gin and bitters
2 and 3 and sequels. The main character's father is the hero of 1.

Lane, Mrs. J.
1 According to Maria
2 Maria again
3 War phases according to Maria

Lane, M.
1 A night at sea 1963
2 A smell of burning 1965
1 Describes a shipwreck and the events leading up to it, while 2 continues the story of the survivors.

Lanham, E. M.
1 The wind blew west
2 Banner at daybreak

Lardner, R. W.
1 Treat 'em rough
2 The real dope

Large, E. C.
1 Sugar in the air
2 Asleep in the afternoon
Paul Pry, the central character of the first book is the supposed author of the second.

Larsson, G.
1 Our daily bread
2 Fatherland, farewell!

Lartéguy, J.
1 The Centurions 1962
2 The Praetorians 1963
Novels of the French army in Algeria.

Lasswell, M.
MRS. FEELEY SERIES:
1 Suds in your eye
2 High time
3 One on the house
4 Wait for the wagon
5 Tooner schooner

Latham, Mrs. A. G.
1 Christabel
2 Christabel in France

Lathen, E.
JOHN THATCHER SERIES:
1 Banking on death 1962
2 A place for murder 1963
3 Accounting for murder 1965

Latta, G.
1 Arnholt makes his bow
2 Re-enter Arnholt

Laverty, M.
THE LIFE OF DELIA SCULLY:
1 Never no more
2 No more than human

Lawrence, D. H.
1 The rainbow
2 Women in love

Lawrence, H.
MARK EAST SERIES:
1 Blood upon the snow
2 Death of a doll
3 A time to die

Lawrence, L.
THE SEED:
1 Morning, moon and night
2 Out of the dust
3 Old father Antic
4 The hoax
5 The sowing

Lawrence, M.
1 Number seven, Queer Street
2 Master of shadows
Short stories featuring Miles Pennoyer.

Lawson, R. N.
1 Beloved shipmates
2 Happy anchorage

Lea, F. H.
1 Good-bye summer
2 Half-angel

Leaser, J.
DR. JASON LOVE:
1 Passport to oblivion 1965
2 Passport to peril 1966

Leblanc, M.
1 Arsène Lupin (by M. Leblanc and E. Jepson]
2 Arsène Lupin versus Sherlock Holmes
3 The exploits of Arsène Lupin
4 The hollow needle
5 813
6 The confessions of Arsène Lupin
7 The crystal stopper
8 The teeth of the tiger
9 Bomb-shell
10 Coffin Island
11 The Golden Triangle
12 The eight strokes of the clock
13 The seven of hearts

Leblanc, M. (*contd.*)
14 The candlestick with seven branches
15 The arrest of Arsène Lupin
16 The double smile [The woman with two smiles]
17 The return of Arsène Lupin
18 Melamare mystery

Le Breton, T.
1 Mrs. May
2 Confessions of Mrs. May
3 Mr. and Mrs. May
4 Mrs. May's lectures to ladies

Le Carré, J.
GEORGE SMILEY:
1 Murder of quality
2 Call for the dead
3 The spy who came in from the cold 1963
4 The looking glass war 1965
1 and 2 reissued in one novel as 'The incongruous spy' 1964 (U.S.). Smiley is only a minor character in 4.

Lee, A.
MISS HOGG SERIES:
1 Sheep's clothing
2 Call in Miss Hogg
3 Miss Hogg and the Bronte murders 1956
4 Miss Hogg and the squash club murder 1957
5 Miss Hogg and the dead dean 1957
6 Miss Hogg flies high 1958
7 Miss Hogg and the Covent Garden murders 1960
8 Miss Hogg and the missing sisters 1961
9 Miss Hogg's last case 1963

Lee, Mrs. J. B. P.
1 Uncle William
2 Happy Island

Lee, N.
BEAUTIFUL GUNNER SERIES:
1 The beautiful gunner
2 Lover, say it with mink
3 Another woman's man

Leeming, J. F.
1 It always rains in Rome
2 A girl like Wigan
3 Arnaldo my brother

Lehmann, J.
1 The whispering gallery 1955
2 I am my brother 1959
N.F. Autobiography

Lehmann, R.
1 Invitation to the waltz
2 The weather in the streets

Leigh, M.
1 Highland homespun
2 Harvest of the moor
3 My kingdom for a horse
4 Spade among the rushes
5 Fruit in the seed
N.F. Autobiography

Leith, Mrs. D.
1 A black Martinmus
2 Lachlan's widow

Leslie, D.
1 Folly's end
2 The Peverills

Leslie, D. S.
1 The devil boat
2 Lovers from the sea
Not precisely sequels. The central character of 2, Alfonso, is the younger brother of the hero of 1.

Leroux, G.
1 The amazing adventures of Carolus Herbert
2 The veiled prisoner
☐
CHÉRI-BIBI SERIES:
1 The floating prison
2 Chéri-Bibi and Cecily
3 Chéri-Bibi, mystery man
4 The dancing girl
5 The new idol
JOSEPH ROULETABILLE SERIES:
1 The mystery of the yellow room
2 The slave bangle
3 The perfume of the lady in black

4 Rouletabille chez le Tsar
5 Le chateau noir
6 Les etranges noces de Rouletabille
7 Rouletabille chez Krupp
8 Rouletabille chez les Bohemiens
9 Le crime de Rouletabille
Only 1–3 have been traced as having been translated.

Leslie, E.
1 Leofwine
2 Elfrida

Leslie, H.
1 Emily in Arlington St.
1 Emily in Arlington Street
2 Martha Plover
3 Young Sam

Leslie, S.
1 The Oppidan
2 The Cantab
3 The Anglo-Catholic

Lessing, D.
CHILDREN OF VIOLENCE:
1 Martha Quest
2 A proper marriage 1956
3 A ripple from the storm 1958
4 Landlocked 1965
'A fifth and final volume is projected' – Author. Volumes 1 and 2 republished (1965) in one volume.

Lester, F.
GEOFFREY SLADE SERIES:
1 The corpse wore rubies 1958
2 Death and the south wind 1958
3 The golden murder 1959

Levene, P.
AMBROSE WEST SERIES:
1 Ambrose in London 1959
2 Ambrose in Paris 1960

Leverson, A.
EDITH OTTLEY TRILOGY:
1 Love's shadow
2 Tenterhooks
3 Love at second sight
Reprinted in 1962 in one volume 'The little Ottleys' with an introduction by

Colin MacInnes. *'In her own right and by her own achievement a very great artist indeed'.*

Lett, G.
1 Rossano
2 The many-headed monster 1957
The Italian Resistance and its post-war effects.

Lewis, C. S.
DR. RANSOM TRILOGY:
1 Out of the silent planet
2 Perelandra
3 That hideous strength

Lewis, E. W.
1 The adventures of Sabo
2 More Sabo stories

Lewis, Mrs. H.
1 Her double life
2 The sunshine of love
□
1 The bailiff's scheme
2 Rosamond's love
□
1 A vixen's treachery
2 Adrift in the world
□
1 The old life's shadows
2 Outside her Eden
□
1 The belle of the season
2 Love before pride

Lewis, M.
EX-SERGEANT HOBBS, V.C. SERIES:
1 The brand of the beast
2 The island of disaster

Lewis, N.
1 Dragon apparent
2 Golden earth
N.F. Travel

Lewis, S.
1 Babbitt
2 The man who knew Coolidge

Lewis, W. H.
1 The splendid century
2 The sunset of the splendid century
N.F. Life and times of Louis XIV.

Lewis, Wyndham
THE HUMAN AGE, A TETRALOGY:
1 The childermass
2 Monstre gai
3 Malign fiesta
4 Trial of man
2 and 3 published in 1 volume. A fantasy of life after death.

Lillie, Mrs. L. C. W.
1 The squire's daughter
2 For honour's sake

Lincoln, J. C.
1 Mr. Pratt
2 Mr. Pratt's patients
□
1 Capt'n Eri
2 The old home house

Lincoln, M.
1 'I, said the sparrow'
2 Nothing ever happens

Lindop, A. E.
1 The singer not the song 1954
2 The Judas figures 1956

Lindsay, H.
1 Methodist idylls
2 More Methodist idylls

Lindsay, Jack
THE BRITISH WAY:
1 Betrayed spring
2 Rising tide
3 Moment of choice
4 A local habitation 1957
5 Choice of times 1963
Novels of post-war Britain, linked by theme, not characters.
□
1 Rome for sale
2 Caesar is dead
3 Last days of Cleopatra
□
1 Life rarely tells
2 The roaring twenties
3 Franfrolico and after
N.F. Autobiography

Lindsay, Joan
1 Time without clocks
2 Facts soft and hard
N.F. Autobiography

Lindsay, P.
SUSSEX SERIES:
1 Devil comes to Winchelsea 1956
2 Bells of Rye 1957
3 Sisters of Rye 1959
□
1 He rides in triumph
2 Whither shall I wander?
Two novels about 15th century London. The same characters appear in both, there is a gap in time between 1 and 2.

Linington, E.
LUIZ MENDOZA:
1 Extra kill 1962
2 The ace of spades 1963
3 Knave of hearts 1963
4 Death of a busybody 1963
5 Double bluff 1964

Linklater, E.
1 Man on my back
2 A year of space
N.F. Autobiography
□
1 Juan in America
2 Juan in China

Linklater, J. L.
SILAS BOOTH SERIES:
1 'Bishop's cap' murder
2 Shadow for a lady
3 Black opal
4 She had a little knife

Linn, J.
1 This was life
2 Winds over the campus

Lippmann, J. M.
1 Martha by-the-day
2 Making over Martha
3 Martha and Cupid

Lisle, D.
ISOLA DERING SERIES:
1 Painter of souls
2 What is love?

Lister, S.
SAINTE MONIQUE SERIES:
1 Mistral Hotel
2 Sunset over France
3 Peace comes to Sainte Monique
4 Marise
5 Miss Sainte Monique
6 Delorme in deep water 1958
Not strictly sequels but connected by the re-appearance of the same characters, particularly Father Delorme.

Livingstone, K.
1 The Dodd papers
2 The Cloze papers

Llewellyn, R.
1 How green was my valley
2 Up, into the singing mountain
3 Down where the moon is small 1966
Trilogy about a Welsh coal mining family.

Lobsang, Rampa, T.
1 The third eye
2 Doctor from Lhasa
3 The Rampa story
N.F. Autobiography

Locherbie-Cameron, M., *see*
Cameron, M. Locherbie-

Lockhart, J. G.
1 Mrs. MacNab and the pirates
2 Mrs. MacNab goes west

Lockhead, M.
1 Their first ten years
2 Young Victorians

Lockley, R. M.
1 Island farm
2 Inland farm
3 The island farmers
4 Golden year
N.F. Autobiography

Lockridge, F. *and* R.
MR. AND MRS. NORTH SERIES:
1 Mr. and Mrs. North
2 The Norths meet murder
3 Murder out of turn
4 Hanged for a sheep
5 Death takes a bow
6 A pinch of poison
7 Death on the aisle
8 Killing the goose
9 Death of a tall man
10 Pay off for the banker
11 Murder within murder
12 Murder is served
13 Dishonest murderer
14 Murder in a hurry
15 Untidy murder
16 Murder comes first
17 Dead as a dinosaur
18 Curtain for a jester
19 Death has a small voice
20 Death of an angel 1957
21 Voyage into violence 1958
22 The long skeleton
23 Murder is suggested
24 The judge is reversed
25 Murder has its points 1962
26 Murder by the book 1964
27 [The ticking clock]
CAPTAIN HEIMRICH SERIES:
1 I want to go home
2 Spin your web, lady
3 Foggy foggy death
4 Client is cancelled
5 Death by association
6 Stand up and die
7 Death and the gentle bull
Continued under the name of Francis Richards.
8 Burnt offering
9 Let dead enough alone
10 Practise to deceive
11 Accent on murder 1960
12 Show red for danger 1961
13 No dignity in death 1962
14 First come first kill 1963
15 The distant clue 1964
16 Murder can't wait 1965

Lodwick, J.
1 Somewhere a voice is calling
2 The starless night

Lofthouse, J.
1 Lancashire countrygoer
2 Countrygoer in the Dales

Lofts, N.
1 The silver nutmeg
2 Scent of cloves 1957
Indonesia in the 18th century.
□
1 Bless this house 1955
2 Afternoon of an autocrat 1956
Story of an 18th century village
□
1 Town house
2 House at Old Vine
3 The house at sunset 1963

London, J.
1 Jerry
2 Michael, brother of Jerry
□
1 Smoke Bellew
2 Smoke and Shorty

Long, E. L.
FLYNN SERIES:
1 Young Flynn
2 The fortunes of Flynn
3 Captain Flynn
4 The vengeance of Flynn
5 Flynn of the Martagon
6 Flynn, A. B.
7 Son of Flynn
8 Flynn's sampler
9 Lieut. Flynn, R.N.
10 Capt. Flynn (ret'd)
11 Ould Flynn
12 The blindness of Flynn
13 Captain Flynn, sheriff 1961
SIMPSON SERIES :
1 Seconds and thirds
2 Trials of the Phidias
LIZZIE COLLINS SERIES:
1 Port of destination
2 Purser's mate
3 Unhappy ship

Long, Mrs. G. M., *see* Bowen, M.

Long, H.
1 Silver face
2 Silverface surrenders

Long, M.
LIZ. PARROTT SERIES:
1 Here's blood in your eye
2 Vicious circle
3 Bury the hatchet
4 Short shrift
5 Dull thud
6 Savage breast

Longford, F. A. P., 1st Baron
1 Born to believe
2 Five lives
N.F. Autobiography

Longhurst, H.
1 It was good while it lasted
2 I wouldn't have missed it
3 You never know till you get there
N.F. Autobiography

Longmate, N.
DET.-SGT. RAYMOND SERIES:
1 Death won't wash 1957
2 A head from death 1958
3 Strip death naked 1959
4 Vote for death 1960

Longstreth, T. M.
1 The scarlet Force
2 The Force carries on
N.F. History of the Royal Canadian Mounted Police.

Loos, A.
1 Gentlemen prefer blondes
2 But, gentlemen marry brunettes

Lorac, E. C. R.
INSPECTOR MACDONALD SERIES:
1 Murder on the barrows
2 Affair on Thor's head
3 Greenwell mystery
4 Murder in St. John's Wood
5 Murder in Chelsea
6 Affair of Colonel Marchand
7 Death on the Oxford Road
8 The organ speaks
9 Death of an author
10 Crime counter crime
11 Post after post mortem
12 A pall for a painter
13 Bats in the belfry

14 The devil and the C.I.D.
15 These names make clues
16 Slippery staircase
17 John Brown's body
18 Black beadle
19 Death at Dyke's corner
20 Tryst for a tragedy
21 Case in the clinic
22 Rope's end rogue's end
23 The sixteenth stair
24 Death came softly
25 Checkmate to murder
26 Fell murder
27 Murder by matchlight
28 Fire in the thatch
29 The theft of the iron dogs
30 Relative to poison
31 Death before dinner
32 Part of a poisoner [Place for a poisoner]
33 Still waters
34 Policemen in the precinct [And then put out the light]
35 Accident by design
36 Murder of a martinet [I could murder her]
37 The dog it was that died
38 Murder in the millrace [Speak justly of the dead]
39 Crook O'lune [Shepherd's crook]
40 Shroud of darkness
41 Dangerous domicile 1957
42 Murder on a monument 1958
43 Death in triplicate 1959
44 Dishonour among thieves 1960
There is an interior sequence by place 'Lunesdale', in some novels – 'Fell murder', 'Crook O'Lune', 'Theft of the iron dogs', and 'Dishonour among thieves', with many minor characters recurring.

Lorimer, G., *and* S.
1 Men are like street cars
2 Stag line
3 Heart specialist

Lorimer, G. H.
1 Letters from a self-made merchant to his son
2 Old Gorgon Graham

Lorimer, N.
1 There was a king in Egypt
2 Shadow of Egypt

Loti, P. *pseud*. [M. J. Viaud]
1 Aziyadé
2 A phantom from the east

Lott, S. M.
STEPHEN RINGWAY SERIES:
1 Twopence for a rat's tail
2 The Judge will call it murder

Lowndes, Mrs. B.
1 Duchess Laura [The Duchess intervenes]
2 Duchess Laura: further days of her life
□
1 I too have lived in Arcadia
2 Where love and friendship dwelt
3 Merry wives of Westminster
4 Passing world
N.F. Autobiography

Lucas, E. V.
1 Listener's lure
2 Over Bemerton's
3 Mr. Ingleside
4 London lavender
5 Landmarks
□
1 The vermilion box
2 Verena in the midst
□
1 Windfall's Eve
2 Down the sky
3 The barber's clock

Lucas, St. J.
1 The first round
2 April folly

Luckner, Count Felix von
1 Sea devil
2 Out of an old sea chest
N.F. Autobiography

Lunn, Sir A.
1 Come what may
2 Now I see
3 And yet so new
N.F. Autobiography

Lushington, F.
1 Pigeon Hoo
2 Pennybridge

Lutyens, E.
1 A blessed girl
2 The birth of Rowland
3 Candles in the sun
N.F. Autobiography

Lyall, E. [A. E. Bayley]
1 Donovan
2 We two

Lyall, G.
1 The wrong side of the sky
2 The most dangerous game

Lyttelton, H.
1 I play as I please
2 Second chorus
N.F. Autobiography

Lytton, Baron
ERNEST MALTRAVERS SERIES:
1 Ernest Maltravers
2 Alice
REAL AND THE IDEAL TRILOGY:
1 The Caxtons
2 My novel
3 What will he do with it
'Zanoni' is 'Zicci' completed.

McArdle, R. Z.
1 My aunt Angie
2 My uncle Oswald

Macaulay, R.
1 Letters to a friend
2 Last letters to a friend
N.F. Autobiography

McBain, E.
THE 87TH PRECINCT:
1 Cop hater
2 The mugger
3 The pusher
4 The con man
5 Killer's choice
6 Killer payoff
7 Lady killer
8 Killer's wedge

9 'Til death
10 King's ransom
11 Give the boys a great big hand
12 The heckler
13 See them die
14 Lady, lady I did it 1963
15 The empty hours 1963
16 Like love 1964
17 Ten plus one 1964
18 Axe 1965
19 He who hesitates 1965
20 Doll 1966

McCarthy, J. H.
1 If I were King
2 Needles and pins
3 Pretty maids all in a row

McCloy, H.
BASIL WILLING SERIES:
1 One for murder
2 The one that got away
3 Through a glass darkly
4 Alias Basil Willing
5 Man in the moonlight
6 Dance of death
7 The Goblin market

McCormick, R.
1 Little coquette
2 Rustle of petticoats

McCulley, J.
1 Black Star
2 Black Star's campaign
3 Black Star's return
4 Black Star again
WELTON PROUSE SERIES:
1 The crimson clown
2 The crimson clown again
□
1 Zorro
2 Further adventures of Zorro
3 Mark of Zorro
THE THUNDERBOLT SERIES:
1 Alias the Thunderbolt
2 The Thunderbolt's jest

McCutchan, P.
COMMANDER SHAW SERIES:
1 Gibraltar Road 1960
2 Redcap 1961

3 Bluebolt one 1961
4 The man from Moscow 1962
5 Warmaster 1963
6 The Moscow coach 1964
7 Deadline 1965

McCutcheon, G. B.
1 The daughter of Anderson Crow
2 Anderson Crow, detective
☐
1 Graustark
2 Beverly of Graustark
3 Truxton King
4 The Prince of Graustark
5 East of the setting sun
6 The inn of the hawk and the raven

McCutcheon, H.
ANTHONY HOWARD SERIES:
1 The angel of light
2 Cover her face
RICHARD LOGAN SERIES:
1 To dusty death 1962
2 Suddenly, in Vienna 1963

MacDonald, B.
1 The egg and I
2 The plague and I
3 Anybody can do anything
4 Onions in the stew
N.F. Autobiography
'Who me?' is a selection from the above made into a connected auto-biography.

MacDonald, G.
1 Annals of a quiet neighbourhood
2 The seaboard parish
3 The vicar's daughter
☐
1 Malcolm
2 The Marquis of Lossie
☐
1 Princess and the goblin
2 Princess and Curdie
☐
1 Sir Gibbie
2 Donal Grant
☐
1 Thomas Wingfold, curate
2 Paul Faber, surgeon

MacDonald, J. R.
LEW ARCHER SERIES:
1 The moving target
2 The drowning pool
3 The way some people die
4 The ivory grin
5 Experience with evil
6 Find a victim
7 The Galton case 1959
8 The zebra striped hearse 1960
9 The far side of the dollar 1965

Macdonald, P.
COL. GETHRYN SERIES:
1 The rasp
2 The white crow
3 The noose
4 The link
5 The Rynox mystery
6 Murder gone mad
7 The choice
8 The wraith
9 The crime conductor
10 Rope to spare
11 Death on my left

Macdonald, S.
1 Sally in Rhodesia
2 My African garden

Macdonald, W. C.
THREE MESQUITEERS SERIES:
1 Restless guns
2 Law of the forty-five
3 Riders of the whistling skull
4 The singing scorpion
5 Powdersmoke range
6 Roarin' lead
7 Ghost-town gold
8 Bullets for Buckaroos
9 The three mesquiteers
10 Bad man's return
11 Mesquiteer mavericks
12 Galloping ghost
CALIPER AND NOGALES SERIES:
1 Punchers of Phantom pass
2 Riddle of Ramrod Ridge
GREGORY QUIST SERIES:
1 Destination danger
2 The Osage bow 1964

Macdonell, J. E.

JIM BRADY TRILOGY:
1 Jim Brady, leading seaman 1954
2 Commander Brady 1956
3 Subsmash 1960
A trilogy of novels about the career of an Australian naval officer.

Mcelroy, H.

INSPECTOR BREWER SERIES:
1 Silver Venus
2 Curtain of the dark
3 Unkindly cup
4 House of Malory

MacEvoy, J. P.

1 Show girl
2 Hollywood girl

McFee, W.

SPENLOVE SERIES:
1 The beachcombers
2 Derelicts
3 Spenlove in Arcady
4 Family trouble
5 The adopted
☐
1 Pilgrims of adversity
2 Sailors of fortune

MacGill, P.

1 The children of the dead end
2 The rat-pit
3 Moleskin Joe

McGovan, J.

1 Hunted down
2 Brought to bay
3 Strange clues
4 Traced and tracked
5 Solved mysteries
6 Criminals caught
7 The invisible pickpocket

McGrath, H.

1 Hearts and masks
2 Deuces wild

MacGregor, A. A.

1 Auld Reekie
2 Vanished waters
3 The goat-wife

4 Turbulent years
5 Go not, happy day
6 The golden lamp 1964
7 Land of the mountain and the flood 1965
N.F. Autobiography

Machado de Assis

1 Epitaph of a small winner
2 Heritage of Quincus Borba

Machen, A.

1 Far off things
2 Things near and far
N.F. Autobiography

McHugh, A.

1 A banner with a strange device 1964
2 The seacoast of Bohemia 1965
Two novels about young people in Boston. Sally Brimmer, the heroine of 1 is an important character in 2.

McIntyre, J. T.

ASHTON–KIRK SERIES:
1 Ashton-Kirk, investigator
2 Ashton-Kirk, secret agent
3 Ashton-Kirk, special detective
4 Ashton-Kirk, criminologist
BUCKSKIN BOOKS:
1 In Kentucky with Daniel Boone
2 In the Rockies with Kit Carson
3 In Texas with Davy Crockett
4 On the borders with Andrew Jackson
YOUNG CONTINENTAL SERIES:
1 The young continentals at Lexington
2 The young continentals at Bunker Hill
3 The young continentals at Trenton
4 The young continentals at Monmouth

Mackail, D.

1 Romance to the rescue
2 Summertime
☐
1 Greenery Street
2 Tales from Greenery Street
3 Ian & Felicity [Peninsular Place]
☐
1 Another part of the wood
2 Summer leaves

Mackay, A.
1 They came to a river
2 Goodbye summer

McKee, R. E.
1 The Lord's anointed
2 After a hundred years

Macken, W.
MACMAHON FAMILY:
1 Seek the fair land 1960
2 The silent people 1962
3 The scorching wind 1964
A trilogy of novels on the foundation of the Irish Republic.

MacKenna, S.
THE REALISTS SERIES:
1 The saviours of society
2 The Secretary of State
3 Due reckoning
THE SENSATIONALISTS SERIES:
1 Lady Lilith
2 The education of Eric Lane
3 The secret victory
☐
1 Sonia
2 Sonia married
3 Midas and son
4 Tomorrow and tomorrow
☐
1 Dermotts rampant
2 The way of the phoenix

Mackenzie, A. M.
1 Lost Kinnellan
2 The falling wind
Published in 1 volume as Keith of Kinnellan.

Mackenzie, C.
SINISTER STREET:
1 Carnival
2 Sinister Street *volume* 1 [Youth's encounter]
3 Sinister Street *volume* 2 [Sinister Street]
4 Guy and Pauline [Plasher's Mead]
5 Sylvia Scarlett
6 Sylvia and Michael
FOUR WINDS OF LOVE:
1 East wind of love

2 South wind of love
3 West wind of love
4 West to north
5 North wind of love *part* 1
6 North wind of love *part* 2
☐
1 Rogues and vagabonds
2 Fairy gold
FAITH, HOPE AND CHARITY TRILOGY:
1 The altar steps
2 The parson's progress
3 The heavenly ladder
☐
1 Poor relations
2 April fools
3 Buttercups and daisies
4 Water on the brain
☐
1 Extremes meet
2 The three couriers
CAPRI SERIES:
1 Vestal fire
2 Extraordinary women
☐
1 Gallipoli memories
2 Athenian memories
3 Greek memories
4 Aegean memories
N.F. Autobiography
HIGHLANDS SERIES:
1 Monarch of the glen
2 Keep the Home Guard turning
3 Whisky galore [Tight little island]
4 Hunting the fairies
5 The rival monster
6 Ben Nevis goes east
7 Rockets galore
8 The stolen soprano 1965
These novels are not strictly sequels but the same characters recur in all.

Mackenzie, D.
1 Fugitives
2 Gentleman at crime
N.F. Autobiography

Maclaren, I. *pseud.* [**Rev. J. Watson**]
1 Beside the bonnie brier bush
2 Days of auld lang syne
3 Kate Carnegie

Maclaughlin, W. R. D.
1 Antarctic raider 1961
2 So thin the line 1963
N.F. Story of the whaling fleet during World War II.

Maclean, N.
1 The former days
2 Set free
3 The years of fulfilment
N.F. Autobiography of Moderator of Church of Scotland.

Macleod, L.
1 Years of peace
2 The crowded hill

Macmanus, S.
1 A lad of the O'Friels
2 The bend of the road
3 Yourself and the neighbours

Macmillan, W. J.
1 Prelude to healing
2 The reluctant healer
N.F. Autobiography
  The story of the life of a faith healer. Not published in this order.

Macnaghten, P.
1 The car that Jack built 1964
2 The right line 1966
  Stories of a racing car.

Macnamara, R. S.
1 The awakening
2 A marriage has been arranged

McNeile, C. H., *see* Sapper, *pseud.*

Macrone, G.
THE MOORHOUSE FAMILY:
1 Antimacassar city
2 The Philistines
3 The Puritans
4 Aunt Bel
5 The Hayburn family
  The first three published as one volume under title 'Wax fruit' ['Red plush']

Macvicar, A.
REV. P. J. MACFARLANE SERIES:
1 The purple rock
2 The temple falls
3 The crouching spy

Madariaga, S. de
THE CONQUEST OF MEXICO:
1 The heart of jade (1492–1522)
2 War in the blood (1537–1541)

Maddock, S.
T. TERREL SERIES:
1 A woman of destiny
2 White siren
3 Gentlemen of the night
4 Danger after dark
5 Conspirators in Capri
6 The eye at the keyhole
7 Conspirators three
8 Forbidden frontiers
9 Conspirators at large
10 Lamp-post 592
11 Doorway to danger
12 Spies along the Severn
13 Spades at midnight
14 Date with a spy
15 Drums beat at dusk
16 Something on the stairs
17 I'll never like Friday again
18 Overture to trouble
  There are three 'Terrel' short stories in other volumes as follows:
1 The picture lady *in* Century of spy stories
2 The unwanted factor *in* My best spy story
3 The man who grew bulbs *in* My best secret service story

Madison, Mrs. L. F.
1 Peggy Owen
2 Peggy Owen, patriot
3 Peggy Owen at Yorktown
4 Peggy Owen and liberty

Maeterlinck, M.
THE BLUE BIRD SERIES:
1 The blue bird
2 The betrothal
  'The children's blue bird' is the play re-written for children. 'The story of Tyltyl' is 'The betrothal' re-written for children.

Maine, C. E.
MIKE DELANEY SERIES:
1 The isotope man 1962
2 Subterfuge 1963
3 Never let up 1964

Mair, G.
1 Doctor goes east
2 Doctor goes north
3 Doctor goes west
N.F. Autobiography

Mair, G. B.
DAVID GRANT SERIES:
1 Death's foot forward 1963
2 Miss Turquoise 1964
3 Live, love and cry 1965

Mais, S. P. B.
1 All the days of my life
2 Buffets and rewards
N.F. Autobiography

Maisky, L.
1 Before the storm
2 Journey into the past
N.F. Autobiography

Malet, L. [Mrs. M. St. L. Harrison]
1 Damaris
2 Deadham Hard
□
1 Boy's love
2 The survivors

Mallet-Joris, F., *see* Joris, F. Mallet-

Malot, H.
1 No relations
2 Her own folk

Maniates, B. K.
1 Amarilly of Clothes-line Alley
2 Amarilly in love

Mann, F. O.
1 Albert Grope
2 Grope carries on
3 Three, the Drive
Grope is only a minor character in (3).

Mann, H.
1 King Wren [Young Henry of Navarre]
2 Last days of Henri Quatre [Henry, King of France]

Mann, M. E.
1 The memories of Ronald Love
2 Avenging children

Mann, T.
JOSEPH AND HIS BRETHREN:
1 Tales of Jacob [Joseph and his brothers]
2 The young Joseph
3 Joseph in Egypt
4 Joseph the provider

Mannering, M. [Mrs. H. P. H. Nowell]
1 Climbing the rope
2 Billy Grimes' favourite
3 Cruise of the *Dashaway*
4 Little Spaniard
5 Salt-water Dick
6 Little maid of Oxbow

Mannin, E.
1 Cactus
2 The pure flame
□
1 Confessions and impressions
2 Privileged spectator
3 Brief voices
N.F. Autobiography

Manning, A. [Mrs. Rathbone]
1 Mary Powell
2 Deborah's diary

Manning, D.
1 Bull Hunter
2 Bull Hunter's romance

Manning, O.
A BALKAN TRILOGY:
1 The great fortune 1960
2 The spoilt city 1962
3 Friends and heroes 1965
The setting is Rumania and Greece as they became involved in World War II.

Manning, R.
R. DRAGON AND SUE SERIES:
1 Green smoke 1957
2 Dragon in danger 1959
3 The dragon's quest 1961

Manor, J.
STEVE SUMMERS SERIES:
1 Too dead to run
2 Red Jaguar
3 Pawns of fear
4 The tramplers 1956

Marguerite, P. *and* **V.**
FRANCO-GERMAN WAR:
1 The disaster
2 Les tronçons du Glaive
3 Strasbourg
4 The commune
No. 2 has apparently never been translated. 3 is only a partial translation of 3 in the original 'Les braves gens'.

Marlow, L.
1 Swan's milk
2 Forth, beast
N.F. Auotobiography

Marquand, J. P.
MR. MOTO SERIES:
1 No hero
2 Thank you Mr. Moto
3 Think fast Mr. Moto
4 Mr. Moto takes a hand
5 Mr. Moto is so sorry
6 Last laugh Mr. Moto
7 Stopover Tokyo 1957

Marric, J. J. *pseud.* [**J. Creasey**]
GIDEON SERIES:
1 Gideon's day 1955
2 Gideon's week 1956
3 Gideon's night 1957
4 Gideon's month 1958
5 Gideon's staff 1959
6 Gideon's risk 1960
7 Gideon's fire 1961
8 Gideon's march 1962
9 Gideon's ride 1963
10 Gideon's vote 1964
11 Gideon's lot 1965
12 Gideon's badge 1966

Mars, A.
1 Unbroken
2 H.M.S. Thule intercepts
N.F. Autobiography of war experiences.

Marsh, J.
RAY FELTON SERIES:
1 Murderer's maze 1957
2 Operation snatch 1958
3 City of fear 1958
4 Small and deadly 1960
SIMON LUCK SERIES:
1 The reluctant executioner 1959
2 Girl in a net 1962

Marsh, N.
INSPECTOR ALLEYN SERIES:
1 A man lay dead
2 Enter a murderer
3 Death in ecstasy
4 Vintage murder
5 Artist in crime
6 Death in a white tie
7 Overture to death
8 Death at the bar
9 Death and the dancing footman
10 Died in the wool
11 Surfeit of lampreys
12 Colour scheme
13 Final curtain
14 Swing brother swing [Wreath for Riviera]
15 Opening night [Night at the Vulcan]
16 Spinsters in jeopardy
17 Scales of justice 1955
18 Off with his head 1957
19 Singing in the shrouds 1958
20 False scent 1959
21 Hand in glove 1960
22 Dead water 1961

Marsh, R.
1 Judith Lee
2 The adventures of Judith Lee
□
1 Sam Briggs: his book
2 Sam Briggs, v.c.

Marshall, A.
THE CLINTON SERIES:
1 The Squire's daughter

2 The eldest son
3 The honour of the Clintons
4 Rank and riches [The old order changeth]
5 The Clintons and others
'Joan and Nancy' is a composite volume made up of parts of 'The Clintons' series. Characters recur in this series and in 'Richard Baldock' and 'Exton Manor'.

□
1 Abingdon Abbey
2 The Graftons

ANOTHONY DARE SERIES:
1 Anthony Dare
2 Anthony Dare's progress
3 Education of Anthony Dare

□
1 Simple stories
2 Simpler stories

□
1 I can jump puddles
2 This is the grass
3 In mine own heart
N.F. Autobiography

Marshall, C.
1 A man called Peter
2 To live again
N.F. Biography of Peter Howard of M.R.A.

Marshall, L.
SUGAR KANE SERIES:
1 Sugar for the lady
2 Sugar on the target
3 Sugar cuts the corners
4 Sugar on the carpet
5 Sugar on the cliff
6 Sugar on the kill
7 Sugar on the loose 1962
8 Sugar on the prowl 1963
9 Ladies can be dangerous 1964
10 Murder is the reason 1964
11 Death strikes in darkness 1965
12 The dead are silent 1966

Marshall, M.
1 Travels of Tramp-royal
2 Tramp-royal on the toby
N.F. Autobiography

Marshall, May
1 Mulberry leaf
2 Youth storms in 1955

Marshall, R.
DON MICKLEM SERIES:
1 Mission to Venice
3 Mission to Sienna

Marston, J.
1 Antonio and Mellida
2 Antonio's revenge

Marston, Jeffery
1 An octave
2 Summer storm
3 No middle way

Martin du Gard, R.
LES THIBAULTS SERIES:
1 Le Cahier gris
2 Le Penitencier
3 La belle Saison
4 Le consultation
5 La Sorellina
6 La mort du pere
7 L'ete
8 Epilogue
There are several translations of this series. The best known American translation is in two volumes containing 1–6 under the title 'The Thibaults, and 7–8 under the title 'Summer'.
The English translation published by Lane in two volumes contains 1–2 and 3–4 only.

Martin, B.
1 Miracle at Carville
2 No one must ever know
N.F. Autobiography

Martin, G. M.
1 Emmy Lou
2 Emmy Lou's road to grace

Martin, M.
1 O rugged land of gold
2 Home in the bear's domain
N.F. Autobiography

Martin, S.

Martin, V., *see* Somerville, E. Œ, *and* Ross, M., *pseud.*

Martindale, C. C.

Martin, W.

Marton, F.

Masefield, J.

Mason, A. E. W.

Mason, F. Van W.

7 The Cairo garter murders
8 The Bucharest ballerina murders
9 Forgotten fleet mystery
10 Rio Casino intrigue
11 Castle Island intrigue
12 Dardanelles derelict
13 Saigon singer
14 Himalayan assignment
15 Two tickets to Tangier 1955
16 The gracious lily affair 1958
17 Secret mission to Bangkok 1960
18 Trouble in Burma 1961
19 Zanzibar intrigue 1964
☐
1 Proud new flags 1954
2 Blue hurricane 1956
3 To whom be glory [The valiant few] 1957
Novels of the naval action in the American Civil War.

Mason, H.
THE SPENCER FAMILY:
1 Fool's gold 1961
2 Our hills cry woe 1963

Masters, J.
THE SAVAGE FAMILY:
1 Coromandel (Jason Savage, 1622–1640)
2 The deceivers (William Savage, 18th century)
3 Night Runners of Bengal (Indian mutiny, 1857 Rodney Savage I)
4 The lotus and the wind (Robin Savage, Afghan Wars, 1879–1881)
5 Far, far the mountain Peak (Peter Savage, 1902–1921)
6 Bhowani Junction (Indian independence, 1945. Rodney Savage II)
7 To the coral strand (Rodney Savage II, 1945–1950)
The story of British rule in India as shown in the lives of successive generations of an English family. The series is intended to comprise about 30 novels. List above is in chronological order, not order of publication. 6 and 7 are direct sequels.
☐
1 Bugles and a tiger 1959

2 The road past Mandalay 1961
N.F. Autobiography of an officer in the Ghurkas.

Masters, R. M.
1 Little Creole
2 Losing fight

Masterman, J. C.
ERNEST BRENDEL SERIES:
1 To teach the senators wisdom
2 The case of the four friends

Mather, B.
ROBINSON FAMILY SERIES:
1 Through the mill
2 Left foot forward

Mather, J. M.
LANCASHIRE IDYLLS:
1 Lancashire idylls
2 By roaring loom

Mathers, H. [Mrs. H. Reeves]
1 The story of a sin
2 Eyre's acquittal

Matheson, H.
GEOFFREY BRANSCOMBE:
1 The third force 1960
2 The balance of fear 1961

Mathew, D.
1 Mango on the mango tree
2 In Valambrosa
3 Prince of Wales feathers

Maud, E. C.
1 An English girl in Paris
2 A daughter of France

Maugham, W. S.
1 Summing up
2 Strictly personal
N.F. Autobiography

Mauriac, C.
LE DIALOGUE INTÉRIEUR:
1 Toutes les femmes sont fatales 1957
2 Le diner en ville 1959
3 La marquise sortit a cinq heures 1961

Mauriac, C. (*contd.*)
4 L'agrandissement 1963
Only No. 2 appears to have been translated under the title 'Dinner in town' 1964

Mauriac, F.
1 Le Baiser au leproux
2 Genetrix
Published in G.B. in one vol.' 'A Kiss for the leper', in U.S. 'The family'.
☐
1 Thérèse Desqueyroux
2 Plongées
Contains two stories 'Thérèse chez le docteur' and 'Thérèse a l'hotel'.
3 La fin de la nuit
Published in Great Britain in one volume under title 'Thérèse'. There is a brief reference to Thérèse in 'That which was lost'.

Maurice, M.
1 Not in our stars
2 But in ourselves

Maurois, A.
1 The silence of Colonel Bramble
2 General Bramble

Mavity, N. B.
PETER PIPER SERIES:
1 Tule Marsh murder
2 Body on the floor
3 Case of the missing sandals
4 The other bullet
5 Fate of Jane Mackenzie

Maxwell, G.
1 Ring of bright water 1962
2 The rocks remain 1963
N.F. Autobiography and natural history.

Maxwell, W. B.
MEN AND WOMEN:
1 Tudor Green
2 The emotional journey
3 Everslade

May, Mrs. C. L.
1 Nellie Milton's house keeping
2 Brownie Sanford

3 Sylvia's burden
4 Ruth Lovell

Mayo, J.
CHARLES HOOD SERIES:
1 Hammerhead 1964
2 Let sleeping girls lie 1965

Mazzetti, L.
1 The sky falls 1963
2 Rage 1964

Meade, L. T. [Mrs. Smith], *and*
Halifax, C.
Stories from the diary of a doctor
Two series

Means, E. K.
1 E. K. Means
2 Further E. K. Means
3 More E. K. Means

Meek, V.
1 Cops and robbers
2 The coppering lark
N.F. Autobiography

Meersch, M. van der
1 The poor girl
2 The hour of love

Mehderi, A. S.
1 From pillar to post
2 Persian adventure
N.F. Autobiography. Not published in this order.

Mehta, V.
1 Face to face
2 Walking the Indian streets
N.F. Autobiography

Melville, H.
1 Typee
2 Omoo

Melville, J.
POLICE SERGEANT CHARMIAN DANIELS:
1 Come home and be killed 1962
2 Burning is a substitute for loving 1963
3 Murders' houses 1964
4 There lies your love 1965

Memmi, A.
1 The pillar of salt
2 Strangers

Menzies-Wilson, T. *see* **Wilson, T. Menzies-.**

Meredith, G.
1 Sandra Belloni. *Same as* Emilia in England
2 Vittoria

Merejkowski, D.
1 The death of the gods. [Julian the apostate]
2 The forerunner. *Same as* The resurrection of the gods. [Romance of Leonardo da Vinci]
3 Peter and Alexis
THE STORY OF DIO:
1 The birth of the gods
2 Akhnaton, King of Egypt

Meriton, P.
1 Captain Duck
2 Conspiracy
3 Plunder

Merriam, L. F.
1 Jenny's bird house
2 Jenny and Tito

Merrick, L.
1 While Paris laughed
2 A chair on the boulevard
3 The little dog laughed
2 and 3 are collections of short stories, some being stories about Tricotrin.

Merriman, Mrs. E. J.
1 The little Millers
2 Mollie Miller

Mersey, C. C.V., 2nd Viscount
1 Picture of life
2 Journal and memories
N.F. Autobiography

Merton, T.
1 Elected silence
2 Sign of Jonas
N.F. Autobiography

Merwin, S.
1 Temperamental Henry
2 Henry is twenty
3 The passionate pilgrim

Metalious, G.
1 Peyton Place
2 Return to Peyton Place

Metcalfe, T. W.
SANTA ANNA TRILOGY:
1 One night in Santa Anna
2 Life and adventures of Aloysius B. Callaghan
3 Fare you well my shining city

Meyerstein, E. H. W.
1 The pleasure lover
2 Terence in love

Meynell, E.
1 Grave fairytale
2 Quintet

Meynell, L. W.
1 Blue feather
2 Odds on Bluefeather

Michael, J.
1 Chokra 1957
2 Chokra and Tags 1958

Michaelis, K.
1 The dangerous age
2 Elsie Lindtner

Middleton, J. A.
1 The grey ghost book
2 Another grey ghost book
3 The white ghost book

Millar, G.
1 Maquis
2 Horned pigeon
N.F. Autobiography
□
1 Isobel and the sea
2 A white boat from England
N.F. Travel

Mille, P.
1 Barnavaux
2 Under the tricolour
3 Louise and Barnavaux

Miller, H.
1 Tropic of cancer
2 Tropic of Capricorn
THE ROSY CRUCIFICTION:
1 Sexus
2 Plexus
3 Nexus
1 and 3 not published in Great Britain.
All these books are connected, being
partly autobiographical.

Miller, H. R.
1 The man higher up
2 His rise to power

Millin, S. G.
1 The dark river
2 Middle class
3 Adam's rest
4 The Jordans
□
1 The night is long
2 World blackout
3 The reeling earth
4 The pit of the abyss
5 The sound of the trumpet
6 Fire out of heaven
7 The seven thunders
8 Measure of my days
N.F. Diary of World War II

Mills, O.
SUPT. ALCOCK SERIES:
1 Misguided missile
2 No match for the law
3 The case of the flying fifteen
4 Unlucky break
5 Stairway to murder 1960

Mills, W.
SIR JOHN HOWDEN SERIES:
1 Shadow crusade
2 French hazard
3 Blind reckoning

Miln, L. J.
1 Mr. and Mrs. Sen
2 Ruben and Ivy Sen

Milne, A. A.
1 The day's play
2 The holiday round
3 Once a week
4 The sunny side
N.F. Essays

Milne, S.
DET. SGT. STEYTLER:
1 The hammer of justice 1963
2 False witness 1964

Mitchell, A.
1 Harley Street hypnotist
2 Harley Street psychiatrist
N.F. Autobiography

Mitchell, G.
MRS. BRADLEY SERIES:
1 Dead man's morris
2 Come away death
3 St. Peter's finger
4 Printer's error
5 Brazen tongue
6 Hangman's curfew
7 When last I died
8 Laurels are poison
9 The worsted viper
10 Sunset over Soho
11 My father sleeps
12 The rising of the moon
13 Here comes a chopper
14 Death and the maiden
15 The dancing druids
16 Tom Brown's body
17 Groaning spinney
18 The devil's elbow
19 The echoing strangers
20 Merlin's furlong
21 Faintley speaking
22 Watson's choice 1955
23 Twelve horses and the hangman's noose 1956
24 The twenty-third man 1957
25 Spotted hemlock 1958
26 The man who grew tomatoes 1959
27 Say it with flowers 1960
28 The nodding canaries 1961
29 My bones will keep 1962
30 Adders on the heath 1963
31 Death of a delft blue 1964
32 Pageant of murder 1965

Mitchell, I. L., *see* Gibbon, L. G., *pseud.*

Mitchell, R. C.
OLD SAN FRANCISCO:
1 Blue for true love (the 40's)
2 Fire (the 50's)
3 Curtain (the 60's)
4 Tell your fortune (the 70's)

Mitchell, S. W.
WAR OF INDEPENDENCE SERIES:
1 Hugh Wynne, Free Quaker
2 The Red City
   □
1 Characteristics
2 Dr. North and his friends
   □
1 Roland Blake
2 West ways

Mitford, B.
1 The King's assegai
2 The white shield

Mitford, N.
1 The pursuit of love
2 Love in a cold climate
   *These are parallel stories rather than
   sequels. The narrator and many of the
   characters are the same, but the central
   characters differ.*
3 Don't tell Alfred 1960
   *In this, the narrator of 1 and 2, becomes
   the principal character.*

Mittelholzer, E.
A SERIES OF NOVELS ON COLONIAL LIFE
IN THE WEST INDIES:
1 Children of Kaywana
2 The harrowing of Hubertus
3 Kaywana blood 1957
   *1 and 3 are direct sequels, telling the
   story of the Van Groenwegel family.*
LEITMOTIV TRILOGY:
1 Latticed echoes
2 Thunder returning 1961
   The author died before completion.

Mitton, G. E. [Lady Scott]
1 Two stringed fiddle
2 The green moth (*with* Sir J. G. Scott)

Moberg, V.
1 The emigrants 1955
2 Unto a good land 1959
3 The last letter home 1961
   *A trilogy on the struggles of a group of
   Swedish emigrants to U.S.A. in the
   19th century.*

Moberg, W.
THE EARTH IS OURS:
1 Memory of youth
2 Sleepless nights
3 The earth is ours

Moffett, C.
1 The master mind
2 Through the wall

Mole, W.
CASSON DUKER SERIES:
1 The Hammersmith maggot
2 Goodbye is not worthwhile 1956
3 Skin trap 1957

Moll, L.
MR. SEIDMAN SERIES:
1 Seidman and son 1958
2 Mr. Seidman and the geisha 1963

Monkhouse, A.
1 My daughter Helen
2 Marmaduke

Montherlant, Henri de
THE YOUNG GIRLS:
1 Young girls
2 Pity for women
   *Published as one volume 'Pity for
   women'.*
3 The demon of good
4 The lepers
   Published as one volume 'The lepers'
   ['*Costals and the hippogriff*'].

Moody, R.
1 Little britches
2 Man of the family
3 The home ranch
N.F. *Autobiography*

Moore, A.
1 Quicksilver
2 Quicksilver justice

Moore, D.
1 Far eastern agent
2 We live in Singapore 1953
N.F Autobiography

Moore, F. F.
CROMWELLIAN IRELAND SERIES:
1 Castle Omeragh
2 Captain Latymer
RAYMOND MONK SERIES:
1 The rise of Raymond
2 The fall of Raymond
□
1 The Jessamy bride
2 Fanny's first novel [Discovering Evalina].

Moore, G.
HAIL AND FAREWELL SERIES:
1 Ave
2 Salve
3 Vale
ANOTHER SERIES:
1 Evelyn Innes
2 Sister Teresa

Moore, J.
1 Portrait of Elmbury
2 Brensham village
3 The blue field
Countryside books about Tewkesbury and district.

Moorman, F. W.
1 Tales of the Ridings
2 More tales of the Ridings

Morgan–de–Groot, J.
1 A lotus flower
2 Even if

Morier, J.
1 The adventures of Hajji Baba of Ispahan
2 Hajji Baba in England

Morland, N.
MRS. PYM SERIES:
1 The moon murders
2 The phantom gunman
3 Street of the leopard
4 Clue of the bricklayer's aunt
5 Clue in the mirror
6 Case without a clue
7 A rope for the hanging
8 A knife for the killer
9 A gun for a god
10 The clue of the careless hangman
11 The corpse on the flying trapeze
12 A coffin for the body
13 Dressed to kill
14 Lady had a gun
15 Call him early for the murder
16 Sing a song of cyanide
17 Look in any doorway 1957
18 Death and the golden boy 1958
19 A bullet for Midas 1958
20 So quiet a death 1960
21 The concrete maze 1960
22 The dear dead girls 1961
ANDY MCMURDO SERIES:
1 She didn't like dying
2 No coupons for a shroud
3 Two dead charwomen
4 The corpse was no lady
5 Blood on the stars
6 He hanged his mother on Monday
7 The moon was made for murder
RORY LUCCAN SERIES:
1 Death when she wakes
2 A girl died singing

Morley C.
ROGER AND HARRIET MIFFLIN:
1 Parnassus on wheels
2 The haunted bookshop

Morley, I.
1 Cry treason
2 We stood for freedom
3 The mighty years

Morris, E.
1 Flowers of Hiroshima 1962
2 Seeds of Hiroshima 1965

Morris, I. J.
1 A kingdom for a song
2 The witch's son

Morris, J.
1 Traveller from Tokyo
2 The Phoenix cup
N.F. Japan before and after the war.

Morrison, A.
1 Martin Hewitt, investigator
2 Chronicles of Martin Hewitt
3 Adventures of Martin Hewitt
4 The red triangle

Morrison, E.
1 There was a veil
2 There lived a lady
☐
1 Light fingers
2 Sir Joseph's guests
☐
1 The last of the Lovells
2 Countisbury
3 An open secret

Morrison, M.
1 Flying high
2 Wider horizons
ELIZABETH CONWAY SAGA:
1 Written for Elizabeth
2 Lady of justice
3 Betsybob
4 The undaunted

Morrow, H. W.
ABRAHAM LINCOLN SERIES:
1 Forever free
2 With malice towards none
3 Last full measure
Published in one volume as 'The Great Captain'.

Mortimer, C.
1 Father Goose
2 Mediterraneo
Not strictly sequels, but some characters reappear.

Morton, A., *pseud.* [J. Creasey,]
THE BARON SERIES:
1 Meet the Baron
2 The Baron returns
3 The Baron at bay
4 The Baron again
5 The Baron at large
6 Alias the Baron
7 Versus the Baron
8 Call for the Baron
9 The Baron comes back
10 A case for the Baron
11 Reward for the Baron
12 Career for the Baron
13 The Baron and the beggar
14 A rope for the Baron
15 Blame the Baron
16 Books for the Baron
17 Cry for the Baron
18 Trap the Baron
19 Shadow the Baron
20 Attack the Baron
21 Warn the Baron
22 The Baron goes East
23 Danger for the Baron
24 The Baron in France
25 The Baron moves fast
26 Nest egg for the Baron
27 Help from the Baron 1955
28 Hide the Baron 1956
29 Frame the Baron 1957
30 Red eye for the Baron 1958
31 Black for the Baron 1959
32 Salute to the Baron 1960
33 A branch for the Baron 1961
34 Bad for the Baron 1962
35 A sword for the Baron 1963
36 The Baron on board 1964
37 The Baron and the Chinese puzzle 1965

Morton, J. B. (**Beachcomber**, *pseud.*)
1 Mr. Thake
2 Mr. Thake again
3 Mr. Thake and the ladies
☐
1 Enchanter's nightshade
2 Penny Royal

Moss, W. S.
1 Ill met by moonlight
2 War of shadows
World War II
Rendel's 'Appointment in Crete' gives another angle on 1.

Motley, Mary, *pseud.*
AUTOBIOGRAPHY:
1 Devils in waiting 1959
2 Morning glory 1961
3 Home to Nurmidia 1963
N.F. Autobiography. 2 describes her early life before the episode in 1.

Motley, W.
1 Knock on any door
2 Let no man write my epitaph 1959
The sequel is about the son of Romano, who dies at the end of 1. Scene is slum area of Chicago.

Mottram, R. H.
1 The Spanish farm
2 D'Archeville
3 Sixty-four, ninety four
4 The winner
5 The crime at Vanderleyden's
6 The stranger
7 Ten years ago . . . a pendant to the Spanish farm trilogy [Armistice and other memories]
1, 3, 5, constitute the Spanish Farm trilogy. 2, 4, 6 are short connecting pieces.
8 Through the Menin Gate (A volume of short stories which the author suggests is also a pendant to *The Spanish Farm*)
The story of Skene is continued in
9 Europa's beast. [A rich man's daughter]
10 Come to the bower
11 Over the wall 1955
☐
1 Our Mr. Dormer
2 The Boroughmonger
3 Castle Island
4 The banquet
5 The headless hound, (contains some short stories continuing the sequence.)
LIFE OBSERVED:
1 The window seat 1954
2 Another window seat 1956
· *N.F. Autobiography*

Mowat, F.
1 The people of the deer
2 The desperate people

Mowbray, J. P. [A. C. Wheeler]
1 A journey to nature
2 Tangled up in Beulah land

Moxon, O.
THE MONSOON TRILOGY:
1 Bitter monsoon

2 The last monsoon
3 After the monsoon 1957
N.F. A trilogy on the war in Burma, particularly the fighting around Imphal.

Moysheh, Oyved
1 Visions and jewels
2 Gems and life

Muhlback, L. [C. M. Mundt]
FREDERICK THE GREAT SERIES:
1 Frederick the Great and his court.
2 Berlin and Sans-Souci
3 Frederick the Great and his family
4 Frederick the Great and his merchant [The Merchant of Berlin]
LOUISA OF PRUSSIA SERIES:
1 Louisa of Prussia and her times
2 Napoleon and the Queen of Prussia
3 Napoleon in Germany
4 Napoleon and Blucher
ANOTHER SERIES:
1 The youth of the Great Elector
2 The reign of the Great Elector
The other works are stories of Prussian history.
There are many sequels untranslated, and the translations given above have been published under various titles, with omissions from the original.

Muir A.
1 Blue bonnet
2 Castles in the air.

Muir, T.
ROGER CRAMMOND SERIES:
1 Death in the reserve
2 Death in the trooper
3 Death in the lock
4 Death without question
5 Death below zero
6 Death under Virgo
7 Death on the agenda
8 Death in Soundings

Mulford, C. E.
1 Bar-20
2 Hop-along Cassidy
3 Bar-20 days
4 The coming of Cassidy – and the others

5 Buck Peters, ranchman: *by* C. E. Mulford, and J. W. Clay
6 The man from Bar-20
7 Johnny Nelson
8 Bar-20 three
9 Tex – of Bar-20
10 Hop-along Cassidy returns
11 Hop-along Cassidy's protege
12 Bar-20 rides again
13 Mesquite Jenkins
14 Mesquite Jenkins tumbleweed
15 Hop-along Cassidy and the eagles brood
16 Trail dust
17 Hop-along Cassidy takes cards
18 Hop-along Cassidy serves a writ
19 Black buttes
20 Beckoning trails
   Continued by Tex Burns.
21 Hop-along Cassidy and the mothers of West Fork
22 Hop-along Cassidy and the trail to Seven Pines
23 Hop-along Cassidy and the riders of High Peak
24 Hop-along Cassidy trouble shooter
   □

1 Corson of the J.C.
2 Me an' Shorty
3 The deputy sheriff
4 The round-up
5 On the trail of the Tumbling T

Mundy, T.
1 The ivory trail
2 The eye of Zeitoon
   □
1 Winds of the world
2 King, of the Khyber Rifles
3 Hirah Singh's tale
   □
1 Guns of the gods
2 Nine unknown
3 Ramsden
1 Ramsden [The devil's guard]
2 The hundred days
3 The woman Ayisha
4 Jimgrim
5 The lion of Petra
6 The king in check

7 The mystery of Khufri's tomb
8 Jungle jest
9 Jimgrim and Allah's peace
1 Jimgrim
2 C.I.D.
3 Red flame of Erinpura
4 The Gunga sahib
   All the above series overlap in characters.
   □
1 Tros of Samothrace
2 The purple pirate

Munn, C. C.
1 Uncle Terry
2 The heart of Uncle Terry

Munnings, Sir A.
1 An artist's life
2 Second burst
3 The finish
N.F. Autobiography

Munro, H.
1 Who told Clutha
2 Clutha plays a hunch 1959
3 A clue for Clutha 1960

Munro, H. H. (Saki, *pseud.*)
1 Reginald
2 Reginald in Russia
   □
1 Chronicles of Clovis
2 Beasts and super-beasts
   Both these series of short stories are now collected in one volume 'The short stories of Saki'.

Munro, J.
1 The man who sold death 1964
2 Die rich, die happy 1965

Murasaki, Lady
1 The tale of Genji
2 The sacred tree
3 A wreath of cloud
4 Blue trousers
5 The lady of the boat
6 The bridge of dreams

Murphy, D. J.
1 Winsome for winners
2 More winners for Winsome

Murray, M.
CORPSE SERIES:
1 Voice of the corpse
2 King and the corpse
3 No duty on a corpse
4 Neat little corpse
5 Right hon. corpse
6 Good luck to the corpse
7 Dr. and the corpse
8 The sunshine corpse
9 Royal bed for a corpse
10 Breakfast with a corpse
11 Wait for a corpse

Murray, W. H.
JOHN TAUNT SERIES:
1 Five frontiers
2 The spurs of Troodos

Musil, R.
MAN WITHOUT QUALITIES:
1 A sort of introduction 1953
2 The like of it now happens 1954
3 Into the millennium [The criminals] 1960
A fourth volume will complete the translation.

Muskett, N.
1 A crown of willow
2 The high fence

Muspratt, S.
1 My south sea island
2 Wild oats
3 Journey home
4 Fire of youth
N.F. Autobiography

Musselman, M. M.
1 I married a redhead
2 Second honeymoon
N.F. Autobiography

Myers, L. H.
THE ROOT AND THE FLOWER:
1 Prince Jali
2 The near and the far
3 Rajah Amar
4 Pool of Vishnu

Mykle, A.
1 Lasso round the moon 1959
2 The song of the red ruby 1961
The story of a young Norwegian schoolmaster.

Myrivillis, S.
1 The mermaid madonna
2 The schoolmistress with the golden eyes

Napier, E.
1 Youth is a blunder
2 Winter is in July
N.F. Autobiography

Nash, S.
INSPECTOR MONTERO AND ADAM LUDLOW:
1 Dead of a counterplot 1961
2 Killed by scandal 1962
3 Death over deep water 1962
4 Dead woman's ditch 1964

Nathan, R.
THE BARLY FIELDS SERIES:
1 Fiddler in barly
2 Wood cutter's house
3 Bishop's wife
4 Orchid
5 There is another heaven
Published in one volume 1938.
□
1 Journey of Tapiola
2 Tapiolas brave regiment
Later published in one volume under title 'Adventures of Tapiola'.

Neale, J. E.
1 Elizabethan House of Commons
2 Queen Elizabeth I and her parliaments (1551-1581)

3 Queen Elizabeth I and her parliaments (1584-1601)
N.F. History

Neame, A.
1 The adventures of Maud Noakes 1963
2 Maud Noakes, guerilla 1965

Neill, A. S.
1 A dominie's log
2 A dominie dismissed
3 A dominie in doubt
4 The booming of Bunkie
5 A dominie abroad
6 A dominie's five

Nelson, L.
1 The physician's daughter
2 Wandering heroines

Nepean, E. M.
TRILOGY ON CHARLES II:
1 Lanterns of horn
2 Ivory and apes
3 My two kings
Not published in this order.

Nethercot, A.
1 The first five lives of Annie Besant
2 The last four lives of Annie Besant
N.F. Autobiography

Neuman, B. P.
PATHS OF THE BLIND SERIES:
1 The greatness of Josiah Porlick
2 The spoils of victory
3 Dominy's dollars

Neumann, A.
NAPOLEON III TRILOGY:
1 The new Caesar
2 Man of December [Gaudy empire]
3 The friends of the people
THE CARBONARI REVOLT IN TUSCANY:
1 The rebels
2 Guerra

Neville, M.
INSPECTOR GROGAN SERIES:
1 Murder and gardenias
2 Murder in Rockwater

3 Murder of a nymph
4 Murder in a blue moon
5 Murder before marriage
6 Come thick night
7 The seagull said murder
8 Murder of the well-beloved
9 Murder of Olympia
10 Murder to welcome her 1959
11 Sweet night to murder her 1959
12 Confession of murder 1962
13 Ladies in the dark 1965

Nevinson, H. W.
1 Changes and chances
2 More changes and chances
3 Last changes and chances
N.F. Autobiography

Newberry, E.
1 Parson's daughter
2 Parson's daughter again
N.F. Autobiography

Newby, P. H.
1 A picnic at Sakkara
2 Revolution and roses
3 A guest and his going
Three novels set in Egypt and London.
Not strictly sequels, but characters in 1,
reappear in 2 and 3.

Newman, B.
PONTIVY SERIES:
1 Maginot line murder
2 Death to the spy
3 Siegfried spy
4 Death to the fifth column
5 Secret weapon
6 Black market
7 Second front – first spy
8 Spy catchers
9 Spy in the brown derby
10 Dead man murder
11 Moscow murder
12 Flying saucer
13 The double menace

Newte, H. W. C.
1 Calico Jack
2 The gentle bigamist

Newton, W. D. B.
1 Phillip in particular
2 Phillip and the flappers

Nexø, M. A.
PELLE, THE CONQUEROR SERIES:
1 Boyhood
2 Apprenticeship
3 The great stuggle
4 Daybreak
*Morten hin Røde (not yet translated)
continues the story.*
ANOTHER SERIES:
1 Ditte: girl alive!
2 Ditte: daughter of man
3 Towards the stars

Nicholas, J.
BILL ANSTRUTHER SERIES:
1 Widow's peak
2 Asbestos mask
3 Whispering steel
4 Deirdre

Nicholls, W. B.
HENRY VII:
1 A wonder for wise men
2 Torryzany

Nichols, B.
1 25
2 All I could never be
☐
1 Down the garden path
2 Thatched roof
3 Village in a valley
☐
1 Merry hall
2 Laughter on the stairs
3 Sunlight on the lawn
*All these books are autobiographical, but
the author agrees with the above
division.*
☐
1 The tree that sat down
2 The stream that stood still
3 The mountain of magic
MR. GREEN SERIES:
1 No man's street
2 Moonflower
3 Death to slow music 1956
4 The rich die hard 1958

5 Murder by request 1959

Nicholson, C. A.
1 Their chosen people
2 The first good joy
☐
1 Hell and the duchess
2 The bridge is lost

Nicholson, M.
1 The house of a thousand candles
2 Rosalind at Red Gate

Nicole, C.
THE AMYOT FAMILY:
1 Amyot's cay 1963
2 Blood Amyot 1964
3 The Amyot crime 1965
*A series of novels on the history of the
Bahamas.*

Nin, A.
1 Ladders to fire 1946
2 Children of the albatross 1947
3 The four chambered heart 1959
4 Spy in the house of love 1954
5 Seduction of the minotaur 1961
*Published in the U.S. under the title
'Cities of the interior'. No. 5 in the U.S.
edition is entitled 'Solar barque'.*

Niven, F.
1 The lost cabin mine
2 Hands up!

Nordhoff, C. and **Hall, J. C.**
THE BOUNTY TRILOGY:
1 Mutiny
2 Men against the sea
3 Pitcairn island

Norman, B.
1 The thousand hands
2 The black pawn

Norman, F.
1 Bang to rights
2 Stand on me 1960
3 The Guntz 1962
N.F. Autobiography

Norris, F.
1 The octopus
2 The pit
The above series was planned as a trilogy, but the author died before writing the third part, to which he intended to give the title of 'The wolf'.

Norris, K.
1 The heart of Rachel
2 Martie the unconquered
□
1 Certain people of importance
2 Hildegarde

North, G.
SERGEANT CLUFF SERIES:
1 Sergeant Cluff stands firm 1960
2 The methods of Sergeant Cluff 1961
3 Sergeant Cluff goes fishing 1962
4 More deaths for Sergeant Cluff 1963
5 Sergeant Cluff and the madmen 1964
Contains two stories, 'Blindness of Sergeant Cluff' and 'Sergeant Cluff laughs last'.
6 Sergeant Cluff and the price of pity 1965

North, S.
1 Plowing on Sunday
2 Night outlasts the whipporwill

Norton, C. L.
1 Jack Benson's log
2 A medal of honour man

Norton, L.
1 Saint-Simon at Versailles
2 Saint-Simon and his world
N.F. History

Norwood, E. P.
DIGGELDY DAN SERIES:
1 Adventures of Diggeldy Dan
2 In the land of Diggeldy Dan
3 Friends of Diggeldy Dan

Norwood, V. Y. C.
1 Man alone
2 A hand full of diamonds
N.F. Autobiography

Novomeysky, M. A.
1 My Siberian life
2 Given to salt
N.F. Autobiography

Obenchain, Mrs. E. C., *see* Hall, E. C., [*pseud.*

O'Brien, E.
1 The country girls 1962
2 The lonely girl 1963
3 Girls in their married bliss 1964
The recurring character is an Irish girl, Cathleen, in Dublin and London.

O'Casey, S.
1 I knock at the door
2 Pictures in the hallway
3 Drums under the window
4 Inishfallen fare thee well
5 Rose and crown
6 Sunset and evening star
7 The green crow
N.F. Autobiography

O'Connor, P.
1 Memoirs of a public baby
2 The lower view
N.F. Autobiography

Odell, S. W.
1 Samson
2 Delilah

O'Donoghue, J.
1 In a quiet land
2 In a strange land
3 In Kerry long ago
N.F. Autobiography

O'Donnell, P.
IRISH PEASANTS ON ARRANMORE:
1 The storm
2 The islanders [The way it was with them]
3 Adrigoole
4 The knife [There will be fighting]

Ogden, R.
1 Courage
2 Little homespun

Ogilvie, E.
1 High tide at noon
2 Storm tide
3 Ebbing tide

O'Grady, S.
THE HEROIC AGE OF IRELAND:
1 The coming of Cuculain
2 The gates of the north
3 The triumph and passing of Cuculain

O'Hara, M.
1 Flicka [My friend Flicka]
2 Thunderhead son of Flicka
3 Green grass of Wyoming

Ohnet, G.
*The series 'Batailles de la vie' is in 39
volumes in the original. Only a few of
these have been translated, viz:*
1 Serge Panine
2 The ironmaster
4 The rival actresses
5 Antoinette
7 Will
8 Dr. Rameau
9 A last love
10 Nimrod and company
11 A debt of hatred
12 Love's depths
14 Lady in grey
19 Pierre's soul
36 Cloud and sunshine
*Possible because of the incompleteness of
translation of the series, it is difficult to
see the connection between them.*

Oldenbourg, Z.
1 The awakened 1957
2 Chains of love 1959
*The story of two lovers in Paris before
and after World War II.*
□
1 World is not enough 1948
2 Corner-stone 1955
*Two novels of France in the 13th
century.*

Oldmeadow, E.
1 Coggin
2 The hare
3 Wild fang

Oliphant, Mrs. M. O. W.
CHRONICLES OF CARLINGFORD:
1 Salem chapel
2 The rector, and doctor's family
3 The perpetual curate
4 Miss Marjoribanks
5 Phoebe, junior
□
STORIES OF THE SEEN AND THE UNSEEN:
1 A beleagured city
2 A little pilgrim in the unseen
3 The land of darkness (contains a
sequel to 2)
□
1 For love and life
2 Squire Arden
□
1 The greatest heiress in England
2 Sir Tom
□
1 The ladies Lindores
2 Lady Car
□
1 Passages in the life of Mistress
Margaret Maitland
2 Lilliesleaf

Oliver, M. M. and **Ducat, E.**
1 The ponies of Bunts
2 Ponies and caravans

Ollivant, A.
1 Two men
2 One woman

Olsen, D. B.
1 Cats don't need coffins
2 Cats don't smile

O'Neill, E.
*'A tale of possessors self-dispossessed'.
This cycle of plays was originally
conceived as five separate plays, but as
the work proceeded O'Neill expanded
it to eleven. Much of the material was
destroyed after his death, and only two
plays have been published. They are
numbers 1 and 6 in the series.*
1 A touch of the poet 1961
2 More stately mansions 1965

Onions, O.

Gandelyn the jester appears in each of these but they are not otherwise sequels.

Onstott, K.

A series of novels about a slave estate in Southern U.S.A.

Oppenheim, E. P.

Orczy, Baroness

Orenburgsky, S. G.

O 'Riordan, C.

The above list is contained in a letter from the author quoted by Mr. F. Seymour Smith. (L.A.R. Oct. 1948). The letter goes on:
"All the novels I have published since 1919 are linked up in so far as at least one character appears in more than one tale. The novel least in the line is 'Rowena Barnes', but Stanistas Priest in that is the friend of the Lord Dagincourt of the 'Age of Miracles' and 'Young Lady Dagincourt' in which Stephen McCarthy and Adam Queen also figure ... I had planned one more novel after 'Married Life' to round off the series and make a complete social history of Anglo-Irish relations during 200 years".

Osborne, D.

N.F. Autobiography

Ostrander, I.

O'Sullivan, J. B.
STEVE SILK SERIES:
1 I die possessed
2 Nerve beat
3 Don't hang me too high
4 The stuffed man
5 Someone walked over my grave 1958
6 Gale fever 1959
7 The long spoon 1960

Ouida *pseud.* [**L. de la Ramée,**]
1 Princess Napraxine
2 Othmar

Owen, H.
JOURNEY FROM OBSCURITY:
1 Childhood 1962
2 Youth 1964
3 War 1965
Chronicles of the Owen family, largely devoted to the story of Wilfred Owen.

Owen, J.
1 The running footman
2 Edward Bringle

Owen, R.
1 Green heart of heaven 1954
2 Worse than wanton 1956
Two novels about the South Seas.

Oxenham, J.
1 My lady of the moor
2 The Twelfth, an amethyst by Beatrice Chase, heroine of *My lady of the moor.*
LIFE OF CHRIST:
1 The hidden years
2 Anno Domini [The master's golden year]
3 The splendour of the dawn
'God's candle' is not part of the series, but is connected with 'Splendour of the dawn'.

Paassen, P. van
1 Days of our years
2 That day alone
N.F. Autobiography

Packard, F. L.
1 The adventures of Jimmy Dale
2 The further adventures of Jimmy Dale
3 Jimmy Dale and the phantom clue
4 Jimmy Dale and the blue envelope murder
5 Jimmy Dale and the missing hour

Packer, J.
1 Pack and follow
2 Grey mistress
3 Apes and ivory
4 Home from sea
N.F. Autobiography of a naval wife

Page, G. [**Mrs. R. A. Dobbin,**]
1 Where the strange roads go down
2 Follow after
　□
1 Jill's Rhodesian philosophy
2 Jill on a ranch

Page, S. H.
CHRISTOPHER HANOT SERIES:
1 Sinister cargo
2 Resurrection murder case

Paget, G.
1 The rose of Raby (1415-1460)
2 The rose of Rouen (1460-1471)
3 The rose of London (1471-1485)
The three volumes are planned as a series covering the history of England from battle of Agincourt to the death of Edward IV. In fictional form but not conceived as novels.

Pagnol, M.
1 The days were too short
2 The time of secrets
N.F. Autobiography

Pain, B.
1 Eliza
2 Eliza's husband
3 Eliza getting on
4 Exit Eliza
5 Eliza's son

Pakenham, F., Earl of Longford
1 Born to believe
2 Five lives
N.F. Autobiography

Pakington, H.
1 Four in family
2 The roving eye
3 In company with Crispin [The eligible bachelor]
1 and 2 were later published in one volume 'The Warmstreys of Romanfield'.
□
1 The Washbournes of Otterley
2 Young William Washbourne
3 Farewell to Otterley

Palacio Valdes, A.
1 Riverita
2 Maxima

Palen, L. S.
THE WHITE DEVIL SERIES:
1 The White Devil of the Black Sea
2 The White Devil's mate

Palmer, S.
MISS H. WITHERS SERIES
1 Penguin pool murders
2 Murder on wheels
3 Puzzle of the pepper tree
4 Murder on a honeymoon
5 The briar pipe
6 Puzzle of the blue banderilla
7 Puzzle of the silver Persian
8 No flowers by request
9 Puzzle of the happy hooligan
10 Death in grease paint
11 Miss Withers regrets
12 Four lost ladies
13 At one fell swoop
14 Nipped in the bud
15 Exit laughing

Palmer, V.
MACY DONOVAN SERIES:
1 Golconda
2 Seedtime
3 The big fellow
Australian novels of a mining township.

Pape, R.
1 Boldness be my friend
2 Sequel to boldness
N.F. Autobiography

Pargeter, E.
1 The eighth champion of Christendom: lame crusade
2 Reluctant odyssey
3 Warfare accomplished
□
1 The heaven tree 1961
2 The green branch 1962
3 The scarlet seed 1963
A trilogy about medieval Wales.

Park, R.
1 The harp in the south
2 Poor man's orange

Parker, Sir G.
1 Pierre and his people
2 An adventure of the north
3 A romany of the snows

Parker, M.
JOHN PICKERING SERIES:
1 Which Mrs. Torr?
2 Invisible red

Parkin, R.
1 Out of the smoke
2 Into the smother
N.F. Autobiography

Parkman, S.
CAPTAIN BOWKER SERIES:
1 Plunder bar
2 Ship ashore
3 The facts about Floyd
4 The passing of Tony Blount
5 Captain Bowker

Parry, L.
1 Fullback
2 The big game

Pasture, Mrs. Henry de la, *afterwards* **Lady Clifford**
1 Catherine of Calais
2 Catherine's child
□
1 Master Christopher
2 Erica, *same as* The Honourable Mrs. Garry

Patterson, I.
SEBALET CROFT SERIES:
1 The Eppworth case
2 The Standish Gaunt case

Patterson, G. N.
1 Tibetan journey
2 God's fool
3 Up and down Asia
N.F. Autobiography

Pattinson, J.
HARVEY LANDON SERIES:
1 Contact Mr. Delgado 1960
2 The liberators 1961

Paul, E.
1 A narrow street
2 Linden on the Saugus branch
3 Ghost town on the Yellowstone
4 My old Kentucky home
5 Sprintime in Paris
6 Desperate scenery
*Autobiographical episodes which together
form a connected story. 1 and 5 are direct
sequels.*
HOMER EVANS SERIES:
1 Mysterious Mickey Finn
2 Hugger-mugger in the Louvre
3 Mayhem in B flat

Paul, L.
1 Living hedge
2 Angry young man
3 The boy down Kitchener street
N.F. Autobiography

Paustovsky, K.
STORY OF A LIFE:
1 Childhood and schooldays
2 Slow approach of thunder

Payne, L.
1 The nose on my face
2 Deep and crisp and even

Payne, R.
1 The great Mogul [Young emperor]
2 The emperor
Two novels on the Emperor Shah Jahan
☐
1 Love and peace
2 The lovers

Peacey, S.
1 Achievement of William Cargoe
2 They are transformed

Peacock, M.
1 Colonel Blood
2 Man of wealth

Peake, M.
1 Titus Groan
2 Gormenghast
3 Titus alone

Pearce, C. E.
INDIAN MUTINY SERIES:
1 A star of the east: Delhi
2 Love besieged: Lucknow
3 Red revenge: Cawnpore

Pearce, M. G.
DANIEL QUORM. TWO SERIES

Pease, H.
1 Magnus Sinclair
2 Of mistress Eve
3 The burning cresset

Peattie, Mrs. E. W.
1 Azalea
2 Annie Laurie and Azalea
3 Azalea at Sunset Gap
4 Lotta Embury's career

Peck, W.
1 A little learning
2 Home for the holidays
N.F. Autobiography

Peeress, A.
1 The shadow on the purple
2 The searchlight on the throne

Pemberton, Sir M.
1 The iron pirate
2 Captain Black

Penn, M.
THE STORY OF HILDA BURTON:
1 Manchester fourteen miles
2 The foolish virgin
3 Young Mrs. Burton

Penton, B.
AUSTRALIAN TRILOGY:
1 Landtakers

2 Giant's stride
3 Inheritors

Pepys, M., 6th Earl of Cottenham
1 All out
2 Sicilian circuit

Pepys, S., Junior, *pseud.*
1 Diary of the Great Warr
2 Second diary of the Great Warr
3 Last diary of the Great Warr

Perez Galdos, B.
CONTEMPORARY NOVELS: THE FIRST
EPOCH
1 Lady Perfecta
2 Gloria
3 Leon Roch
4 Marianela
*Of the second epoch, comprising 18
novels, I can only trace two in translation.*
□
1 The spendthrifts 1952
2 Miau 1963
□
1 Trafalgar
2 The court of Charles IV
3 Saragossa
*These are the only volumes translated
of the series. National Episodes, 46
volumes, which covers the history of
Spain from the Napoleonic wars to 1900.*

Perham, M.
1 Lugard, the years of adventure 1959
2 Lugard, the years of authority 1960
N.F. Biography

Perowne, S.
1 The life and times of Herod the
Great
2 The later Herods 1958
N.F. History

Perri, F.
"THE TRIPTYCH OF THE FAITH"
1 The unknown disciple
To follow
2 Epicharis
3 The death of Rome
A trilogy on the rise of Christianity.

Petrie, R.
INSPECTOR MACLURG SERIES:
1 Death in Deakins Wood 1963
2 Murder by precedent 1964
3 Running deep 1965

Peyrefitte, R.
1 Diplomatic diversions
2 Diplomatic conclusions

Phelan, J.
1 Criminals in real life
2 Fetters for twenty

Philby, H. St. J.
1 Arabian days
2 Forty years in the wilderness
N.F. Autobiography

Philips, J.
PETER STYLES SERIES:
1 The laughter trap 1963
2 The black glass city 1964
3 The twisted people 1965
*Unusual in a detective series in that
there is a connected theme as well as a
recurring character.*

Phillips, H. W.
1 Mr. Scraggs introduced by Red
Saunders
2 Red Saunders: his adventures West
and East
3 Red Saunders' pets and other
critters
4 Plain Mary Smith

Phillpotts, E.
THE HUMAN BOY SERIES:
1 The human boy
2 The human boy again
3 From the angle of seventeen
4 The human boy and the War
5 A human boy's diary
CHILDREN OF THE MIST SERIES:
1 Children of the mist
2 Children of men
THE BOOK OF AVIS:
1 Bred in the bone
2 Witches' cauldron
3 A shadow passes

Phillpotts, E. (*contd.*)

INDUSTRIES OF ENGLAND SERIES:

1 Old Delabole
2 Brunel's tower
3 Green alleys
4 The nursery [Banks of Colne]
5 The spinners
6 Storm in a teacup

☐

1 There was an old woman
2 There was an old man

Pickles, W.

1 Between you and me
2 Sometime never
3 Ne'er forget the people
N.F. Autobiography

Pidgin, C. F.

1 Quincey Adams Sawyer and Mason's Corner folks
2 The further adventures of Quincey Adams Sawyer and Mason's Corner folks
3 The chronicles of Quincey Adams Sawyer, detective; *by C. F. Pidgin and J. M. Taylor*

Pilgrim, D.

1 No common glory
2 The grand design

Pilkington, R.

1 Small boat through Belgium
2 Small boat through Holland
3 Small boat to the Skagerrack
4 Small boat through Sweden
5 Small boat to Alsace
6 Small boat through France
7 Small boat through Germany
8 Small boat through Southern France
N.F. Travel

Pinney, P.

1 Dust on my shoes
2 Who wanders alone
3 Anywhere but here
N.F. Autobiography

Piper, M. R.

1 Sylvia's experiment
2 Sylvia of the Hilltop
3 Sylvia Arden decides

Piper, W.

1 New lives [The son of John Wintringham]
2 Full flower [The sun in his own house]
These are modernized sequels to 'Pride and Prejudice', by Jane Austen.

Plaidy, J.

LUCREZIA BORGIA SERIES:

1 Madonna of the seven hills
2 Light on Lucrezia 1958

ISABELLA OF CASTILE AND FERDINAND OF ARAGON:

1 Castile for Isobella
2 Spain for the sovereigns
3 Daughters of Spain 1961

TRILOGY ON CATHERINE DE MEDICI:

1 Madame Serpent
2 The Italian woman
3 Queen Jezebel

KATHERINE OF ARAGON SERIES:

1 Katherine, the virgin widow 1961
2 The shadow of the pomegranate 1962
3 The king's secret matter 1962

TRILOGY ON CHARLES II:

1 The wandering prince
2 A health unto his majesty
3 Here lies our sovereign lord

LOUIS XV SERIES:

1 Louis the well-beloved
2 The road to Compiegne 1959

SPANISH INQUISITION:

1 The rise of the Spanish Inquisition
2 The growth of the Spanish Inquisition 1960
3 The end of the Spanish Inquisition 1962
N.F. History

Platts, W. C.

1 The Tuttlebury tales
2 Tuttlebury troubles
3 The whims of Erasmus
4 More Tuttlebury tales

Plivier, T.

TRILOGY ON WORLD WAR II:

1 Moscow
2 Stalingrad

3 Berlin
Documentary novels on the Eastern Campaign.

Plomer, W.
AUTOBIOGRAPHY:
1 Double lives
2 At home
N.F. Autobiography

Plumb, J. H.
1 Sir Robert Walpole: The making of a statesman
2 Sir Robert Walpole: the King's minister
N.F. Biography

Plummer, T. A.
FRAMPTON SERIES:
1 Shadowed by the C.I.D.
2 Shot at night
3 Frampton of the Yard
4 Dumb witness
5 Was the Mayor murdered?
6 Death symbol
7 Man they put away
8 Five were murdered
9 Man they feared
10 Two men from the East
11 Muse theatre murder
12 Melody of death
13 Black ribbon murders
14 Crime at 'Crooked Gables'
15 Fool of the Yard
16 Devil's tea party
17 Man who changed his face
18 Murder limps by
19 Murder by an idiot
20 Simon takes the 'rap'
21 Murder in the village
22 The strangler
23 Man with the crooked arm
24 J. for Jennie murders
25 The Barissh mystery
26 The pierced ear murders
27 Who fired the factory
28 The silent four
29 Hunted!
30 Strychnine for one
31 Death haunts the repertory
32 Yellow disc murders
33 Murder of Doctor Gray

34 Murder through room 45
35 Frampton sees red
36 Murder at Marlington
37 The Westlade murders
38 Murder in Windy Coppice
39 A scream at midnight
40 The black rat
41 Where was Fruit murderd?
42 Murder in the surgery
43 Pagan Joe
44 Condemned to live 1956
45 Murder at Lantern Corner
46 The elusive killer 1958
47 The hospital thief 1959
48 The vestry murder 1959
49 The spider man 1960
50 Murder at Brownhill 1962

Plunkett, E. J., *18th Baron* **Dunsany**, *see* Dunsany, 18th Baron

Plympton, A. G.
1 Dear daughter Dorothy
2 Dorothy and Anton

Poe, E. A.
1 The narrative of Arthur Gordon Pym. *Cont. by Jules Verne.*
2 Sphinx of the ice-fields
Published in one volume as 'The mystery of Arthur Gordon Pym' 1962.

Polney, Peter de
1 Death and tomorrow
2 Fools of choice
N.F. Autobiography

Ponsonby, D. A.
1 Family of Jaspard
2 Bristol cousins

Pontoppidam, H.
1 Emmanuel
2 The promised land
3 Dommens day (not translated)

Pook, P.
1 Banking on form
2 Pook in boots
3 Pook in business 1963
4 Bwana Pook 1965
N.F. Autobiography

Pool, M. L.
1 Roweny in Boston
2 Mrs. Keats Bradford
□
1 The two Salomes
2 Out of step

Pope-Hennessy J., *see* Hennessy, J. Pope-

Porteous, C.
1 The farm by the lake
2 The snow
3 The earth remains
□
1 Farmer's creed
2 Teamsman
3 Land truant
N.F. Autobiography
THE STORY OF JONUS WISHET:
1 The cottage
2 Sons of the farm
3 The battle mound

Porter, E. H.
1 Pollyanna
2 Pollyanna grows up
Continued by H. L. Smith
3 Pollyanna of the orange blossoms
4 Pollyanna's jewels
5 Pollyanna's debt of honour
6 Pollyanna's western adventure
Continued by E. Borton
7 Pollyanna in Hollywood
8 Pollyanna's castle in Mexico
9 Pollyanna's door to happiness
10 Pollyanna's golden horseshoe
11 Pollyanna and the secret mission
Continued by M. P. Chalmers
12 Pollyanna's protegee
Continued by V. M. Moffitt
13 Pollyanna at Six Star Ranch
14 Pollyanna of Magic Valley
□
1 Cross-currents
2 The turn of the tide

Porter, G. Stratton-
1 Freckles
2 The girl of the Limberlost
By J. Stratton-Porter
3 Freckles comes home

Porter, J.
DET. CHIEF INSPECTOR DOVER:
1 Dover one 1964
2 Dover two 1965
3 Dover three 1965

Porter, R.
1 Summer drftwood
2 Winter fire

Porter, S., *see* Henry, O., *pseud.*

Portman, L.
1 Hugh Rendal
2 The progress of Hugh Rendal

Post, M. B.
1 Annie Jordan
2 Matt Regan's woman

Post, M. D.
1 The strange schemes of Randolph Mason
2 The clients of Randolph Mason
3 Randolph Mason: corrector of destinies

Poultney, C. B.
1 Mrs. 'Arris
2 More Mrs. 'Arris
3 Mrs. 'Arris again
4 Mrs. 'Arris carries on

Pound, A.
1 Once a wilderness
2 Second growth

Powell, A.
THE MUSIC OF TIME:
1 A question of upbringing
2 A buyer's market
3 The acceptance world 1951
Published (1962) in one volume. 'A dance to the music of time.'
4 At Lady Molly's 1957
5 Casanova's Chinese restaurant 1960
6 The kindly ones 1962
These form a second trilogy in the series.
7 The valley of bones 1964
This begins the six volume trilogy

planned as the second half of the work,
and is itself the first volume in a trilogy
dealing with World War II.

Powell, L.
PHILLIP ODELL SERIES:
1 A count of six
2 Shadow play
3 Spot the lady
4 Still of height
5 The black casket

Powell, R.
ARAB AND ANDY SERIES:
1 Don't catch me
2 All over but the shooting
3 Shoot if you must
4 And hope to die
5 Lay that pistol down
6 Leave murder to me

Powys, L. C.
1 The joy of it
2 Still the joy of it
N.F. Autobiography

Pratt, L.
1 Ezekiel
2 Ezekiel expands

Preedy, G., *pseud., see* **Bowen M.**
[Mrs. G. M. Long,]

Prescot, J.
CASE BOOKS:
1 Both sides of the case
2 The case continued 1959
3 The case proceeding 1960
4 Case for the accused 1961
5 Case for trial 1962
6 Case for hearing 1963
7 Case for court 1964
8 The case re-opened 1965

Prescott, H. F. M.
PILGRIMAGES OF FRIAR FELIX FABIO:
1 Jerusalem journey [Friar Felix at large] 1955
2 Once to Sinai 1957

Preston, F.
1 Harvest of daring

2 Great refusals 1958
Novels of a New Zealand family.

Prevost, M.
1 Frederique
2 Lea
2 has not been translated.

Prichard, K. S.
AUSTRALIAN TRILOGY:
1 The roaring nineties
2 Golden miles
3 Winged seeds

Priestley, J. B.
1 Midnight on the desert
2 Rain upon Godshill
3 Margin released, 1962
N.F. Autobiography

Prior, L. F. L.
1 Law unto themselves
2 The valley of exile
3 These times of travail
1 is set in medieval times, 2 and 3 are modern, but all relate events in the history of the Fielmar family.

Pritchard, K. *and* **H.**
1 The chronicles of Don Q
2 New chronicles of Don Q
3 Don Q's love story

Proctor, M.
INSPECTOR MARTINEAU SERIES:
1 Killer at large
2 The midnight plumber
3 Moonlight flitting 1963
4 His weight in gold 1966

Propper, M.
TOMMY RANKIN SERIES:
1 Murder in sequence
2 You can't gag the dead

Proudfoot, W.
INSPECTOR VALLIANT SERIES:
1 Crime in the arcade
2 Trail of the ruby
3 Arrest

Proust, M.
REMEMBRANCE OF THINGS PAST SERIES:
1 Swann's Way
2 Within a budding grove
3 The Guermantes Way, 2 volumes
4 Cities of the Plain, 2 volumes
5 The captive
6 The sweet cheat gone.
7 Time regained [The past recaptured]

Prouty, O. H.
THE VALE FAMILY:
1 White fawn
2 Lisa Vale
3 Now voyager
4 Homeport
5 Fabia

Pryde, H. W.
MCFLANNEL SERIES:
1 First book of the McFlannels
2 McFlannels see it through
3 McFlannels united
4 McFlannel family affairs
5 Maisie McFlannel

Pugh, E.
1 The eyes of a child
2 The secret years

Punshon, E. R.
BOBBY OWEN SERIES:
1 Information received
2 Death among the sunbathers
3 Crossword mystery
4 Mystery villa
5 Death of a beauty queen
6 Death comes to Cambers
7 The Bath mysteries
8 Mystery of Mr. Jessop
9 The dusky hour
10 Dictator's way
11 Comes a stranger
12 Suspects nine
13 Murder abroad
14 Four strange women
15 Ten star clues
16 The dark garden
17 Diabolic candelabra
18 Conqueror inn
19 Night's cloak
20 Secrets can't be kept
21 There's a reason for everything
22 It might lead anywhere
23 Helen passes by
24 Music tells all
25 The house of Godwinsson
26 So many doors
27 Everybody always tells
28 The secret search
29 The golden dagger
30 The attending death
31 Strange ending
32 Brought to light
33 Dark is the clue
34 Six were present
CARTER AND BELL SERIES:
1 Unexpected legacy
2 Proof counterproof
3 Cottage murder
4 Genius in murder
5 Truth come out

Q. (Quiller-Couch, Sir A. T.)
1 The astonishing history of Troy Town
2 Noughts and crosses
3 The delectable Duchy
4 Wandering Heath
5 The white wolf; and other fireside tales
6 The mayor of Troy
7 Corporal Sam, and other stories
8 Brother Copas
9 Hocken and Hunken
□
1 Major Vigoureux
2 Tom Tiddler's ground

Quantrill, M.
THE GOTOBED TRIPTYCH:
1 Gotobed Dawn 1959
2 Gotobedlam 1961
3 John Gotobed alone 1963

Queen, E.
1 The Roman hat mystery
2 The French powder mystery
3 The Dutch shoe mystery
4 The Greek coffin mystery
5 The Egyptian cross mystery
6 The American gun mystery
7 The Siamese twin mystery
8 Adventures of Ellery Queen

9 The Chinese orange mystery
10 The Spanish cape mystery
11 Halfway house
12 Door between
13 Devil to pay
14 The four of hearts
15 The dragon's teeth
16 The new adventures of Ellery Queen
17 Calamity town
18 There was an old woman
19 The murderer is a fox
20 Cat of many tails
21 Casebook of Ellery Queen
22 Ten days wonder
23 Double double
24 Origin of evil
25 The king is dead
26 The scarlet letters
27 Adventures of Ellery Queen
28 New adventures of Ellery Queen
29 Inspector Queen's own case 1956
30 The finishing stroke 1957
31 Queen's Bureau of investigation
32 The player on the other side 1963
33 And on the eighth day 1964
There is an inner sequence in the three novels set in Wrightsville, 'Calamity Town', 'Murderer is a fox', 'Ten days wonder'.

Quennell, P.
1 Byron: the years of fame
2 Byron in Italy
N.F. Biography

Quentin, P.
PETER DULUTH SERIES:
1 Puzzle for fools
2 Puzzle for players
3 Puzzle for puppets
4 Puzzle for wantons
5 Puzzle for fiends
6 Puzzle for pilgrims
7 Run to death
8 Fatal woman [Black widow]
9 The follower
10 The wife of Ronald Sheldon
11 The man in the net 1956
12 Highly suspicious circumstances 1957

Quick, H.
IOWA PIONEER LIFE:
1 Vandemark's folly
2 Hawkeye
3 The invisible woman

Quin, D. [Lewis, A. H.]
1 Wolfville
2 Wolfville days
3 Wolfville nights
4 Black Lion Inn
5 Sandburrs

Quinain, P.
1 Country beat
2 Policeman on the green
N.F. Autobiography of a policeman.

Radford E. M. *and* A.
DR. MANSON SERIES:
1 Inspector Manson's success
2 Murder jigsaw
3 Crime pays no dividends
4 John Kyeling died
5 Who killed Dick Whittington
6 Murder to live
7 Murder isn't cricket
8 Look in on murder 1955
9 The heel of Achilles 1956
10 Death on the Broads 1958
11 Death of a frightened editor 1959
12 Death at the Chateau Noir 1959
13 Murder on my conscience 1960
14 Death's inheritance 1960
15 Death takes the wheel 1961
16 From information received 1962
17 A cosy little murder 1963
18 Murder of three hosts 1963
19 The hungry killer 1964
20 Mask of murder 1965
SUPT. CARMICHAEL SERIES
1 Look in on murder 1955
2 Married to murder 1959
1 is also Dr. Manson

Raimond, C. E., *pseud., see* Robins, E.

Ramee, L. de la, *see* Ouida, *pseud.*

Rankin, Mrs. C.
1 Dandelion Cottage
2 Adopting of Rosa Marie
3 The castaways of Pete's Patch

Ransome, S.
SCHUYLER COLE SERIES:
1 False bounty
2 The deadly Miss Ashley
3 Lilies in her garden grew
4 Tread lightly, angel
5 Drag the dark
6 Deadly bedfellows 1955
7 The tragic acquittal 1955
8 Night drop 1956
9 So deadly my love 1958
10 The men in her death 1959
11 I'll die for you 1959

Rasmussen, A. H.
1 Sea fever
2 China trader
3 Return to the sea
N.F. Autobiography

Ratel, S.
1 The high house [The house in the hills]
2 The green grape
Published in France under general title 'Isabelle Comtat'.

Rattray, S.
HUGO BISHOP SERIES:
1 Knight sinister
2 Queen in danger
3 Bishop in check
4 Dead silence
5 Dead circuit 1955

Raven, S.
ALMS FOR OBLIVION:
1 The rich pay late 1964
2 Friends in low places 1965
Planned as series of ten novels of the English scene since the war.

Rawson, C.
THE GREAT MERLINI SERIES:
1 Death from a top hat
2 Footprints on the ceiling
3 Headless lady
4 Death out of thin air
5 No coffin for the corpse

Rawson, M. S.
1 Tales of Rye Town
2 Adventures at Rye Town

Raymond, E.
A LONDON GALLERY:
1 We, the accused
2 The marsh
3 Gentle Greaves
4 The witness of Canon Welcome
5 A chorus ending
6 The Kilburn tale
7 Child of Norman's End
8 For them that trespass
9 Was there love once?
10 The corporal of the guard
11 A song of the tide
12 The chalice and the sword
13 To the wood no more
14 The Lord of Wensley
15 The old June weather
16 The city and the dream
A series of novels portraying the variety of London life over the last half century. Not otherwise connected.
☐
1 Daphne Bruno
2 The fulfilment of Daphne Bruno
☐
1 A family that was
2 The jesting army
3 Mary Leith

Raymond, W.
1 Two men o' Mendip
2 No soul above money

Rayter, J.
JOHNNY POWERS:
1 The victim was important
2 Asking for trouble

Read, Miss *pseud.* [D. J. Saint,]
FAIRACRE SERIES:
1 Village school
2 Village diary
3 Storm in the village
4 Miss Clare remembers 1962
5 Over the gate 1964
☐
1 Thrush Green
2 Winter in Thrush Green 1961

Read, C.
1 Mr. Secretary Cecil and Queen Elizabeth

2 Lord Burghley and Queen Elizabeth
N.F. Biography

Reade, C.
  1 It is never too late to mend
  2 The autobiography of a thief
  ☐
  1 Love me little love me long
  2 Hard cash

Reeve, A. B.
  1 Craig Kennedy, detective
  2 The poisoned pen
  3 The silent bullet
  4 The gold of the gods
  5 The dream doctor
  6 The adventuress
  7 The treasure train
  8 The black hand
  9 The Panama plot
10 Exploits of Elaine
11 Romance of Elaine
12 Triumph of Elaine
13 The film mystery
14 Craig Kennedy listens in
15 The boy scout's Craig Kennedy

Reeve, D.
  1 Smoke in the lanes
  2 No place like home

Reid, F.
  1 Young Tom
  2 Retreat
  3 Uncle Stephen

Reid, P. R.
  1 The Colditz story
  2 The latter days
N.F. Escape

Reid, W. S. Hill-
  1 Letters of an economic father
  2 Letters from a bank parlour
N.F

Reilly, H.
INSPECTOR MCKEE SERIES:
  1 McKee of Centre St.
  2 Dead man control
  3 All concerned notified
  4 Dead can tell

  5 Murder in Shinbone Alley
  6 Death demands an audience
  7 Mourned on Sunday
  8 Opening door
  9 Murder on Angler's Island
10 Silver leopard
11 The farm house
12 Staircase 4
13 Murder at Arroways
14 The velvet hand
15 Not me Inspector
16 Compartment K
17 Follow me 1961
18 The day she died 1963

Remarque, E. M.
  1 All quiet on the Western front
  2 The road back
  3 Three comrades

Rémy, *pseud.*
  1 Silent company
  2 Courage and fear
  3 Portrait of a spy
N.F. Autobiography

Renault, M.
  1 The King must die 1960
  2 The bull from the sea 1962
The story of Theseus

Renton, *pseud.* [**E. M. Channing,**]
  1 The girl of the caravan
  2 Years later

Revell, L.
MISS JULIA TYLER SERIES:
  1 Bus station murders
  2 No pockets in shrouds
  3 A silver spade

Reynolds, S.
  1 A poor man's house
  2 Alongshore
  3 How 'twas
  4 Seems so

Rhode, J.
DR. PRIESTLEY SERIES:
  1 The Paddington mystery
  2 Dr. Priestley's quest
  3 The Ellerby case

Rhode, J. (*contd.*)
4 The Davidson case
5 Tragedy on the line
6 The hanging woman
7 Mystery at Greycombe farm
8 Dead men at the folly
9 Motor rally mystery
10 The Claverton mystery
11 Death in the hopfields
12 Invisible weapons
13 Bloody tower
14 Death on Sunday
15 Death pays a dividend
16 Death on the boat train
17 Murder at the cottage
18 Death at the helm
19 They watched by night
20 The fourth bomb
21 Death on the track
22 Men die at Cypress Lodge
23 Death invades the meeting
24 Vegetable duck
25 Bricklayers' arms
26 The lake house
27 Death in Harley St.
28 Nothing by the truth
29 Death of an author
30 The telephone call
31 Blackthorn house
32 Up the garden path
33 The two graphs
34 Family affairs
35 Dr. Goodwood's locum
36 The secret meeting
37 Death in Wellington Road
38 Death at the dance
39 By registered post
40 Death at the inn
41 The Davidson murders
42 Death on the lawn 1954
43 The domestic agency 1955
44 Death of a godmother 1955
45 Open verdict 1956
46 An artist dies 1956
47 Death of a bridegroom 1957
48 Robbery with violence 1957
49 Murder at Derivale 1958
50 Death takes a partner 1958
51 Licensed for murder 1959
52 Three cousins die 1959
53 Twice dead 1960
54 The fatal pool 1960

55 The vanishing diary 1961
Inspector Waghorn is also a major character in the later novels.

Rhodes, K.
MARTIN RYOTT SERIES:
1 Wild heart of youth
2 The golden flower

Rice, A. H.
1 Mrs. Wiggs of the Cabbage Patch
2 Lovey Mary

Rice, C.
1 Innocent bystander
2 My kingdom for a hearse 1959

Rich, L. D.
1 We took to the woods
2 Happy the land
3 My neck of the woods
4 Only parents
5 Innocence under the elms
N.F. Autobiography

Richards, F., *see* Lockridge, F. and R.
The early novels in the 'Captain Heimrich' series were by these joint authors and have been retained there for convenience.

Richards, L. E.
CALVIN PARKS SERIES:
1 The wooing of Calvin Parks
2 'Up to Calvin's.'
3 On board the *Mary Sands*
CAPTAIN JANUARY SERIES:
1 Captain January
2 Melody
3 Marie
4 Rosin, the beau
MRS. TREE SERIES:
1 Mrs. Tree
2 Mrs. Tree's will
QUEEN HILDEGARDE SERIES:
1 Queen Hildegarde
2 Hildegarde's holiday
3 Hildegarde's home
4 Hildegarde's neighbours
5 Hildegarde's harvest
THREE MARGARETS SERIES:
1 Three Margarets

2 Margaret Montfort
3 Peggy
4 Rita
5 Fernley House
6 The Merryweathers

Richardson, D. M.
PILGRIMAGE:
1 Pointed roofs
2 Backwater
3 Honeycomb
4 The tunnel
5 Interim
6 Deadlock
7 Revolving lights
8 The trap
9 Oberland
10 Dawn's left hand
11 Clear horizon
12 Dimple hill
Later collected in four volumes.

Richardson, H. H.
THE CHRONICLES OF THE FORTUNES OF
RICHARD MAHONEY:
1 Australia felix
2 The way home
3 Ultima Thule
*The story of Richard's son Cuffy is
continued in:*
4 The end of a childhood

Richer, C.
1 Ti-Coyo and his shark
2 Son of Ti-Coyo

Richmond, Sir A.
1 Twenty-six years (1879–1905)
2 Another sixty years 1965
N.F Autobiography

Richmond, Mrs. G. S.
JULIET SERIES:
1 The indifference of Juliet
2 With Juliet in England
RED PEPPER BURNS SERIES:
1 Red Pepper Burns
2 Mrs. Red Pepper
3 Red Pepper's patients
4 Red and black
5 The Redfields

6 Red Pepper returns
□
1 On Xmas day, in the morning
2 On Xmas day, in the evening
3 Under the Xmas stars

Richter, C.
AMERICAN PIONEER TRILOGY:
1 The trees
2 The fields
3 The town

Rickard, Mrs. V.
1 Bird of strange plumage
2 The perilous elopement

Rietz, D.
1 Commando
2 Trekking on
3 No outspan
N.F. Autobiography

Riley, W.
1 Windyridge
2 Windyridge revisited
□
1 Thro' a Yorkshire window
2 A Yorkshire suburb

Rinehart, M. R.
1 Amazing adventures of Lilian Carberry
2 Tish
3 More Tish
4 Tish plays the game
5 Tish marches on

Ripperget, Mrs. H.
1 112, Elm Street
2 The Bretons of Elm Street
Short stories of life in U.S. today.

Rita *pseud.* [Humphreys, Mrs. D.]
1 Sheba
2 Countess Pharamond
VICTORIA SAGA SERIES:
1 The grandmothers
2 The wand'ring darlin'
3 Jean and Jeanette

Ritson, K.
TESSA SERIES:
1 Tessa in South Africa
2 Tessa to the rescue 1957
3 Tessa and some ponies
4 The Runnoth dude ranch 1960

Rives, A., *afterwards* **Princess Troubetz-koy**
1 The quick and the dead
2 Barbara Dering

Robb, J.
1 Red Radford and the Black Legion
2 Red Radford and operation kidnap
3 Red Radford and the Iron Guard

Robbins, C.
CLAY HARRISON SERIES:
1 Dusty death
2 The man without a face
3 Death on the highway
4 Six signpost murder
5 Death forms threes

Robbins, Mrs. S. S.
1 Mabel Hazard's thoroughfare
2 Mabel's stepmother

Roberts, B.
1 A.B.C's test case
2 A.B.C. investigates

Roberts, C.
1 Victoria fourthirty
2 They wanted to live
□
1 Pilgrim cottage
2 The guests arrive
3 Volcano
□
1 Spears against us
2 Pamela's spring song
□
1 Gone rustic
2 Gone rambling
3 Gone afield
□
1 And so to Bath
2 And so to America
□
1 Halfway

2 One year of life
N.F. Autobiography

Roberts, C. G. D.
1 The forge in the forest
2 A sister to Evangeline [Lovers in Acadie]
□
1 The wisdom of the wilderness
2 They that walk in the wild

Roberts, K.
CHRONICLES OF ARUNDEL:
1 Arundel
2 Rabble in arms
3 The lively lady
4 Captain Caution

Roberts, M.
1 Midsummer madness
2 More midsummer madness

Robertson, C.
PETER GAYLEIGH SERIES:
1 The temple of dawn
2 The amazing corpse
3 Zero hour
4 Alibi in black
5 Explosion
6 Two must die
7 Dark knight
8 Devil's lady
9 Knaves' castle
10 Calling Peter Gayleigh
11 Sweet justice
12 Death wears red shoes
13 Dusky limelight
14 Peter Gayleigh flies high
15 Demons moon
16 The tiger's claws
VICKY MCBAIN SERIES:
1 Venetian mask
2 The Eastlake affair
3 Who rides a tiger 1957
4 The threatening shadows 1959
5 Night trip 1960
6 You can keep the corpse 1961
DETECTIVE SUPERINTENDENT BRADLEY:
1 Time to kill 1961
2 Conflict of shadows 1962
3 The frightened widow 1963
4 Dead on time 1964

5 Sinister moonlight 1965
6 Killer's mask 1966

Robins, E. [Parks, Mrs. G. R.] Raimond, C. E., *pseud.*
1 The new moon
2 Milly's story

Robinson, P.
INDIAN GARDEN SERIES:
1 Chasing a fortune
2 Tigers at large
3 Under the punkah
4 Valley of the Teetotum Trees

Robinson, R. E.
1 Uncle Lisha's shop
2 Uncle Lisha's camps
3 Uncle Lisha's outing

Rodney, J.
AUTOBIOGRAPHY:
1 To heal the sick
2 Next patient, please
N.F. Autobiography

Rohmer, S.
1 Tales of secret Egypt
2 Brood of the witch queen
FU-MANCHU SERIES:
1 The mysterious Dr. Fu-Manchu
2 The devil doctor
3 The Si-Fan mysteries
4 Daughter of Fu-Manchu
5 Return of Dr. Fu-Manchu
6 Insidious Dr. Fu-Manchu
7 Hand of Dr. Fu-Manchu
8 Mask of Fu-Manchu
9 The bride of Fu-Manchu
10 President Fu-Manchu
11 The drums of Fu-Manchu
12 The island of Fu-Manchu
13 Shadow of Fu-Manchu
14 Emperor Fu-Manchu
15 Re-enter Dr. Fu-Manchu 1957
SUMURU SERIES:
1 Sins of Sumuru
2 Slaves of Sumuru
3 Virgin in flames
4 The moon is red
5 Sand and satin
6 Sinister Madonna 1956

Rolfe, F. W. (Baron Corvo, *pseud.***)**
1 Stories Toto told me
2 In his own image

Rolland, R.
* JOHN CHRISTOPHER SERIES:
1 Dawn and morning
2 Storm and stress
3 John Christopher in Paris
4 Journey's end
*The above list is the British edition.
There are other editions in one and
three volumes. The original French
edition was in 10 volumes as follows:*
1 L'autre
2 Le malin
3 L'adolescent
4 La revolte
5 La foire sur la place
6 Antoinette
7 Dans la maison
8 Les amis
9 Le buisson ardent
10 La nouvelle journée
THE SOUL ENCHANTED SERIES:
1 Annette and Sylvie
2 Summer
3˙ Mother and son
4 The combat [Death of a world]
5 Via Sacra [World in birth]
*4 and 5 were published in one volume
as 'Death of a world'.*

Rolvaag, O. E.
1 Giants in the earth
2 Peder victorious
3 Their father's god

Romains, J.
MEN OF GOODWILL:
1 Book 1 Sixth of October [Le 6
Octobre]
Book 2 Quinette's crime [Crime de
Quinette]
2 Book 3 Childhood's loves [Les
amours enfantines]
3 Book 4 Eros in Paris [Eros de Paris]
4 Book 5 The proud of heart [Les
Superbes]
5 Book 6 The humbles [Les humbles]
6 Book 7 The lonely [Recherche d'une
église]

Romains, J. (*contd.*)
7 Book 8 Provincial interlude [Province]
8 Book 9 Flood warning [Montée des perils]
Book 10 The powers that be [Les Pouvoirs]
9 Book 11 To the gutter [Recours a l'abime]
Book 12 To the stars [Les créateurs]
10 Book 13 Death of a world [Mission a Rome]
Book 14 Death of a world [Le drapeau noir]
11 Book 15 Verdun. The prelude [Prelude a Verdun]
Book 16 Verdun. The battle [Verdun]
12 Book 17 The aftermath [Vorge contre Quinette]
Book 18 The aftermath [La douceur de la vie]
The following are published only in U.S. commencing with volume 10 of the U.S. edition.
10 The new day
Book 19 Promise of dawn [Cette grande lueur a l'est]
Book 20 The world is your adventure
11 Work and play
Book 21 Mountain days
Book 22 Work and play
12 The Wind is rising
Book 23 The gathering of the gangs [Naissance de la bande]
Book 24 Offered in evidence [Compurations]
13 Escape in passion
Book 25 The magic carpet
Book 26 Francoise
14 Book 27 Seventh of October
The difference in numbering of the U.K. and U.S. editions is due to Books 3, 4, 5 and 6 being separate volumes in the U.K. and in two volumes in the U.S.
Early U.S. titles differ slightly. The final volume of American edition contains an index of characters.
The titles in brackets are the original French titles, given when these were published as separate volumes.

Ronald, J.
1 Young Quentin [Man born of woman]
2 Sparks fly upward

Ronan, T.
1 Deep of the sky 1962
2 Pack horse and pearling boat 1964
N.F. 1 is a biography of his father, 2 his own early life on his father's sheep station, in Australia.

Roosevelt, E.
1 On my own
2 You learn by living
N.F. Autobiography

Roper, N.
1 Dianys
2 Wish

Rose, A. P.
1 Room for one more
2 The gentle house
N.F. The adoption of a displaced child.

Ross, B.
DRURY LANE SERIES:
1 The tragedy of X
2 The tragedy of Y
3 The tragedy of Z
4 Drury Lane's last case

Ross, C.
1 The haunted seventh
2 When the devil was sick

Ross, I. T.
BEN GORDON SERIES:
1 Requiem for a schoolgirl 1960
2 Murder out of school 1961
3 Old students never die 1963

Ross, J.
1 The major
2 The major steps out

Ross, Jean
1 Under a glass dome
2 The garden by the river

Ross, L.
1 The stranger
2 Blaze Allan

Ross, S.
CIVIL WAR TRILOGY:
1 Vagabond treasure
2 Sword is king 1958
3 Drum and trumpet sound! 1960

Rosten, L., *pseud.* [**L. Q. Ross**]
1 The education of Hyman Kaplan
2 The return of Hyman Kaplan

Roth, L.
1 I'll cry tomorrow
2 Beyond my worth
N.F. Autobiography

Rothenstein, Sir W.
1 Men and memories
2 Since fifty
N.F. Autobiography

Rougvie, C.
ROBERT BELCOURT SERIES:
1 Medal from Pamplona 1963
2 Tangier assignment 1965
3 The Gredos reckoning 1966

Rover, W.
1 The *Neptune* outward bound
2 The *Neptune* afloat

Rowse, A. L.
1 The England of Elizabeth
2 The expansion of Elizabethan England 1956
N.F. History
1 The early Churchills 1957
2 The later Churchills 1958
N.F. Biography
☐
1 A Cornish childhood
2 A Cornishman at Oxford 1965
N.F. Autobiography

Rowland, J.
INSPECTOR SHELLEY SERIES:
1 Grim souvenir
2 Bloodshed in Bayswater
3 Professor dies

4 Death on Dartmoor
5 Suicide alibi
6 Dangerous company
7 Murder in the museum
8 Slow poison
9 Cornish Riviera mystery
10 Crooked house
11 Spy with a scar
12 Gunpowder alley
13 Death of Neville Norway
14 Death beneath the river
15 Time for killing
16 Calamity in Kent
17 The orange tree mystery
18 Puzzle in pyrotechnics

Royde-Smith, N., *see* Smith, N. Royde-

Royle, E. M.
1 The squaw man
2 The silent call

Ruark, R.
1 The old man and the boy
2 The old man's boy grows older
N.F. Autobiography

Rushton, C.
DETECTICE INSPECTOR CADMAN SERIES:
1 No beat so fierce
2 Devil's power
3 Furnace for a foe

Russell, Countess, *see* Arnim, M. A.,
Baroness von

Russian, A., *and* **Boyle, F.**
1 The orchid seekers
2 The riders

Rutherford, M., *pseud.* [**W. H. White,**]
1 Autobiography of Mark Rutherford
2 Mark Rutherford's deliverance

Rutter, O.
1 The song of Tiadatha
2 The travels of Tiadatha

Rutzebeck, H.
1 Alaska man's luck
2 My Alaskan idyll

Ryan, I.
1 Black man's country
2 Black man's town
3 Black man's palaver

Ryland, C.
CHIEF INSPECTOR SHANNON SERIES:
1 The Notting Hill murder
2 The murders at the manor

Rynd, E. E.
1 Mrs. Green
2 Mrs Green again

Sabatini, R.
CESARE BORGIA SERIES:
1 Shame of motley
2 Justice of the Duke
3 Banner of the Bull
□
1 Scaramouche
2 Scaramouche the kingmaker
□
1 Captain Blood
2 Chronicles of Captain Blood
3 The fortunes of Captain Blood

Sahgal, N.
1 Prison and chocolate cake
2 From fear set free
N.F. Autobiography

Saint, D. J., *see* Read, Miss, *pseud.*

St. Laurent, Cecil, *pseud.* **[Laurent-Cely]**
CHERIE SERIES:
1 Caroline Cherie 1959
2 Caroline in Italy 1960
3 The loves of Caroline cherie 1960
4 Caroline cherie and Juan 1961
5 Intrigues of Caroline cherie 1962
□
1 Clotilde 1959
2 Encore Clotilde 1960
Although the atmosphere is romantic, the background of Vichy France in World War II is authentic.

St. Reymont, L.
THE PEASANTS SERIES:
1 Autumn

2 Winter
3 Spring
4 Summer

Saki, *pseud. see* Munro, H. H.

Sale, E.
1 Recitation from memory
2 My mother bids me bind my hair

Salinger, J. D.
THE GLASS FAMILY:
1 For Esme with love and squalor 1953
2 Franny and Zooey 1962
3 Raise high the roof beam carpenters *and* Seymour 1963
This series of short stories and novels tells the story of a New York family of six precocious children. In (1) a collection of short stories, there are several allusions to them, but only one, 'A perfect day for banana fish' is a complete episode, describing the death of the eldest, Seymour. 'Franny and Zooey' consists of two stories about the two youngest members. 'Raise high the roof beam, carpenters', tells the story of Seymour's wedding, as seen by Buddy, the second of the family, and a detailed story of Seymour.
There are six short stories leading up to 'The catcher in the rye', concerning Vincent and Holden Caulfield. They are: 'The last day of the last furlough', 'A day in France', 'This sandwich has no mayonnaise', 'The stranger', 'I'm crazy', and 'Slight rebellion off Madison'.

Salisbury, D.
MRS. NORRIS SERIES:
1 Death of an old sinner
2 A gentleman called

Salmond, J. B.
1 My man Sandy
2 Bawbee Bowden

Salter, E.
INSPECTOR HORNSLEY SERIES:
1 Voice of the peacock
2 Once upon a tombstone 1965

Sampson, E. S., *and* **Calhoun, F. B.**
1 Miss Minerva and William Green Hill
2 Billy and Major
3 Miss Minerva's baby
4 Miss Minerva on the old plantation

Sanborn, K. A.
1 Adopting an abondoned farm
2 Abandoning an adopted farm

Sand, George, *pseud.* **[Mm. Dudevant]**
BERRICHON IDYLLS:
1 Little Fadette
2 The devil's pool
3 Francis, the waif
SOCIALIST NOVELS:
1 The master mosaic workers
2 The journeyman joiner
3 The miller of Angibault
A WOMAN SINGER SERIES:
1 Consuelo
2 The Countess of Rudolstadt

Sandel, C.
1 Alberta and Jacob 1962
2 Alberta and freedom 1963
3 Alberta alone 1964

Sanders, B.
WARD AND SALLY DIGBURN:
1 Code of dishonours 1965
2 Feminine for spy 1966

Sanders, D. L.
MONTGOMERY FAMILY:
1 Six for heaven
2 Shining river
3 Waterfall
4 Ribbons in her hair 1957
5 Pepper tree bay 1959
Novels about an Australian family.

Sanders, J.
NICHOLAS PYM SERIES:
1 A firework for Oliver 1964
2 The hat of authority 1965
Stories of a Cromwellian secret service agent.

Sandstrom, F.
PONT–CLERY SERIES:
1 Midwife of Pont-Clery
2 The virtuous women of Pont-Clery

Sandys, O.
·1 The pleasure garden
2 Old roses

Santayana, Y.
1 Persons and places
2 The middle span
3 My host the world
N.F. Autobiography

Sapper, *pseud.* **[McNeile, C. H.]**
1 Bull-dog Drummond
2 The Black gang
3 The third round
4 The final count
5 The female of the species
6 Temple Tower
7 The return of Bull-dog Drummond
8 Knockout
9 Bull-dog Drummond at bay
10 Challenge
Continued by Gerald Fairlie
11 Bull-dog Drummond on Dartmoor
12 Bull-dog Drummond attacks
13 Captain Bull-dog Drummond
14 Bull-dog Drummond stands fast
15 Hands off Bull-dog Drummond
16 Calling Bull-dog Drummond
17 Return of the Black gang
☐
1 Jim Maitland
2 The island of terror
☐
1 Ask for Ronald Standish
2 Ronald Standish

Saroyan, W.
1 Mama, I love you 1956
2 Papa, you're crazy 1957
Two novels about the same family, told by the small daughter in 1 and by the small son in 2.

Sartre, J. P.
THE ROADS TO FREEDOM: A TETRALOGY
1 The age of reason
2 The reprieve
3 Iron in the soul [Troubled sleep]
4 The last chance
A sequence of novels about France before, during and after World War II.

Sassoon, S.
1 Memoirs of a foxhunting man
2 Memoirs of an infantry officer
3 Sherston's progress

Sava, G.
1 Healing knife
2 The love of surgery
N.F. Autobiography
PETER SLAVINE:
1 A boy in Samarkand
2 Caught by revolution
3 Flight from the palace
4 Pursuit in the desert

Sawyer, E. A.
1 The Christmas makers' club
2 Elsa's gift home

Saxe, R. B.
1 The ghost knows his greengages
2 The ghost does a Richard III

Sayers, D. L.
LORD PETER WIMSEY SERIES:
1 Unnatural death [The Dawson pedigree]
2 Whose body
3 Clouds of witness
4 Unpleasantness at the Bellona Club
5 Lord Peter views the body
6 Have his carcase
7 Five red herrings [Suspicious characters]
8 Strong poison
9 Murder must advertise
10 Hangman's holiday (some stories in series)
11 The nine tailors
12 Gaudy night
13 Busman's honeymoon
14 The haunted policeman (in *Detective Medley*, edited by John Rhode)
8, 12 and 13, form an internal sequence, being the love story of Peter Wimsey and Harriet Vane.

Scanlon, N. M.
NEW ZEALAND SERIES:
1 Top step
2 Primrose Hill
3 Pencarrow

4 Tides of youth
5 Winds of heaven
6 Ambition's harvest

Scannell, F.
1 Cinderella's sister
2 Peter's predicament

Scapel, Æsculapius, *pseud.* [**E. Berdoe.**]
1 St. Bernard's
2 Dying scientifically

Schechtman, J. B.
1 Rebel and statesman
2 Fighter and prophet
N.F. Autobiography

Scherf, M.
MARTIN BUELL SERIES:
1 Always murder a friend
2 Gilbert's last toothache
3 Curious custard pie
4 The elk and the evidence
5 Green plaid pants

Schickele, R.
THE RHINELAND HERITAGE:
1 Marie Capponi
2 The heart of Alsace
Original German edition is in three volumes.

Schildt, G.
1 In the wake of Odysseus
2 In the wake of a wish
3 The sun boat
N.F. Autobiography

Schiddel, E.
1 The devil in Buck's County 1962
2 Scandal's child 1963
3 Devil's summer 1965
A trilogy of novels about a country area in the U.S.A.

Schneour, S.
1 Noah Pandre
2 Noah Pandre's village

Schnitzler, A.
1 Bertha Garlan

2 Beatrice
3 Fraulein Elsie

Schonstedt, W.
1 In praise of life
2 The cradle builder

Schumacher, H.
1 The fair enchantress
2 Nelson's last love

Schweitzer, A.
1 On the edge of the primeval forest
2 More from the primeval forest 1941
N.F. Autobiography

Scott, B. M.
1 Which then, be fool?
2 And which, the knave

Scott, Mrs. C. A. Dawson-
SOME WOMEN STUDIES:
1 The maiden [The story of Anne Bearnes]
2 The mother [The burden]
3 The matron [Treasure trove]

Scott, Sir H.
1 Your obedient servant
2 Scotland Yard
N.F. Autobiography

Scott, J. M.
1 Snowstone
2 The silver land

Scott, J. R.
1 The colonel of the Red Hussars
2 The Princess Dehra

Scott, M.
FREDDIE SERIES:
1 Families are fun 1963
2 No sad songs 1964
3 Freddie 1965

Scott, R. T. M.
1 Secret service Smith
2 The black magician
3 Ann's crime
4 Aurelius Smith—detective
5 Murder stalks the Mayor

Scott, S.
SEPTIMUS DODDS:
1 Tincture of murder
2 Influenza mystery
3 Operation urgent
4 Blood in their ink
5 The mass radiography murders
6 Doctor Dodd's experiment 1955

Scott, Sir W.
1 The monastery
2 The abbot
CHRONICLES OF THE CANONGATE INCLUDE:
1 Chrystabel Croftangry
2 The fair maid of Perth
3 The Highland widow
4 My Aunt Margaret's mirror
5 The surgeon's daughter
6 The tapestried chamber
7 The two drovers
TALES OF MY LANDLORD INCLUDE:
1 The black dwarf
2 The bride of Lammermoor
3 Castle Dangerous
4 Count Robert of Paris
5 The heart of Mid-Lothian
6 The legend of Montrose
7 Old Mortality
TALES OF THE CRUSADERS INCLUDE:
1 The betrothed
2 The talisman
See also Fowler, S.

Scott, Will
1 Disher – detective
2 Shadows

Seafarer, *pseud.*
CAPTAIN FIREBRACE SERIES:
1 Captain Firebrace
2 Firebrace and the Java Queen
3 Firebrace and Father Kelly 1957
4 Smuggler's pay for Firebrace 1959

Seagrave, G. S.
1 Burma surgeon
2 Burma surgeon returns
3 My hospital in the hills
N.F. Autobiography

Sedges, J., *pseud. see* Buck, P. S.

Selby, J.
THE TRACE FAMILY:
  1 Elegant journey 1944
  2 Island in the corn 1941
  3 Starbuck 1943
  Not published in this order.

Sellwood, A. V.
  1 Atlantic
  2 Dynamite for hire
  N.F. story of a captain of a German raider in World War II and his subsequent career.

Sender, R.
  1 Chronicle of dawn 1945 [Cronica del Alba 1942]
  2 Hipogripo Violento 1954
  3 La Quinta Julieta 1957
  Published in one volume under the title 'Before noon' (1959).

Service, R. W.
  1 Ploughman of the moon
  2 Harper of heaven
  N.F. Autobiography

Seton, G., *pseud.* **[G. S. Hutchinson]**
COLONEL GRANT SERIES:
  1 The W plan
  2 According to plan
  3 Scar 77
  4 Colonel Grant's tomorrow
  5 The K code plan
  6 The V plan
  7 The red colonel

Setoun,, G. *pseud.* **[T. N. Hepburn,]**
  1 Barncraig
  2 Sunshine and Haar

Sewell, E. M.
  1 The journal of a home life
  2 After life

Seymour, B. K.
  1 Three wives
  2 Youth rides out
  ☐
  1 Maids and mistresses
  2 Interlude for Sally
  3 Summer of life

MALLING–GAYWOOD FAMILY:
  1 Buds of May
  2 Tumbled house
  3 Children grow up

Seymour, J.
  1 On my own terms
  2 The fat of the land
  N.F. Autobiography

Shafer, Mrs. S. A.
  1 The day before yesterday
  2 Beyond chance of change

Shannon, D.
MENDOZA SERIES:
  1 Case pending 1964
  2 Mark of murder 1965

Sharber, K. T.
  1 The annals of Ann
  2 At the age of Eve

Sharp, M.
  1 The eye of love 1961
  2 Martha in Paris 1962
  3 Martha, Eric and George 1964
  ☐
  1 Miss Bianca
  2 The rescuers
  3 The turret 1965

Shaw, G. B.
  Note – Sir H. Johnston's 'Mrs. Warren's daughter' is a sequel to Shaw's 'Mrs. Warren's profession'.

Sheehan, P. A.
  1 Geoffrey Austin, student
  2 The triumph of failure

Sheldon, C. M.
  1 In His steps
  2 'Jesus is here'

Shepard, E. H.
  1 Drawn from memory
  2 Drawn from life
  N.F. Autobiography

Shepherd, Eric
  1 Murder in a nunnery
  2 More murder in a nunnery

Sheppard, A. T.
1 The rise of Ledgar Dunstan
2 The quest of Ledgar Dunstan

Sheridan, C.
1 Stella defiant
2 Stella triumphant

Sherrard, O. A.
BIOGRAPHY OF PITT THE ELDER:
1 A War Minister in the making
2 Pitt and the Seven Years' War
3 Lord Chatham and America

Sherwood, J.
MR. BLESSINGTON SERIES:
1 Disappearance of Dr. Bruderstein
2 Mr. Blessington's plot
3 Ambush for Anatol
4 Vote for poison 1956

Shillaber, B. P.
1 Ike Partington
2 Cruises with Captain Bob
3 Double-runner Club
4 The Partington patchwork
5 Ike Partington and his friends

Sholokhov, M.
1 And quiet flows the Don
2 The Don flows home to the sea
3 Virgin soil upturned [Seeds of tomorrow]
4 Harvest on the Don
5 Tales from the Don
This is better regarded as two series. 1 and 2, describe events up to the end of the Civil War, 3–5 are the story of the effort to organise collective farms.

Shulman, I.
1 The Amboy Dukes
2 Cry tough
3 The big brokers
A trilogy on a group of juvenile delinquents. Not published in Great Britain.

Shurtleff, B.
'AWOL' SERIES:
1 Short leash
2 Awol at large
3 Long leash

Sidgwick, E.
ASHWIN SERIES:
1 A lady of leisure
2 Duke Jones
3 The accolade
TONY EDGWELL SERIES:
1 Promise
2 Succession
WICKFORD (OR IVEAGH) SERIES:
1 Hatchways
2 Jamesie
THE SHERIFF FAMILY SERIES:
1 Laura
2 The bells of Shoreditch [When I grow rich]
3 Dorothy's wedding [A tale of two villages]

Sidney, Sir P.
Note – Mrs. Deames' 'Arcadia, written by a young gentleman', is a continuation of Sir P. Sidney's 'Arcadia'.

Siedel, I.
1 The labyrinth
2 The wish child

Sienkiewicz, H.
1 With fire and sword (Poland and Russia)
2 The deluge (Poland, Sweden and Russia)
3 Pan Michael (Poland, Russia and the Ukraine)

Silberrad, U. L.
1 The wedding of the Lady of Lovell
2 The second book of Tobiah
3 Green pastures

Silone, I., *pseud.* [S. Tranquilli.]
1 Bread and wine
2 The seed beneath the snow

Simenon, G.
The sequence of the 'Maigret' series in translation is difficult, since they have been produced by different publishers, and the early volumes contained two stories, usually one Maigret story and one a regional novel or thriller. The following list is a complete one of the

Simenon, G. (*contd.*)

chronological order of publication of the French titles, with the English translation. This is not necessarily the order of publication in England. Where a Maigret story is in another volume, this is indicated.

1 Pietr-le-letton. The strange case of Peter the Lett *in* Inspector Maigret investigates
2 M. Gallet, décédè. The death of M. Gallet *in* Introducing Inspector Maigret
3 Le Pendu de St. Pholien. The crime of Inspector Maigret *in* Introducing Inspector Maigret
4 Le Charretier de la Providence. The crime at Lock 14 *in* Triumph of Inspector Maigret
5 La Tete d'un homme. A battle of nerves *in* Patience of Maigret
6 Le chien jaune. A face for a clue *in* Patience of Maigret
7 La nuit du carrefour. The cross road murders *in* Inspector Maigret investigates
8 Un crime en Hollande. The crime in Holland *in* Maigret abroad
9 Au rendevous de Terreneuvas. The sailor's rendezvous *in* Maigret keeps a rendezvous
10 La danseuse du Gai-Moulin. At the Gai-Moulin *in* Maigret abroad
11 La Guinguette a deux sous. Guinguette by the Seine *in* Maigret to the rescue
12 Le port de Brumes. Death of a harbourmaster *in* Maigret and M. l'abbé
13 L'Ombre chinois. The shadow on the courtyard *in* Triumph of Inspector Maigret
14 L'affaire St. Fiacre. The St. Fiacre affair *in* Maigret keeps a rendezvous
15 Chez les Flamands. The Flemish shop *in* Maigret to the rescue
16 Le fou de Bergerac. The madman of Bergerac *in* Maigret travels south
17 Liberty bar. Liberty bar *in* Maigret travels south
18 L'ecluse No. 1. The lock at Charenton *in* Maigret sits it out

19 Maigret. Maigret returns *in* Maigret sits it out
20 Signe Picpus. To any lengths *in* Maigret on holiday
21 Les vacances de Maigret. Maigret on holiday
22 Maigret et son mort. Maigret's special murder
23 La première enquete du Maigret. Maigret's first case
24 Mon ami Maigret. My friend Maigret
25 Maigret et le vieille dame. Maigret and the old lady
26 L'ami de Mme Maigret. Madame Maigret's friend
27 Les mémoirs de Maigret. Maigret's memoirs
28 Maigret au Picratts. Maigret in Montmartre *in* Maigret right and wrong
29 Maigret en meublé. Maigret takes a room
30 Maigret et la grande perche. Maigret and the burglar's wife
31 Le revolver de Maigret. Maigret's revolver
32 Maigret a peur. Maigret afraid
33 Maigret se trompe. Maigret's mistake *in* Maigret right and wrong
34 Maigret a l'école. Maigret goes to school
35 Maigret et la jeune mort. Maigret and the young girl
36 Un échec de Maigret. Maigret's failure
37 Maigret s'amuse. Maigret's little joke
38 Les scrupules de Maigret. Maigret has scruples
39 Maigret et les témoins recalcitrantes. Maigret and the reluctant witnesses
40 Maigret aux assizes. Maigret in court
41 Maigret et les viéillards. Maigret in society
42 Maigret et le voleur paresseux. Maigret and the lazy burglar
43 Maigret et le client du Samedi. Maigret and the Saturday caller
44 Maigret en colère. Maigret loses his temper

45 Maigret sets a trap 1965
46 Maigret on the defensive 1966
Four Maigret titles have been published in paperbacks under different titles. These are Nos. 1, 7, 13 and 42.

Simms, W. G.
AMERICAN REVOLUTION STORIES:
1 The partisan
2 Mellichampe
3 The kinsman *same as* The scout
4 Katherine Walton
5 The sword and the distaff *same as* Woodcraft
6 The forayers
7 Eutaw
KENTUCKY SERIES:
1 Charlemonte
2 Beauchampe
☐
1 Pelayo
2 Count Julian

Simon, B.
1 Abbe Pierre and the ragpickers
2 Ragman's city
N.F. Social studies. The work of rehabilitation of the homeless in Paris.

Simonds, W., *see* Ainwell, W., *pseud.*

Simons, R.
INSPECTOR WACE SERIES:
1 The houseboat killings 1959
2 A frame for murder 1960
3 Murder joins the chorus 1960
4 Gamble with death 1960
5 The killing chase 1961
6 Silver and death 1963

Simpson, A.
1 I threw a rose into the sea
2 Red dust of Africa
N.F. Not published in this order.

Simpson, J. Hope-
1 The Bishop of Kenelminster
2 The Bishop's picture

Sims, G. R.
MARY JANE SERIES:
1 Mary Jane's memoirs

2 Mary Jane married

Sinclair, H.
1 American years
2 The years of growth
3 Years of illusion

Sinclair, Harold
1 The horse soldiers 1956
2 The cavalryman 1958
Novels of the American Army in the Civil War and shortly after. Not published in Great Britain.

Sinclair, J. G.
1 Easingden
2 Love in Easingden

Sinclair, M.
1 Mr. Waddington of Wyck
2 Rector of Wyck
☐
1 Mary Oliver
2 Arnold Waterlow
Not strictly sequels, but companion books.

Sinclair, U.
NEW YORK TRILOGY:
1 The metropolis
2 The money-changers
3 The machine
SYLVIA SERIES:
1 Sylvia
2 Sylvia's marriage
'WORLD'S END' SERIES:
1 World's end (1913–1919)
2 Between two worlds (1919–1929)
3 Dragon's teeth (1929–1934)
4 Wide is the gate (1934–1937)
5 Presidential agent (1937–1938)
6 Dragon harvest (1939–1940)
7 A world to win (1940–1942)
8 Presidential mission (1942–1943)
9 One clear call (1943–1946)
10 O shepherd speak (1945–1946)
11 Return of Lanny Budd (1946–1947)

Sinderby, R.
'DOGSBODY' SERIES:
1 'Dogsbody'
2 The vagrant lover

Singer, B.
1 You're wrong Delaney
2 Have patience, Delaney
3 Don't slip Delaney

Sitwell, Sir O.
1 Left hand, right hand
2 The scarlet tree
3 Great morning
4 Laughter in the next room
5 Noble essences
6 Tales my father taught me 1961
N.F. Autobiography. No. 6 is a pendant to the series, including material omitted from the main work.
1 England reclaimed 1929
2 Wrack at Tidesend 1933
3 On the Continent 1958
N.F. A trilogy of poems.

Skidmore, H.
1 I will lift up mine eyes
2 Heaven came so near
☐
1 River rising
2 Hill doctor

Sladen, D.
1 A Japanese marriage
2 Playing the game

Slate, J.
1 Black Maria, M.A.
2 Maria marches on
3 Death in silhouette

Slater, Mrs. C. P.
1 Margaret Pow in furrin' parts
2 Margaret Pow comes home
3 Margaret Pow looks back

Slaughter, F. G.
AMERICAN CIVIL WAR:
1 In a dark garden
2 The stubborn heart
BIBLICAL SERIES:
1 Road to Bithynia
2 The Galileans
3 The song of Ruth
4 The scarlet cord

Smeeton, M.
1 A taste of the hills
2 A change of jungles
N.F. Autobiography

Smith, A.
1 Alfred Hagart's household
2 Miss Oona McQuarrie

Smith, A. D. H.
1 The doom trail
2 Beyond the sunset

Smith, C. Gibbs-
PAUL HARVARD PSYCHOLOGIST:
1 Operation Caroline 1955
2 Escape and be secret 1957

Smith, C. P.
1 Artillery of time
2 Ladies' day

Smith, D.
1 No rain in these clouds
2 Same sky all over
N.F. Autobiography

Smith, E.
LENSMAN SERIES:
1 Triplanetary 1955
2 First lensman 1957

Smith, F. H.
1 Colonel Carter of Cartersville
2 Colonel Carter's Christmas
☐
1 Kennedy Square
2 The fortunes of Oliver Horn

Smith, F. R., *see* Ackworth, J., *pseud.*

Smith, H. M.
INSPECTOR FROST SERIES:
1 Inspector Frost's jig-saw
2 Inspector Frost in the city
3 Inspector Frost and Lady Brassing-ham
4 Inspector Frost and the fire brigade
5 Inspector Frost and the Waverdale fire
6 Inspector Frost in Crevenna Cove

7 Inspector Frost and the Whitburne murder
8 Inspector Frost in the background

Smith, H. Z.
'SKINNY' SERIES:
1 'Not so quiet'
2 Luxury ladies

Smith, J. P.
1 Widow Goldsmith's daughter
2 Chris and Otho

Smith, N. Royde-
1 Children in the wood
2 Summer holiday
3 The island
☐
1 Jake 1936
2 How white is my sepulchre 1958
The narrator of 2 is a character in 1.

Smith, S. Kaye-
1 Johanna Godden
2 Johanna Godden married, and other stories
☐
1 Children's summer [Summer holiday]
2 Selina is older [Selina]
☐
1 Superstition corner
2 Galleybird
3 The end of the House of Alard

Smith, T.
1 The jovial ghosts
2 Topper takes a trip

Smith, V. C.
1 Song of the unsung
2 Candles to the dawn

Smith, W.
1 When the lion feeds 1965
2 The sound of thunder 1966
Two novels of the Boer War.

Smollett, T. G.
1 The adventures of Roderick Random
2 The history of Peregrine Pickle
Connected by the minor character, Morgan.

Smyth, E.
1 Impressions that remained
2 Streaks of life
3 Final burning of boats
4 As time went on
5 What happened next
N.F. Autobiography

Smythe, P.
1 Jump for joy
2 Jump ahead
3 Jumping round the world
N.F. Autobiography

Snaith, J. C.
1 Love Lane
2 The council of seven

Snow, C. P.
STRANGERS AND BROTHERS SERIES:
1 Strangers and brothers
2 The light and the dark
3 Time of hope
4 The masters
5 The new men
6 Homecomings 1956
7 The conscience of the rich 1958
8 The affair 1960
9 Corridors of power 1964
Nos. 4 and 8 are direct sequels.
A series of novels depicting various aspects of the contemporary scene in which the narrator, Lewis Eliot takes part. In some, 'Time of hope' for example, he is the principal character, in others hardly more than a spectator.
The Series will comprise 10 or 12 novels. The general theme is the manifestation and corruption of power.

Snow, E.
1 Red star over China
2 The other side of the river 1962
N.F. Travel and politics. 1 was published in the '30's. 2 tells the story of changes since the first visit.

Snowden, K.
1 King Jack
2 Jack the outlaw

Somers, D.
MAJOR JOHN FALCONBRIDGE:
1 Falcon–Queen's messenger
2 Falcon and the diamond necklace

Somers, P.
HUGH CURTIS AND MOLLIE BROWN,
REPORTERS:
1 Beginners' luck 1957
2 Operation piracy 1958
3 The shivering mountain 1959

Somerville, E. Œ., and **Ross, M.,**
pseud. [**V. Martin**]
1 Some experinces of an Irish R.M.
2 Further experiences of an Irish R.M.
3 The Irish R.M. and his experiences
4 In Mr. Knox's country
*3 is a collection of the stories in 1 and 2
with one addition.*

Soubiran, A.
THE STORY OF JEAN NERAC:
1 The doctors
2 The healing oath
3 Bedlam

South, A.
1 Broken house
2 The dwelling place
3 Renewal

Southworth, Mrs. E. D. E. N.
1 A beautiful friend
2 Victor's triumph
□
1 The bride's fate
2 The changed brides
□
1 Cruel as the grave
2 Tried for her life
□
1 Fair play
2 How he won her
□
1 The family doom
2 The maiden widow
□
1 The hidden hand
2 Capitola's peril
□
1 Ishmael

2 Self-raised
□
1 The lost heir of Linlithgow
2 A noble lord
□
1 Only a girl's heart
2 The rejected bride
3 Gertrude Haddon
□
1 Unknown
2 The mystery of Raven Rocks
3 The phantom wedding
4 A perfect love

Souvestre, P., *and* **Allain, M.**
1 Fantomas
2 The exploits of Juve
3 Messengers of evil
4 A nest of spies
5 A royal prisoner
6 Slippery as sin
7 A limb of Satan
8 The lord of terror
9 Juve in the dock
10 Fantomas captured
11 The revenge of Fantomas
12 Bulldog and rats

Spain, N.
MIRIAM BIRDSEYE SERIES:
1 Cinderella goes to the morgue
2 R. in the month
3 Not wanted on voyage
4 Out damned tot

Spearman, F. H.
1 Held for orders
2 Nerve of Foley, etc.

Spears, Sir E.
WORLD WAR I:
1 Liaison 1914
2 Prelude to victory
ASSIGNMENT TO CATASTROPHE:
1 Prelude to Dunkirk
2 The fall of France
Memoirs of two World Wars.

Sperber, M.
1 Wind and the flame
2 To dusty death
3 The lost boy 1956
A trilogy on the Partisans in Yugoslavia.

Sperry, A.
CHAD POWELL:
1 Rain forest
2 Thunder country

Spicer, B.
CARNEY WILDE SERIES:
1 The dark light
2 Blues for the Prince
3 The golden door
4 The long green
5 Blacksheep run
6 Taming of Carney Wilde
7 Exit, running

Spielhagen, F.
1 Problematic characters
2 Through night to light

Spiller, A.
CHIEF INSPECTOR 'DUCK' MALLARD
SERIES:
1 You can't get away with murder
2 And thereby hangs
3 Brief candle
4 Phantom circus
5 Murder without malice
6 Muder is a shady business
7 Black cap for murder 1955
8 Brains trust for murder 1955
9 Ring twice for murder 1956
10 The black rat 1956
11 It's in the bag 1956
12 Murder on a shoestring 1958

Spring, H.
1 Heaven lies about us
2 In the meantime
3 And another thing
N.F. Autobiography
☐
1 Shabby tiger
2 Rachel Rosing
☐
1 Hard facts
2 Dunkerley's
3 Time and the hour

Springs, E. W.
1 Warbirds
2 Warbirds and ladybirds
3 Above the bright blue sky

Spykman, E. C.
THE CARES FAMILY:
1 A lemon and a star 1958
2 Wild angel 1960
3 Terrible, horrible Edie 1961

Stacpoole, H. de V.
1 The blue horizon
2 In blue waters
☐
1 The blue lagoon
2 The garden of God
3 The gates of morning
☐
1 The order of release
2 Monsieur de Rochefort

Stafford, A.
1 Light me a candle
2 Bess
3 Great Mrs. Pennington
4 The time it takes
Novels of Victorian and Edwardian London.

Stagge, J.
DR, WESTLAKE SERIES:
1 Murder gone to earth
2 Murder or mercy
3 Murder in the stars
4 Funeral for five
5 Call and Hebise
6 Light from a lantern
7 Death and the dear girls
8 Death's old sweet song
9 The three fears

Standish, R.
1 The three bamboos
2 The small general

Stanford, J. K.
LT.-COL. JAMES GORE-BUNBURY SERIES:
1 Guns wanted 1956
2 Jimmy Bundobust 1958
A minor character in 1 is the hero of 2, where he is trying to settle in village life after retirement.

Stannard, Mrs. H. E. V., *see* Winter, J. S.

Stapledon, O.
1 Last and first men
2 Last men in London
The sequel is an expanded section of the first book.

Stark, F.
1 Traveller's prelude (1893–1927)
2 Beyond Euphrates (1928–1933)
3 Coast of incense (1933–1939)
N.F. *Autobiography*
1 Ionia
2 The Lycian shore
N.F. *Travel in Greece and Asia Minor.*

Starr, L.
1 To please myself
2 To please myself again
N.F. *Autobiography*

Steen, M.
THE FLOOD TRILOGY:
1 The sun is my undoing
2 Twilight on the floods
3 Phoenix rising [Jehovah blues]
SPANISH TRILOGY
1 Matador
2 One-eyed moon
3 The tavern

Steen, S.
1 Sailor, beware!
2 Watch it, sailor! 1961

Steinbeck, J.
1 Cannery Row
2 Sweet Thursday

Stendhal, *pseud.* [**H. Beyle,**]
LUCIEN LEUWEN:
1 The green huntsman
2 The telegraph

Stern, G. B.
THE RAKONITZ FAMILY:
1 Tents of Israel [The matriarch]
2 A deputy was king
3 Mosaic
4 Shining and free
5 The young matriarch
☐
1 Monogram

2 Another part of the forest
3 Trumpet voluntary
4 Benefits forgot
5 A name to conjure with
6 All in good time
7 The way it worked out
"The ragbag chronicles that apparently I am under compulsion to write every three or four years". From 'A name to conjure with'.

Stevenson, D. E.
DRUMBERLEY SERIES:
1 Vittoria cottage
2 Music in the hills
3 Winter and rough weather [Shoulder the sky]
☐
1 Celia's house
2 Listening valley
☐
1 Mrs. Tim
2 Mrs. Tim carries on
3 Mrs. Tim gets a job
4 Mrs. Tim flies home
1 was originally published as two volumes, 'Mrs. Tim of the Regiment' and 'Golden days'.
☐
1 Miss Buncle's book
2 Miss Buncle married
3 The two Mrs. Abbotts
☐
1 Five windows
2 The tall stranger 1957
N.B. The first volume contains a brief appearance of the main character (Barbie France) in volume 2.
☐
1 Katharine Wentworth 1964
2 Katharine's marriage 1965
One of the characters Mac Aslan, appears in an earlier book 'Smouldering fire', reissued 1966.
☐
1 Amberwell 1954
2 Summerhills 1956
Not sequels in plot, but the Ayrton family appears in both novels.

Stevenson, R. L.
1 An inland voyage

2 Travels with a donkey
N.F. Travel

Steward, P.
1 Gaboreau
2 Gaboreau the terrible

Stewart, A.
1 Alicella
2 Family tapestry
N.F. Autobiography

Stewart, A. M.
1 Gerald
2 Eustace

Stewart, C.
1 The residency 1962
2 Jethro's daughters 1964
Novels of Victorian India

Stewart, F. L.
1 I wore my rabbit
2 Flowering in the sun
3 Bees in our bonnet 1961
N.F. Farming in Natal

Stewart, M.
1 Adam Square
2 Mysterious way

Stil, A.
THE FIRST CLASH:
1 The water tower
2 A gun is unloaded
3 Paris is with us

Stinde, J.
1 The Buchholz family
2 The Buchholzes in Italy
3 Frau Wilhelmine
Masterful Wilhelmine [The hausfrau rampant] edited by E. V. Lucas, is a condensation of the series. In view of the date [1916] the selection is probably not calculated to show the best of the author's work.

Stockley, C.
DALLA SERIES:
1 Dalla the lion cub
2 The leopard in the bush

Stockton, F. R.
1 The adventures of Captain Horn
2 Mrs. Cliff's yacht
□
1 Captain Chap
2 The young master of Hyson Hall
□
1 The casting away of Mrs. Lecks and Mrs. Aleshine
2 The Dusantes
□
1 Rudder Grange
2 The Rudder Grangers abroad; and other stories
3 Pomona's travels
□
1 The casting away of Mrs. Lecks and Mrs. Aleshine 1886
2 The Dusantes 1888
Re-issued in one volume 1956.

Stoekl, Baroness de
1 Not all vanity
2 My dear Marquis
3 When men had time to love

Stoker, B.
1 Dracula
2 Dracula's guest; and other stories

Stong, P.
1 State fair
2 Return in August
The sequel is set 20 years later.
1 Buckskin breeches
2 Ivanhoe Keeler
The hero of 2 is a minor character in 1.

Storm, J.
SARAH VANESSA SERIES:
1 Dark emerald
2 Bitter rubies
3 Deadly diamond

Story, J. T.
ALBERT ARGYLE:
1 Live now, pay later 1961
2 Something for nothing 1963
3 The urban district lover 1964

Stout, R.
NERO WOLFE SERIES:
1 Fer-de-Lance
2 The league of frightened men
3 The rubber band
4 The red box
5 Some buried Caesar
6 Over my dead body
7 Black orchids
8 Where there's a will
9 Not quite dead enough
10 Too many cooks
11 The silent speaker
12 Too many women
13 More deaths than one [And be a villain]
14 Trouble in triplicate
15 The second confession
16 Three doors to death
17 In the best families
18 Curtains for three
19 Murder by the book
20 Triple jeopardy
21 Out goes she [Prisoner's base]
22 The golden spiders
23 Three men out
24 The black mountain
25 The final deduction
26 Before midnight
27 The black mountain 1955
28 Three witnesses 1956
29 Might as well be dead 1957
30 Three for the choir 1958
31 If death ever slept 1959
32 Crime and again 1959
33 Champagne for one 1959
34 Murder in style 1960
35 Three at Wolfe's door 1960
36 Too many clients 1961
37 Homicide trinity 1962
38 Gambit 1963
39 Trio for blunt instruments 1964
40 A right to die 1965
41 The doorbell rang 1966
TECUMSEH FOX SERIES:
1 Double for death

2 Broken vase
3 Bad for business

Stowe, Mrs. H. B.
HARRY HENDERSON SERIES:
1 My wife and I
2 We are our neighbours
□
1 Uncle Tom's cabin
2 Key to Uncle Tom's cabin
□
1 Oldtown folks
2 Sam Lawson's fireside stories

Strachey, J., *see* Blake, *pseud.*

Straker, J. F.
DAVID WRIGHT SERIES:
1 A coil of rope 1962
2 Final witness 1963
INSPECTOR PITT SERIES:
1 Postman's knock
2 Pick up the pieces
3 Ginger horse 1955
4 A gun to play with 1956
5 Good-bye Aunt Charlotte 1958

Strange, J. S.
GEORGE HONEGGER SERIES:
1 Murder gives a lovely light
2 Come to judgement

Strange, N. K.
KENYA SERIES:
1 Kenya dawn
2 Kenya calling
3 A wife in Kenya
4 Kenya moon
5 Courtship in Kenya
6 Youth comes to Kenya

Strange, O.
1 Sudden
2 Sudden gold-seeker
3 Sudden outlawed
4 Sudden makes war
5 Sudden rides again
6 Sudden takes the trail
7 Sudden plays a hand

Stratford, E. Wingfield-
1 Charles, King of England

2 King Charles and King Pym
3 King Charles the martyr
N.F.

Strathesk, J. [J. Todd]
1 Bits from Blinkbonny
2 More bits from Blinkbonny

Stratton-Porter, G., *see* Porter, G.
Stratton-

Streatfield, N.
1 The vicarage family
2 Away from the vicarage
N.F. *Autobiography*

Street, J. H.
DABNEY FAMILY SERIES:
1 Oh promised land (War of 1812)
2 Tap roots (1858–1865)
3 By valour and arms (Civil War)
4 Tomorrow we reap (1890).
   By J. H. Street and J. S. Childers
5 Mungo Dabney (Spanish-American War)
WINGO SERIES:
1 The gauntlet
2 High calling

Street, P.
1 Between the tides
2 Beyond the tides
N.F. *Books on the fishing industry*

Streeter, E.
1 Dere Mable
2 That's me all over
3 Same old Bill, eh Mable!

Stretton, H. [*pseud.*** S. Smith,]**
1 Jessica's first prayer
2 Jessica's mother

Stribling, T. S.
COLONEL MILT VAIDEN TRILOGY:
1 The forge
2 The store
3 Unfinished cathedral

Strindberg, A.
1 Son of a servant
2 Red room

3 Confession of a fool
4 Fair haven and foul strand
   These are all parts of Strindberg's autobiographical novel 'Tjanstikinnan's son'. A further title 'Growth of a soul' is presumably a condensation, but the compiler has been unable to consult it.

Stringer, A.
1 The prairie wife
2 The prairie mother
3 The prairie child

Strode, W. Chetham-
1 Three men and a girl
2 Top of the milk

Strong, L. A. G.
1 The garden
2 Sea wall
   Not a sequel but a companion volume.

Stuart, E. [Leroy, A. C.]
1 Harum Scarum
2 Harum Scarum's fortune
3 Harum Scarum married

Stuart-Wortley, V., *see* Wortley, V.
Stuart-

Stuart-Young, J. M., *see* Young, J. M.
Stuart-

Studley, E.
1 Teddy Boy's picnic
2 Life is for living
N.F. *Autobiography*

Stuntz, S. C., *see* Conrad, S., *pseud.*

Sue, E.
MYSTERIES OF THE PEOPLE SERIES:
1 The gold sickle
2 The brass bell
3 The iron collar
4 The silver cross
5 The casque's lark
6 The poniard's hilt
7 The branding needle
8 The abbatical crozier
9 The Carlovingian coins
10 The iron arrowhead

Sue, E. (*contd.*)
11 The infant's skull
12 The pilgrim's shell
13 The iron pincers
14 The iron trivet
15 The executioner's knife
16 The pocket bible
17 The blacksmith's hammer
18 The sword of honour
19 The galley slave's ring
*These books are a chronicle of a family
from 57 B.C. to 1851 A.D.*

Suhl, Y.
1 One foot in America
2 Cowboy on a wooden horse

Sullivan, T. F.
Day and night stories
Two series.

Supervielle, J.
1 Colonel's children
2 Survivor

Surtees, R. S.
1 Jorrock's jaunts and jollities
2 Handley Cross
3 Hillingdon Hall

Sutcliffe, H.
1 An episode in Arcady
2 A bachelor in Arcady
3 A benedick in Arcady
□
1 A man of the moors
2 Through sorrow's gates
□
1 Shameless Wayne
2 Red o' the feud

Sutherland, H.
1 The arches of the years
2 A time to keep
3 In my path
N.F. Autobiography

Sutton, G.
1 The rowan tree
2 Shepherd's warning
3 Smoke across the fell
4 North star

5 Fleming of Honister
*Chronicles of the Fleming family in the
Fell country.*
*This is chronological order, not order of
publication.*

Sutton, M.
1 Children of Ruth
2 The promised land

Swan, A. S. [Smith, Mrs. B.]
1 Elizabeth Glen
2 Mrs. Keith Hamilton, M.B.
□
1 A son of Erin
2 An American woman
□
1 A maid of the isles
2 Macleod's wife

Swanson, N. H.
1 The Judas tree
2 The silent drum
3 Unconquered
*The first three of a projected series of
novels on American pioneer life. Not
completed.*

Swinnerton, F.
1 The woman from Sicily 1956
2 A tigress in Prothero 1958
3 The Grace divorce 1960
4 Quadrille 1965
*A sequence of novels about a family in
four generations – all actors. The scene
is a small country town in East Anglia.*
□
1 Background with chorus
2 Figures in the foreground
N.F. Autobiography

Sykes, W. S.
INSPECTOR DRURY SERIES:
1 The missing money-lender
2 The harness of death

Syrett, N.
1 The Victorians
2 Rose Cottingham married

Tabori, P.
SPIDER AND MOONLIGHT: A TRILOGY:
1 Two forests
2 Uneasy giant
3 Heritage of mercy

Taffrail, *pseud.* **[T. Dorling,]**
1 Pincher Martin, O.D.
2 'Oh, Joshua!'
　□
1 Pirates
2 The lonely bungalow

Tangye, D.
1 A gull on the roof
2 A cat in the window
3 A drake at the door
4 A donkey in the meadow

Tarkington, B.
1 Penrod 1914
2 Penrod and Sam 1916
3 Penrod Jashber 1929
　Later published in one volume, 'Penrod,
　his complete story' 1931.
GROWTH TRILOGY:
1 The turmoil
2 The magnificent Ambersons
3 The Midlander

Tasaki, H.
THE STORY OF PRIVATE TAKEO:
1 Long the imperial way
2 The mountains remain

Taylor, D.
1 Lights across the Delaware 1954
2 Farewell to Valley Forge 1955
3 Storm the last rampart 1960
　A trilogy of the American War of
　Independence.

Taylor, P. A.
ASEY MAYO SERIES:
1 Mystery of the Cape Cod tavern
2 Tinkling symbol
3 Sandbar majestic
4 Figure away
5 Octagon house
6 Annulet of guilt
7 Banbury bog
8 Spring harrowing

9 The criminal C.O.D.
10 Deadly sunshade
11 Perennial boarder
12 Six iron spiders
13 Going going gone
14 Proof of the pudding
15 Asey Mayo trio
16 Punch with care
17 Diplomatic corpse

Taylor, P. M.
INDIAN HISTORY TRILOGY:
1 Tara
2 Ralph Darnell
3 Seeta

Teilhet, D. *and* **H.**
BARON VON KAZ SERIES:
1 The ticking terror murders
2 The feather cloak murders
3 The crimson hair murders
4 The broken face murders

Telscombe, A.
MISS BAGSHOT SERIES:
1 Miss Bagshot goes to Moscow 1960
2 Miss Bagshot goes to Tibet 1961

Temple, P.
1 The Tyler mystery 1957
2 East of Algiers 1959

Tempski, A. von
1 Born in Paradise
2 Aloha (My love to you)
N.F. Autobiography

Terhune, A. P.
1 Lad
2 Bruce
3 Buff
4 Further adventures of Lad
5 Wolf
6 Gray Dawn
7 Lad of Sunny bank
8 The way of a dog
　Stories of dogs owned by Sunny bank
　Kennels

Tey, J.
DETECTIVE INSPECTOR GRANT SERIES:
1 The man in the queue

Tey, J. (*contd.*)
2 A shilling for candles
3 The Franchise affair
4 To love and be wise
5 The daughter of time
6 The singing sands

Thackeray, W. M.
1 The history of Henry Esmond
2 The Virginians
☐
1 The history of Pendennis
2 The Newcomes
3 The book of Philip
Though not sequels, many of the characters appear in all three books.

Thane, E.
WILLIAMSBURG SERIES:
1 Dawn's early light (American Revolution)
2 Yankee stranger (Civil War)
3 Ever after (Spanish-American War)
4 The light heart (World War I)
5 Kissing kin (1920–1930)
6 This was tomorrow (1934–1938)
7 Homing (1938–1941) 1958

Thayer, C.
1 Bears in the caviar
2 Hands across the caviar
N.F. Wartime experiences of a diplomatist.

Thayer, L.
PETER CLANCY SERIES:
1 The mystery of the thirteenth floor
2 The unlatched door
3 The puzzle
4 Sinister mark
5 The key
6 Poison
7 Alias Dr. Ely
8 The darkest spot
9 Set a thief
10 Dead men's shoes
11 The last shot
12 The glass knife
13 To catch a thief
14 The Scrimshaw millions
15 Hell-gate tides
16 The counterfeit bill

17 The second shot
18 The death weed
19 Red-handed
20 Murder in the mirror
21 Death in the gorge
22 Last trump
23 This man's doom
24 Ransom racket
25 The strange Sylvester affair
26 Lightening strikes twice
27 Stark murder
28 X marks the spot
29 Guilty
30 Persons unknown
31 Halowee'n homicide
32 Murder is out
33 Murder on location
34 Accessory after the fact
35 Hanging's too good
36 A plain case of murder
37 Accident, manslaughter or murder
38 Five bullets
39 A hair's breadth
40 The jaws of death
41 Murder stalks the circle
42 Out, brief candle
43 A clue for Clancy
44 Death within the vault
45 Civil root
46 Too long endured
47 Clancy's secret mission
48 Prisoner pleads not guilty
49 No holiday for death
50 Murder in the Pacific
51 Web of hate
52 Two ways to die
53 Dead on arrival
54 Fatal alibi
55 And one cried murder 1962

Thibault, J. A. *see* France, A., *pseud.*

Thiess, F.
TETRALOGY OF 20TH CENTURY GERMANY:
1 Farewell to Paradise
2 Gateway to life
3 The devil's shadow
4 Der Zentaur (not yet translated)

Thirkell, A.
BARSETSHIRE SERIES:
1 High rising

2 Wild strawberries
3 The demon in the house
4 August folly
5 Summer half
6 Pomfret Towers
7 The Brandons
8 Before lunch
9 Cheerfulness breaks in
10 Northbridge Rectory
11 Marling Hall
12 Growing up
13 The headmistress
14 Miss Bunting
15 Peace breaks out
16 Private enterprise
17 Love among the ruins
18 The old bank house
19 County chronicle
20 Duke's daughter
21 Happy returns
22 Jutland cottage
23 What did it mean?
24 Enter Sir Robert 1955
25 Never too late 1956
26 A double affair 1957
27 Close quarters 1958
28 Love at all ages 1959
29 Three score and ten (originally announced as 'The vicar's daughter')
Completed by C. A. Lejeune 1961
Many characters recur throughout these novels, 'Each is a separate entity, but it is perhaps less confusing to read them in order, as it gives more clue to the people'. Author.

Thomas, H.
1 As it was
2 World without end

Thomas, L.
1 The sea devil
2 Sea devil's foc'sle
N.F.

Thompson, E.
1 Introducing the Arnisons
2 John Arnison
□
1 In Araby Orion
2 Lament for Adonis

1 An Indian day 1927
2 A farewell to India 1931
3 An end of the hours 1938

Thompson, F.
1 Lark rise
2 Over to Candleford
3 Candleford Green
4 Still glides the stream
N.F. Autobiography

Thompson, J. M.
1 The French Revolution
2 Napoleon Bonaparte: his rise and fall
3 Louis Napoleon and the second empire
A trilogy on modern French history.

Thompson, K.
1 Great house
2 Mandevilla
3 Sugarbird 1963
4 Richard's way 1965

Thompson, L. S.
1 Death stops the show
2 Hear not my steps

Thomson, A. A.
1 Marigold cottage
2 Trust Tilty
3 Steeple Thatchby

Thomson, Sir B.
1 P.C. Richardson's first case
2 Richardson scores again
3 Richardson goes abroad
4 Richardson solves a Dartmoor mystery

Thomson, D.
1 Daniel
2 Break in the sun

Thorndyke, R.
1 Dr. Syn on the high seas
2 Dr. Syn returns

Thorndyke, R. (*contd.*)
3 Further adventures of Dr. Syn
4 Dr. Syn
5 Amazing quest of Dr. Syn
6 Courageous exploits of Dr. Syn
7 The shadow of Dr. Syn

Thowald, J.
1 Century of the surgeon
2 Triumph of surgery
N.F. Medicine

Thurston, E. T.
1 The antagonists
2 Richard Furlong
3 The achievement
   Published in one volume as 'The achievement of Richard Furlong'.
BELLWATTLE AND CRUIKSHANK SERIES:
1 The garden of resurrection
2 Tares
3 The patchwork papers
4 Sheepskins and grey russet
JOHN GREY SERIES:
1 The city of beautiful nonsense
2 The world of wonderful reality

Thurston, L. M.
1 How Charley Roberts became a man
2 How Eva Roberts gained her education
3 Charley and Eva's home in the West
4 The children of Amity Court

Tibber, R.
1 No white coat 1958
2 Love on my list 1959
3 Patients of a saint 1961
N.F. Autobiography. Story of a doctor.

Tilman, H. W.
1 Mischief in Patagonia
2 Mischief among the penguins
3 Mischief in Greenland

Tilsley, F.
1 Voice of the crowd
2 Brother Nap

Tiltman, M. H.
1 Quality Chase

2 Quality Chase's daughter
   Stories of an antique dealer.
COUNTRY LIFE TRILOGY:
1 Cottage pie
2 Little place in the country
3 The birds began to sing

Tilton, A.
LEONIDAS WITHERALL SERIES:
1 Cut direct
2 Cold steal
3 Left leg

Timms, E. V.
AUSTRALIAN SAGA:
1 Forever to remain
2 Pathway of the sun
3 Beckoning shore
4 Valleys beyond
5 The challenge
6 Scarlet frontier
7 The fury
8 They came from the sea 1956
9 Shining harvest 1957
10 Robina 1958
11 The big country 1959
   Series of novels on the development of Australia since 1831.

Tinker, F. M. *and* **E.**
OLD NEW ORLEANS:
1 Widows only
2 Strife
3 Closed shutters
4 Mardi Gras masks

Tolkein, J. R. R.
THE LORDS OF THE RING:
1 The Hobbit 1950
2 The fellowship of the ring 1952
3 The two towers 1954
4 The return of the King 1955
   An allegory of a mythical world. 1 describes the finding of the ring, the sequels which are a separate cycle, its consequences.

Tomkinson, C.
1 Les girls
2 African follies
3 What a performance
N.F. Autobiography

Topelius, Z.
1 Times of Gustaf Adolf
2 Times of battle and of rest
3 Times of Charles XII
4 Times of Frederick I
5 Times of Linnaeus
6 Times of alchemy

Torgerson, E. D.
CAPTAIN MONTIGNY SERIES:
1 The murderer returns
2 The cold finger curse
3 Murder for profit

Tourgee, A. W.
1 A fool's errand
2 The invisible empire

Tovey, D.
1 Cats in the belfry
2 Cats in May
3 Life with grandma 1964
N.F. Autobiography

Townend, P.
MCGILL SERIES:
1 Man on the end of a rope 1960
2 The road to El Suida 1961

Townsend, E. W.
1 Chimmie Fadden explains, Major Max expounds
2 Chimmie Fadden, Major Max, and other stories

Toy, B.
1 A fool on wheels
2 A fool in the desert
3 A fool strikes oil
N.F. Travels in North Africa and Arabia.

Toye, F.
1 For what we have received
2 Truly thankful
N.F. Autobiography

Toynbee, P.
1 Pantaloon 1962
2 Two brothers 1964
Two novels in verse.

Tracey, L.
1 An American emperor
2 The lost provinces
DETECTIVES FURNEAUX AND WILSON SERIES:
1 Passing of Charles Lanson
2 Park Lane mystery
3 The second baronet
4 The black cat
5 The Gleave mystery
6 The third miracle
7 Law of the talon
8 Women in the case
9 One girl in a million

Traill, P.
MR. CRIBBAGE SERIES:
1 Wedding of the jackal
2 So sits the turtle
3 Under the plane trees
MR PRENTICE SERIES:
1 The portly peregrine
2 Wings of tomorrow
3 Rope of sand

Train, A.
EPHRAIM TUTT, ATTORNEY-AT-LAW:
1 Tutt and Mrs. Tutt
2 Adventures of Ephraim Tutt
3 The hermit of Turkey Hollow
4 By advice of counsel
5 Tut tut Mr. Tutt
6 Page Mrs. Tutt
7 When Tutt meets Tutt
8 Tutt for Tutt
9 Mr. Tutt takes the stand
10 Old man Tutt
11 Mr. Tutt comes home
12 Mr. Tutt finds a way
13 Yankee lawyer
Collections of short stories. Some may be repeated in various volumes.

Tranquilli, S., *see* Silone, I., *pseud.*

Tranter, N.
1 MacGregor's gathering
2 The clansman
Scotland in the 18th century.
□
1 Cheviot chase

Tranter, N. (*contd.*)
2 Night riders
    □
1 The master of Gray 1961
2 The courtesan 1963
3 Past master 1965
    Scotland in the 16th century.

Trapp, M. A.
1 The Trapp family singers
2 The Trapp family on wheels
N.F. Autobiography

Treat, L.
MITCH TAYLOR AND JUB FREEMAN:
1 V as in victim
2 H as in hunted
3 Q as in quicksand
4 F as in flight
5 T as in trapped
    There is a short story, 'L as in loot' in
    Ellery Queen's mystery annual, 1965.

Treger, A.
1 Probationer nurse
2 Maternity nurse
N.F. Autobiography

Trench, J.
MARTIN COTTERELL SERIES:
1 Docker dead
2 Dishonoured bones
3 What rough beast

Treneer, A.
1 School house in the wind
2 Cornish years
3 Stranger in the Midlands
N.F. Autobiography

Trevelyan, G. M.
1 Garibaldi and the defence of the Roman Republic
2 Garibaldi and the thousand
3 Garibaldi and the making of Italy
N.F. History
ENGLAND UNDER QUEEN ANNE:
1 Blenheim
2 Ramillies and the Union with Scotland
3 The peace and the protestant succession

Trevena, J. [E. G. Henham]
DARTMOOR TRILOGY:
1 Furze the cruel
2 Granite
3 Heather

Trewin, J. C.
1 Up from the Lizard
2 Down to the lion
N.F. Autobiography

Trollope, A.
CHRONICLES OF BARSETSHIRE:
1 The warden
2 Barchester Towers
3 Dr. Thorne
4 Framley Parsonage
5 The small house at Allington
6 Last chronicle of Barset
7 Barchester pilgrimage, by R. A. Knoxe
MANOR HOUSE NOVELS:
1 Orley Farm
2 The Vicar of Bullhampton
3 Is he Popenjoy?
4 John Caldigate
5 The Belton estate
PARLIAMENTARY NOVELS:
1 The Eustace diamonds
2 Can you forgive her?
3 Phineas Finn
4 Phineas Redux
5 The Prime Minister
6 The Duke's children
    Parliamentary Novels are also known
    as 'Palliser' group. O.U.P. edition
    contains a 'Who's Who of characters'
    with cross references to the novels by
    R. W. Chapman.

Trollope, Mrs. F.
1 Widow Barnaby
2 Adventures of the Barnabys in America

Troubetzkoy, Princess, *see* Rives, A.

Troy, S.
INSPECTOR SMITH SERIES:
1 Half way to murder
2 Tonight and tomorrow
3 Drunkard's end

4 Second cousin removed
5 Waiting for Oliver
6 Don't play with the rough boys
7 Cease upon midnight
8 No more a roving

Troyat, H.
THE SEED AND THE FRUIT:
1 Amèlie in love
2 Amèlie and Pierre
3 Elizabeth
4 Tender and violent Elizabeth
5 The encounter
The original French order is:
1 Les semelles et les moissons
2 Amèlie
3 La grive
4 Tendre et violente Elizabeth
5 La rencontre
*The English and French volumes do not
exactly correspond. There is a connection with 'The Danov family' series in
that a member of that family appears in 5.*
LA LUMIÈRE DES JUSTES:
1 Les compagnons de Coquelicot
2 La Barynia
3 La gloire des vaincus
4 Les dames de Siberie
5 Sophie ou la fin des combats
*1 and 2 have been translated under the
titles 'The brotherhood of the red poppy',
and 'The baronness'.*
THE DANOV FAMILY SERIES:
1 My father's house
2 Sackcloth and ashes
3 Strangers in the land
*The 'Red and the white' and 'Strangers
on earth' are parts of the above under
different titles. The original French
order is:*
TANT QUE LA TERRE DURERA:
1 Tant que la terre durera
2 Le sac et la cendre
3 Etrangers sur la terre

Truman, H. S.
1 Year of decisions
2 Years of trial and hope
N.F. *Autobiography*

Truss, S.
INSPECTOR GIDLEIGH SERIES:

1 The hidden men 1959
2 One man's death 1960

Tucker, A.
1 The man Miss Susie loved
2 Miss Susie Slagle's

Tucker, C., (A. L. O. E., *pseud.*)
1 The giant killer
2 Battling with the world

Tuite, H.
1 The Pottleton bridge club
2 Mr. Pottleton's bridge parties
□
1 Helpless Annie
2 Helpless Annie's ideas

Turgenev, I. S.
1 Dimitri Roudine. *Same as* Rudin
2 A house of gentlefolk. *Same as* A
nobleman's retreat
□
1 Fathers and children. *Same as* Fathers
and Sons
2 Virgin soil

Turner, E. T.
1 Legal T leaves
2 More T leaves

Turner, J.
RAMPION SAVAGE SERIES:
1 Murder at Landred Hall
2 A death by the sea
3 The dark index
4 The glass interval 1961
5 The nettleshade 1962
6 The slate landscape 1964
7 The blue mirror 1965

Turner, James
THE STORY OF NICHOLAS DE LA HAYE:
1 The crimson moth 1962
2 The long avenues 1964
A study of childhood and adolescence.

Turner, J. V.
AMOS PETRIE SERIES:
1 Death must have laughter
2 Who spoke last
3 Amos Petrie's puzzle

Turner, M.
1 Story of David Blythe
2 Another moon
Not strictly sequels but characters recur.

Turner, P.
1 Colonel Shepperton's clock 1964
2 The Grange at High Force 1965

Turner, S.
1 Over the counter 1962
2 A farmer's wife 1963
3 The farm at King's Standing 1964
N.F. Autobiography

Turner, W. J.
1 Blow for balloons
2 Henry Airbubble in search of a circumference to his breath

Turpin, A.
1 My flat and her apartment 1963
2 The box 1965
The narrator is the same in both novels.

Tute, W.
1 The Felthams
2 The younger Felthams

Tuttle, W. C.
HASHKNIFE SERIES:
1 The medicine man
2 Ghost trails
3 Thicker than water
4 Morgan trail
5 Santa Dolores stage
6 Hashknife of Stormy river
7 Tumbling river range
8 The dead line
9 Arizona ways [Hashknife of Double Bar]
10 Hashknife lends a hand
11 Hashknife of the canyon trail
12 Bluffer's luck
13 Hidden blood
14 Trouble trailer
15 Shot gun gold
16 Valley of suspicion 1964
17 Double-crossers of Ghost Tree 1965

Twain, M. *pseud.* **(S. L. Clemens,)**
1 Adam's diary

2 Eve's diary
□
1 Adventures of Tom Sawyer
2 Adventures of Huckleberry Finn
3 Tom Sawyer abroad
4 Tom Sawyer, detective
5 Tom Sawyer grows up, *by* C. Wood
There is a sequel to Huckleberry Finn by C. Wood.
□
1 The American claimant
2 The gilded age; *by* Twain *and* Warner

Tweedsmuir, John Buchan, 1st Baron,
see Buchan, J., 1st Baron Tweedsmuir

Tweedsmuir, Lady, *see* Buchan, S. C.

Tyler, C.
CLINT LACEY SERIES:
1 Showdown at Singing Sands
2 Ride stem stranger

Tyler, C. W.
1 Quality Bill's girl
2 Blue Jean Billy

Tytler, A. F.
1 Leila
2 Leila in England
3 Leila at home
4 Mary and Florence
5 Mary and Florence at sixteen

Ulbach, L.
1 The steel hammer
2 For fifteen years

Undset, S.
KRISTIN LAVRANSDATTER:
1 The garland [The bridal wreath]
2 The mistress of Husaby
3 The cross
Later published in one volume.
THE MASTER OF HESTVIKEN SERIES:
1 The axe
2 The snake pit
3 In the wilderness
4 The son avenger
THE MODERN SCENE:
1 Gymnadenia [The wild orchid]
2 The burning bush

Upfield, A. W.

NAPOLEON BONAPARTE SERIES:
1 Murder down under
2 Footprints in the bush
3 Death of a swagman
4 The devil's steps
5 Widows of Broome
6 Mountains have a secret
7 The new shoe
8 Murder must wait
9 Venom House
10 Death of a lake
11 Bone is pointed
12 Cake in the hatbox
13 Bony buys a woman 1957
14 The bachelors of Broken Hill 1958
15 Bony and the mouse 1959
16 Bony and the black virgin 1959
17 Bony and the white savage 1959
18 Winds of evil 1960
19 Bony and the Kelly Gang 1960
20 The mystery of Swordfish reef 1961
21 Death of a swagman 1961
22 The will of the tribe 1962
23 Madman's bend 1962
24 Bush ranger of the skies 1963
25 Mr. Jelly's business 1964
26 The Barakee mystery 1965
(*First printed in 1929 and the first of the series, but not previously published in the U.K.*)

Upson, W. H.

ALEXANDER BOTTS SERIES:
1 Alexander Botts
2 Earthworms in Europe
3 Keep 'em crawling
4 Botts in war
5 Earthworms through the ages
6 Hello, Mr. Henderson
7 No rest for Botts
All volumes of short stories.

Urquhart, F.

THE STORY OF BESSIE HIPKISS:
1 The ferret was Abraham's daughter
2 Jezebel's dust

Urquhart, M.

1 Trail on north circular
2 Girl on the waterfront
3 Dig the missing

Usher, F.

DAYE SMITH SERIES:
1 Ghost of a chance 1956
2 The lonely cage 1956
3 Portrait of fear 1957
4 The price of death 1957
5 Death is waiting 1958
6 First to kill 1959
7 Death in error 1959
8 Dig my darling 1960
9 Shot in the dark 1961
10 The faceless stranger 1961
11 Fall into my grave 1962
12 Who killed Rosie Gray 1962
13 Stairway to murder 1964

Usher, G.

DETECTIVE-SUPERINTENDENT DREXEL SERIES:
1 Death in the straw 1954
2 The Restmaster riddle 1955

Uttley, A.

1 Country child
2 Farm on the hill

Vachell, H. A.

ENGLISH COUNTRY LIFE SERIES:
1 Fishpingle
2 The soul of Susan Yellam
HARROW SCHOOL SERIES:
1 The hill
2 John Verney
3 Lord Samarkand
QUINNEY SERIES:
1 Quinney's
2 Quinney's adventures
3 Quinney's for quality
□
1 Now still came evening on
2 Twilight grey
3 In sober livery
4 Methuselah's diary
5 More from Methuselah
6 Quests
N.F. Autobiography

Vail, A.

1 Love me a little
2 The bright young things

Vaizey, Mrs. G. de H.
1 About Peggy Saville
2 More about Peggy
□
1 Pixie O'Shaughnessy
2 More about Pixie
3 Love affairs of Pixie

Vanardy, V.
1 The two-faced man
2 Something doing

Vance, L. J.
1 Lone wolf
2 The false faces
3 Lone Wolf's daughter. *Same as* Red masquerade
4 Alias the Lone Wolf
5 The Lone Wolf returns
□
1 The adventures of Terence O'Rourke
2 The pool of flame
3 The romance of Terence O'Rourke

Vandercook, J. W.
BERTRAM LYNCH SERIES:
1 Murder in Trinidad 1953
2 Murder in Fiji 1955
3 Murder in New Guinea 1959

Van der Meersch, M.
1 The poor girl
2 The hour of love 1956

Van der Post, L.
1 A bar of shadow 1956
2 The seed and the sower 1957
3 The sword and the doll 1959
Published in one volume in 1962, under title of 2. Wartime experiences of a soldier.
□
1 The lost world of the Kalahari 1958
2 The heart of the hunter 1960
N.F. Travel

Van derWater, F. F.
AMERICAN REVOLUTION SERIES:
1 Reluctant rebel 1948
2 Wings of the morning 1955
3 Day of battle 1958
4 Catch a falling star 1949

Mainly centred on the history of the State of Vermont.

Van Dine, S. S.
PHILO VANCE SERIES:
1 Benson murder case
2 Canary murder case
3 The Greene murder case
4 Bishop murder case
5 Scarab murder case
6 Dragon murder case
7 Casino murder case
8 Kennel murder case
9 Garden murder case
10 Kidnap murder case
11 Gracie Allen murder case
12 Winter murder case

Van Druten, J.
1 The vicarious years
2 The widening circle
The first volume is an autobiographical novel, the second, autobiography.

Van Gulik, R.
JUDGE DEE SERIES:
1 The Chinese bell murders 1958
2 The Chinese gold murders 1959
3 The Chinese lake murders 1960
4 The Chinese nail murders 1961
5 The Chinese maze murders 1961
6 The Emperor's pearl 1962
7 The haunted monastery 1963
8 The lacquer screen 1964
9 The red pavilion 1964
10 The willow pattern 1965
11 The monkey and the tiger 1965
12 The phantom of the temple 1966
An unusual series in that the scene is medieval China. Nos. 8 and 9 are direct sequels within the sequence.

Vanvogt, A. E.
1 The weapon shops of Isher
2 The weapon makers
Science fiction

Varé, D.
1 Maker of heavenly trousers
2 Gate of happy sparrows
3 Temple of costly experience
Later collected in one volume as 'Novels of Yen Ching'.

□
1 Laughing diplomat
2 Two imposters
N.F. *Autobiography*

Varnham, J.
INSPECTOR SEMLAKE SERIES:
1 Death rehearses
2 Travelling dead man
3 Beware of the dog.

Vaughan, C. A.
1 The invincibles
2 The wilderness

Vaughan, R.
1 Moulded in earth
2 Son of Justin
2 is about the son of Justin Peele, main character in 1.

Velikovsky, I.
1 Worlds in collision
2 Earth in upheaval
N.F. *Cosmography. A third volume has been announced but not yet published.*

Verga, G.
THE VINTI FAMILY SERIES:
1 The house by the medlar tree
2 Maestro-don Gesnaldo
Volume 2 was translated by D. H. Lawrence.

Verne, J.
CAPTAIN HATTERAS SERIES:
1 The English at the North Pole. *Same as* At the North Pole
2 The ice desert. *Same as* The field of ice. *Same as* The desert of ice
CAPTAIN NEMO SERIES:
1 20,000 leagues under the sea
2 Dropped from the clouds
3 Abandoned
4 The secret of the island
THE CRYPTOGRAM SERIES:
1 The conspirators of Trieste
2 The captives of Antekirtta
GIANT RAFT SERIES:
1 800 leagues on the Amazon
2 The cryptogram
J. R. KASALLON SERIES:
1 The survivors of the Chancellor
2 Martin Paz

KÉREBAN THE INFLEXIBLE SERIES:
1 Captain of the Guidara
2 Scarpante, the spy
THE MOON SERIES:
1 From the earth to the moon
2 Round the moon
NORTH AGAINST SOUTH SERIES:
1 Burbank the Norterner
2 Texar the Southerner
STEAM HOUSE SERIES:
1 The demon of Cawnpore
2 Tigers and traitors
THE BARSAC MISSION:
1 The city in the Sahara
2 Into the Niger bend
Both republished in 1959.
□
1 Into the abyss 1963
2 Leader of the resistance 1963
Republication in two volumes of 'A family without a name', historical novel on the 1837 rising in Quebec.
□
1 Anomalous phenomena
2 Homeward bound
Reprinted in this form, 1965, but they are parts of the novel 'Hector Servadac'.

Verner, G.
1 The cleverness of Mr. Budd
2 The return of Mr. Budd
3 Mr. Budd again
4 Mr. Budd investigates

Verney, J.
1 Going to the wars
2 A dinner of herbs 1966
N.F. *Autobiography. In 2 the author revisits the scene of his wartime imprisonment and tells the story of his escape.*

Vickers, R.
INSPECTOR CURWEN SERIES:
1 They can't hang Caroline
2 Murder in two flats
3 Gold and wine
4 Six came to dinner
DEAD ENDS SERIES:
1 The department of dead ends
2 Murder will out
There is a story in this series in Ellery Queen's 'Double Dozen', 1965.

Viereck, G. S. *and* **Eldridge, P.**
THE WANDERING JEW:
1 My first two thousand years
2 Salome the wandering Jewess
3 The invincible Adam

Vines, F.
1 The lonely shore 1959
2 So wild the sea 1961
Historical novels on Western Australia.

Vivian, E. C.
INSPECTOR HEAD SERIES:
1 Seventeen cards
2 Cigar for Inspector Head
3 Who killed Gatton
4 Tramp's evidence
5 .38 automatic
6 Evidence in blue
7 Rainbow puzzle
8 Problem by rail
9 Touch and go

Vivian, F.
INSPECTOR KNOLLIS SERIES:
1 Death of Mr. Lomas
2 Sable messenger
3 The threefold cord
4 The ninth enemy
5 Laughing dog
6 Singing masons
7 Sleeping island
8 Elusive bowman
9 The ladies of Locksley

Voynich, E. L.
1 Put off thy shoes
2 The gadfly
3 An interrupted friendship
Nos. 2 and 3 are about the Italian Revolution of 1848. No. 1 is about the great grandmother of 'The Gadfly'. There were to have been two other novels connecting the series, which have not been published. It is worthy of note that 'The Gadfly' was published in 1897, 'Put off thy shoes' in 1945.

Wade, H.
INSPECTOR POOLE SERIES:
1 The Duke of York's steps
2 No friendly drop

3 Policeman's lot
4 Constable, guard thyself
5 Bury him darkly
6 Lonely Magdalen
7 New graves at Great Norme
8 Be kind to the killer
9 Diplomat's folly
10 Too soon to die
11 Gold was our grave
12 The Litmore snatch

Waine, C.
1 Breed of the inshore
2 Sweepers

Waldman, E.
1 The land is large
2 Broad is the way

Waldy, F. H.
1 Bonnie Editha Copplestone
2 Frolic

Wall, M.
FURSEY SERIES:
1 The unfortunate Fursey
2 The return of Fursey
Humorous novels of medieval Ireland.

Wallace, D.
1 Ungava Bob
2 The gaunt gray wolf

Wallace, E.
BONES SERIES:
1 Sanders of the river
2 People of the river
3 Bosambo of the river
4 Bones
5 Keepers of the King's peace
6 Lieut. Bones
7 Bones in London
8 Sandi, the King maker
9 Bones of the river
10 Again Sanders
Continued by Francis Gerard
11 Return of Sanders of the river
12 The law of the river
13 Another Sanders
14 Justice of Sanders
FOUR JUST MEN SERIES:
1 Four just men

2 The council of justice
3 The four just men of Cordova
4 Some adventures of the four just men
5 The law of the four just men
6 The three just men
7 Again the three just men
EVANS SERIES:
1 Educated Evans
2 Good Evans
3 More Educated Evans
SUPERINTENDENT MINTER SERIES:
1 Big foot
2 Lone house mystery
RINGER SERIES:
1 The gaunt stranger
2 Again the ringer
MR. J. G. REEDER SERIES:
1 Room 13
2 Mind of Mr. J. G. Reeder
3 Terror keep
4 Red aces
5 The Gov'nor

Wallace, K.
1 I walk alone
2 Without a stair
☐
1 Grace on their doorsteps
2 And after that, the dark

Walling, R. A. J.
PHILIP TOLEFREE SERIES:
1 The fatal five minutes
2 Follow the blue car
3 The Tolliver case
4 Eight to nine
5 The five suspects
6 The cat and the corpse
7 Mr. Tolefree's reluctant witnesses
8 The corpse in the crimson slippers
9 The corpse with the dirty face
10 The mystery of Mr. Mock
11 Bury him deeper
12 The crime in Cumberland Court
13 The Coroner doubts
14 More than one serpent
15 Dust in the vault
16 They liked Entwistle
17 Why did Trelawney die
18 By hook or by crook
19 Castle-Dinas
20 The doodled asterisk

21 A corpse without a clue
22 The late unlamented

Walmsley, L.
1 Foreigners
2 Three fevers
3 Sally Lunn
4 Phantom lobster
5 Love in the sun
6 The golden waterwheel
7 The happy ending
8 Paradise Creek 1963
'Phantom lobster' was the box that held
'Three fevers,' but 'Three fevers' was
also to hold 'Foreigners'. 'Love in the
sun' fitted over the lot, but later, I was
to squeeze in a sequel to 'Three fevers',
'Sally Lunn', wherein I resolved the
age-long quarrel between the Fosdycks
and the Lunns.
From 'So Many Loves', by J. Walmsley.
6, 7, and 8 are pendants to the series.

Walpole, H.
JEREMY SERIES:
1 Jeremy
2 Jeremy and Hamlet
3 Jeremy at Crale
RUSSIA SERIES:
1 The dark forest
2 The secret city
From 'The Inquisitor'.
'My intention was to write nine novels
concerned with contemporary England,
three of them with London for a background, three dealing with provincial
town life, and three with country life.
Then the scheme developed and there
have been four novels in each division'.
LONDON GROUP:
1 The Duchess of Wrexe
2 The young enchanted
3 Wintersmoon
4 Captain Nicholas
PROVINCIAL GROUP:
1 The cathedral
2 Harmer John
3 The old ladies
4 The inquisitor
COUNTRY GROUP, KNOWN AS THE
HERRIES SAGA:
1 Rogue Herries

Walpole, H. (*contd.*)
2 Judith Paris
3 The fortress
4 Vanessa
Characters overlap in the above series.
MARADICK SERIES:
1 The captives
2 Maradick at forty
3 Fortitude
4 Portrait of a man with red hair
The following series was later classified by the author as the London Group. It overlaps the Maradick series and the original London group.
1 Fortitude
2 The Duchess of Wrexe
3 The green mirror
4 The captives
5 The young enchanted
6 Wintersmoon
7 Hans Frost
8 Captain Nicholas
9 The joyful Delaneys
The Trenchard family appears in 'Green mirror', 'Young enchanted', and again in 'Dark Forest'. Peter Westcott appears in 'Fortitude' and 'Young enchanted', and is mentioned in 'Duchess of Wrexe', 'Hans Frost', and 'Captain Nicholas'.
☐
The following two books, set in Elizabethan times, form a prelude to the 'Herries Saga'.
1 The bright pavilions
2 Katharine Christian

Walsh, J. M.
1 Once in Tiger Bay
2 Return to Tiger Bay
3 King of Tiger Bay
COLONEL ORMISTON SERIES:
1 Spies are abroad
2 The secret service girl
3 King's messenger
4 Spies in pursuit
5 The man from Whitehall
6 Spies never return
7 The silent man
8 Tiger of the night
9 The half ace
10 Spies' vendetta

11 Spies in Spain
'O.K.' KEENE SERIES:
1 Island of spies
2 Black dragon
3 Dial 999
4 Bullets for breakfast
5 King's enemies
6 Secret weapons
7 Death at his elbow
8 Spies from the skies
9 Danger zone
10 Island alert
11 Face value
12 Whispers in the dark

Walsh, M.
1 Thomasheen James
2 The smart fellow

Waltari, M. T.
1 Michael the Finn [The adventurer]
2 The Sultan's renegade [The wanderer]

Walter, W. W.
1 The pastor's son
2 The doctor's daughter
3 The arbiter of your fate

Walton, Mrs. O. F.
1 Christie's old organ
2 Christie, the King's servant

Ward, C.
1 The strange adventures of Jonathan Drew
2 Jonathan Drew, rover [Yankee rover]

Ward, Mrs. H.
1 Marcella
2 Sir George Tressady
☐
1 Robert Elsmere
2 The case of Richard Meynell

Ward, R. C.
1 Swallows eaves
2 Snow on the high ground

Ward, R. H.
NEIL FALDER: VARIATIONS ON A LIFE:
1 The conspiracy 1964

2 The wilderness 1962
3 The offenders 1963
1 published last, is about Neil as a young boy.

Ware, W.
1 Zenobia
2 Aurelian
Historical novels The Queen of Palmyra and the Emperor Aurelian.

Warfield, C. A.
1 Ferne Fleming
2 Cardinal's daughter
□
1 Monford Hall
2 Miriam's memoirs
3 Sea and shore

Warner, A.
1 Susan Clegg and her friend Mrs. Lathrop
2 Susan Clegg and her neighbours' affairs
3 Susan Clegg and a man in the house
□
1 Seeing England with Uncle John
2 Seeing France with Uncle John

Warner, A. B.
STORIES OF VINEGAR HILL:
1 The old church door
2 Golden thorns, etc.
3 An hundredfold, etc.

Warner, C. D.
1 A little journey in the world
2 The golden house
3 That fortune

Warner, R.
1 The young Caesar 1959
2 Imperial Caesar 1960
1 covers the period to his first Consulship 2 to his death.

Warner, S. *and* **A. B.**
1 Wych Hazel
2 The gold of Chickaree

Warren, C. H.
1 England is a village

2 The land is yours
3 Miles from anywhere
N.F. Descriptions of Essex country.

Warren, L.
THE WHETSTONE SAGA:
1 Foundation stone 1940
2 Whetstone walls 1952

Warren, R.
1 Where no mains flow
2 A lamb in the lounge 1959
N.F. Autobiography

Warren, V.
BRANDON SERIES:
1 Brandon takes over
2 Brandon in New York
3 Brandon returns

Warriner, T.
AMBO, MR. SCOTTER AND THE ARCH-DEACON SERIES:
1 Method in his murder
2 Ducats in her coffin
3 Death's dateless night
4 The doors of sleep
5 Death's bright angel 1956
6 She died, of course 1958

Wasserman, J.
1 The Maurizius case
2 Etzel Andergast [Doctor Kerkoven's]
3 Joseph Kerkoven's third existence

Waters, F.
1 The wild earth's nobility
2 Below grass roots
3 Dust within the rock

Watson, E. H. L.
1 An attic in Bohemia
2 Benedictine

Watson, E. Lacon-
1 The Strange family
2 Rudolph Strange
3 Last of the Stranges

Watson, H. B. M.
DICK RYDER, HIGHWAYMAN, SERIES:
1 Galloping Dick
2 The High Toby
3 The King's highway
4 As it chanced

Watson, K.
1 Litanies of life
2 Later litanies

Watson, S.
1 In the twinkling of an eye
2 The mark of the beast

Waugh, E.
BASIL SEAL SERIES:
1 Black mischief
2 Put out more flags
Basil Seal also makes a brief appearance in 'Work suspended'. A new short story, 'Basil Seal rides again', appeared in the 'Sunday Telegraph' February 10th and 17th, 1963, and was later published in a limited edition. Several characters from other novels also appear.
□
1 A handful of dust
2 Mr. Loveday's little outing
A volume of short stories one of which is an alternative last chapter to 'Handful of dust'.
WORLD WAR II TRILOGY:
1 Men at arms 1952
2 Officers and gentlemen 1955
3 Unconditional surrender 1961
A revised edition was published in 1965 under the title 'Sword of honour'. 'The product is intended (as it was originally) to be read as a single story'. Author.

Waugh, H.
CHIEF OF POLICE FELLOWS SERIES:
1 Born victim
2 The late Mrs. D. 1959
3 Road block 1960
4 Sleep long my love 1961
5 Last seen wearing 1962
6 Death and circumstance 1963
7 The missing man 1964
8 End of a party 1965

Waugh, J. L.
1 Robbie Doo
2 Cracks wi' Robbie Doo

Wawn, F. T.
1 The masterdillo
2 The road to the stars

Waye, C.
CHRISTOPHER PERRIN SERIES:
1 Figure of eight
2 Murder of Monk's Barn
3 The end of the chase
4 The Prime Minister's pencil

Weale, P. [B. L. Simpson]
1 The eternal Princess
2 The altar fire
3 The temple bells
□
1 Wang the ninth
2 Her closed hands
3 Crucifixion

Webb, A.
MR. PENDLEBURY SERIES:
1 Verdict without jury
2 Mr. Pendlebury's second case
3 Mr. Pendlebury's hat trick
4 Thank you Mr. Pendlebury
5 Mr. Pendlebury makes a catch
6 Mr. Pendlebury saw them die
7 Mr. Pendlebury and the suicide club
8 Murder in reverse
9 A queer bag of bodies

Webb, B.
1 My apprenticeship
2 Our partnership
N.F. Autobiography

Webb, G. *and* Mason, E. J.
1 The Archers of Ambridge 1955
2 The Archers intervene 1956

Webb, H. B. L. (J. Clayton, *pseud.*)
13TH CENTURY PROVENCE:
1 Gold of Toulouse
2 Dew in April
3 Anger of the north

Webb, J.
FATHER SHANLEY SERIES:
1 The big sin
2 Such women are dangerous
3 The damned lovely
4 The bad blonde

Webster, F. A. M.
1 Old Ebbie, detective up-to-date
2 Old Ebbie returns
3 The crime scientist

Webster, H. M.
SHAMUS BURKE SERIES:
1 Ballycubin mystery
2 Secret of Baron's folly
3 Tontine treasure

Webster, J.
1 Daddy Long-legs
2 Dear enemy
□
1 Just Patty
2 When Patty went to school
3 Patty and Priscilla [When Patty went to college]

Wedgwood, V.
1 The King's peace
2 The King's war
N.F. Charles I and the Civil War.

Weidman, J.
1 I can get it for you wholesale
2 What's in it for me?

Weiser, F. X.
1 The Christmas book
2 The Easter book
3 The holyday book
N.F. A trilogy on the cycle of Christian feasts.

Welcome, J.
RICHARD GRAHAM SERIES:
1 Run for cover
2 Hard to handle 1964
3 Wanted for killing 1965

Wellman, P.
1 The walls of Jericho
2 The chain

3 Jericho's daughter 1957
Novels about the town of Jericho, Kansas.

Wells, C.
FLEMING STONE SERIES:
1 Roll-top desk mystery
2 Fuller's earth
3 The curved blade
4 Clue of the eyelash
5 Black night murders
6 Broken O
7 Calling all suspects
8 Crime incarnate
9 Crime tears on
10 Devil's work
11 Gilt edged quilt
12 Importance of being murdered
13 Killer
14 Missing link
15 Murder at the casino
16 Murder in the bookshop
17 Murder on parade
18 Murder plus
19 Murder will in
20 Who killed Caldwell?

Wells, D. D.
1 Her Ladyship's elephant
2 His Lordship's leopard

Wentworth, P.
MISS SILVER SERIES:
1 Grey mask
2 The case is closed
3 Lonesome road
4 Danger point
5 The Chinese shawl
6 Miss Silver intervenes
7 The clock strikes twelve
8 The key
9 The traveller returns
10 Pilgrim's rest
11 Latter end
12 Spotlight
13 Eternity ring
14 The case of William Smith
15 Miss Silver comes to stay
16 The catherine wheel
17 The Brading collection
18 Through the wall
19 The ivory dagger

Wentworth, P. (*contd.*)
20 Anna where are you?
21 The watersplash
22 Ladies' bane
23 Out of the past
24 Vanishing point
25 The silent pool 1955
26 The Benevent treasure 1956
27 Poison in the pen 1956
28 The listening eye 1957
29 The gazebo 1957
30 The fingerprint 1958
31 Alington inheritance 1959
32 The girl in the cellar 1960
33 Miss Silver detects 1961
THE WAVENEYS SERIES:
1 A little more than kin
2 Anne Belinda

Wentworth, W.
1 Kibbo Ganey
2 Drifting Island

Wernher, H.
1 My Indian family
2 My Indian son-in-law

Weschberg, J.
1 Looking for a bluebird
2 Sweet and sour
3 Blue trout and black truffles
Autobiographical sketches and stories.

Wesker, A.
1 Chicken soup with barley
2 Roots
3 I'm talking about Jerusalem
A play trilogy

Westall, W.
1 With the Red Eagle
2 A red bridal

Westron, C.
1 Toombe Hamlet
2 Salty
3 More Salty
4 Salty ashore

Westrup, M.
1 Elizabeth's children
2 Elizabeth in retreat

Wetjen, A. R.
1 Shark Gotch of the islands
2 Chronicles of Shark Gotch
3 Shark Gotch and Typhoon Bradley
4 Shark Gotch shoots it out
5 In the wake of Shark Gotch

Weymouth, A.
INSPECTOR TREADGOLD SERIES:
1 Frozen death
2 Doctors are doubtful
3 Inspector Treadgold investigates

Wharton, E.
OLD NEW YORK SERIES:
1 False dawn
2 The old maid
3 The spark
4 New year's day

□
1 Hudson River bracketed
2 The Gods arrive

Wheatley, D.
ROGER BROOK SERIES:
1 Launching of Roger Brook
2 Shadow of Tyburn tree
3 The rising storm
4 Man who killed the king
5 Dark secret of Josephine 1958
6 The rape of Venice 1959
7 The sultan's daughter 1963
8 The wanton princess 1966
DUC DE RICHLIEU SERIES:
1 Three inquisitive people
2 The forbidden territory
3 The devil rides out
4 The golden Spaniard
5 Strange conflict
6 Code-word golden fleece
7 The second seal
8 Dangerous inheritance 1965
The earlier adventures of the Duc de Richlieu are told in:
1 Prisoner in the mask 1957
2 Vendetta in Spain 1961
JULIAN DAY SERIES:
1 The quest of Julian Day
2 The sword of fate
3 Bill for the use of a body 1964
GREGORY SALLUST SERIES:
1 The scarlet imposter

2 Faked passports
3 The black baroness
4 V for vengeance
5 Come into my parlour
6 The island where time stands still
7 Traitor's gate 1958
8 They used dark forces 1964
Gregory Sallust also appears in 'Black August' and 'Contraband', but these are not part of the same series.

Whitby, M. [Mrs. P. Hicks]
1 Awakening of Mary Fenwick
2 Mary Fenwick's daughter

White, A.
1 The lost traveller
2 The sugar house
3 Beyond the glass
'Frost in May' should be considered as part of the series, since the central character is the same, though under a different name.

White, E.
1 The path
2 The pilgrimage to Premnath

White, G. M.
1 Tess of the Storm Country
2 Secret of the Storm Country

White, J. D.
ROGER KELSO SERIES:
1 Brave Captain Kelso 1959
2 Captain of marine 1960
3 Princess of Persia 1961
4 Young Mr. Kelso 1963

White, P.
1 The infatuation of the Countess
2 The Countess and the King's diary
☐
1 Mr. Bailey Martin
2 Mr. Bailey Martin, O.B.E.

White, S. E.
1 Gold 1913
2 The gray dawn 1915
3 The rose dawn 1920
Later published in one volume as 'Story of California'.

Bobby Orde, a character in 'Gold' and 'Gray dawn', is the central character of 'The adventures of Bobby Orde'.
1 The leopard woman
2 Simba
3 Back of beyond
TRILOGY OF AMERICAN LUMBERING:
1 The blazed trail
2 The riverman
3 The rules of the game
ANDY BURNETT SERIES:
1 The long rifle
2 Ranchero
3 Folded hills
4 Stampede
☐
1 Skookum Chuck
2 Secret harbour
☐
1 Silent places
2 The conjuror's house

White, T. H.
1 Earth stopped
2 Gone to ground
☐
1 Age of scandal
2 The scandal monger
N.F. 18th century essays.

White, W. H., *see* Rutherford, M., *pseud.*

White, W. P.
1 Paradise Bend
2 Lynch lawyers
3 The heart of the range
4 Hidden trails

Whiteing, R.
1 The island
2 No. 5 John Street

Whitelaw, D.
1 The little hour of Peter Wells
2 Wolf's crag

Whitlock, P. and Hull, K., *see* Hull, K.

Whitney, Mrs. A. D. T.
1 A summer in Leslie Goldthwaite's life
2 We girls
3 Real folks
4 The other girls

Wibberley, L.
1 Beware of the mouse 1958
2 The mouse that roared 1959
*Stories about the mythical Duchy of
Grand Fenwick. 1 is in medieval times,
2 is contemporary.*

Wickham, H.
FERRIS MCCLURE SERIES:
1 The clue of the crimson petal
2 The scarlet X

Widdemer, M.
WINONA SERIES – 5 VOLUMES
1 The rose-garden husband
2 The wedding-ring man
□
1 The years of love
2 The other lovers

Wiesel, E.
1 Night
2 Dawn
N.F. Autobiography

Wigg, T. I. G.
1 For the sons of gentlemen 1960
2 A job with the boys 1959
Autobiographical novels on teaching.

Wiggin, K. D. [Riggs, Mrs.]
PENELOPE SERIES:
1 A cathedral courtship
2 Penelope's English experiences
3 Penelope's experiences in Scotland
4 Penelope's Irish experiences
5 Penelope's postscript
REBECCA SERIES:
1 Rebecca of Sunnybrook Farm
2 New chronicles of Rebecca
□
1 A summer in a canon
2 Polly Oliver's problem

Wightman, F.
THE VOYAGES OF 'WYLO':
1 The wind is free
2 My way leads me seaward
N.F. Travel

Wilder, R.
1 Drum 1963

2 Wind from the Carolinas 1964

Wiley, H.
1 The wildcat
2 The prowler

Wilkerson, D.
1 The cross and the switchblade
2 Twelve angels from hell

Wilkins, V.
1 And so Victoria 1936
2 Husband for Victoria 1958

Wilkinson, B.
GEOFFREY MILDMAY SERIES:
1 Proceed at will
2 Run, mongoose
3 Last clear chance

Willard, B.
1 Proposed and seconded
2 Echo answers

Williams, A.
RUPERT QUINN SERIES:
1 The long run south 1960
2 Barbouze 1962

Williams, B. A.
1 Come spring
2 Thread of scarlet
3 Strange woman
4 Time of peace
THE CURRAIN FAMILY SERIES:
1 House divided 1947
2 The unconquered 1953
*Two novels of a southern family in the
Civil War.*

Williams, E.
1 Valley of animals
2 Pig in paradise

Williams, H.
1 The merrymakers in New York
2 The merrymakers in Chicago

Williams, P.
1 I am Canute
2 God's warrior

Williams, R.
1 Border country 1962
2 Second generation 1964

Williams, T.
1 Baby Doll
2 The milk train doesn't stop here
Two plays.

Williams, V.
THE CLUBFOOT SERIES:
1 The man with the club foot
2 The secret hand
3 The return of Clubfoot
4 Clubfoot the avenger
5 The three of clubs
6 The crouching beast ·
7 The gold comfit box
8 The spider's touch
9 Courier to Marrakesh
MANDERTON SERIES:
1 The yellow streak
2 The orange divan
3 The eye in attendance
4 Death answers the bell
TREVOR DANE SERIES:
1 The clock ticks on
2 Masks off at midnight
3 The clue of the rising moon
MR. TREADGOLD SERIES:
1 Mr. Treadgold cuts in
2 Skeleton out of the cupboard

Williams, W. C.
1 White mule
2 In the money

Williamson, C. N. *and* A. M.
1 The lightning conductor
2 The Princess passes
3 My friend the chauffeur
4 The lightning conductress [Lightning conductor discovers America]
5 The lightning conductor comes back
□
1 Lord Loveland discovers America
2 Lady Betty across the water

Williamson, G.
SILVA D'CROY SERIES:
1 The lovable outlaw
2 Grand trunk knight

Williamson, H.
THE FLAX OF DREAM SERIES:
1 Beautiful years
2 Dandelion days
3 Dream of fair women
4 The pathway
5 The star-born
5 is not part of the tetralogy but is a pendant to it. 'Dark lantern' starts a new series on Phillip Maddison cousin of Willie Maddison of 'Flax of dream'.
A CHRONICLE OF ANCIENT SUNLIGHT:
1 Dark lantern
2 Donkey boy
3 Young Philip Maddison
4 How dear is life
5 Fox under my cloak
6 The golden virgin 1957
7 Love and the loveless 1958
8 A test of destruction 1960
9 The innocent moon 1961
10 It was the nightingale 1962
11 The power of the dead 1963
12 The phoenix generation 1965
Chronicle of a family from Victorian times to World War II.

Williamson, T. R.
1 Hunky
2 In Krusach's house

Willis, C. M.
SUPERINTENDENT BOSCOBELL SERIES:
1 Author in distress. *Same as* No. 18
2 Death at the Pelican
3 The Chamois murder
4 Death treads . . .
5 Then came the police
6 Defeat of a detective
7 Fatal accident
8 On the night in question
9 A body in the dawn
10 The case of the Calabar bean
11 The case of the R.E. pipe
This introduces a new main character, Roger Ellerdine.
12 The clue of the lost hour
Mainly Roger Ellerdine.
ROGER ELLERDINE AND SERGEANT BLOSSOM SERIES:
1 The clue of the golden ear-ring
2 Who killed Brother treasurer

Willis, C. M. (*contd.*)
3 What say the jury?
4 The dead voice
5 It pays to die
6 Death in the dark 1955
7 The dyer strikes again 1956
8 Mere murder 1959
9 Case of the empty bee hive 1959
10 Death of a best seller 1959

Willis, F.
1 101, Jubilee Road
2 Pence and dripping toast
3 London journal
N.F. *A trilogy of life in Edwardian London.*

Willis, T.
DIXON OF DOCK GREEN SERIES:
1 The devil's churchyard 1957
2 Seven gates to nowhere 1958

Wilmot, R. P.
STEVE CONSIDINE SERIES:
1 Blood in your eye 1954
2 Death rides a painted horse 1955

Wilson, A.
1 Wallace of the secret service
2 His excellency Governor Wallace

Wilson, C.
GERALD SORME SERIES:
1 Ritual and the dark 1960
2 Man without a shadow 1963

Wilson, G. M.
INSPECTOR LOVICK SERIES:
1 Murder on Monday 1963
2 Shot at dawn 1964
3 The devil's skull 1965

Wilson, H. L.
1 Ruggles of Red Gap
2 Somewhere in Red Gap
3 Ma Pettengill

Wilson, I.
GREGORY FLAMM SERIES:
1 But not for love 1962
2 That feeds on men 1963
3 Lilies that fester 1964
4 Empty tigers 1965

Wilson, M.
1 The able McLaughlins
2 The law and the McLaughlins
□
1 The Kenworthys
2 The painted room

Wilson, P.
1 The ringside seat
2 More ringside seats

Wilson, T. Menzies-
1 September to September
2 The eye of a needle
3 At first light

Wingfield-Stratford, E., *see* Stratford, E. Wingfield-

Winn, G.
1 Dreams fade
2 Fly away, youth

Winter, B.
STEVE CRAIG SERIES:
1 Darker grows the street
2 The dead sleep for keeps
3 Redheads cool fast
4 Next stop the morgue
5 The night was made for murder
6 Sleep long, my lovely

Winter, J. S. [Mrs. H. E. V. Stannard]
BINKS SERIES:
1 The Binks family
2 The married Miss Binks
BLANKHAMPTON SERIES:
1 Army society
2 Beautiful Jim
3 Garrison gossip
4 In quarters
5 On the march
6 The other man's wife
7 The soul of the bishop
8 Little Joan
9 The love of Philip Hampden
10 A simple gentleman
BOOTLES SERIES:
1 A blameless woman
2 Bootles' baby
3 Bootles's children
4 A born soldier, etc.

5 Cavalry life
6 Ferrers Court
7 Heart and sword
8 Houp-la!
9 The major's favourite
10 Mignon's husband
11 Mignon's secret
12 Pluck
13 Regimental legends

Winther, S. K.
NEBRASKA TRILOGY:
1 Take all to Nebraska
2 Mortgage your heart
3 This passion never dies

Winthrop, T.
1 John Brent
2 Love and skates

Winton, J.
1 We joined the navy 1959
2 We saw the sea 1960
3 Down the hatch 1961
4 All the nice girls 1962
N.F. *Humorous adventures of a group of submariners.*

Wise, D. *and others*
GLEN MORRIS STORIES:
1 Guy Carlton
2 Dick Duncan
3 Jessie Carlton
4 Walter Sherwood
5 Kate Carlton
HOLLYWOOD SERIES:
1 Stephen and his tempter
2 Florence Baldwin's picnic
3 Lionel's courage
4 Florence rewarded
5 Nat and his chum
6 Elbert's return
LINDENDALE STORIES:
1 Sidney de Grey,
2 Nellie Warren
3 Louis Sinclair
4 Cousin Clara
5 Peter Clinton

Wister, O.
1 Lin McLean
2 The Jimmjohn boss

3 The Virginian
4 Members of the family

Witting, C.
INSPECTOR CHARLTON SERIES:
1 Murder in blue
2 Midsummer murder
3 Case of the Michaelmas goose
4 Cat out of the bag
5 Measure for murder
6 Subject murder
7 Let X be the murderer
8 Dead on time
9 A bullet for Rhino
10 Case of the 'Busy bees'
11 Silence after dinner
12 Mischief in the offing 1957

Wittlin, J.
1 Salt of the earth
2 Healthy death
3 Hole in the sky

Witwer, H. C.
1 From baseball to Boches
2 'A smile a minute'

Wodehouse, P. G.
JEEVES SERIES:
1 The inimitable Jeeves
2 Carry on Jeeves
3 Very good Jeeves
4 Thank you Jeeves
5 Right-ho Jeeves
6 Code of the Woosters
7 Joy in the morning
8 The mating season
9 Ring for Jeeves
10 Jeeves and the feudal spirit
11 A few quick ones
12 Jeeves in the offing 1962
13 Stiff upper lip, Jeeves 1963
12 includes stories about Jeeves, Mr. Mulliner and the Oldest Member.
SCHOOL SERIES:
1 The gold bat
2 The white feather
UKRIDGE SERIES:
1 Love among the chickens
2 Ukridge
OLDEST MEMBER SERIES:
1 The heart of a goof

Wodehouse, P. G. (*contd.*)

2 The clicking of Cuthbert

The above is based on the main characters, but Wodehouse characters recur in many of the novels and short stories, and some minor characters appear in stories under several of the above headings.

Wogan, C.

Wolfe, H.

Wolfe, T.

Wood, A.

Wood, Mrs. H.

Wood, J.

1 Tipple in the deep
2 Beer for Christmas
N.F. Autobiography

Woodard, C.
1 A doctor heals by faith
2 A doctor's faith holds fast
3 A doctor's faith is challenged
N.F. Autobiography

Woodberry, J.
1 Rafferty takes to fishing 1959
2 Floodtide for Rafferty 1960
3 Rafferty rides a winner 1961
4 Rafferty makes a landfall 1962

Woodroofe, Mrs. A. T.
1 Michael Kemp
2 Michael, the married man

Woodrooffe, T.
1 River of golden sand
2 Naval odyssey
3 In good company
4 Maonalua
N.F. Autobiography

Woodruff, P.
THE MEN WHO RULED INDIA:
1 The founders
2 The guardians
N.F. History

Woods, S.
SIR NICHOLAS HARDING AND ANTONY
MAITLAND SERIES:
1 Bloody instructions 1961
2 Malice domestic 1962
3 The taste of fears 1963
4 Error of the moon 1963
5 Twisted like the fox 1964
6 This little measure 1964
7 The windy side of the law 1965
8 Though I know she lies 1965

Woolf, L.
1 Sowing (1880–1904) 1959
2 Growing (1904–1911) 1961
3 Beginning again (1911–1919) 1964
N.F. Autobiography

Worboise, E. J., *afterwards* **Mrs. Guyton**
1 Grace Hamilton's schooldays
2 Kingsdown Lodge
☐
1 Mr. Montmorency's money
2 Emilia's inheritance

Worby, J.
1 The other half
2 Spiv's progress
N.F. Autobiography

Wortley, V. Stuart-
1 Life without purpose
2 Grow old along with me
N.F. Autobiography

Wray, I.
INSPECTOR DIGBY SERIES:
1 The Vye murder
2 Murder – and Ariadne

Wren, P. C.
BEAU GESTE SERIES:
1 Beau Geste
2 Beau Sabreur
3 Beau Ideal
4 Good Gestes
5 Spanish Maine
5 Spanish Maine [The desert heritage]
☐
1 Soldiers of misfortune
2 Valiant dust
☐
1 Dew and mildew
2 The young stagers
SINCLAIR DYSART SERIES:
1 Action and passion
2 Sinbad the soldier
3 The fort in the jungle
☐
1 The man of a ghost [Spur of pride]
2 Worth while [To the hilt]

Wright, B.
1 The world's my football pitch
2 Captain of England
3 Football is my passport
4 One hundred caps and all that
N.F. Autobiography

Wright, H. B.
DAN MATTHEWS SERIES:
1 The shepherd of the hills
2 The calling of Dan Matthews
3 God and the groceryman

Wright, J. M.
1 Making of a man
2 A made man

Wright, M. O.
1 Tommy – Anne and the three hearts
2 Wabeno, the magician

Wright, S. F., *see* Fowler, S., *pseud.*

Wylie, I. A. R.
1 Towards morning
2 Brodie and the deep sea
□
1 The undefeated
2 Home are the hunted 1959

Wylie, P.
CRUNCH AND DES SERIES:
1 The big ones get away!
2 Salt water daffy
3 Fish and tin fish
4 Crunch and Des
Short stories about deep sea fishing.
Selection published under title 'The
best of Crunch and Des'.

Wynne, A.
DR. HAILEY SERIES:
1 Mystery of the evil eye [Sign of
evil]
2 The double thirteen
3 Sinners go secretly
4 The mystery of the ashes
5 The horsemen of death
6 The red scar
7 The dagger
8 The fourth finger
9 Room with iron shutters
10 The yellow crystal
11 The blue Vesuvius
12 Murder of a lady [Silver scale
mystery]
13 The silver arrow [The white arrow]
14 The case of the green knife

15 The Cotswold case
16 The loving cup [Death out of the
night)
17 Case of the gold coins
18 Death of a banker
19 The Holbein mystery [The red lady]
20 The toll house murder
21 Door nails never die
22 Death of a king
23 Death of a golfer
24 House on the hard
25 Emergency exit
26 Murder in a church

Wynne, M.
1 Comrades from Canada
2 A cousin from Canada
□
1 The story of Heather
2 Heather the second

Wynnton, P.
1 Black Turret
2 Ten jewels

Wyss, J. D.
1 Swiss family Robinson
Sequels by other authors are as follows:
2 Willis the pilot; *by* Frith
3 The island home; *by* Jules Verne
4 The castaways of the flag; *by*
Jules Verne

Yates, D.
BERRY SERIES:
1 Brother of Daphne
2 Courts of idleness
3 Berry and Co.
4 Jonah and Co.
5 Adele and Co.
6 And Berry came too
7 The house that Berry built
8 The Berry scene
9 As Berry and I were saying
10 B-Berry and I look back 1958
This is autobiographical, but contains
many sidelights on the series.
□
1 Anthony Lyveden
2 Valerie French
RICHARD CHANDOS SERIES:
1 Blind corner

2 Perishable goods
3 Blood royal
4 Fire below [By royal command]
5 She fell among thieves
6 Gale warning
7 An eye for a tooth
8 Red in the morning
9 Cost price
10 Ne'er do well
Jonathan Mansel, though not the main character, occurs in all the 'Berry' series and in other books as follows:
'Blind corner', 'Perishable goods', 'Gale warning', 'Shoal water', 'An eye for a tooth', 'Red in the morning'.
John Bagot is the hero of 'Gale warning', and appears in 'Red in the morning'. Richard Chandos and Jonathan Mansel appear in 'Ne'er do well' but do not play an active part.

Yonge, C. M.
The novels are nearly all related by the means of the characters who reappear, but it is impossible to compile a list of direct sequels. The following notes however will show how the many characters develop.
1 Scenes and characters
Characters from this book reappear in 'Two sides of the shield', 'Beechcroft at Rockstone' and 'Long vacation'.
2 The castle builders
A character in this, Lady Herbert Somerville, reappears in 'The pillars of the house.'
3 The daisy chain
The sequel to this is
4 The trial
Characters from both books appear in others, notably 'Pillars of the house'.
5 Dynevor Terrace
Characters reappear in 'Beechcroft at Rockstone'.
6 Hopes and fears
Characters reappear in 'Pillars of the house'.
7 The Stokesley secret
Characters reappear in 'Two sides of the shield' and 'Beechcroft at Rockstone'.
8 Countess Kate

Characters reappear in 'Pillars of the house'.
9 The chaplet of pearls
This has a sequel in
10 Stray pearls
11 The pillars of the house
Old and new characters appear again in 'Two sides of the shield', 'Beechcroft at Rockstone' and 'Modern Broods'.
12 Two sides of the shield
13 Beechcroft at Rockstone
The characters in these two books are nearly all taken from earlier ones.
14 The long vacation
15 Modern broods
These are direct sequels of the previous two, and bring in characters also from other earlier books.
There is a sequel to 'The heirs of Redclyffe' by Mrs. Hicks Beach, 'Anabel and Mary Verena'.

York, J.
SUPERINTENDENT FOLLY SERIES:
1 Find the body
2 Run away to murder
3 Close the door on murder
4 Let's kill Uncle Lionel
5 The gallows are waiting

Young, A.
1 A prospect of flowers
2 A retrospect of flowers
N.F. Botany

Young, E. H.
1 Jenny Wren
2 The Curate's wife

Young, F. B.
1 Wood smoke
2 Pilgrim's rest
☐
1 They seek a country
2 City of gold

Young, G.
1 Wild blood
2 Hurricane Williams
3 Hurricane Williams' revenge

Young, S.
1 So red the rose
2 Feliciana

Zangwill, I.
CELIBATES CLUB SERIES:
1 The Bachelors' Club
2 The Old-maids' Club
GHETTO SERIES:
1 Children of the ghetto
2 Dreamers of the ghetto
3 Ghetto comedies
4 Ghetto tragedies
5 They that walk in darkness

Zilahy, L.
1 The donkeys 1949
2 The angry angel 1953
The story of an aristocratic Hungarian family in two World Wars.

Zola, E.
FOUR GOSPELS SERIES:
1 Fruitfulness
2 Work
3 Truth
4 Intended to be entitled 'Justice'– author died before writing it.
ROUGON MACQUART SERIES:
1 The fortunes of the Rougons
2 In the swim. *Same as* Rush for the spoil
3 The fat and the thin
4 The conquest of Plassans
5 Abbe Mouret's transgression
6 His Excellency

7 The dram shop
8 A love episode
9 Nana
10 Piping hot
11 Ladies paradise
12 How jolly life is!
13 Germinal
14 The masterpiece
15 The soil
16 The dream
17 The human beast
18 Money
19 The downfall
20 Dr. Pascal
In the preface to 1 Zola explains the whole series, and in 20 concludes and sums up the results of the Rougon Macquart cycle – Bakers guide to best fiction.
Direct sequels are 1 and 6 which deal with the Rougons, and 2 and 18, which are about the financier Saccard.
The appearances of the various characters are traced in 'A Zola dictionary', by J. G. Patterson.
THREE CITIES TRILOGY:
1 Lourdes
2 Rome
3 Paris

Zweig, A.
A TRILOGY OF THE TRANSITION:
1 Young woman of 1914
2 Education before Verdun
3 The case of Sergeant Grischa
4 The crowning of a king [Winfried]

NOTES

NOTES

NOTES

NOTES

Sequels

Abbott, E.
LONG LOOK BOOKS:
1 Long Look House
2 Out of doors at Long Look
3 A trip eastwards

Abbot, J.
THE AUGUST STORIES – four volumes
FLORENCE STORIES – six volumes
FRANCONIA SERIES – ten volumes
JONAS SERIES – six volumes
MARCO POLO SERIES – six volumes
RAINBOW AND LUCKY STORIES – five volumes
ROLLO SERIES – fourteen volumes
ROLLO'S TOUR IN EUROPE – ten volumes
YOUNG CHRISTIAN SERIES – four volumes

Adam, R.
1 A stepmother for Susan of St. Bride's
2 Susan and the wrong baby

Adams, A.
1 Doddles: a school story
2 Doddles makes things hum
☐
1 Ella of Berry Farm
2 Our Lil
3 That Barbara Moore
The last three also in one volume as 'Those Shepton children'.

Adams, H.
THE PIONEER BOY SERIES – six volumes

Adams, H. C.
TALES OF CHARLTON SCHOOL:
1 The cherry-stones
2 The first of June

TALES OF NETHERCOURT:
1 The lost rifle
2 The chief of the school
TALES OF WALTER'S SCHOOLDAYS:
1 The doctor's birthday
2 Walter's friend

Adams, Q.
OUTDOOR CHUMS SERIES – eight volumes

Adams, W. T., *see* Optic, O., *pseud.*

Adamson, G.
MR. BUDGE SERIES:
1 Mr. Budge builds a house
2 Mr. Budge buys a car

Adamson, J. *and* **G.**
TOPSY AND TIM SERIES:
1 Topsy and Tim's Friday book
2 Topsy and Tim's Saturday book
3 Topsy and Tim's Sunday book
4 Topsy and Tim's Foggy day
5 Topsy and Tim at the football match
6 Topsy and Tim go fishing
7 Topsy and Tim's bonfire night
8 Topsy and Tim's snowy day
9 Topsy and Tim go on holiday
10 Topsy and Tim at the seaside

Ainsworth, R.
RUFTY TUFTY SERIES:
1 Rufty Tufty the golliwog
2 Rufty Tufty at the seaside
3 Rufty Tufty goes camping
4 Rufty Tufty runs away
5 Rufty Tufty flies high
6 Rufty Tufty's Island
7 Rufty Tufty and Hattie
8 Rufty Tufty makes a house 1964

Akers, F.
1 The boy fortune hunters in Alaska
2 The boy fortune hunters in Panama
3 The boy fortune hunters in Egypt

Alcott, L. M.
AUNT JO'S SCRAP-BAG SERIES:
1 My boys, etc.
2 Shawl straps
3 Cupid and Chow-chow, etc.
4 My girls
5 Jimmy's cruise in the Pinafore, etc.
6 An old fashioned thanksgiving, etc.
THE COUSINS SERIES:
1 Eight cousins
2 Rose in bloom
LITTLE MEN AND WOMEN SERIES:
Different publishers issue the books with varying titles, but mostly as
1 Little women
2 Good wives
3 Little men
4 Jo's boys

Alden, Mrs. G. M., *see* Pansy, *pseud.*

Alden, W. L.
1 Adventures of Jimmy Brown
2 Jimmy Brown in Europe. *Same as* Jimmy Brown trying to find Europe
☐
1 Moral pirates
2 Cruise of *The Ghost*
3 Cruise of the Canoe Club

Aldous, A.
MCGOWAN SERIES:
1 McGowan goes to sea
2 McGowan goes fishing
3 McGowan goes motor racing
4 McGowan goes to Henley
5 McGowan climbs a mountain

Aldridge, J.
THE MEADOW-BROOK GIRLS' SERIES – six volumes

Alger, H., *Junior*
ATLANTIC SERIES – four volumes
BRAVE AND BOLD SERIES – four volumes
CAMPAIGN SERIES – three volumes
FRANK AND FEARLESS SERIES – three volumes
GOOD FORTUNE SERIES – three volumes
HOW TO RISE SERIES – three volumes
LUCK AND PLUCK SERIES – eight volumes
NEW WORLD SERIES – three volumes
PACIFIC SERIES – four volumes
RAGGED DICK SERIES – six volumes
TATTERED TOM SERIES – eight volumes
VICTORY SERIES – three volumes

Allain, M. E.
BALLET FAMILY SERIES:
1 The Ballet family 1963
2 The Ballet family again 1964

Allen, A.
1 Story of the village
2 Story of painting
3 Story of our parliament
Characters in each volume are the same, but not otherwise sequels.

Allen, A. E.
1 Joe, the circus boy
2 The Martie twins
3 Marjory, the circus girl
4 Marjory at the Willows

Allen, E.
PEPE MORENO SERIES:
1 Pepe Moreno 1957
2 Pepe Moreno and the roller skates 1958
3 Pepe on the run 1959
4 Pepe Moreno and the dilapidated donkey 1960
5 Pepe Moreno's Quixotic adventure 1962

Allen, W. B.
CAMP AND TRAMP SERIES:
1 Lost in Umbagog
2 The mammoth hunters
PINE CONE SERIES:
1 Pine cones
2 Silver rages
3 Northern Cross
4 Kelp
5 Cloud and cliff
6 Gulf and glacier

SIEGE OF BOSTON SERIES:
1 A son of liberty
2 Called to the front

Allum, N.
MONICA SERIES:
1 Monica joins the W.R.A.C. 1964
2 Monica takes a commission 1965

Allum, T.
HURRICANE HARLAND SERIES:
1 Hurricane Harland blows in
2 Hurricane Harland hits out
3 Hurricane Harland takes the plunge
4 Hurricane Harland crashes the gate
CAPTAIN MICHAEL TRIGGINGTON SERIES:
1 Introducing Trigger
2 Trigger blazes the trail

Anckarsvard, K.
BONIFACIUS SERIES:
1 Bonifacius the green 1962
2 Bonifacius and little Bonnie 1963

Anderson, C. W.
BLAZE SERIES:
1 Billy and Blaze
2 Blaze and the forest fire
3 Blaze and the gypsies
4 Blaze finds the trail
5 Blaze and the mountain lion

Anderson, V.
THE YORK FAMILY SERIES:
1 Vanload to Venice 1961
2 Nine times never 1963
3 The Yorks in London 1964
BROWNIE SERIES
1 Amanda and the Brownies 1962
2 The Brownies and the golden hand 1963
3 The Brownies way abroad 1964
4 The Brownies and the ponies 1965

Andom, R. [A. W. Barrett]
TRODDLES SERIES:
1 We three and Troddles
2 Troddles and us and others
3 Cruise of the Mock Turtle
4 Lighter days with Troddles
5 Four men with a van

6 The runaways. *Same as* At school with Troddles
7 On tour with Troddles
8 Our flat
9 Troddles' farm
10 Adrift with Troddles
11 Just Troddles
12 Three men and Troddles
13 With Troddles in the trenches
14 Same old Troddles
15 Out and about with Troddles

Andrew, P.
GINGER SERIES:
1 Ginger over the wall 1962
2 Ginger and Batty Billy 1963
3 Ginger and No. 10 1964

Andrews, J.
SEVEN LITTLE SISTERS SERIES:
1 Seven little sisters
2 Each and all
3 The seven little sisters who live on the round ball
4 The seven little sisters prove their sisterhood

Anglund, J. W.
1 Cowboy and his friend
2 Cowboy's secret life

Appleton, V.
TOM SWIFT SERIES – 27 volumes

Arthur, R. M.
CAROLINA SERIES:
1 Carolina's holiday 1957
2 Carolina's golden bird 1958
3 Carolina and Roberto 1959
4 Carolina and the sea-horse 1960

Arundel, L.
MOTOR BOAT BOYS' SERIES – six volumes

Atkinson, J. C.
1 Walks and talks of two schoolboys
2 Play-hours and half-holidays

Atkinson, M. E.
THE LOCKETT FAMILY SERIES:
1 August adventure
2 Mystery manor
3 The compass points north
4 Smuggler's gap
5 Going gangster
6 Crusoe Island
7 Challenge to adventure
8 Monster of Widgeon Weir
9 Nest of the scarecrow
10 Problem party
11 Chimney cottage
12 House on the moor
13 The thirteenth adventure
14 Steeple folly
FRICKA SERIES:
1 Castaway camp
2 Hunter's moon
3 The barnstormers
4 Unexpected adventure
5 Riders and raids

Avery, G.
1 The warden's niece 1962
2 The Italian spring 1964

Awdry, W.
ENGINE SERIES:
1 The three railway engines
2 Thomas the tank engine
3 Janet the red engine
4 Tank engine Thomas again
5 Troublesome engines
6 Henry the green engine
7 Toby the tram engine
8 Gordon the big engine
9 Edward the blue engine
10 Tom the little engine
11 Percy the small engine
12 Eight famous engines
13 Duck and the diesel engine
14 Little old engine
15 The twin engines
16 Branch line engines
17 Gallant old engine
18 Stepney the 'bluebell' engine
19 Mountain engines
20 Very old engines 1965

Aymé, M.
1 Wonderful farm
2 Return to Wonderful farm

B. B., *pseud.*
BILL BADGER SERIES:
1 Wandering wind
2 Bill Badger's winter cruise
3 Bill Badger and the pirates
4 Bill Badger's finest hour
5 Bill Badger's whispering reeds adventure
6 Bill Badger's big mistake
7 Bill Badger's last adventure
□
1 The little grey men
2 Down the bright stream
3 The Forest of Boland Light Railway 1958
4 The Wizard of Boland 1959
□
1 Monty Woodpig and his bubblebuzz car
2 Monty Woodpig's caravan

Baker, C.
THUNDERBIRD SERIES:
1 The venture of the Thunderbird 1959
2 The return of the Thunderbird 1959

Baker, M. J.
THE RIDLEY FAMILY SERIES:
1 Castaway Christmas 1963
2 Cut off from crumpets 1964
HOMER SERIES:
1 Homer sees the Queen
2 Homer goes to Stratford
3 Homer in orbit
4 Homer goes west 1965

Baker, W. F.
BOY RANCHERS SERIES – six volumes

Baldwin, M.
1 Follies of Fifi
2 Golden Square High School
□
1 A popular girl
2 Sybil

Ballantyne, J.
MAITLAND CHILDREN SERIES:
1 Holiday trench
2 Kidnapped at Coombe 1960
3 No mystery to the Maitlands 1961

Ballantyne, R. M.
1 The coral island
2 The gorilla hunters
☐
1 Sunk at sea
2 Lost in the forest
3 Over the Rocky Mountains
☐
Tales of adventure. *Four series*

Bancroft, E.
JANE ALLEN SERIES – three volumes

Bancroft, J.
JAMES STEEL SERIES:
1 Guardian of honour 1961
2 The ring of truth 1962

Bancroft, L.
1 Prince Mud-Turtle
2 Mr. Woodchuck
3 Bandit Jim Crow
4 Twinkle's enchantment
5 Sugar-loaf mountain
6 Prairie Dog Town

Banner, A.
ART AND BEE SERIES:
1 Art and Bee
2 More Art and Bee
3 More and more Art and Bee
4 Art and Bee and the rainbows
5 Art and Bee and the kind dog

Barbour, R. H.
BIG FOUR SERIES – three volumes
ERSKINE SERIES – three volumes
GRAFTON SCHOOL SERIES – three volumes
HILTON SCHOOL SERIES – three volumes
HUDSON RIVER SERIES – three volumes
PURPLE PENNANT (HIGH SCHOOL) SERIES –
    three volumes
YARDLEY HALL SERIES – eight volumes

Barclay, I.
WORLDS WITHOUT END SERIES:
1 The early explorers
2 The great age of discovery
3 Filling in the map 1959
N.F. Geography

Barker, K. F.
BELLMAN SERIES:
1 Bellman
2 Bellman carries on

Barne, K.
ROSINA SERIES:
1 Rosina Copper
2 Rosina and son
FARRAR FAMILY SERIES:
1 Family footlights
2 Visitors from London
3 Dusty's windmill

Barnum, V.
JOE STRONG SERIES – seven volumes

Barr, N.
WE FOUR SERIES:
1 We four on Mouse Island
2 We four and the King's treasure

Barrington, G. W.
RUSTY AND PETER SERIES:
1 Broken voyage
2 Desert ghost

Barton, O. R.
NANCY AND NICK SERIES – 4 vols.

Batchelor, M.
1 Little Rhodesian
2 Gwenda's friend from home

Bateman, R.
ARCHIBALD MCGILLICUDDY SERIES:
1 Archie young detective 1961
2 Mystery for Archie 1963
3 Archie abroad 1964
4 Archie and the missing stamps 1964

Bates, G.
THE KHAKI BOYS SERIES – five volumes

Bates, H. E.
ACHILLES SERIES:
1 Achilles the donkey 1962
2 Achilles and Diana 1963
3 Achilles and the twins 1964

Baum, L. F.
OZ SERIES – 21 volumes

Baumann, H.
AMERICA–ASIA–AFRICA TRILOGY:
1 Son of Columbus
2 Sons of the steppe
3 The barque of the brothers 1958

Bawden, N.
THE MALLORY CHILDREN SERIES:
1 The secret passage 1963
2 On the run 1964

Baxter, G.
1 Jump to the stars 1961
2 The difficult summer 1962
3 The perfect horse 1963

Bayley, V.
'ADVENTURE' SERIES:
1 Paris adventure 1954
2 Lebanon adventure 1955
3 Kashmir adventure 1956
4 Corsican adventure 1956
5 Turkish adventure 1957
6 London adventure 1962
7 Swedish adventure 1963
8 Italian adventure 1964
9 Scottish adventure 1965
   Not strictly sequels, but characters recur.

Bayliss, C. K.
LOLAMI SERIES:
1 Lolami, the little cliff dweller
2 Lolami in Tusayan

Beach, E. L.
ANNAPOLIS SERIES:
1 An Annapolis plebe
2 An Annapolis youngster
3 An Annapolis second classman
4 An Annapolis first classman
ROGER PAULDING SERIES:
1 Roger Paulding, apprentice seaman
2 Roger Paulding, gunner's mate
3 Roger Paulding, gunner
4 Roger Paulding, ensign
UNITED STATES NAVAL SERIES:
1 Ralph Osborn, midshipman at Annapolis
2 Midshipman Ralph Osborn at sea
3 Ensign Ralph Osborn
4 Lieutenant Ralph Osborn

Beaman, B., *and* S. G.
TOYTOWN SERIES:
1 Ernest the brave *and* The Toytown mystery
2 Tea for two *and* A portrait of the mayor
3 The Theatre Royal *and* Punch and Judy
4 Toytown goes west
5 The enchanted ark
6 The mayor's sea voyage
7 Larry the plumber
8 The Toytown treasure
9 Mr. Noah's holiday
10 The conversion of Mr. Growser
11 The great Toytown war
12 How the radio came to Toytown
13 The extraordinary affair of Ernest the policeman
14 Pistols for two
15 A Toytown Christmas party
16 Mr. Growser moves house
17 Dreadful doings in Ark Street
18 The Arkville dragon
19 The showing up of Fanny the lamb
20 Toytown pantomime

Beardmore, G.
BELLE OF THE BALLET SERIES:
1 Belle of the ballet's gala performance 1956
2 Belle of the ballet's country holiday 1957

Beech, M.
PETER SERIES:
1 Peter and Veronica
2 Peter the cub

Bell, R. S. W.
1 Tales of Greyhouse
2 Green at Greyhouse
3 The secret seven
4 Greyhouse days
5 Polson of Greyhouse
6 J. O. Jones
7 Smith's week
   Note – 6 and 7 relate to Greyhouse boys who went to other schools as masters.

Bellhouse, L. W.
1 Caravan children
2 Caravan again
3 Caravan goes west
4 Caravan comes home
5 Christmas Caravan
6 Winter Caravan
HELICOPTER SERIES:
1 The helicopter children
2 The helicopter flies again 1957
Belloc, H.
1 The bad child's book of beasts
2 More beasts (for worse children)
Bemelmans, L.
MADELINE SERIES:
1 Madeline
2 Madeline's rescue
3 Madeline and the bad lot
4 Madeline and the gypsies
5 Madeline in London

Benary, M.
THE LECHOWS SERIES:
1 The ark
2 Rowan farm
Story of a German family after the War.

Benedict, D.
1 Pagan the black 1962
2 Fabulous 1963
3 Bandoleer 1964
A trilogy on a ranch in Montana.

Benham, W.
BEN LIGHTBOY SERIES:
1 Ben Lightboy, special
2 Ben Lightboy's biggest puzzle

Bennet, G. M., *see* Sea-lion, *pseud.*

Bennett, R.
MISS PINK SERIES:
1 Little Miss Pink
2 Little Miss Pink at Greytoes
3 Little Miss Pink at the Great House
4 Little Miss Pink's school
5 Little Miss Pink's splendid summer
6 Little Miss Pink's wedding

Beresford, E.
GAPPY, JIM AND JANE SERIES:
1 Television mystery 1957

2 Flying doctor mystery 1958
3 Trouble at Tullington Castle 1958
4 Gappy goes west 1959
5 The Tullington film-makers 1960
6 Strange hiding place 1962
7 The missing formula mystery 1963
8 Flying doctor to the rescue 1964

Berna, P.
1 Threshold of the stars
2 Continent in the sky 1959
GABY SERIES:
1 A hundred million francs 1958
2 The street musician 1960
3 The mystery of Saint Salgue 1963

Berrisford, J. M.
SKIPPER SERIES:
1 Skipper the dog from the sea
2 Skipper and the Headlan four 1957
3 Skipper's exciting summer 1958
4 Skipper and the runaway boy 1960
5 Skipper and son 1961
TAFF SERIES:
1 Taff the sheepdog 1958
2 Son of Taff 1959
3 S.O.S. for sheepdog Taff 1960
4 Taff and the stolen ponies 1965
JACKIE AND BABS SERIES:
1 Jackie won a pony
2 Ten ponies and Jackie 1961
3 Jackie's pony patrol 1963
4 Jackie and the pony trekkers 1963
THE BROOKE FAMILY:
1 A pony in the family 1962
2 A colt in the family 1963
3 A showjumper in the family 1964

Bertram R.
ANN THORNE SERIES:
1 Ann Thorne, reporter
2 Ann Thorne in America
3 Scoop for Ann Thorne
4 Front page Ann Thorne

Biggs, M.
MELLING SCHOOL SERIES:
1 New prefect at Melling
2 The Blakes come to Melling
3 Susan in the sixth

Bird, M.

ANDY PANDY SERIES:

1 Andy Pandy and his hobby horse 1953
2 Andy Pandy and the gingerbread man 1953
3 Andy Pandy's washing day 1953
4 Andy Pandy's nursery rhymes 1954
5 Andy Pandy and the ducklings 1954
6 Andy Pandy's tea party 1954
7 Andy Pandy's jumping up book 1954
8 Andy Pandy in the country 1955
9 Andy Pandy's Jack in the box 1955
10 Andy Pandy's shop 1955
11 Andy Pandy and Teddy at the zoo 1956
12 Andy Pandy and the white kitten 1956
13 Andy Pandy and the willow tree 1956
14 Andy Pandy builds a house for Looby Loo 1956
15 Andy Pandy's kite 1957
16 Andy Pandy paints his house 1958
17 Andy Pandy's shopping bag 1958
18 Andy Pandy and the hedgehog 1959
19 Andy Pandy's puppy 1960
20 Andy Pandy and the woolly lamb 1960
21 Andy Pandy and the teddy dog 1960
22 Andy Pandy's dovecote 1960
23 Andy Pandy and the baby pigs 1961
24 Andy Pandy's little goat 1961
25 Andy Pandy and the patchwork cat 1962
26 Andy Pandy and the snowman 1962
27 Andy Pandy plays lions and tigers 1964
28 Andy Pandy's play-house 1964
29 Andy Pandy and the green puppy 1965
30 Andy Pandy and the badger 1965

Bishop, G.

CAPTAIN COMSTOCK SERIES – two volumes

Bisset, D.

1 Anytime stories
2 Sometime stories
3 Next time stories

Bjorn, T.

PAPA SERIES:

1 Papa's wife
2 Papa's daughter 1958

Blake, J.

GARRY HALLIDAY SERIES:

1 Garry Halliday and the disappearing diamonds 1960
2 Garry Halliday and the ray of death 1961
3 Garry Halliday and the kidnapped five 1962
4 Garry Halliday and the sands of time 1963
5 Garry Halliday and the flying foxes 1965

Blanchard, A. E.

CARITA SERIES – two volumes
THE CORNERS SERIES – two volumes
GIRL SCOUT SERIES – two volumes
THE PIONEERS SERIES – three volumes
REVOLUTIONARY SERIES FOR GIRLS – three volumes
WAR OF 1812 SERIES – two volumes

Blyton, E.

PIP SERIES:

1 Adventures of Pip
2 More adventures of Pip

HAPPY HOUSE SERIES:

1 Children of happy house
2 Happy house children again

FAMOUS FIVE SERIES:

1 Five on a Treasure Island
2 Five go adventuring again
3 Five run away together
4 Five go to Smuggler's Top
5 Five go off in a caravan
6 Five on Kirrin Island again
7 Five go off to camp
8 Five get into trouble
9 Five fall into adventure
10 Five on a hike together
11 Five have a wonderful time
12 Five go down to the sea
13 Five go to mystery moor
14 Five have plenty of fun
15 Five on a secret trail
16 Five go to Billycock Hill
17 Five get into a fix

18 Five on Finston Farm
19 Five go to Demon's rocks 1961
20 Five have a mystery to solve 1962
21 Five are together again 1963
'BARNEY' SERIES:
1 The Rilloby Fair mystery 1950
2 The Rubadub mystery 1952
3 The Rockingdown mystery 1954
4 The Ring o'bells mystery 1955
5 The Rat-a-tat mystery 1956
6 The Ragamuffin mystery 1959
FARAWAY TREE SERIES:
1 Enchanted wood
2 Magic faraway tree
3 Folk of the faraway tree
□
1 Caravan family 1953
2 Runabout's holidays 1955
3 Four in a family 1956
MALORY TOWERS SERIES:
1 First term at Malory Towers
2 Second form at Malory Towers
3 Third year at Malory Towers
4 Upper fourth at Malory Towers
5 In the fifth at Mallory Towers
6 Last term at Malory Towers
ADVENTURE SERIES:
1 Island of adventure
2 Castle of adventure
3 Valley of adventure
4 Sea of adventure
5 Mountain of adventure
6 Ship of adventure
7 Circus of adventure
8 River of adventure
□
1 Mischief
2 Mischief again
3 The laughing kitten
4 Let's have a party 1956
'FATTY' SERIES
1 Mystery of the burnt cottage
2 Mystery of the disappearing cat
3 Mystery of the secret room
4 Mystery of the spiteful letters
5 Mystery of the missing necklace
6 Mystery of the hidden house
7 Mystery of the pantomime cat
8 Mystery of the invisible thief
9 Mystery of the vanished prince
10 Mystery of the strange bundle
11 Mystery of Holly Lane

12 Mystery of Tally-Ho cottage
13 Mystery of the missing man 1956
14 Mystery of the strange messages 1957
15 Mystery of the Buncher Towers 1961
NAUGHTIEST GIRL SERIES:
1 Naughtiest girl in the school
2 Naughtiest girl again
3 Naughtiest girl is a monitor
NODDY SERIES:
1 Noddy and his car 1951
2 Noddy's colur ship book 1952
3 New big Noddy book 1954
4 Noddy goes to the fair 1954
5 Noddy and the magic rubber 1955
6 You funny little Noddy 1955
7 Noddy meets Father Christmas 1955
8 Noddy in Toyland 1956
9 Noddy and Teddy Bear 1956
10 Be brave like Noddy 1956
11 A day with Noddy 1957
12 Noddy and the bumpy dog 1957
13 Do look out Noddy 1957
14 You're a good friend Noddy 1958
15 Noddy has an adventure 1958
16 Noddy's own nursery rhymes 1959
17 Noddy goes to sea 1959
18 Big Noddy book 1959
19 Noddy and the donkey 1960
20 Cheer up little Noddy 1960
21 Mr. Plod and little Noddy 1961
22 Noddy and the Tootles 1962
23 Noddy and the aeroplane 1963
WISHING CHAIR SERIES:
1 Adventures of the wishing chair
2 The wishing chair again
AMELIA JANE SERIES:
1 Naughty Amelia Jane
2 More about Amelia Jane
3 Amelia Jane again
CIRCUS SERIES:
1 Come to circus
2 Hurrah for circus
3 Circus days again
4 Mr. Galliano's circus
ADVENTUROUS FOUR SERIES:
1 The adventurous four
2 The adventurous four again
MR. MEDDLE SERIES:
1 Merry Mister Meddle
2 Mister Meddle's mischief

Blyton, E. (*contd.*)
  3 Mister Meddle's muddles

MR. PINKWHISTLE SERIES:
  1 Mr. Pinkwhistle interferes
  2 The adventures of Mr. Pinkwhistle

SECRET SEVEN SERIES:
  1 The Secret Seven
  2 Secret Seven adventures
  3 Well done Secret Seven
  4 Secret Seven on the haul
  5 Go ahead Secret Seven
  6 Good work, Secret Seven
  7 Three cheers Secret Seven
  8 Secret Seven mystery
  9 Puzzle for the Secret Seven
  10 Secret Seven fireworks
  11 Secret Seven win through
  12 Shock for the Secret Seven
  13 Good old Secret Seven
  14 Born at the seaside
  15 Look out Secret Seven
  16 Fun for the Secret Seven

SIX COUSINS SERIES:
  1 Six cousins at Mistletoe farm
  2 Six cousins again

ST. CLARE'S SERIES:
  1 Twins at St. Clare's
  2 O'Sullivan twins again
  3 Summer term at St. Clare's
  4 Second term at St. Clare's
  5 Claudine at St. Clare's
  6 Fifth formers at St. Clare's

Boden, H.
MARLOWS SERIES:
  1 Marlows at Newgate
  2 Marlows win a prize
  3 Marlows dig for treasure
  4 Marlows in danger
  5 Marlows at Castle Cliff
  6 Marlows and the regatta
  7 Marlows' Irish holiday
  8 Marlows in town

NOEL SERIES:
  1 Noel and the donkeys
  2 Noel's happy day
  3 Noel's Christmas holiday

JOANNA SERIES:
  1 Joanna's special pony 1960
  2 Joanna rides the hills 1961

Bond, G.
LUCK SERIES:
  1 Sergeant Luck 1956
  2 Luck of the Legion's desert adventure 1958
  3 Carry on, Sergeant Luck 1962
  4 The return of Sergeant Luck 1964

Bond, M.
PADDINGTON SERIES:
  1 A bear called Paddington 1958
  2 More about Paddington 1959
  3 Paddington helps out 1960
  4 Paddington abroad 1961
  5 Paddington at large 1962
  6 Paddington marches on 1964

Bonehill, R.
BOY HUNTER SERIES:
  1 Four boy hunters
  2 Guns and snowshoes
  3 Young hunters of the lake

FRONTIER SERIES:
  1 Pioneer boys of the goldfields
  2 Pioneer boys of the Great Northwest
  3 With Boone on the frontier

YOUNG HUNTERS SERIES:
  1 Gun and sled
  2 The young hunters in Porto Rico

ANOTHER SERIES:
  1 The island camp
  2 The winning run

Bonner, R.
BOY INVENTORS SERIES – six volumes

Boscawen, L.
HOLLINGBURY FAMILY SERIES:
  1 We never knew Uncle
  2 We live in Lemon Yard

Bosco, H.
PASCALET AND AUNT MARTINE SERIES:
  1 The fox in the island
  2 The boy and the river
  3 Barboche 1959

Boston, L. M.
GREEN KNOWE SERIES:
  1 Children of Green Knowe
  2 Chimneys of Green Knowe 1957

3 River at Green Knowe 1959
4 A stranger at Green Knowe 1961
5 An enemy at Green Knowe 1964

Boucher, A.
THE STORY OF HALLI THORDARSON:
1 The path of the raven 1959
2 The Greenland farers 1961
3 The vineland venture 1963
4 The raven's flight 1964
A series about the Vikings in the 11th century.

Bowes, J.
ANZAC SERIES:
1 The young Anzacs
2 The Anzac war trail
3 The Aussie crusaders

Boyd, E.
WANDERLUST BROWN SERIES:
1 Introducing Wanderlust Brown
2 Wanderlust goes south
3 Wanderlust's third innings

Boylston, H. K.
CAROL PAGE SERIES:
1 Carol goes on the stage
2 Carol comes to Broadway
3 Carol in repertory
4 Carol on tour
SUE BARTON SERIES:
1 Sue Barton student nurse
2 Sue Barton senior nurse
3 Sue Barton visiting nurse
4 Sue Barton rural nurse
5 Sue Barton superintendent nurse
6 Sue Barton neighbourhood nurse
7 Sue Barton staff nurse

Bradburne, E. S.
ELIZABETH ANN SERIES:
1 Elizabeth Ann
2 More of Elizabeth Ann

Braddock, G.
REX KINGDOM SERIES – five volumes

Brady, C. T.
BOB DASHAWAY SERIES – three volumes
BOYS OF THE SERVICE SERIES – four volumes

ANOTHER SERIES:
1 The blue ocean's daughter
2 The adventures of Lady Susan

Braene, B.
1 Trina finds a brother 1963
2 Little sister Tai-Mi 1964

Brambleby, A.
THREE SERIES:
1 Three for trouble
2 Three pack for holiday

Bramston, M.
1 Snowball society
2 Home and school

Brandon, G.
SENGLER'S CIRCUS SERIES:
1 Sengler's circus
2 Sengler's sawdust ring
3 Sengler's rising star
4 Sengler's comes to town
5 Sengler's buys Babette

Bray, E. O.
1 Willie and May
2 A month at the seaside

Breckenridge, G.
RADIO BOYS SERIES – nine volumes

Breitenbach, L. M.
ALMA SERIES – four volumes

Brenda *pseud.* [**Mrs. Castle Smith**]
1 Froggy's little brother
2 More about Froggy

Brent-Dyer, E. M., *see* Dyer, E. M. Brent-

Brereton, F. S.
GREAT WAR OF 1914–18 SERIES:
1 With French at the front
2 Under French's command
3 With Joffre at Verdun
4 At grips with the Turk
5 On the road to Bagdad
6 Under Haig in Flanders
7 Under Foch's command
8 With the Allies to the Rhine

Brereton, F. S. (*contd.*)
   9 With Allenby in Palestine
   10 From the Nile to the Tigris
   11 The armoured car scouts

Bright, R.
   GEORGIE SERIES:
   1 Georgie
   2 Georgie to the rescue
   3 Georgie and the robbers

Brims, B.
   1 Runaway riders 1964
   2 Red rosette 1965

Brisley, J. L.
   MILLY-MOLLY-MANDY SERIES:
   1 Milly-Molly-Mandy stories
   2 More of Milly-Molly-Mandy
   3 Milly-Molly-Mandy again
   4 Further doings of Milly-Molly-
     Mandy

Brooks, A.
   DAINTY DOROTHY SERIES – 16 volumes
   PRINCESS POLLY SERIES – six volumes
   PRUE BOOKS – six volumes
   RANDY BOOKS – eight volumes

Brooks, A. R.
   FREDDY SERIES:
   1 Freddy's first adventure
   2 Freddy the explorer
   3 Freddy the detective
   4 Freddy and Freginald

Brooks, E.
   KHAKI GIRLS SERIES – four volumes

Brooks, E. S.
   YOUNG DEFENDER SERIES:
   1 With Lawson and Roberts
   2 In defence of the flag
   3 Under the allied flag
   GROUSER SERIES:
   1 Grouser investigates
   2 Strange case of the antlered man

Brown, H. D.
   1 Little Miss Phoebe Gay
   2 Her sixteenth year

Brown, P.
   1 Swish of the curtain
   2 Golden pavements
   3 Blue door venture
   4 Maddy alone
   5 Maddy again 1956

Brown, R.
   TWO CHILDREN SERIES:
   1 Amazon adventures of two children
   2 Two children and their jungle zoo

Brown, R. Haig-
   1 Saltwater summer
   2 Starbuck Valley winter

Brown, T. B.
   PETER AND TIM SERIES:
   1 Adventures of Peter and Tim
   2 Peter and Tim's schooldays
   3 Peter and Tim on the trail

Bruce, D. F.
   DIMSIE SERIES:
   1 Dimsie goes to school
   2 Dimsie moves up
   3 Dimsie moves up again
   4 Dimsie among the prefects
   5 Dimsie grows up
   6 Dimsie head girl
   7 Dimsie goes back
   8 Dimsie intervenes
   9 Dimsie carries on
   NANCY SERIES:
   1 Nancy at St. Bride's
   2 Nancy returns to St. Bride's
   3 Nancy calls the tune
   SPRINGDALE SERIES:
   1 The New house captain
   2 The best house in the school
   3 Captain of Springdale
   4 The New house at Springdale
   5 Prefects at Springdale
   6 Captain Anne
   SALLY SERIES:
   1 Sally Scatterbrain
   2 Sally again
   3 Sally's summer term

Bruce, M. G.
   BILLABONG SERIES – eight volumes

Bruna, D.
MIFFY SERIES:
1 Miffy 1963
2 Miffy at the seaside 1964
3 Miffy at the zoo 1965
4 Miffy in the snow 1965

Bryson, C. L.
TAN AND TECKLE SERIES:
1 Tan and Teckle
2 Woodsy neighbours of Tan and Teckle

Buckels, A.
BUNNY BUFFIN SERIES:
1 Stories of Bunny Buffin
2 Adventures of Bunny Buffin

Buckeridge, A.
REX MILLIGAN SERIES:
1 Rex Milligan's busy term
2 Rex Milligan raises the roof
3 Rex Milligan holds forth 1957
4 Rex Milligan reporting 1961
JENNINGS SERIES:
1 Jennings goes to school
2 Jennings and Darbishire
3 Jennings follows a clue
4 Jennings' little hut
5 Jennings diary
6 According to Jennings
7 Our friend Jennings
8 Thanks to Jennings 1957
9 Take Jennings for instance 1958
10 Jennings as usual 1959
11 The trouble with Jennings 1960
12 Just like Jennings 1961
13 Leave it to Jennings 1963
14 Jennings, of course 1964
15 Especially Jennings 1965

Buhet, G.
1 The honey siege
2 The grand catch

Bullingham, A.
PENELOPE SERIES:
1 Penelope
2 Penelope and Curlew 1957
3 Summer on the hills 1960

Burgess, F. G.
GOOP SERIES – five volumes

Burgess, T. W.
ANIMAL STORIES SERIES – 20 volumes
BED-TIME STORY BOOKS – 20 volumes
BOY SCOUT SERIES – four volumes
GREEN MEADOW SERIES – four volumes
MOTHER WEST WIND SERIES – eight volumes

Burgoyne, P.
1 The school mystery
2 Fighting formula
3 Schoolmaster spy
4 Contraband castle 1960

Burleigh, C. B.
NORMAN CARVER SERIES:
1 All among the loggers
2 With pickpole and peavey
3 The young guide
RAYMOND BENSON SERIES:
1 The camp on Letter K
2 Raymond Benson at Krampton
3 The Kenton pines

Burman, B. L.
CATFISH BEND SERIES:
1 High water at Catfish Bend 1960
2 The owl hoots twice at Catfish Bend 1962
3 Seven stars for Catfish Bend 1962

Burr, S.
HOLLY GORDON SERIES:
1 Lantern of the North
2 My candle the moon
3 The Saint Bride Blue 1956

Burrett, E. C.
1 Boy Scout Crusoes
2 Cameron Island

Burton, C. P.
BOB'S HILL SERIES:
1 The boys of Bob's Hill
2 The Bob's Cave boys
3 The Bob's Hill braves
4 The boy scouts of Bob's Hill
5 Camp Bob's Hill
6 Raven patrol of Bob's Hill
7 The trail makers

227

Bush, A. M.
1 High school
2 The three friends

Butterworth, H.
ZIG–ZAG SERIES – 18 volumes

Byers, I.
PENNY AND GILIAN SERIES:
1 Adventure at Fairborough's Farm
2 Adventure at Dilingdon Dene
3 Adventure at the Blue Cockatoo
TONY AND MELISSA SERIES:
1 Jewel of the jungle
2 Flowers for Melissa
3 Kennel maid Sally
JEREMY AND FENELLA SERIES:
1 The strange story of Pippin Wood
2 The missing masterpiece 1957
   □
1 Tim of Tamberly Forest 1961
2 Tim returns to Tamberly 1962
3 Trouble at Tamberly 1964

Caldwell, P. K.
VIVIAN SERIES:
1 Prefects at Vivian's 1956
2 Head girl at Vivian's 1957

Campbell, B.
KEN HOLT SERIES:
1 Clue of the marked claw
2 Clue of the coiled cobra
3 Secret of Hangman's Inn
4 Mystery of the galloping horse
5 The black thumb mystery
6 The clue of the phantom car
7 Mystery of the iron box
8 Secret of Skeleton Island
9 Mystery of the green flame
10 Mystery of the grinning tiger
11 Mystery of the vanishing magician
12 Riddle of the stone elephant
13 Mystery of the invisible enemy
14 Mystery of the shattered glass
15 Mystery of Gallows Cliff
16 Clue of the silver scorpion

Campbell, J.
1 Four ponies 1959
2 The Merrow ponies 1961

Campbell, M.
RICHARD DE BRUN SERIES:
1 Wide blue road 1962
2 Lamas and longships 1963
3 The squire of Val 1963

Capon, P.
1 Warrior's moon
2 Kingdom of the bulls
3 Lord of the chariots
4 The golden cloak 1963

Carlson, N. S.
ORPHELINES SERIES:
1 The happy Orphelines 1960
2 A brother for the Orphelines 1961
3 A pet for the Orphelines 1963
4 The Orphelines in the enchanted castle 1965
   Stories about a French orphanage.

Carr, A. R.
NAN SHERWOOD SERIES – five volumes

Carroll, L. *pseud.* [C. L. Dodgson,]
ALICE SERIES:
1 Alice's adventures in Wonderland. *Originally published under the title, 'Alice's adventures underground'.*
2 Through the looking-glass and what Alice found there.
3 (Davy and the Goblin, or what followed reading 'Alice in Wonderland': by C. E. Carryl)
4 More Alice *by* G. Wilson 1959
SYLVIE SERIES:
1 Sylvie and Bruno
2 Sylvie and Bruno, concluded

Carruth, J.
SALLY SERIES:
1 Sally and her puppy
2 Sally on holiday
3 Sally on the farm

Carson, J.
SADDLE BOY SERIES – five volumes

Carter, B.
1 Perilous descent
2 Speed six!

Carter, H.
BOY SCOUTS SERIES – 12 volumes

Case, C. M.
1 Wolf the Saxon boy
2 The banner of the White Horse

Casserley, A.
BARNEY SERIES:
1 About Barney
2 Barney the donkey 1960

Castlemon, H. [C. A. Fosdick]
AFLOAT AND ASHORE SERIES – three volumes
BOY TRAPPER SERIES – three volumes
FOREST AND STREAM SERIES – three volumes
FRANK NELSON SERIES – three volumes
GO-AHEAD SERIES – three volumes
GUNBOAT SERIES – six volumes
HOUSEBOAT SERIES – three volumes
LUCKY TOM SERIES – three volumes
PONY EXPRESS SERIES – three volumes
ROCKY MOUNTAIN SERIES – three volumes
ROD AND GUN SERIES – three volumes
ROUGHING IT SERIES: – three volumes
SPORTSMAN'S CLUB SERIES – three volumes
WAR SERIES – six volumes

Catherall, A.
'S.S. BULLDOG' SERIES:
1 Ten fathoms deep 1954
2 Jackals of the sea 1955
3 Forgotten submarine 1955
4 Java sea duel 1957
5 Sea wolves 1958
6 Dangerous cargo 1960
7 China sea jigsaw 1962
8 Prisoners under the sea 1963
9 The strange invader 1964
10 Tanker trap 1965

Catling, G.
THE GANG SERIES:
1 The gang on the Broads
2 The gang in the Western isles

Chadwick, D.
EARLY AUSTRALIAN SERIES:
1 John of the Sirius
2 John of Sydney Cove 1957
3 John and Nanbaree 1962

Chadwick, L.
BASEBALL JOE SERIES – 11 volumes

Champney, Mrs. E. W.
GREAT-GRANDMOTHER'S GIRLS SERIES –
two volumes
THREE VASSAR GIRLS SERIES – 11 volumes
WITCH WINNIE SERIES – nine volumes

Chance, J. N.
BUNST SERIES:
1 The black ghost
2 The dangerous road
3 Bunst the bold
4 Bunst and the brown voice
5 Bunst and the secret six
6 Bunst and the flying eye

Channel, A. R.
1 The fighting four
2 The turret busters
3 Operation V.2.

Channon, F. E.
1 An American boy at Henley
2 Jackson and his Henley friends
3 Henley's American captain
4 Henley on the battle line

Chapman, A.
DAREWELL CHUMS SERIES – two volumes
FRED FENTON ATHLETIC SERIES – five
volumes
RADIO BOYS SERIES – seven volumes
RAILROAD SERIES – eight volumes
TOM FAIRFIELD SERIES – five volumes

Chapman, E.
MARMADUKE SERIES:
1 Marmaduke goes to France
2 Adventures with Marmaduke
3 Marmaduke and Joe
4 Marmaduke and his friends
5 Marmaduke and the elephant
6 Marmaduke and the lambs
7 Marmaduke and the lorry
8 Marmaduke goes to Holland
9 Marmaduke goes to America

Chauncy, N.
1 They found a cave
2 World's end was home
3 A fortune for the brave
Tasmanian stories.

Chaundler, C.
1 The fourth form detectives
2 The fourth form rebel

Chell, M.
SLIMTAILS SERIES:
1 Slimtails
2 More Slimtails
3 Merry Slimtails
4 Slimtail's triplets
5 Slimtail's friends
6 Slimtails at home 1956

Chrystie, M.
LEATHERS AUCKLAND SERIES:
1 Leathers steps in 1957
2 Leathers again 1958
3 Leathers after big game 1958
4 Leathers in Mozambique 1959
5 Leathers on the wild coast 1960

Church, R.
1 The cave
2 Down river 1958

Claire, H.
FIVE DOLLS SERIES:
1 Five dolls in a house
2 Five dolls and the monkey
3 Five dolls in the snow
4 Five dolls and their friends
5 Five dolls and the Duke

Clarke, E. L.
DROWSY SERIES:
1 Drowsy and Timmy go south
2 Farmer Drowsy
3 Drowsy's Christmas Eve
4 Drowsy and the beanstalk
5 Drowsy goes to school

Clarke, M.
LITTLE BEAR SERIES:
1 A big book about little bear
2 Another book about little bear

Clarke, P.
JAMES SERIES:
1 James the policeman
2 James and the robbers
3 James and the smugglers

Claudy, C. H.
TELL ME WHY SERIES – four volumes

Cleaver, H.
1 Brother o' mine
2 Captains of Harley
3 Roscoe makes good
4 The Harley First XI

Clewes, D.
THE HADLEY FAMILY SERIES:
1 The adventures of the Blue Admiral 1955
2 Adventure on Rainbow Island 1957
3 The jade green Cadillac 1958
4 The lost tower treasure 1959
5 Adventure of the scarlet daffodil 1960
6 The singing strings 1961

Coatsworth, E.
1 Away goes Sally
2 Five bushel farm
☐
1 The littlest house 1962
2 Plum daffy adventure 1965

Cobb, B. F.
JACK HENDERSON SERIES – six volumes

Coblentz, C.
1 Beggars' Penny
2 Bells of Leyden sing

Cockett, M.
Rolling on 1961
2 Cottage by the lock 1963

Cole, M. A.
JUDY LAWLER SERIES:
1 Holiday camp mystery
2 Thrilling holiday
3 Another thrilling holiday

Coleridge, C. R.
1 Green girls of Greythorpe
2 Fifty pounds

Collins, F.
THE WOODLAND PACK:
1 The Pack that ran itself
2 The Woodland Pack
3 The Brownie year 1957
4 Barny and the Big House Pack 1960

Comfort, M. H.
THE DUSTIN FAMILY:
1 Winter on the Johnny Smoker
2 Treasure on the Johnny Smoker

Conway, E. C.
1 The little ways
2 More little ways
Stories of the Saints.

Coolidge, S. [S. C. Woolsey]
KATY SERIES:
1 What Katy did
2 What Katy did at school
3 What Katy did next
4 What Katy did at home
5 Clover
6 In the high valley

Cooper, E. H.
WYMARKE SERIES – four volumes

Corcoran, B.
1 The boy scouts of Kendallville
2 The boy scouts of the Wolf Patrol

Corson, H. W.
PETER SERIES:
1 Peter and the moon trip 1962
2 Peter and the unlucky rocket 1963
3 Peter and the big balloon 1963

Cory, D.
PUSS IN BOOTS, JUNIOR, SERIES—six volumes

Courtney, G.
WILD LORINGS SERIES:
1 The wild Lorings at school
2 The wild Lorings – detectives

Cox, J.
SKIPPER SERIES:
1 Dangerous waters
2 Calamity camp 1956

Cox, P.
BROWNIE SERIES – 11 volumes

Cox, S. A.
DARE BOYS SERIES – 12 volumes

Cradock, Mrs. H. C.
JOSEPHINE SERIES – seven volumes
TEDDY BEAR SERIES:
1 Adventures of a teddy bear
2 More adventures of a teddy bear
3 In teddy bear's house
4 Teddy bear's shop
5 Teddy bear's farm

Craigie, D.
NICKY AND NIGGER SERIES:
1 Nicky and Nigger join the circus 1958
2 Nicky and Nigger and the pirates 1960
CAPTAIN FLINT SERIES:
1 Captain Flint to the rescue 1958
2 Captain Flint detective 1959
3 Captain Flint shipwrecked 1960
TIM HOOLEY SERIES:
1 Tim Hooley's hero 1957
2 Tim Hooley's haunting 1958

Crane, L. D.
THE AUTOMOBILE GIRLS SERIES – six volumes

Creed, Mrs. J. P. [L. Mack]
1 Teens
2 Girls together

Cresswell, H.
JUMBO SPENCER SERIES:
1 Jumbo Spencer 1964
2 Jumbo back to nature 1965

Creswell, H. B.
MARYTARY SERIES:
1 Marytary
2 Johnny and Marytary

Creswick, P.
1 In Aelfred's days
2 Under the Black Raven
3 Hasting, the pirate

Crisp, F.
DIRK ROGERS SERIES:
1 Java Wreckmen
2 The demon wreck
3 Manila menfish
4 Sea ape
5 Giant of Jembu gulf
6 The ice diners 1960
7 The coral wreck 1964
8 The samguman 1965

Crockett, S.
TWO AMERICAN BOYS SERIES –
five volumes

Crompton, R.
WILLIAM SERIES:
1 Just William
2 More William
3 William again
4 William the Fourth
5 Still William
6 William – the Conqueror
7 William – in trouble
8 William – the outlaw
9 William – the good
10 William
11 William the bad
12 William's happy days
13 William's crowded hours
14 William the pirate
15 William the rebel
16 William the gangster
17 William the detective
18 Sweet William
19 William the showman
20 William the dictator
21 William and A.R.P., *republished*
   1956 *as* William the film star
22 William and the evacuees *republished*
   1956 *as* William's bad resolution
23 William carries on
24 William does his bit
25 William and the Brains Trust
26 Just William's luck
27 William the bold
28 William and the tramp
29 William and the moon rocket
30 William and the space animal 1956
31 William the explorer 1960
32 William's television show 1961
33 William's treasure trove 1962

34 William and the witch 1964
35 William and the pop singers 1965
JIMMY SERIES:
1 Jimmy
2 Jimmy again

Cross, J. K.
1 Angry planet
2 S.O.S. from Mars
   Adventures of 'Albatross' explorers.
   Science fiction.

Cumming, P.
SILVER EAGLE SERIES:
1 Silver Eagle riding school
2 Silver Eagle carries on
3 Rivals to Silver Eagle

Curlewis, Mrs. H. R., *see* Turner, E.

Currey, E. H.
IAN HARDY SERIES:
1 Ian Hardy, naval cadet
2 Ian Hardy, midshipman
3 Ian Hardy, senior midshipman
4 Ian Hardy fighting the Moors

Curtis, Mrs. A. T.
GRANDPA'S LITTLE GIRLS SERIES –
   six volumes
LITTLE MAIDS' HISTORICAL SERIES—
   three volumes
MARJORIE SERIES – four volumes

Cuthbert, D.
1 Six in a castle
2 Six and a secret

Dale, J.
SHIRLEY FLIGHT SERIES:
1 Shirley Flight, air hostess 1958
2 Shirley Flight and the diamond
   smugglers 1958
3 Shirley Flight and the desert adventure 1958
4 Shirley Flight in Hollywood 1958
5 Shirley Flight and the Flying Doctor
   1959
6 Shirley Flight and the Rajah's
   daughter 1959

7 Shirley Flight in Congo rescue 1960
8 Shirley Flight and the great bullion mystery 1960
9 Shirley Flight and the fjord adventure 1961
10 Shirley Flight and the Pacific castways 1961
11 Shirley Flight and the Chinese puzzle 1962
12 Shirley Flight and the flying jet 1962
13 Shirley Flight in Canadian capers 1962
14 Shirley Flight in storm warning 1963
15 Shirley Flight in Hawaiian mystery 1963
16 Shirley Flight in Spain 1963

Dale, N.
TIM FOREST SERIES:
1 The exciting journey
2 Mystery Christmas
3 Skeleton Island
ADVENTURES OF PETER, GINGER AND VERONICA:
1 Secret service
2 Dangerous treasure
3 The best adventures
□
1 The clock that struck fifteen
2 The Medenham carnival
3 The Pied Piper of Medenham
4 All change for Medenham
5 A Medenham secret

Dalton, C.
1 Malay canoe
2 Malay boy
3 Malay island
4 Malay cruise

Daniell, D. S.
DRUMMER OLIVER GROVE:
1 Mission for Oliver
2 Polly and Oliver
3 Polly and Oliver at sea 1960
4 Polly and Oliver beseiged 1963
5 Polly and Oliver pursued 1964
The adventures of Drummer Oliver Grove of the 111th Regiment of Foot and his cousin Polly.
JIMIMY SERIES:
1 By Jimimy

2 Saved by Jimimy
3 By Jimimy ahoy 1963

Danielsson, B.
1 Terry in the South Seas 1960
2 Terry in Australia 1961

Darbois, D.
1 Nick in Africa
2 Nick in Tahiti

Daringer, H. F.
THE ENDICOTT FAMILY SERIES:
1 Pilgrim Kate
2 Debbie of the Green Gate
3 Country cousin
A chronicle of the early American settlers.

Darling, M. G.
1 Battles at home
2 In the world
□
1 We four girls
2 A girl of this century

Darlington, E. B. P.
THE CIRCUS BOYS SERIES – four volumes

Darwin, B., *and* E.
1 The tale of Mr. Tootleoo
2 Tootleoo two

Davis, J.
1 Tadgy the mystery boy
2 Detective Tadgy
3 Tadgy on the trail

Dawlish, P.
1 Captain Peg-leg's war
2 Peg-leg and the fur pirates
3 Peg-Leg sweeps the sea
□
1 MacClellan's lake
2 The Bagodia episode
DAUNTLESS SERIES:
1 Dauntless finds her crew
2 Dauntless sails again
3 Dauntless and the Mary Baines
4 Dauntless takes recruits
5 Dauntless sails in
6 Dauntless in danger
7 Dauntless goes home 1960

Dawson, H.
NOREEN AND AUNT JOAN:
1 Noreen's first case 1959
2 The house in Haven Street 1960
3 Noreen and the Barclay affair 1963
4 Noreen and the missing schoolgirl 1963
5 Noreen and the Henry affair 1965
6 Noreen and the mystery hero 1965

Daykin, L.
1 The fairground family
2 More about the fairground family

Dehn, O.
TABBY SERIES:
1 Tabby magic 1959
2 More Tabby magic 1960
THE CARETAKERS SERIES:
1 The caretakers
2 The caretakers and the poacher
3 The caretakers and the gypsy
4 The caretakers to the rescue

De Jong, D.
LEVEL LAND SERIES:
1 The level land
2 Return to the level land

Delahaye, G.
MARY SERIES:
1 Mary's mountain holiday 1962
2 Mary goes camping 1963
3 Mary's happy year 1964
4 Mary's seaside holiday 1965

De La Mahotiere, M.
1 The newspaper children 1960
2 Round-up on Exmoor 1961

Delderfield, R. F., *see* Stevenson, R. L.

Delgado, A.
MIKE AND CAROLINE SERIES:
1 The very hot water bottle
2 Hide the slipper 1963

De Mille, J.
BRETHREN OF THE WHITE CROSS SERIES:
1 The B.O.W.C.
2 Boys of Grand Pré School
3 Lost in the fog
4 Fire in the woods
5 Picked up adrift
6 Treasure of the seas
YOUNG DODGE SERIES:
1 Among the brigands: Italy
2 The seven hills: Rome
3 The winged lion: Venice

Deming, T.
INDIAN LIFE SERIES:
1 Little Eagle
2 Indians in winter camp
3 Red people of the wooded country
4 Indians of the pueblos
5 Indians of the wigwams

Denes, G.
JOHN AND JENNIFER
1 Jennifer goes to school
2 John and Jennifer at the zoo
3 Christmas at Timothy's
4 John and Jennifer at the farm
5 John and Jennifer at the circus
6 John and Jennifer and their pets
7 John and Jennifer's treasure hunt
8 John and Jennifer go camping
9 John and Jennifer's pony club
10 John and Jennifer go to London 1956
11 John and Jennifer go sailing 1957
12 John and Jennifer's concert party
13 John and Jennifer go travelling 1957
14 John and Jennifer at London Airport 1958

Denison, M.
SUSANNAH SERIES:
1 Susannah of the mounties
2 Susannah rides again
3 Susannah of the Yukon

Denton, J.
JAMIE SERIES:
1 Jamie: the story of a puffer 1958
2 Jamie and Jock's present 1959

Denton, P.

THE TWINS SERIES:
1 Tales of the twins
2 The twins again 1959

Derwent, L.

MACPHERSON SERIES:
1 Macpherson
2 Macpherson's funnybone
3 Macpherson's highland fling
4 Macpherson in Edinburgh
5 Macpherson in America

De Selincourt, A.

1 Family afloat
2 Three green bottles
3 One good 'Tern'
4 One more summer
5 Calicut lends a hand
6 Micky
7 Kestrel

Diack, H.

1 Boy in a village
2 That village on the Don
N.F. Autobiography

Dick, A.

ALASTAIR MACALASTAIR SERIES:
1 And only man
2 Old-fashioned Christmas
3 Curate's crime
4 MacAlastair looks on
5 Cross purposes

Dickins, J.

1 Jill and Prince and the pony 1963
2 Jill and Prince triumph again 1964

Dickson, H.

SUNSHINE RANCH SERIES:
1 Doris of Sunshine Ranch
2 Family at Sunshine Ranch

Dirks, R.

KATZEMJAMMER KIDS SERIES:
1 The cruise of the Katzemjammer kids
2 The Komical Katzemjammers
3 The tricks of the Katzemjammer kids

Dixon, F. W.

HARDY BOYS SERIES:
1 Secret of the lost tunnel
2 Sign of the crooked arrow
3 Phantom freighter
4 House on the cliff
5 Tower treasure
6 Secret of the old mill
7 Missing chums
8 Hunting for hidden gold
9 Shore Road mystery
10 Secret of the caves
11 Mystery of Cabin Island
12 Great airport mystery
13 Secret of skull mountain
14 Secret panel
15 What happened at midnight
16 While the clock ticked
17 Footprints under the window
18 Mark on the door
19 Hidden harbour mystery
20 Sinister signpost
21 Figure in hiding
22 Secret warning
23 Twisted claw
24 Disappearing floor
25 Mystery of the flying express
26 Clue of the broken blade
27 Flickering torch mystery
28 Melted coins
29 Short-wave mystery
30 Wailing siren mystery
31 Secret of wild cat swamp
32 Pursuit patrol
33 Mystery of the desert giant
34 The clue of the screeching owl
35 The secret of Pirate's hill
36 The ghost at skeleton creek
37 The Viking symbol mystery
38 The mystery of the Aztec warrior
39 The mystery at Devil's Paw
40 The mystery of the Chinese junk
41 The crisscross shadow 1965
42 The yellow father mystery 1965
43 The hooded hawk mystery 1965
44 The clue in the embers 1965

Dixon, R.

POCOMOTO SERIES:
1 Pocomoto – pony express rider
2 Pocomoto – tenderfoot
3 Pocomoto and the canyon treasure

Dixon, R. (*contd.*)
4 Pocomoto and the night riders
5 Pocomoto – Bronco buster
6 Pocomoto – brush poppa
7 Pocomoto and the l'il fella
8 Pocomoto – buffalo hunter
9 Pocomoto – cowboy cavalier
10 Pocomoto and the lazy river
11 Pocomoto and the snow wolf
12 Pocomoto and the Indian trails
13 Pocomoto and the Sierra pioneers
14 Pocomoto and the Spanish steed
15 Pocomoto and the golden herd
16 Pocomoto and the robbers' trail 1956
17 Pocomoto and the desert gold 1957
18 Pocomoto and the circus folk 1957
19 Pocomoto and the lazy sheriff 1958
20 Pocomoto and the lost hunters 1959
21 Pocomoto and the cowboy herd 1960
22 Pocomoto and the desert braves 1961
23 Pocomoto and the Mexican bandits 1963

Dodgson, C. L., *see* Carroll, L., *pseud.*

Donman, G.
CARMELO SERIES:
1 Shattering silence
2 Swooping vengeance

Donovan, J. B.
BILL SPEED SERIES:
1 Meet Bill Speed, C.I.D.
2 The laughing horses
3 Bill Speed on hot ice
4 Bill Speed – special squad

Douglas, A. M.
HELEN GRANT SERIES – nine volumes
KATHIE STORIES – seven volumes
LITTLE GIRL SERIES – 14 volumes
LITTLE RED HOUSE SERIES – five volumes
SHERBURNE HOUSE SERIES – 12 volumes

Douglas, F.
1 Alarms and excursions
2 The sentimental smuggler

Dowd, E. C.
POLLY SERIES:
1 Polly of the Lady Gay Cottage
2 Polly of the hospital staff
3 Polly and the princess

Downie, J. M.
GAUNT SERIES:
1 Gaunt of the Pearl Seas patrol
2 Secret of the loch
3 Gaunt of Pacific Command

Drake, J.
MR. GRIMPWINKLE SERIES:
1 The jiggle woggle bus
2 Mr. Grimpwinkle
3 Mr. Grimpwinkle's marrow
4 Mr. Grimpwinkle – pirate cook
5 Mr. Grimpwinkle buys a house
5 Mr. Grimpwinkle buys a bus
6 Mr. Grimpwinkle's holiday
7 Mr. Grimpwinkle's visitor

Drysdale, W.
1 The young reporter
2 The fast mail
3 The beach patrol
4 The young supercargo

Dubois, I. M.
LITTLE GREY MOUSE SERIES:
1 Little grey mouse
2 More adventures of the little grey mouse family

Dudley, A. T.
PHILLIPS EXETER SERIES:
1 Following the ball
2 Making the nine
3 In the line
4 With mask and mitt
5 The great year
6 The Yale cup
7 A full-back afloat
8 The Pecks in camp
STORIES OF THE TRIANGULAR LEAGUE:
1 The school four
2 At the home plate

Dudley, C., *and* **Elwell, F. R.**
MR. COLLINS AND TONY SERIES:
1 Mr. Collins and Tony go fishing
2 Mr. Collins and Tony visit Heron Wood

Duff, D.V.

BILL BERENGER SERIES:
1 Bill Berenger's first case
2 Berenger to the rescue
3 Berenger's toughest case
4 Bill Berenger wins command

ADAM MACADAM, NAVAL CADET:
1 Sea serpent island 1956
2 Ocean haul 1956
3 The *San Matteo* 1957
4 Sea-bed treasure 1957
5 Black ivory 1958
6 Undersea oil tanker 1959
7 At close grips 1959
8 Crusader's gold 1959
9 The king's rescue 1959
10 Pirates aboard 1960
11 The stolen aircraft carrier 1961
12 Red sea blackbirders 1961
13 The pale grey man 1962

JEREMY SERIES:
1 The ship-slayers
2 The miracle man
3 Operation sunpower

SHELLBACK SERIES:
1 Yarns of a shellback
2 More yarns of a shellback 1960

Dugdale, P. M.

DUNKEL SERIES:
1 Dunkel
2 Dunkel again

Du Jardin, R.

TOBEY HEYDON SERIES:
1 Class ring
2 Boy trouble

PAM AND PENNY SERIES:
1 Double date
2 Double feature

MARCEY SERIES:
1 Wait for Marcy
2 Marcy catches up

Duncan, J.

CAMERONS SERIES:
1 Camerons on the train 1962
2 Camerons on the hills 1963
3 Camerons at the castle 1964

Duncan, K. M.

1 Secrets at Saxon Hill 1963
2 The lordly isle 1964

Duncan, N.

1 Adventures of Billy Topsail
2 Billy Topsail and Co.
3 Doctor Luke of the Labrador
4 Billy Topsail, M.D.

Dunn, M.

1 We go to Paris
2 We go to Belgium
3 We go to Denmark
4 We go to the Channel Islands
N.F. The main character is the same.

Durham, V. C.

THE SUBMARINE BOYS SERIES – eight
volumes

Dutton, L.

RAGS SERIES:
1 Rags, M.D.
2 Again Rags

Duvoisin, R.

VERONICA SERIES:
1 Veronica 1963
2 Veronica goes to Petunia's farm 1964
3 Veronica's smile 1965

Dyer, E. M. Brent-

CHALET SCHOOL SERIES:
1 School at the Chalet
2 Jo of the Chalet School
3 Princess of the Chalet School
4 Rivals of the Chalet School
5 Head girl of the Chalet School
6 Euastacia goes to the Chalet School
7 Chalet School and Jo
8 Chalet School in camp
9 Exploits of the Chalet girls
10 Chalet School and the Lintons
11 New House at the Chalet School
12 Jo returns to the Chalet School
13 New Chalet School
14 Chalet School in exile
15 Chalet School goes to it
16 Highland twins and the Chalet School
17 Lavender laughs in Chalet School
18 Gay from China in the Chalet School
19 Jo to the rescue
20 Three go to the Chalet School
21 Chalet School and the island

Dyer, E. M. Brent- (*contd.*)
22 Peggy of the Chalet School
23 Carola storms the Chalet School
24 Wrong Chalet School
25 Shocks for the Chalet School
26 Chalet School in the Oberland
27 Bride leads the Chalet School
28 Changes for the Chalet School
29 Joey goes to the Oberland
30 Chalet School and Barbara
31 Chalet School does it again
32 Tom tackles the Chalet School
33 Chalet girl from Kenya
34 Mary Lou at the Chalet School
35 Genius at the Chalet School 1956
36 Problem for the Chalet School 1956
37 New mistress at the Chalet School 1957
38 Excitements at the Chalet School 1957
39 The coming of age of the Chalet School 1958
40 Chalet School and Richenda 1958
41 Trials at the Chalet School 1959
42 Theodora and the Chalet School 1959
43 Joey and Co. in the Tyrol 1960
44 Ruby Richardson Chaletian 1960
45 A leader in the Chalet School 1961
46 The Chalet School wins a trick 1961
47 A future Chalet schoolgirl 1962
48 The feud in the Chalet School 1962
49 The Chalet School triplets 1963
50 The Chalet School reunion 1963
51 Jane and the Chalet School 1964
52 Redheads at the Chalet School 1964
53 Adrienne of the Chalet School 1965
54 Summer term at the Chalet School 1965

LA ROCHELLE SERIES:

1 Maids of La Rochelle
2 Janie of La Rochelle
3 Heather leaves school
4 Head girl's difficulties
5 Gerry goes to school
6 Seven scamps
7 Janie steps in

SKELTON HALL SERIES:

1 The school at Skelton Hall 1962
2 Trouble at Skelton Hall 1963

Eager, E.
1 Magic or noté
2 The well-wishers

Earl, J. P.
THE SCHOOL TEAM SERIES – four volumes

Eaton, S.
BEARS SERIES – seven volumes

Eaton, W. P.
BOY SCOUTS SERIES – five volumes

Eddy, D. C.
WALTER SERIES – six volumes

Eden, C. H.
1 At sea with Drake
2 Queer chums

Edwards, D.
THE APPLEYARDS SERIES:
1 The Appleyards 1955
2 The Appleyards again 1956

Edwards, L.
JERRY TODD BOOKS – two volumes

Edwards, M.
PUNCHBOWL FARM SERIES:
1 No mistaking Corker
2 Black hunting whip
3 Punchbowl midnight
4 Spirit of Punchbowl Farm
5 The wanderer
6 Punchbowl harvest
7 Frenchman's secret 1956
8 The cownappers 1958
9 The outsider 1961
    Includes characters from Romney Marsh series.
10 Fire in the Punchbowl 1965
ROMNEY MARSH SERIES:
1 Wish for a pony
2 Summer of the great secret
3 The midnight horse
4 The white riders
5 Hidden in a dream
6 Cargo of horses
7 Storm ahead
8 No entry
9 The nightbird
10 Operation seabird 1957

11 Strangers to the Marsh 1958
12 No going back 1960
13 The hoodwinkers 1961
14 Killer dog 1962
15 Dolphin summer 1963

Edwards, S.
SALLY BAXTER, GIRL REPORTER SERIES:
1 Sally Baxter in Canada 1958
2 Sally Baxter and the mystery heiress 1958
3 Sally Baxter and the runaway princess 1958
4 Sally Baxter on location 1958
5 African alibi 1959
6 The holiday family 1959
7 In Australia 1959
8 Underwater adventure 1959
9 The golden yacht 1961
10 Secret island 1961
11 The Shamrock mystery 1961
12 Strangers in Fleet Street 1961

Edwin, M.
1 Curlew Jon
2 The Zig-zag path
3 The double halfpenny

Eggleston, E.
1 The Hoosier schoolmaster
2 The Hoosier schoolboy

Eigl, K.
MORO SERIES:
1 Moro the little black donkey 1965
2 Moro at the holiday camp 1966

Eiloart, Mrs. E.
ERNIE ELTON SERIES:
1 Ernie Elton, the lazy boy
2 Ernie Elton at school
3 Ernie Elton at home and school

Einberg, E.
THE KENNEDYS ABROAD SERIES:
1 Ann and Peter in Holland
2 Ann and Peter in Southern Spain
3 Ann and Peter in Southern Germany 1959

Eldon, M.
BUMBLE SERIES:
1 Bumble
2 Snow Bumble
3 Highland Bumble

Eldred, W. L.
1 The crimson ramblers
2 Classroom and campus
3 St. Dunstan boy scouts
4 Camp St. Dunstan

Eliot, H. E.
LAURA SERIES:
1 Laura's holidays
2 Laura in the mountains

Elliott, E. C.
KEMLO SERIES:
1 Kemlo and the zones of silence
2 Kemlo and the crazy planet
3 Kemlo and the sky horse
4 Kemlo and the Martian ghosts
5 Kemlo and the craters of the moon
6 Kemlo and the space lanes
7 Kemlo and the star men
8 Kemlo and the gravity rays
9 Kemlo and the purple dawn
10 Kemlo and the end of time
11 Kemlo and the zombie men 1958
12 Kemlo and the space men 1960
13 Kemlo and the satellite builders 1961
14 Kemlo and the space invaders 1962
15 Kemlo and the masters of space 1963

Ellis, E. S. *pseud.* [H. R. Gordon]
ARIZONA SERIES – three volumes
AUTOMOBILE SERIES – two volumes
BOONE AND KENTON SERIES – three volumes
BOUND TO WIN SERIES – three volumes
BOY PATROL SERIES – two volumes
BOY PIONEER SERIES – three volumes
BRAVE AND HONEST SERIES – three volumes
COLONIAL SERIES – three volumes
DEERFOOT SERIES – three volumes
FOREIGN ADVENTURE SERIES – three volumes
FOREST AND PRAIRIES SERIES – three volumes
GREAT RIVER SERIES – three volumes

Ellis, E. S. *pseud.* [**H. R. Gordon**]
(*contd.*)

LOG CABIN SERIES – three volumes
NEW DEERFOOT SERIES – three volumes
NORTHWEST SERIES – three volumes
PADDLE YOUR OWN CANOE SERIES – three
volumes
RIVER AND WILDERNESS SERIES – three
volumes
STRANGE ADVENTURE SERIES – two volumes
THROUGH ON TIME SERIES – two volumes
TRUE GRIT SERIES – three volumes
WAR CHIEF SERIES – three volumes
WILD ADVENTURE SERIES – two volumes
WILD WOODS SERIES – three volumes
WYOMING VALLEY SERIES – – three volumes

Ellis, E. S., *and* **Chipman, W. P.**

UP AND DOING SERIES:
1 A hunt on snow shoes
2 The cruise of the *Firefly*

Ellis, K. R.

THE WIDE AWAKE GIRLS SERIES – three
volumes

Ellis, V.

HILARY SERIES:
1 Hilary's tune
2 Hilary's holidays 1961

Ellison, M. (Nomad, *pseud.***)**

NOMAD SERIES:
1 Wandering with Nomad
2 Out of doors with Nomad
3 Over the hills with Nomad
4 Roving with Nomad
5 Adventuring with Nomad
6 Northwards with Nomad

Ellsberg, E.

SALVAGE SERIES:
1 Thirty fathoms deep
2 Ocean gold
3 Spanish ingots
4 Treasure below

Elwell, F. R.

MR. COLLINS AND TONY SERIES:
1 Mr. Collins and Tony go tracking

2 Mr. Collins and Tony and the
sleeping mouse
3 Mr. Collins and Tony by the sea
1960
4 Mr. Collins and Tony in London
1960

Emerson, A. B.

BETTY GORDON SERIES – seven volumes
RUTH FIELDING SERIES – 20 volumes

Endicott, R. B.

CAROLYN SERIES:
1 Carolyn of the Corners
2 Carolyn of the sunny heart

Enright, E.

THE MELENDY FAMILY SERIES:
1 The Saturdays
2 The four storey mistake
3 Then there were five
4 Spiderweb for two
PORTIA AND JULIAN SERIES:
1 Gone-away lake
2 Return to Gone-away 1962

Estes, E.

THE MOFFATS SERIES:
1 The Moffats
2 Middle Moffat 1960
3 Rufus, M. 1960

Estoril, J.

DRINA SERIES:
1 Ballet for Drina 1957
2 Drina's dancing 1958
3 Drina dances in exile 1959
4 Drinas dances in Italy 1959
5 Drina dances again 1960
6 Drina dances in New York 1961
7 Drina dances in Paris 1962
8 Drina dances in Madeira 1963
9 Drina dances in Switzerland 1964
10 Drina goes on tour 1965

Euphan, J., *pseud., see* Todd, B.

Evens, G. K. (Romany, *pseud***)**

ROMANY SERIES:
1 Out with Romany
2 Out with Romany again
3 Out with Romany once more

4 Out with Romany by the sea
5 Out with Romany by moor and dale
6 Out with Romany by meadow and stream
7 Romany, Muriel and Doris
8 Romany turns detective
9 Romany caravan returns

Everett-Green, E., *see* Green- E., Everett

Falkner, F. B.
AQUALUNG TWINS SERIES:
1 Aqualung twins find Chinese treasure 1956
2 Aqualung twins and the vanishing people 1957
3 Aqualung twins and the iron crab 1958

Farjeon, E.
MARTIN PIPPIN SERIES:
1 Martin Pippin in the apple orchard
2 The King's barn
3 Young Gerard
4 The mill of dreams
5 Martin Pippin in the daisy field

Farley, W.
BLACK STALLION SERIES:
1 Black stallion
2 Black stallion returns
3 Son of the Black stallion
4 Black stallion and Satan
5 Blood Bay colt
6 Black stallion's filly 1952
7 Little Black, a pony 1964
8 Little Black goes to the circus 1965

Farmer, B. J.
1 The vanished policeman
2 Policeman's holiday
3 Tony Ward, policeman
4 Policeman's hobby 1960

Farrar, F. W.
1 Darkness and dawn
2 Gathering clouds

Farrow, G. E.
PANJANDRUM SERIES – two volumes
WALLYPUG SERIES – 11 volumes

Fation, L.
HAPPY LION SERIES:
1 The happy lion
2 The happy lion roars
3 The three happy lions
4 The happy lion's quest
5 The happy lion in Africa
6 The happy lion and the bear

Fearn, J.
GOLDEN AMAZON SERIES:
1 Golden Amazon
2 Golden Amazon returns
3 Golden Amazon's triumph
4 Amazon's diamond quest
5 Amazon strikes again
6 Twin of the Amazon
MERRIDEW SERIES:
1 Valley of the doomed
2 Merridew rides again
3 Merridew marches on
4 Merridew fights again
5 Merridew follows the trail

Fearon, E.
PLUCKROSE SERIES:
1 The sheepdog adventure
2 Pluckrose's horse
3 Secret of the Chateau

Feist, A.
JEREMY SHAFTO SERIES:
1 High Barbary
2 Spread Eagle

Felsen, G.
BERTIE SERIES
1 Bertie comes through
2 Bertie takes care

Ferguson, R.
JILL SERIES:
1 Jill's gymkhana
2 A stable for Jill
3 Jill has two ponies
4 Jill enjoys her ponies
5 Jill's riding club 1956
6 Rosettes for Jill 1957
7 Jill and the perfect pony 1959
8 Pony jobs for Jill 1960
9 Jill's pony trek 1962

Fidler, K.

THE BRYDONS SERIES:

1 The borrowed garden 1944
2 St. Jonathan's in the country 1945
3 The Brydons at Smuggler's Creek 1946
4 More adventures of the Brydons 1947
5 The Brydons in summer 1948
6 The Brydons do battle 1949
7 The Brydons in a pickle 1950
8 The Brydons look for trouble 1950
9 The Brydons hunt for treasure 1951
10 The Brydons catch queer fish 1952
11 The Brydons stick at nothing 1952
12 The Brydons abroad 1953
13 The Brydons get things going 1954
14 Surprises for the Brydons 1955
15 Challenge to the Brydons 1956
16 The Brydons go camping 1958
17 The Brydons at Blackpool 1960
18 The Brydons on the Broads 1961
19 The Brydons go canoeing 1963

DEANS SERIES:

1 Deans move in
2 Deans follow a clue
3 Deans solve a mystery
4 Deans defy danger
5 Deans dive for treasure 1956
6 Deans to the rescue 1957
7 Deans lighthouse adventure 1959
8 Deans and Mr. Popple 1960
9 The Dean's Dutch adventure 1962

HERITAGE SERIES:

1 Tales of the North Country
2 Tales of London
3 Tales of the Midlands

Finlay, C. K.

JOHN MCINNES SERIES:

1 Fisherman's gold 1961
2 Shepherd's purse 1963
3 Farewell to the Western Isles 1964

Finlay, W.

GILLIAN LINDSAY SERIES:

1 The Witch of Redesdale
2 Peril in the Pennines
3 Peril in Lakeland

JUDITH NORTON SERIES:

1 Cotswold holiday
2 Judith in Hanover

3 Lost silver of Langdon
4 Storm over the Cheviot

NARROW BOAT SERIES:

1 Canal holiday 1955
2 Cruise of the *Susan* 1958

Finly, M.

ELSIE BOOKS – 28 volumes
MILDRED SERIES – seven volumes
ANOTHER SERIES:

1 An old-fashioned boy
2 Our Fred

Finnemore, J.

TEDDY LESTER SERIES:

1 Three school chums
2 His first term
3 Teddy Lester's chums
4 Teddy Lester's schooldays
5 Teddy Lester in the fifth
6 Teddy Lester, captain of cricket

Fitzgerald, H.

1 Home farm 1956
2 Faraway farm 1957

Fitzhugh, P. K.

BOY SCOUT SERIES – three volumes
PEE WEE HARRIS SERIES – seven volumes
ROY BLAKELY SERIES – 11 volumes
TOM SLADE SERIES – 13 volumes
WEETY MARTIN BOOKS – two volumes

Fitzroy, O.

1 The island of birds 1955
2 The hunted head 1956
Historical stories of the '45.

Flack, M.

ANGUS SERIES:

1 Angus and the cat
2 Angus and the ducks
3 Angus and Topsy
4 Angus and Way-Tail-Bess
5 Angus lost

Flandrau, C. M.

1 The diary of a freshman
2 Sophomores abroad

Flower, J. G.
GRACE HARLOWE SERIES:
Group 1 (High School) –
four volumes
Group 2 (College) –
seven volumes
Group 3 (Overland) – 10 volumes

Flynn, M.
CORNELIUS RABBIT SERIES:
1 Cornelius Rabbit of Tang
2 Cornelius on holidays
3 Cornelius in charge

Forest, A.
THE MARLOWE FAMILY SERIES:
1 Autumn term 1956
2 Falconer's lure 1957
3 Peter's room 1961
4 The Marlows and the traitor 1962
5 The Thursday kidnapping 1964
6 The Thuggery affair 1965

Forester, D. J.
THE BUNGALOW BOYS SERIES – six volumes

Forrester, I. L.
THE POLLY PAGE SERIES – four volumes

Fosdick, C. A., *see* Castlemon, H.

Foster, E. F.
1 Mary'n' Mary
2 Marigold
3 Marigold's winter

Foster, K.
JONATHAN LAMB SERIES:
1 Dangerous waters
2 Danger for two
3 Jonathan Lamb adventurer
4 Jonathan Lamb detective
5 Jonathan Lamb in peril

Foster, W. B.
1 Swept out to sea
2 The frozen ship
3 From sea to sea
4 The sea express

Fox, F. M.
COSY CORNER SERIES – two volumes
LITTLE BEAR SERIES – three volumes

Fox, G. M.
MOUNTAIN GIRL SERIES:
1 Mountain girl
2 Mountain girl comes home

Francoise, *pseud.*
JEANNE-MARIE SERIES:
1 Jeanne-Marie counts her sheep
2 Springtime for Jeanne-Marie
3 Jeanne-Marie in gay Paris
4 Jeanne-Marie at the fair

Fraser, C.
1 The underground explorers
2 The underground river

Fraser, E.
DAVID JOHN SERIES:
1 David John 1962
2 David John hears about Jesus 1963
3 David John again 1964
4 David John finds out 1965

Freehoff, W. A.
YOUNG FARMER SERIES:
1 The young farmer
2 The young farmer at college

Frees, H. W.
1 The Sandman: his puppy stories
2 The Sandman: his animal stories
3 The Sandman: his bunny stories
4 The Sandman: his kittycat stories

Frewer, G.
ADVENTURE SERIES:
1 Adventure in Forgotten Valley 1963
2 Adventure in the Barren Lands 1964

Frey, H. C.
CAMP FIRE GIRLS SERIES – ten volumes

Frey, H. C., and Vandercook, M., *see* Vandercook, M.

Frith, H.
1 Captains of cadets
2 The log of the *Bombastes*

Frost, F. M.
WINDY FOOT SERIES:
1 Windy Foot at the county fair
2 Sleigh bells for Windy Foot
3 Maple sugar for Windy Foot

Frost, K. D.
1 Drinker of the wind
2 Sahara hostage

Fry, R.
1 Lucinda and the painted bell 1957
2 Lucinda and the sailor kitten 1958
3 Fly home Colombina 1959

Fyson, J.
1 The three brothers of Ur 1964
2 The journey of the eldest son 1965

Gall, A. C.
MOTHER MCGREW BOOKS – ten volumes

Gallico, P.
1 The day the guinea-pig talked 1962
2 The day Jean-Pierre was kidnapped 1963
3 The day Jean-Pierre went round the world 1965

Gardner, H.
1 Beyond the marble mountain
2 Back to the marble mountain

Garis, H. R.
BED TIME STORIES – 24 volumes
CURLY CAPS SERIES – six volumes
DADDY SERIES – ten volumes
GIRL SCOUT SERIES – five volumes
GLORIA SERIES – two volumes
JOAN BOOKS – two volumes
NEWSPAPER SERIES – two volumes
YOUNG REPORTER SERIES – six volumes

Garner, A.
1 The wierdstone on Brisingamen 1962
2 The moon of Gomrath 1964

Garnett, E.
RUGGLES FAMILY SERIES:
1 The family from One-End street
2 Further adventures of the family from One-End Street
3 Holiday at the Dew-Drop Inn 1962

Garnett, H.
1 Rough water brown
2 Secret of the rocks 1958

Garnett, R.
1 The silver kingdom
2 The white dragon 1963

Garrard, P.
HILDA SERIES:
1 Doings of Hilda
2 Hilda at school
3 Hilda fifteen
4 Hilda's adventures

Garrison, F.
WEST POINT SERIES:
1 Off for West Point
2 A cadet's honour
3 On guard
4 The West Point treasure
5 The West Point rivals

Gates, J. S.
THE LIVE DOLLS SERIES – 11 volumes

Gaunt, M.
BRIM SERIES:
1 Brim's boat 1964
2 Brim sails out 1965
□
1 Belle Isle
2 The Invaders

Geijerstam, C.
1 Northern summer
2 Storevik: another Northern summer
3 Northern winter

Gervaise, M.
'G' FOR GEORGIA SERIES:
1 A pony of your own
2 Ponies and holidays
3 Ponies in clover
4 Ponies and mysteries
5 Pony from the farm
6 Pony clue 1956
7 Pony island 1957
8 Vanishing pony 1958
9 A puzzle for ponies 1964
10 Secret of pony pass 1965
MARSTON CHILDREN SERIES:
1 Golden path adventure
2 Secrets of Golden path
3 Strangers at Golden path 1958
4 Golden path pets 1959

FARTHINGALE SERIES:
1 Fireworks at Farthingale
2 Farthingale fête
3 Farthingale feud 1957
4 Farthingale find 1960
BELINDA SERIES:
1 A pony for Belinda 1959
2 Belinda rides to school 1960
3 Belinda's other pony 1961
4 Belinda wins her spurs 1962

Gibbs, S., *see* Rhodes, J.

Gibson, M.
1 Ian Munro's Monte Carlo rally
2 Le Mans 24 hours

Gifford, G.
1 The youngest Taylor 1964
2 Ben's expedition 1965

Gilbert, E. L.
1 The frolicsome four
2 The making of Meenie

Gilchrist, B. B.
HELEN SERIES:
1 Helen over-the-wall
2 Helen and the uninvited guests
3 Helen and the Find-out Club
4 Helen and the fifth cousins

Gillespie, T. H.
ZOO-MAN SERIES:
1 Zoo-man talks
2 Zoo-man stories
3 Zoo-man tales 1959
4 Zoo-man again 1961

Gilson, C.
1 Submarine U93
2 The mystery of Ah Jim
3 The fire gods
4 In the power of the Pigmies

Ginther, P.
BETH ANNE SERIES – three volumes
BETSY HALE SERIES – three volumes
MISS PAT SERIES – ten volumes

Godfrey, H.
1 Jack Collerton's engine

2 Dave Morell's battery

Golden Gorse., *pseud.*
1 Mousie
2 Older Mousie

Gollomb, J.
LINCOLN HIGH SERIES – two volumes

Goolden, B.
THE TABOR FAMILY:
1 Minty 1961
2 Five pairs of hands 1962
3 Minty and the missing picture 1963
4 Minty and the secret room 1964

Gould, E. L.
ADMIRAL STORIES – four volumes
FELICIA SERIES – four volumes
POLLY PRENTICE SERIES – four volumes

Goulding, F. R.
MAROONERS SERIES:
1 The young marooners
2 Marooners Island
WOODRUFF STORIES:
1 Sapelo
2 Nachoochee
3 Sal-o-quah

Govan, M.
1 The trail of the red canoe
2 The trail of the broken snowshoe 1956

Graeme, L.
HELEN SERIES:
1 Helen, ballet student
2 Helen in musical comedy
3 Helen, television dancer

Graeme, R.
BRANDY SERIES:
1 Brandy ahoy!
2 Where's Brandy?
3 Brandy goes a cruising
Junior novels about Sea-cadet Brandy.

Graham, R.
1 The furry forest bears
2 Mustard and company

Gramatky, H.
LITTLE TOOT SERIES:
1 Little Toot 1964
2 Little Toot on the Thames 1965

Grannan, M.
1 Just Mary stories
2 More just Mary stories

Graveson, C. C.
1 The Farthing family
2 London to Philadelphia

Gray, W. T.
BAD BOY SERIES:
1 The bad boy's diary
2 The bad boy abroad

Green, E. Everett-
1 The Castle of the White Flag
2 Ringed by fire
☐
1 Dickie and Dorrie
2 Dickie and Dorrie at school
☐
1 Dulcie's little brother
2 Dulcie and Tottie
3 Dulcie's love story
☐
1 Maud Kingslake's collect
2 Cuthbert Coningsby
☐
1 Tom Tufton's travels
2 Tom Tufton's toll

Green, R. L.
THE SPEARLAKE CHILDREN SERIES:
1 The wonderful stranger
2 The luck of the Lynns
3 Theft of the golden cat

Gregor, E. R.
CAMPING SERIES – two volumes
EAST INDIAN SERIES – six volumes
WEST INDIAN SERIES – two volumes

Grey, P.
KIT HUNTER, SHOW JUMPER:
1 Bush adventure 1959
2 Rival riders 1959
3 South American mission 1959
4 The wild one 1959

5 Kit Hunter and the mystery of the mine 1960
6 Kit Hunter and the phantom horse 1960
7 Kit Hunter in fiesta for wild one 1960
8 Kit Hunter in Moor Grange mystery 1960
9 Kit Hunter in the homing trail 1961
10 Kit Hunter in the last hurdle 1961
11 Kit Hunter in little outlaw 1961
12 Kit Hunter in Royal Command 1961

Griffiths, H. S.
LETTY SERIES – ten volumes

Griffiths, J.
GRIFF AND TOMMY SERIES:
1 Griff and Tommy 1963
2 Griff and Tommy and the golden image 1964

Grinnell, G. B.
JACK SERIES – seven volumes

Grove, H. P.
THE GREYCLIFFE GIRLS SERIES – five volumes

Gunn, J.
1 Humpty in the hills 1962
2 The goodbye island 1963
PETER KENT SERIES:
1 Barrier Reef espionage
2 Battle in the ice 1956
3 Gibraltar sabotage 1957
4 Submarine island 1958
5 Peter Kent's command 1960
6 City in danger 1962

Hackforth-Jones, G., *see* Jones, G. Hackforth-

Hadfield, A. M.
THE WILLIVER CHRONICLES:
1 Williver's luck 1964
2 Williver's quest

Hakansson, G.
POMANDER SERIES:
1 Mr. Pomander
2 The Pomanders of Little Chipping

Haig-Brown, R., *see* Brown, R. Haig-

Hale, E. E., *and* **S.**
FAMILY FLIGHT SERIES – five volumes

Hale, H.
JACK RACE SERIES – five volumes

Hale, K.
ORLANDO SERIES:
1 Orlando's home life
2 Orlando's camping holiday
3 Orlando's trip abroad
4 Orlando buys a farm
5 Orlando becomes a doctor
6 Orlando's silver wedding
7 Orlando keeps a dog
8 Orlando the judge
9 Orlando's evening out
10 Orlando's invisible pyjamas
11 Orlando's seaside holiday
12 Orlando buys a cottage
13 Orlando and the three graces 1965

Hale, L. P.
PETERKIN SERIES – three volumes
*A selection of this series published under
the title 'The Peterkin papers' 1965.*

Hale, S.
CAROLINE SERIES:
1 Caroline takes to dancing 1960
2 Caroline joins the stars 1961
□
1 Painter's mate 1964
2 Mystery boxes 1965

Haley, G. E.
CORMORANT SERIES:
1 Cormorant ahoy!
2 Cormorant's commandos
3 Cormorant sails again 1955
4 Cormorant on patrol 1956

Hall, A.
1 The admiral's secret
2 The K.F. Conspiracy

Hall, G. L.
PETER SERIES:
1 Peter's jumping horse
2 Peter at the stampede

Hallard, P.
1 Coral Reef castaway 1959
2 Barrier Reef bandits 1960

Hamilton, E.
1 Speedy
2 Rainbow and Speedy
3 Starlight
4 Children at Maywish 1957

Hamlin, Mrs. M. S.
NAN SERIES – three volumes

Hammond, H.
PINKEY PERKINS SERIES – three volumes

Hamre, L.
PETER HOVDEN SERIES:
1 Otter three two calling 1961
2 Blue two bale-out 1961
3 Ready for take-off 1962

Hancock, H. I.
ANNAPOLIS SERIES – four volumes
BOYS OF THE ARMY SERIES – eight volumes
GRAMMAR SCHOOL BOYS SERIES – four
volumes
HIGH SCHOOL BOYS SERIES – four volumes
HIGH SCHOOL VACATION SERIES – four
volumes
MOTOR BOAT CLUB SERIES – seven vol-
umes
SQUARE DOLLAR BOYS SERIES – two vol-
umes
WEST POINT SERIES – four volumes
YOUNG ENGINEERS SERIES – four volumes

Hardy, D. M.
CHRISTABEL SERIES:
1 Christabel at Cleave
2 Christabel's Cornish adventure

Hare, T. T.
1 Making the freshman team
2 A sophomore half-back
3 A senior quarter-back
4 A junior in the line
5 A graduate coach

Harper, T. A.
1 Siberian gold
2 Kubirk the outlaw
3 His excellency and Peter
4 Red sky

Harris, J. C.
AARON SERIES:
1 The story of Aaron
2 Aaron in the woods
UNCLE REMUS STORIES:
1 Uncle Remus, his songs and sayings
2 Night with Uncle Remus
3 Uncle Remus and his friends
4 Mr. Rabbit at home
3 The Tar-baby and other rhymes of Uncle Remus
6 Uncle Remus and Brer Rabbit
7 Uncle Remus returns
These are the original volumes. Collections have been published under several different titles.
'The Chronicles of Aunt Minery Ann' consists of tales told by a sister of Uncle Remus.

Harris, R.
TURKEY SERIES:
1 Adventures of Turkey 1958
2 Turkey and partners 1959
3 Turkey and Co. 1961

Hastings, V.
JO SERIES:
1 Jo and the skiffle group 1958
2 Jo and Coney's cavern 1959
3 Jo and the jumping boy 1960
WENDY AND JINX SERIES:
1 Wendy and Jinx and the Dutch stamp mystery 1956
2 Wendy and Jinx and the missing scientist 1957

Hatch, R. W.
CURIOUS LOBSTER SERIES:
1 The curious lobster
2 The curious lobster's island

Hatcher, J.
GASWORKS ALLEY GANG SERIES:
1 The Gasworks Alley gang

2 The Gasworks Alley gang goes west 1961

Hawley, M. C.
FOUR LITTLE BLOSSOMS SERIES – four volumes

Hawthorn, M.
CARLOTTI SERIES:
1 Carlotti joins the team
2 Carlotti takes the wheel

Hawthorne, N.
1 A wonder book for boys and girls
2 Tanglewood tales
□
1 Twice-old tales
2 Mosses from an old manse
3 The snow image and other twice-told tales

Hayes, C. W.
BOY TROOPERS SERIES – four volumes

Haywood, C.
BETSY SERIES:
1 'B' is for Betsy
2 Betsy and Billy
3 Back to school with Betsy
4 Betsy and the boys
5 Betsy's little star
EDDIE SERIES:
1 Little Eddie
2 Eddie and the fire engine
3 Eddie and the gardenia
PENNY SERIES:
1 Here's a Penny
2 Penny and Peter
3 Penny goes to camp

Heap, J. W.
DINGLEFLOP SERIES:
1 Dingleflop chimes
2 Dingleflop moon

Helmericks, B.
1 Oolak's brother 1955
2 Arctic hunter 1956
3 Arctic bush pilot 1957

Hemyng, B.
JACK HARKAWAY SERIES – 13 volumes

Henderson, Le G.
AUGUSTUS SERIES:
1 Augustus and the river
2 Augustus and the mountains
3 Augustus goes South

Henry, M.
MISTY SERIES:
1 Misty of Chincoteague 1964
2 Stormy, Misy's foal 1965

Henson, J.
THE HOLLOWAY CHILDREN SERIES:
1 River detectives
2 Detectives in the hills
3 Detectives by the sea
4 Detectives abroad
5 Detectives in Wales

Henty, G. A.
DUTCH REPUBLIC SERIES:
1 By pike and dyke
2 By England's aid
PENINSULAR WAR SERIES:
1 With Moore at Corunna
2 Under Wellington's command
THIRTY YEARS' WAR SERIES:
The lion of the North
2 Won by the sword

Harge, *pseud.*
1 The adventures of TinTin
2 Prisoners of the sun
3 TinTin in Tibet
4 The seven crystal balls
5 The Castafione emerald

Heyliger, W.
DON STRONG SERIES – three volumes
HIGH BENTON SERIES – two volumes
SCHOOL TEAM SERIES – four volumes

Hickson, Mrs. M.
1 Concerning Teddy
2 Chronicles of Teddy's village

Higgins, A. C.
LITTLE PRINCESS STORIES – four volumes

Hildick, E. W.
JIM STARLING SERIES:
1 Jim Starling

2 Jim Starling and the agency
3 Jim Starling's holiday 1960
4 Jim Starling and the colonel 1960
5 Jim Starling goes to town 1964
6 Jim Starling takes over 1964
7 Jim Starling and spotted dog 1964
LEMON KELLY SERIES:
1 Meet Lemon Kelly 1963
2 Lemon Kelly digs deep 1964

Hill, G. B.
CORNER HOUSE GIRLS SERIES – 12 volumes

Hill, L.
MARJORIE SERIES:
1 Marjorie and Co.
2 Stolen holiday
3 Border Peel
4 No medals for Guy 1962
PATIENCE SERIES:
1 They called her Patience
2 It was all through Patience
3 Castle in Northumbria
4 So Guy came too
5 The 5/- holiday
ANNETTE DANCES SERIES:
1 Dancing Peel 1952
2 Dancer's luck 1955
3 Little dancer 1956
4 Dancer in the wings 1958
5 Dancer in danger 1959
6 Dancer on holiday 1961
SADDLERS WELLS SERIES:
1 A dream of Sadlers Wells
2 Veronica at the Wells
3 Masquerade at the Wells
4 No castanets at the Wells
5 Jane leaves the Wells
6 Ella at the Wells
7 Return to the Wells
8 Principal role
9 Susan fearless
10 Dress rehearsal
11 Back stage
12 Vicki in Venice
13 The secret 1964
THE VICARAGE CHILDREN SERIES:
1 The Vicarage children 1962
2 More about Mandy 1963
3 The Vicarage children on Skye 1966

Hill, M. B.
JUDY JO SERIES:
1 Down-along Apple Market Street
2 Summer comes to Apple Market Street
3 Surprise for Judy Jo
4 Jacka' Lantern for Judy Jo
5 Along comes Judy Jo
6 Snowed-in family

Hillyard, M. D.
PEGGY SERIES:
1 Peggy's giant
2 Peggy and the giant's aunt
MINIKIN SERIES:
1 Minikin's visit
2 Minikin's new home
3 A treat for Minikin 1958

Hinkle, T.
DR. RABBIT SERIES – six volumes

Hoare, R. J.
ROBBY OF THE GLOBE SERIES:
1 Sinister hoard 1958
2 Desperate venture 1959
3 Secret in the Sahara 1960

Hodgson, W. H.
1 The boats of the Glen Carrig
2 The house on the borderland
3 The ghost pirates

Hofmeyer, H.
1 Garibaldi's ski-boat
2 Fly away Paul 1963

Hogarth, A.
MUFFIN SERIES:
1 Red Muffin book
2 Blue Muffin book
3 Green Muffin book
4 Purple Muffin book

Hogg, G.
EXPLORERS SERIES:
1 Explorers awheel
2 Explorers on the wall
3 Explorers afloat
JONTY SERIES:
1 Sealed orders
2 Secret of Hollow Hill

3 Norwegian holiday
4 Riddle of Dooley Castle
5 The granite men

Holland, M.
MR. HARE SERIES:
1 Mr. Hare makes stare soup
2 Mr. Hare and the honey bees
3 Mr. Hare has a bright idea
WIZARD WINKLE SERIES:
1 Wizard Winkle won't tell
2 Wizard Winkle goes north
3 Wizard Winkle's wishing ring
BILLY SERIES:
1 Billy had a system
2 Billy's clubhouse

Holland, R. S.
BOY SCOUTS SERIES:
1 Boy scouts of Birch Bark Island
2 Boy scouts of Snow Shoe Lodge

Hooper, M.
AMELIA SERIES:
1 Amelia and the angels
2 Amelia and the robber rats

Hope, L. L.
BOBBSEY TWINS SERIES:
1 Bobbsey twins at school
2 Bobbsey twins at the circus
3 Bobbsey twins at the seashore
4 Bobbsey twins on a houseboat
5 Bobbsey twins in the country
6 Bobbsey twins camping out
7 Bobbsey twins wonderful secret
8 Bobbsey twins solve a mystery
9 Bobbsey twins at Meadow Brook
10 Bobbsey twins at Snow Lodge
11 Bobbsey twins at Blueberry Point
12 Bobbsey twins at Lighthouse Point
13 Bobbsey twins in Echo Valley
14 Bobbsey twins in Eskimo Land
15 Bobbsey twins on the Pony trail
16 Bobbsey twins at Big Bear Pond
17 Bobbsey twins at Sugar Maple Hill
18 Bobbsey twins go treasure hunting
19 Bobbsey twins on a bicycle trip
20 Bobbsey twins and the horse shoe riddle
21 Bobbsey twins at Mystery Mansion
22 Bobbsey twins at Whitesail harbour

23 Bobbsey twins in Rainbow Vally
24 Bobbsey twins at Pilgrim Rock
25 Bobbsey twins at the Tower of London
26 Bobbsey twins' forest adventure
27 Bobbsey twins' own little ferryboat
28 Bobbsey twins at Indian Hollow
29 Bobbsey twins in the Mystery Cave
30 Bobbsey twins in Tulip Land
31 Bobbsey twins' own little railway
32 Bobbsey twins at the Ice Carnival
33 Bobbsey twins' big adventure at home
34 Bobbsey twins' search in the great city
□

BUNNY BROWN SERIES – 13 volumes
MAKE BELIEVE STORIES – seven volumes
MOVING PICTURE GIRLS SERIES – seven volumes
OUTDOOR GIRLS SERIES – 14 volumes
SIX LITTLE BUNKERS SERIES – nine volumes

Hopkins, W. J.
SANDMAN STORIES:
1 The sandman: his farm stories
2 The sandman: more farm stories
3 The sandman: his ship stories
4 The sandman: his sea stories
ANOTHER SERIES:
1 The clammer
2 The meddlings of Eve
3 The clammer and the submarine

Hornibrook, I.
DRAKE SERIES – three volumes

Horrabin, J. F.
1 Some adventures of the Noah family
2 The Noahs on holiday – with Japhet
3 More about the Noahs – and Tim Tossett

Horseman, E.
1 Hubble's bubble 1964
2 The Hubbles' treasure hunt 1965

Hough, E.
THE YOUNG ALASKANS SERIES – four volumes

Houston, E. J.
1 Five months on a derelict
2 Wrecked on a coral island
3 In captivity in the Pacific
4 At school in the Cannibal Islands

How, R. W.
FRIENDLY FARM SERIES:
1 The Friendly farm
2 Adventures at Friendly farm

Hoyland, R.
ETHELBERT SERIES:
1 Ethelbert
2 Ethelbert under the sea
3 Ethelbert goes to the moon
4 Ethelbert and the witch doctor

Hoyle, F.
OUR BROTHER NICK SERIES:
1 Our brother Nick and the tolling bell
2 Our brother Nick and the old quarry
3 Our brother Nick and the tattooed gardener
4 Our brother Nick and the African drums

Hughes, F.
BILL HOLMES SERIES:
1 The adventures of Bill Holmes
2 Bill Holmes and the red panthers
3 Bill Holmes and the fortune teller

Hughes, T.
1 Tom Brown's schooldays
2 Tom Brown at Oxford

Hull, K. *and* Whitlock, P.
1 The far-distant Oxus
2 Escape to Persia
3 Oxus in summer

Hunt, M. L.
ROMANO FAMILY SERIES:
1 Stars for Cristy 1959
2 Cristy at Skippinghills 1960

Hunting, G.
SANDSY SERIES:
1 Sandsy's pal
2 Sandsy himself

Hurt, A.
JEANETTE'S SERIES:
1 Jeanette's first term 1961
2 Jeanette in the summer term 1962

Hurt, F. M.
'PINETOPS' SERIES:
1 The wonderful birthday 1954
2 Fun next door 1955
3 Two to make friends 1955
4 The exciting summer 1956
5 Thirteen for luck 1957
6 Intruders at Pinetops 1958
ANDY SERIES:
1 Andy in trouble 1956
2 Andy keeps a secret 1956
3 Andy takes the lead 1957
4 Andy gets the blame 1958
5 Andy finds a way 1959
6 Andy wins the prize 1960
7 Andy and her twin 1961
8 Andy in danger 1962
9 Andy goes abroad 1964
10 Andy meets a hero 1964
11 Andy looks for gold 1965
MR. TWINK SERIES:
1 Clever Mr. Twink 1954
2 Mr. Twink takes charge 1955
3 Mr. Twink finds out 1956
4 Mr. Twink, detective 1957
5 Mr. Twink and the kitten mystery 1958
6 Mr. Twink and the pirates 1959
7 Mr. Twink and the jungle garden 1960
8 Mr. Twink finds a family 1961
9 Mr. Twink and the cat thief 1962

Irwin, I. H.
MAIDA SERIES:
1 Maida's little shop
2 Maida's little house

3 Maida's little school
4 Maida's little island
5 Maida's little camp
6 Maida's little houseboat
7 Maida's little theatre
8 Maida's little village
9 Maida's little cabins

Jacberns, R.
1 Becky Compton, ex dux
2 An uncomfortable term
3 Schoolgirls' battlefield

Jackson, F. G.
WEE WINKLES SERIES:
1 Wee Winkles and Wideawake
2 Wee Winkles and Snowball
3 Wee Winkles and her friends

Jackson, Mrs. G. E. S.
MISS CRICKET SERIES:
1 Little Miss Cricket
2 Little Miss Cricket's new home
3 Little Miss Cricket at school
□
1 Peggy Stewart at home
2 Peggy Stewart at school
□
1 Three Graces
2 Three Graces at college
□
1 Three little women
2 Three little women at work
3 Three little women's success
4 Three little women as wives

Jacobs, C. E.
BLUE BONNET SERIES – six volumes
JOAN SERIES – two volumes

Jacobs, J.
1 Celtic fairy tales
2 More Celtic fairy tales
□
1 English fairy tales
2 More English fairy tales

James, G.
JOHN AND MARY SERIES:
1 John and Mary
2 More about John and Mary
3 John and Mary abroad

4 John and Mary detectives
5 New friends for John and Mary
6 John and Mary's visitors
7 John and Mary and Miss Rose Brown
8 John and Mary's secret society
9 John and Mary's youth club
10 John and Mary at school
11 John and Mary at Riverton
12 Adventures of John and Mary
13 John and Mary's aunt
14 John and Mary in Rome
15 John and Mary's fairy-tales
16 John and Mary's Japanese fairy tales
17 John and Mary and Lisetta
18 John and Mary by land and sea
19 John and Mary's treasures 1960
20 John and Mary revisit Rome 1963

James, M., [Doyle, Mrs. M. C. M.]
1 Jimmie Suter
2 The boys of Pigeon Camp
3 The hero of Pigeon Camp

James, W.
UNCLE BILL SERIES:
1 Uncle Bill
2 In the saddle with Uncle Bill

Jameson, E. M.
PENDLETON SERIES:
1 The Pendletons
2 The Pendleton twins
3 Peggy Pendleton's plan

Jansson, T.
MOOMIN SERIES
1 Moominland 1956
2 Moominland midwinter 1958
3 Tales from Moominvalley 1963

Jayne, R. H.
WAR WHOOP SERIES – four volumes
WILD ADVENTURE SERIES – three volumes

Jeffery, G.
1 On the ball!
2 Up the Town!

Johns, W. E.
REX CLINTON SERIES:
1 Kings of space
2 Return to Mars

3 Now to the stars
4 To outer space
5 The edge of beyond
6 The death rays of Ardilla
7 To worlds unknown
8 Quest for the perfect planet
9 Worlds of wonder
10 Man who vanished into space
ADVENTURE SERIES:
1 Adventure bound 1956
2 Adventure unlimited 1957
GIMLET SERIES:
1 King of the Commandos
2 Gimlet goes again
3 Gimlet comes home
4 Gimlet mops up
5 Gimlet's oriental quest
6 Gimlet bores in
7 Gimlet lends a hand
8 Gimlet off the map
9 Gimlet gets the answer
10 Gimlet takes a job
WORRALS SERIES:
1 Worrals of the W.A.A.F.
2 Worrals carries on
3 Worrals flies again
4 Worrals on the warpath
5 Worrals goes east
6 Worrals of the islands
7 Worrals in the wilds
8 Worrals down under
9 Worrals goes afoot
10 Worrals in the wastelands
11 Worrals investigates
*'Comrades in arms' contains stories of
'Biggles', 'Worrals' and 'Gimlet'.*
BIGGLES SERIES:
1 The rescue flight
2 Biggles flies east
3 Biggles hits the trail
4 Biggles and Co.
5 Biggles in Africa
6 Biggles – Air Commodore
7 Biggles flies west
8 Biggle flies south
9 Biggles goes to war
10 Biggles flies north
11 Biggles in Spain
12 Biggles in the Baltic
13 Biggles in the south seas
14 Biggles – secret agent
15 Biggles defies the swastika

Johns, W. E. (*contd.*)
16 Biggles sees it through
17 Biggles in the jungle
18 Spitfire parade
19 Biggles – charter pilot
20 Biggles in Borneo
21 Biggles sweeps the desert
22 Biggles fails to return
23 Biggles in the Orient
24 Biggles delivers the goods
25 Sergeant Bigglesworth, C.I.D.
26 Biggles second case
27 Biggles hunts big game
28 Biggles takes a holiday
29 Biggles breaks the silence
30 Biggles gets his men
31 Another job for Biggles
32 Biggles goes to school
33 Biggles works it out
34 Biggles takes the case
35 Biggles – air detective
36 Biggles flies again
37 Biggles follows on
38 Biggles and the black raider
39 Biggles in the blue
40 Biggles in the Gobi
41 Biggles cuts it fine
42 Biggles and the pirate treasure
43 Biggles – foreign legionnaire
44 Biggles of special air police
45 Biggles and the black pencil
46 Biggles and leopards of Zinn
47 Biggles and poor rich boy
48 Biggles at World's end
49 Biggles buries the hatchet
50 Biggles hits the trail
51 Biggles learns to fly
52 Biggles of the Interpol
53 Biggles presses on
54 Biggles on mystery island
55 Biggles' Chinese puzzle
56 Biggles takes charge
57 Biggles in Mexico
58 Biggles' combined operation
59 Biggles goes home
60 Biggles in Australia
61 Biggles makes ends meet
62 Biggles on the home front
63 Biggles forms a syndicate
64 Biggles and the missing millionaire
65 Biggles sets a trap
66 No rest for Biggles

67 Orchids for Biggles
68 Biggles goes alone
69 Biggles and the lost sovereigns
70 Biggles and black mask
71 Biggles investigates
72 Biggles takes it rough
73 Biggles takes a hand
74 Biggles' special case
75 Biggles and the plane that disappeared
76 Biggles looks back
77 Biggles and the plot that failed
78 Biggles scores a bull
    *Issued by several different publishers,
    and so not listed in chronological order.*
    ☐
1 Worlds of wonder
2 The men who vanished into space

Johnson, C.
BEDTIME WONDER TALES – 15 volumes
    ☐
1 Ellen's lion
2 The lion's own story

Johnson, O. M.
1 The prodigious Hickey. *Same as* The
    eternal boy
2 The Tennessee shad
3 Skippy Bedelle
4 The varmint
5 Stover at Yale

Johnston, A. Fellows-
GEORGINA SERIES – two volumes
THE LITTLE COLONEL SERIES – 14 volumes
THE LITTLE COLONEL STORY HOUR BOOKS
    – 12 volumes

Jones, G. Hackforth-
GREEN SAILORS SERIES:
1 The Green sailors
2 The Green sailors on holiday
3 Green sailors ahoy!
4 Green sailors, beware
5 Green sailors and blue water
6 Green sailors and fair winds 1956
7 Green sailors go west 1956
8 Green sailors go to Gibraltar 1957
9 Green sailors in the Caribbean 1958
10 Green sailors in the Galapagos 1959
11 Green sailors in the South Seas 1960

Jones, H.
DR. JOHN HADDON:
1 Beware the hunter
2 The web of Caesar

Jones, J. C.
JAMES AND SUSAN SERIES:
1 James and Susan in the country
2 James and Susan at the seaside

Jones, P.
TALES OF TERRY TROTTER:
1 Wheldon the weed 1961
2 Crump the Crock 1962
3 Wheldon the wizard 1963
4 Mathematics or blood? 1964

Jordan, E. G.
MARY IVERSON SERIES:
1 Mary Iverson: her book
2 Mary Iverson tackles life
3 Mary Iverson's career

Judah, A.
BASIL CHIMPY SERIES:
1 Basil Chimpy isn't bright
2 Basil Chimpy's comic right
□
1 Henrietta in the snow
2 Adventures of Henrietta Hen
3 Henrietta in love

Judd, A.
TODDY SERIES:
1 Toddy
2 Toddy scores again

Judson, C.
AMERICAN IMMIGRANT SERIES:
1 They came from Sweden
2 They came from France
3 They came from Scotland
4 Petar's treasure: they came from Dalmatia
5 Michael's victory: they came from Ireland
6 Lost violin: they came from Bohemia

Judson, C. I.
MARY JANE SERIES – nine volumes

Kaeser, H. J.
MIMFF SERIES:
1 Mimff
2 Mimff in charge
3 Three cheers for Mimff!
4 Mimff takes over
5 Mimff Robinson

Kantor, McK.
BUGLE ANN SERIES:
1 The voice of Bugle Ann
2 Daughter of Bugle Ann

Kastner, E.
EMIL SERIES:
1 Emil and the detectives
2 Emil and the three twins
3 The 35th of May

Kaufmann, H.
CAPTAIN GEVERT SERIES:
1 The lost Sahara trail 1964
2 The city under the desert sands 1965

Kay, B.
ELIZABETH SERIES:
1 Elizabeth: her folks
2 Elizabeth: her friends

Kay, R.
BIG WAR SERIES – nine volumes
GO-AHEAD BOYS SERIES – six volumes

Keene, C.
NANCY DREW SERIES:
1 Secret of the old clock
2 Hidden staircase
3 Bungalow mystery
4 Mystery at Lilac Inn
5 Secret at Shadow Ranch
6 Secret of Red Gate farm
7 Clue in the diary
8 Nancy's mysterious letter
9 Sign of the twisted candles
10 Password to Larkspur Lane
11 Clue of the broken locket
12 Message in the hollow oak
13 Mystery of the ivory charm
14 The whispering statue
15 The haunted bridge
16 Clue of the tapping heels
17 Mystery of the brass-bound trunk

Keene, C. (*contd.*)
18 Mystery of the moss-covered mansion
19 Quest of the missing map
20 The clue in the jewel box
21 The secret in the old attic
22 Clue in the crumbling wall
23 Mystery of the tolling bell
24 The clue in the old album
25 The ghost of Blackwood Hall
26 The clue of the leaning chimney
27 The secret of the wooden lady
28 The clue of the black key
29 The mystery at the ski jump
30 The clue of the velvet mask
31 Mystery of the fire dragon
32 The clue of the dancing puppet
33 The hidden window mystery
34 The haunted showboat
35 The moonstone castle mystery
36 The clue of the whistling bagpipes
37 The secret of the golden pavilion
38 The clue in the old stage coach
39 The clue of the velvet mask 1965
40 The ringmaster's secret 1965
41 The scarlet slipper mystery 1965
42 The witchtree symbol 1965
DANA GIRLS SERIES:
1 By the light of the study lamp
2 The secret at Lone Tree cottage
3 In the shadow of the tower
4 A three-cornered mystery

Kelland, C. B.
MARK TIDD SERIES – six volumes
CATTY ATKINS SERIES – five volumes
□
1 Hard money
2 Gold
3 The jealous house

Kellogg, E.
ELM ISLAND STORIES – six volumes
FOREST GLEN SERIES – six volumes
GOOD OLD TIME SERIES – four volumes
PLEASANT COVE SERIES – six volumes
WHISPERING PINE SERIES – six volumes

Kent, M.
FOUR SEASONS AT CHERRY-TREE FARM:
1 Spring at Cherry-Tree Farm
2 Summer at Cherry-Tree Farm

3 Autumn at Cherry-Tree Farm
4 Winter at Cherry-Tree Farm
THE TWINS SERIES:
1 The twins at Hillside Farm
2 The twins at home
3 The twins at the seaside
4 The twins on the move 1962

Kenyon, J. W.
PETER TRANT SERIES:
1 Peter Trant, cricketer-detective
2 Peter Trant heavyweight champion
3 Peter Trant speed king

Kidell-Monroe, J., *see* Monroe, J. Kidell-

Killbourne, C. E.
ARMY BOY SERIES – four volumes

Kingston, W. H. G.
1 Three midshipmen
2 Three lieutenants
3 Three commanders
4 Three admirals

Kirk, E. O.
DOROTHY DEAN SERIES:
1 Dorothy Deane
2 Dorothy Deane and her friends

Kirkland, J.
1 Zury
2 The McVeys

Kirkman, M. M.
1 The romance of Alexander the Prince
2 The romance of Alexander the King
3 The romance of Alexander and Roxana

Kitchen, F.
FOXENDALE FARM SERIES:
1 Foxendale Farm
2 More adventures at Foxendale Farm 1961
3 Winter at Foxendale 1964

Kjelgaard, J. A.
1 Snow dog
2 Wild trek

Knight, C.
PEPE AND RONNIE SERIES:
1 The quest of the golden Condor
2 The secret of the buried tomb
3 Sky road to mystery

Knight, F.
'CLIPPER SHIP' SERIES:
1 Golden monkey
2 Voyage to Bengal
3 Clippers to China
4 The bluenose pirate 1956
5 He sailed with Blackbeard 1958
Stories telling in fiction the history of the Merchant Navy.
CHICHESTER HARBOUR SERIES:
1 Mudlarks and mysteries
2 Family on the tide 1956
3 Please keep off the mud 1957
4 Shadows on the mud 1960

Knight, P.
1 Gold of the snow goose 1961
2 Assassin's castle 1962
ANTHONY DAINTREY SERIES:
1 Bramble fortress 1962
2 The Boreas adventure 1963

Knowles, G.
THE ISLANDERS SERIES:
1 The Islanders
2 The Islanders' secret cave
3 The Islanders' strange holiday
4 The Islanders in danger
5 The Islanders follow a clue

Knox, T. W.
THE BOY TRAVELLER SERIES – 15 volumes

Kyle, E.
FURZE SERIES:
1 Visitors from England
2 Holly hotel
3 West wind
4 House on the hill
5 Vanishing island
6 The seven sapphires

Laan, D.
1 Adventures of Fingerling 1960
2 Fingerling and his friends 1960
3 Fingerling at the zoo 1960

4 Travels of Fingerling 1960
5 Fingerling goes home 1961
6 Fingerling and the sandman 1962

La Belle, C. A.
RANGER BOYS SERIES – five volumes

Lamplugh, L.
THE ALLEN FAMILY:
1 Pigeongram puzzle
2 Nine bright shiners 1959
3 Vagabond's castle 1960
4 Rockets on the dunes 1961
5 The sixpenny runners 1962
6 Midsummer madness 1963

Lancaster, F. B.
BUFFEY BOY SERIES:
1 Buffey-boy
2 Buffey-boy's treasure

Lane, C. D.
ALTAIR SERIES:
1 Treasure cave
2 Black tide

Langworthy, J. L.
THE BIRD BOYS SERIES – five volumes

Larom, H. V.
MOUNTAIN PONY SERIES:
1 Mountain pony
2 Mountain pony and the pinto
3 Mountain pony and the rodeo mystery

Lattimore, E. F.
LITTLE PEAR SERIES:
1 Little Pear
2 Little Pear and his friends

Lavell, E.
GIRL SCOUTS SERIES – eight volumes

Lawton, W.
BOY AVIATOR SERIES – eight volumes
DREADNOUGHT BOYS SERIES – six volumes
OCEAN WIRELESS SERIES – six volumes

Le Baron, G.
1 Little Miss Faith
2 Little daughter
3 The Rosebud Club
☐
1 Queer Janet
2 Jessica's triumph
3 The children of Bedford Court

Lee, A. L.
CO-ED SERIES – four volumes

Le Feuvre, A.
1 Odd
2 Odd made even
☐
1 Us, and our charge
2 Us, and our donkey
3 Us, and our empire

Leigh, R.
1 The adventures of Mr. Hero
2 Mr. Hero and the Raggler children
SARA AND HOPPITY SERIES:
1 Sara and Hoppity
2 Sara and Hoppity make new friends
3 Sara and Hoppity get lost
4 Sara and Hoppity find a cat
TOMAHAWK SERIES:
1 Tomahawk and the river of gold 1960
2 Tomahawk and the tomb of White Moose 1961
3 Tomahawk and the animals of the wild 1961

Leighton, R.
1 Gildersley's tenderfoot
2 The Red Patrol
☐
1 Kiddie of the camp
2 Kiddie the scout
3 Kiddie, the prairie rider

Leonard, M. F.
1 Everyday Susan
2 Christmas Tree House
3 Susan grows up

Leonard, N. M.
GRAYMOUSE SERIES – five volumes

Leslie, Mrs. M. [Mrs. H. N. W. Blake]
LITTLE AGNES SERIES:
1 Little Agnes
2 Trying to be useful
3 I'll try
4 Art and artlessness
PLAY AND STUDY SERIES:
1 Howard and his teacher
2 Jack, the chimney sweeper
3 Motherless children
4 Play and study
WOODBINE SERIES:
1 Live and learn
2 The governor's pardon
3 Paul Barton
4 Walter and Frank

Lester, P.
MARJORIE DEAN – SCHOOL SERIES – four volumes
MARJORIE DEAN – COLLEGE SERIES – four volumes

Lethbridge, P.
1 The holiday adventurers
2 Lakeland adventure
3 Boy from London
4 Danger in the hills
5 The Beresfords in Tarndale

Lewis, C.
BLUNDERLAND SERIES:
1 Clara in Blunderland
2 Lost in Blunderland

Lewis, C. S.
NARNIA SERIES:
1 The lion, the witch and the wardrobe 1950
2 Prince Caspian 1951
3 Voyage of the *Dawn Treader* 1952
4 The silver chair 1953
5 The horse and his boy 1954
6 Magician's nephew 1955
7 The last battle 1956
No. 6 contains a plan and explanation of the series. Awarded Carnegie Medal. Allegorical fantasy of two children in an imaginary 'fairy country'.

Lewis, L.
SHIRLEY SERIES:
1 Shirley goes travelling 1960
2 Shirley in America 1961

Leyland, E.
1 Gentlemen of Sussex
2 Hazard royal
SKINNY SERIES:
1 Well done Skinny
2 Skinny's Xmas Eve
3 Skinny on the warpath
FLAME SERIES:
1 Flame takes over
2 Flame of the Amazon
3 Flame of the Sierras
4 Flame wins through
5 Flame takes a chance
6 Flame over Africa
7 Flame hits the trail
8 Flame hits back
9 Flame takes command 1957
10 Flame makes the grade 1958
11 Flame secret agent 1958
12 Flame sets the pace 1959
13 Flame of the Sahara 1959
14 Flame and League of five 1960
15 Flame and the treasure trail 1961
16 Flame and the king's ransom 1962
'RED' LAWSON SERIES:
1 No quarter
2 Case for 'Red' Lawson
3 Versus the shadow
4 Calling Red lawson
5 Red Lawson and sons of the desert
ABBEY SERIES:
1 Abbey sees it through
2 Conspiracy at Abbey
3 Abbey on the warpath
4 Abbey turns the tables 1959
5 Abbey makes the grade 1960
6 Oddman out at the Abbey 1961
STEVEN GALE SERIES:
1 Calling Steven Gale 1961
2 Gale hits the headlines 1961
3 Scoop for Steven Gale 1962
4 Gale and the sword of Mars 1962
SIX-GUN GAUNTLET SERIES:
1 Six gun Gauntlet strikes the trail
2 Six gun Gauntlet rides again
3 Six gun Gauntlet gets his man
4 Six gun Gauntlet hits back

'CAPTAIN' SERIES:
1 The Captain on guard
2 The Captain rides again
3 The Captain intervenes
4 The Captain strikes back
RIP RANDALL SERIES:
1 Challenge
2 Counter-attack
3 Sabotage
4 Madman's peak
5 Rip Randall and the Pharaoh's tomb 1956

Leyland, E. *and* **Scott-Chard, T. E.**
HUNTER HAWK, SKYWAY DETECTIVE SERIES:
1 Outlaws of the air 1956
2 Atom plant mystery 1957
3 Smugglers of the skies 1958
4 Commandos of the clouds 1958
5 Comet round the world 1959
6 The secret weapon 1960
7 Bandit gold 1961

Lillington, K.
1 Conjurer's alibi
2 A man called Hughes 1961

Lincoln, A. C.
MOTORCYCLE CHUMS SERIES – six volumes

Lincoln, Mrs. J. T. G.
1 Marjorie's quest
2 A genuine girl
□
1 An unwilling maid
2 The luck of Rathcoole

Lindgren, A.
KATI SERIES:
1 Kati in Italy 1962
2 Kati in America 1963
3 Kati in Paris 1965
BULLERBY SERIES:
1 The six Bullerby children 1961
2 Christmas at Bullerby 1962
3 Cherry time at Bullerby 1964
4 Happy days at Bullerby 1965

Lindsay, M.
1 Mother stories
2 More mother stories

Lister, G.
STARLIGHT SERIES:
1 Starlight belongs to me
2 A Star for Starlight
3 Quest for Starlight 1956

Little, F.
1 The lady of the decoration
2 The lady married. *Same as* The lady and Sada San
3 Little Sister Snow
4 Jack and I in Lotus Land

Little, S.
STANTONS SERIES:
1 Stantons' comes of age
2 Stantons' pulls it off
3 Masquerade at Stantons
HIGHCLIFF SERIES:
1 Puzzles at Highcliff 1959
2 Highcliffe on tour 1960
CASTLE SCHOOL SERIES:
1 Castle school gets going
2 The twins at Castle school
3 Castle school on holiday
4 Castle school at the cross-roads
5 Blood royal at Castle school
6 Castle school on the screen
7 Castle school on the warpath
8 Castle school in the news

Lloyd, J.
CATHERINE SERIES:
1 Catherine goes to school
2 Catherine, head of the house

Lofting, H.
DR. DOLITTLE SERIES:
1 The story of Dr. Dolittle
2 The voyages of Dr. Dolittle
3 Dr. Dolittle's post office
4 Dr. Dolittle's circus
5 Dr. Dolittle's zoo
6 Dr. Dolittle's caravan
7 Dr. Dolittle's garden
8 Adventures of Dr. Dolittle
9 Dr. Dolittle in the moon
10 Return of Dr. Dolittle
11 Dr. Dolittle and the secret lake
12 Dr. Dolittle's Puddlebury adventure
13 Dr. Dolittle and the green canary

Lounsberry, L.
KIT CAREY SERIES:
1 Cadet Kit Carey
2 Lieut. Carey's luck
3 Captain Carey
4 Kit Carey's protégé
TOM TRUXTON SERIES:
1 Tom Truxton's schooldays
2 Tom Truxton's ocean trips

Lovelace, M. H.
BETSY TACY AND TIB SERIES:
1 Betsy-Tacy
2 Betsy-Tacy and Tib
3 Over the big hill
4 Down town
5 Heaven to Betsy
6 Betsy in spite of herself
7 Betsy was a junior
8 Betsy and Joe
9 Emily of Deep Valley

Lowndes, J. S.
1 Royal chase
2 Tudor star
Adventures of the Tudor children Francis and Anne Woodward and the Stafford family.

Lunt, A.
1 Jeannette's first term
2 Jeannette in the summer term

Lynch, P.
BROGEEN THE LEPRECHAUN SERIES:
1 Brogeen follows the magic tune
2 Brogeen and the green shoes
3 Brogeen and the black enchanter
4 Brogeen and the lost castle
5 The stone house at Kilgobbin 1959
6 The longest way round 1961
7 Brogeen and the red fez 1963
8 Guests at the beech tree 1964
THE TURF-CUTTER'S DONKEY SERIES:
1 The turf-cutter's donkey goes visiting
2 The turf-cutter's donkey
3 The turf-cutter's donkey kicks up his heels

Lynn, E.
1 In khaki for the King
2 Oliver Hastings, V.C.

3 Knights of the air
4 Tommy of the tanks
5 Lads of the Lothians

Lyon, E.
IAN AND SOVRA SERIES:
1 The house in hiding
2 We daren't go a hunting
3 Runaway home
4 Cathie runs wild
MEREDITH FAMILY:
1 Green grow the rushes 1964
2 Echo valley 1965

Macarthur, W.
LARRY PEARSON SERIES:
1 Zambesi adventure
2 The valley of hidden gold
3 Guns for the Congo 1963

McCormick, D. J.
1 Paul Bunyan swings his axe
2 Tall timber tales

McCulloch, D.
DOODLE MCCLINK SERIES:
1 Doodle McClink
2 Doodle McClink in cloudland
☐
1 Cornish adventure
2 Cornish mystery
Macdonald, B.
MRS. PIGGLE-WIGGLE SERIES:
1 Mrs. Piggle-Wiggle
2 Mrs. Piggle-Wiggle's magic
3 Hello, Mrs. Piggle-Wiggle 1957

Macdonald, U.
1 Alys-all-alone
2 Alys in Happyland

MacGregor, E.
MISS PICKERELL SERIES:
1 Miss Pickerell goes to Mars
2 Miss Pickerell and the geiger counter
3 Miss Pickerell goes undersea
4 Miss Pickerell goes to the Arctic

McGregor, R. J.
CHI-LO SERIES:
1 Chi-lo the admiral
2 Chi-lo the general

McGuire, E.
1 Brave young land
2 Full grown nation
N.F. American history.

McIlvane, J.
CAMMIE SERIES:
1 Cammie's choice 1963
2 Cammie's challenge 1964

MacKenzie, K.
THE PENTIRE FAMILY SERIES:
1 Four Pentires and Jimmy
2 We four and Sandy
3 A green fox
4 Vicky and the Pentires

Mackenzie, K.
1 The Starke sisters 1963
2 Charlotte 1964

Mackinnon, A.
1 The boys of Glen Morrock
2 Cracksman's holiday

Maclean, C. M.
1 Seven for Cordelia
2 Three for Cordelia (The Tharrus three)
3 Farewell to Tharrus

Macleod, A. W.
1 Parlicoot
2 Parlicoot's house

MacNeill, J.
1 My friend Specs McCann 1957
2 Specs fortissimo 1958
3 Various specs 1961

Macnell, J.
METTLE SERIES:
1 Captain Mettle, V.C. 1955
2 Mettle dives deep 1956
3 Mettle at Woomera 1957

Macvicar, A.

JEREMY GRANT AND DR. MCKINNON
SERIES:
1 Lost planet
2 Return to the lost planet
3 Red fire on the lost planet 1959
4 Peril on the lost planet 1960
5 Space agent and the lost planet 1961
6 Space agent and the Isles of fire 1962
7 Space agent and the ancient peril 1963

Madden, M. S.

SIR GUYON SERIES:
1 Sir Guyon, the interloper
2 Sir Guyon in snowland

Maddock, R. B.

CORRIGAN SERIES:
1 Corrigan and the black riders 1957
2 Corrigan and the white cobra 1958
3 Corrigan and the yellow peril 1958
4 Corrigan and the dream makers 1959
5 Corrigan and the golden pagoda 1959
6 Corrigan and the blue crater 1960
7 Corrigan and the red legions 1961
8 Corrigan and the green tiger 1961
9 Corrigan and the little people 1963
ROCKY SERIES:
1 Rocky and the lions
2 Rocky and the elephant

Malone, P. B.

WEST POINT SERIES:
1 Winning his way to West Point
2 A plebe at West Point
3 A West Point yearling
4 A West Point cadet

Mansbridge, P.

CAROLINE SERIES:
1 A crime for Caroline 1958
2 Flowers from Caroline 1959
3 Caroline and the auction sale 1961
4 No clues for Caroline 1966

Mantle, W.

THE LESTERS AND THE WESTCOTTS:
1 The hiding place

2 Tinker's castle 1963
3 The chateau holiday 1964

Manuel, E.

TRISHA TRELAWNEY SERIES:
1 The green feather
2 The crimson petal

Marlitt, E. [*pseud.* H. E. John]
1 The Princess of the Moor
2 The little Princess

Marokvia, M. *and* A.

ANN AND PAUL SERIES:
1 Grococo
2 A French crow
3 Nanette
4 A French goat
5 Belle Arabelle

Marryat, Capt. F.

Note: 'The little savage, concluded,' by R. F. Williams, is a sequel to Capt, Marryat's 'Little savage.'

Marsh, J.

RICK AND PETE CLAYTON SERIES:
1 In the trail of the Albatross
2 Secret of the Pygmy herd

Martin, E. Le Breton-

OTTER PATROL SERIES:
1 The boys of the Otter Patrol
2 Otters to the rescue

Martin, N.
1 Call the vet.
2 Vet. in the making 1957
JEAN SERIES:
1 Jean behind the counter 1963
2 Jean, teen-age fashion buyer 1964
YOUNG FARMERS SERIES:
1 Young farmers at Gaythorne
2 Young farmers in Denmark
3 Young farmers in Scotland 1956

Martin, R.

JOEY SERIES:
1 Joey of Jasmine Street
2 Joey and the river pirates
3 Joey and the mail robbers
4 Joey and the Blackbird gang

5 Joey and the helicopter
6 Joey and the square of gold
7 Joey and the magic eye 1956
8 Joey and the city ghosts 1957
9 Joey and the Royalist treasure 1957
10 Joey and the squib 1958
11 Joey and the smugglers' legend 1958
12 Joey: soap box driver 1959
13 Joey and the magic pony 1960
14 Joey and the secret engine 1960
15 Joey and the master plan 1961
16 Joey and the detectives 1962
17 Joey and the magician 1963
18 Joey and pickpocket 1964
19 Joey and the trainrobbers 1965
TONY SERIES:
1 Tony and the champ
2 Tony and the secret money
TREW TWINS SERIES:
1 The gold elephant
2 The money mystery
3 The secret boat
DANCE AND CO. DETECTIVES:
1 Mystery of the car bandits 1958
2 Mystery of the poisoned puppet 1959
3 Mystery of the pay-snatchers 1963
4 Mystery of the missing passenger 1964

Mason, A. B.
TOM STRONG SERIES – five volumes

Mason, S. W.
KESTREL SERIES:
1 Kestrels over the beacon
2 Kestrels jetty
3 Kestrels dare danger
4 The Kestrels plot adventure

Masters, E. L.
1 Mitch Miller
2 Skeeters Kirby

Mathews, J. H.
BESSIE SERIES – six volumes
KITTY AND LULU BOOKS – six volumes
UNCLE RUTHERFORD SERIES – two volumes

Mathews, M. E.
1 Redheads of Windyridge
2 Island in the lake
3 Sixpenny holiday

Matthewman, P.
THE 'DANESWOOD' SERIES:
1 Chloe takes control
2 Queerness of Rusty
3 Josie moves up
4 New role for Natasha
5 Justice for Jacqueline
6 Pat at the helm
7 The intrusion of Nicda
THE 'MR. JONES' SERIES
1 Thanks to Mr. Jones
2 Peter – new girl
3 Mr. Jones tips the scales
4 Peter plays sleuth
THE 'PRIORY' SERIES:
1 Because of Vivian
2 The turbulence of Tony
3 The coming of Lys
4 The amateur prefects

Mattsar, O.
1 The brig *Three Lilies* 1960
2 Mickel seafarer 1961

Mauzey, M.
1 Oil field boy
2 Cotton farm boy
3 Texas ranch boy

May, S. [*pseud.* **R. S. Clarke**]
DOTTY DIMPLE SERIES – six volumes
FLAXIE FRIZZLE SERIES – six volumes
LITTLE PRUDY FLYAWAY SERIES – six volumes
LITTLE PRUDY STORIES – six volumes
LITTLE PRUDY'S CHILDREN SERIES – six volumes
QUINNEBASSET SERIES – six volumes

Mayhew, R. *and* **Johnson, B.**
BUBBLE BOOKS – 12 volumes

Mayne, W.
1 Swarm in May
2 Chorister's cake
3 Cathedral Wednesday

Mears, J. R.
THE IRON BOYS SERIES – four volumes

Meherin, E.
1 Chickie
2 Chickie: a sequel

Meyler, E.
1 The Gloriet tower
2 The castle on the rock 1957
Historical novels of the reign of Edward III.
THE ELWOOD FAMILY:
1 Adventure in Purbeck
2 Adventure in Dale House 1956
3 Adventure on ponies 1958
4 Adventure next door 1960

Meynell, L. W.
SMOKY JOE SERIES:
1 Smoky Joe
2 Smoky Joe in trouble
3 Smoky Joe goes to school 1956
NURSE ROSS SERIES:
1 Nurse Ross takes over
2 Nurse Ross shows the way
3 Nurse Ross saves the day
4 Nurse Ross and the doctor 1962
5 Good luck, Nurse Ross 1963
ROBIN WESTON SERIES:
1 Scoop 1964
2 The suspect scientist 1965

Meynell, L. W., *see also* Tring, A. S.,
[*pseud.*
Miller, A.
LINGER-NOTS SERIES – three volumes

Miller, A. G.
1 Fury
2 Fury and the mustangs 1961

Miller, M. J.
1 The Queen's music
2 The powers of the sapphire
3 Doctor Boomer

Miller, O. T.
KRISTY SERIES:
1 Kristy's rainy day picnic
2 Kristy's surprise party
3 Kristy's queer Christmas

Mills, A.
MUFFIN THE MULE SERIES:
1 Muffin the mule
2 More about Muffin
3 Muffin and the magic hat
4 Here comes Muffin
5 Muffin at the seaside

Milray, C.
1 A highland guest 1956
2 The secret of the caves 1957

Mitchell, E.
SILVER BRUMBY SERIES:
1 The silver Brumby 1961
2 Silver Brumby's daughter 1963
3 Silver Brumbies of the south 1965

Mitchell, G.
CATHY SERIES:
1 Cathy away 1963
2 Cathy at home 1965

Mitchell, L.
JIMMY GRIER SERIES:
1 Boys of the big top
2 Codeword – Bontry

Moffit, V. M. *see* Borton, E. H.

Mogridge, S.
NEW FOREST SERIES:
1 New Forest adventures 1953
2 New Forest mystery 1954
3 New Forest quest 1955
4 New Forest exploits 1956
5 New Forest discoveries 1957
6 New Forest smugglers 1958
7 New Forest pirates 1959
8 New Forest vagabond 1960
9 New Forest detectives 1962
10 New Forest treasure 1963
11 New Forest spies 1964
BARRY SERIES:
1 Barry and the Hurricane Squadron 1960
2 Barry and the 'Circus' raids 1961
3 Barry and the V weapons 1963
PETER SERIES:
1 Peter and the bomb
2 Peter's Denmark adventure 1958

Molesworth, Mrs.
1 Grandmother dear
2 A Christmas posy

Monckton, E.
TIM SERIES:
1 Tim minds the shop
2 Tim minds the baby
3 Tim thinks of something

Monroe, J. Kidell-
LITTLE BLACK WAISTCOAT SERIES:
1 In his little black waistcoat
2 In his little black waistcoat in Tibet

Montgomery, F. T.
BILLY WHISKERS (stories about goats), SERIES – 22 volumes

Montgomery, J.
FOXY SERIES:
1 Foxy 1960
2 My friend Foxy 1961

Montgomery, G.
GOLDEN STALLION SERIES:
1 Capture of the Golden Stallion
2 Golden Stallion's revenge
3 Golden Stallion to the rescue
4 Golden Stallion's victory
5 Golden Stallion and the wolf dog
6 Golden Stallion's adventure at Redstone 1960

Montgomery, L. M.
1 Anne of Green Gables
2 Anne of Avonlea
3 Chronicles of Avonlea
4 Anne of the Island
5 Anne's house of dreams
6 Rainbow Valley
7 Rilla of Ingleside
8 Further chronicles of Avonlea
9 Anne of Ingleside
10 Anne of Windy Willows
11 June of Lantern Hill
12 Kilmeny of the Orchard
☐
1 Story girl
2 Golden road
☐
1 Emily of New Moon

2 Emily climbs
3 Emily's quest
☐
1 Pat of Silver Bush
2 Mistress Pat

Moore, D.
1 A plucky schoolgirl
2 Terry, the girl guide

Moore, P.
GRENFELL AND WRIGHT SCIENCE FICTION SERIES:
1 Master of the moon
2 The Island of fear
MAURICE GRAY SERIES:
1 Mission to Mars 1955
2 The domes of Mars 1956
3 The voices of Mars 1957
4 Peril on Mars 1958
GREGORY QUEST SERIES:
1 Quest of Spaceways
2 World of mists
ROBIN NORTH AND REX REDMAYNE SERIES:
1 Wanderer in space 1961
2 Crater of fear 1962
3 Invader from space 1963
4 Caverns of the moon 1964

Morecamp, A.
1 Live boys
2 Live boys in the Black Hills

Morgan, G.
CONWAYS SERIES:
1 Cameras on the Conways
2 Conways ahoy

Morley, L.
SKID WILD SERIES:
1 Skid Wild, speedway rider
2 Skid Wild, speedway captain

Morrison, G. W.
GIRLS OF CENTRAL SERIES – seven volumes

Morrison, J. S.
1 Wind force seven
2 The monach light 1961

Morrison, S. E.
CHILHOWEE SERIES:
1 Chilhowee boys
2 Chilhowee boys in war time

Morrow, C.
1 The singing and the gold
2 The noonday thread

Moss, N.
CLIFF HOUSE SERIES:
1 School on the precipice
2 Susan's stormy term
3 Strange quest at Cliff House
4 The Cliff House monster
5 The riddle of Cliff House 1957

Moss, R.
JENNY SERIES:
1 Jenny of the fourth
2 Jenny's exciting term
*Stories of Jenny Fairfax and her friends
Lorna and Isobel at Southdown school.*

Moulton, Mrs. L.
Bed time stories. THREE SERIES

Muir, M.
1 Pam, Pot and Kettle 1964
2 Kettle's great adventure 1965
TORRIDONS SERIES:
1 Torridons' triumph
2 Torridons' surprise
3 Torridons in Spain 1962
4 Torridons in trouble 1963

Muirden, J.
ERIC KENDALL SERIES:
1 Space intruder 1964
2 The moon-winners 1965

Mullins, I. M.
1 The Blossom shop
2 Anne of the Blossom shop
3 Anne's wedding
4 The Mt. Blossom girls

Munro, K.
MATES SERIES:
1 Campmates
2 Dorymates
3 Canoemates
4 Raftmates

PACIFIC COAST SERIES:
1 The fur-seal's tooth
2 Snow-shoes and sledges
3 Rick Dale
4 The painted desert
RAIL AND WATER SERIES:
1 Under orders
2 Prince Dusty
3 Cab and caboose
4 The coral ship
WHITE CONQUEROR SERIES:
1 With Crockett and Bowie
2 Through swamp and glade
3 At war with Pontiac
4 The white conquerors
ANOTHER SERIES:
1 Two about Crockett
2 Lost treasure cave

Murray, L.
1 In the track of the huskies 1960
2 Ginnie and the snow gypsies 1961

Musson, M.
MR. POPPLECORN SERIES:
1 Mr. Popplecorn and four little hens
2 Mr. Popplecorn, Tasker and Moo

Nash, F. O. H.
AUDREY SERIES:
1 How Audrey became a guide
2 Audrey in camp
3 Audrey at school

Needham, V.
1 The black riders 1956
2 Red rose of Ruvina 1957

Nesbit, E. [Bland, Mrs.]
TREASURE SEEKERS SERIES:
1 The story of the treasure seekers
2 The would-be goods
3 The new treasure seekers
4 Oswald Bastable and others
　□
1 Five children and it
2 The Phoenix and the carpet
3 The amulet
　□
1 The house of Arden
2 Harding's luck

Nichols, W. T.
SAFETY FIRST SERIES – three volumes

Nicholson, J.
1 Adventures at Gull's Point
2 Gull's Point and pineapple

Nolan, W.
1 Rich inheritance
2 Exiles come home
Historical stories of period of Elizabeth I and James I from Catholic viewpoint. Not strictly sequels but characters reappear.

Nomad, *pseud. see* Ellison, M.

Noonan, M.
1 Flying doctor 1961
2 Flying doctor on the Great Barrier Reef 1962
3 Flying doctor and the secret of the pearls 1962
4 Flying doctor shadows the mob 1963
5 Flying doctor hits the headlines 1965

Norris, S.
THE SHOWMAN SERIES:
1 Phil, the showman
2 The young showman's rivals
3 The young showman's pluck
4 The young showman's triumph

North, G. M.
VIRGINIA DARE SERIES – five volumes

Nortje, P. H.
1 The green ally 1962
2 Wild goose summer 1964

Norton, M.
THE 'BORROWERS' SERIES:
1 The borrowers
2 The borrowers afield
3 The borrowers afloat
4 The borrowers aloft 1961
Stories of the tiny people who live in human houses and are responsible for 'borrowing' the things that get lost. Carnegie Medal winner 1949.

Nuttall, N.
1 Severn holiday 1962
2 Mendip holiday 1963

Oakeshott, R. E.
1 A knight and his armour 1961
2 A knight and his horse 1962
3 A knight and his weapons 1963
N.F. History

Ober, F. A.
THE KNOCKABOUT CLUB SERIES – nine volumes

O'Brien, J. S.
SILVER CHIEF SERIES:
1 Silver Chief dog of the North
2 Silver Chief to the rescue
3 Return of Silver Chief

O'Farrell, K.
THE LATTIMER CHILDREN:
1 Off to the sea with Annabelle
2 Three cheers for Annabelle
3 Cousin Annabelle's Xmas 1959

Ogden, A.
MRS. FLUSTER SERIES:
1 Mrs. Fluster and family
2 Mrs. Fluster's circus

Ohlson, E. E.
PIPPA SERIES:
1 Pippa at home
2 Pippa in Switzerland 1955
3 Pippa at Brighton 1956

Ohlson, H.
THUNDERBOLT SERIES:
1 Thunderbolt of the spaceways
2 Thunderbolt and the rebel planet

Oliver, M. M.
1 Menace on the moor 1962
2 Riddle of the tired pony 1963

Oliver, S.
SMOKY SEA SERIES:
1 Son of the smoky sea
2 Back to the smoky sea

Oman, C.
1 Johel
2 Ferry the fearless

Optic, O. *pseud.* **[W. T. Adams]**
ALL OVER THE WORLD SERIES – 12 volumes
ARMY AND NAVY STORIES – six volumes
BLUE AND THE GRAY (AFLOAT) SERIES –
  six volumes
BLUE AND THE GRAY (ON LAND) SERIES –
  six volumes
BOAT BUILDERS SERIES – six volumes
FAMOUS BOAT CLUB SERIES – six volumes
FLORA LEE SERIES – six volumes
GREAT WESTERN SERIES – six volumes
HOUSEHOLD LIBRARY – three volumes
LAKE SHORE SERIES – six volumes
ONWARD AND UPWARD SERIES – six
  volumes
RIVERDALE SERIES – six volumes
STARRY FLAG SERIES – six volumes
WOODVILLE SERIES – six volumes
YACHT CLUB SERIES – six volumes
YOUNG AMERICAN ABROAD SERIES – 12
  volumes

Osgood, M. A.
LITTLE CANARY SERIES:
  1 Little Canary's daisy
  2 Little Canary
  3 Little Canary's Cousin Eugene
  4 Little Canary's black cats

Oterdahl, J.
  1 April adventure 1962
  2 Tina and the latchkey child 1963

Otis, J. *pseud.* **[J. O. Kaler]**
BOY SCOUT SERIES – two volumes
BOYS VENTURE SERIES – two volumes
NAVY BOYS SERIES – two volumes
PIONEER SERIES – nine volumes
SILVER FOX FARM SERIES – four volumes
STORIES OF AMERICAN HISTORY – 12
  volumes
STORIES OF NEWSBOY LIFE – six volumes
TOBY TYLER SERIES – two volumes

Otis, J. *and* **Stratemeyer, E.**
THE MINUTE BOYS SERIES – ten volumes

Outcault, R. F.
BUSTER BROWN SERIES:

Oxenham, E. J.
ABBEY GIRLS SERIES:

  1 The Abbey girls
  2 Abbey girls at home
  3 School days at the Abbey
  4 Abbey girls play up
  5 Two Joans at the Abbey
  6 Robins in the Abbey
  7 A Fiddler in the Abbey
  8 Stowaways for the Abbey
  9 Abbey girls in town
  10 Abbey girls go back to school
  11 Abbey girls on trial
  12 Abbey girls win through
  13 Secrets of the Abbey
  14 Maid of the Abbey
  15 Jen of the Abbey school
  16 Schoolgirl Jen at the Abbey
  17 Guardians of the Abbey
  18 Strangers at the Abbey
  19 Rachel in the Abbey
  20 Selma at the Abbey
  21 A dancer from the Abbey
  22 Song of the Abbey 1955
  23 Jandy Mac comes back 1956
  24 Tomboys at the Abbey 1957
  25 Two queens at the Abbey 1958

Packer, J.
PEPPER SERIES:
  1 No pony like Pepper 1963
  2 Gymnkhana trek 1964
  3 Pepper leads the string 1965

Page, T. N.
SANTA CLAUS SERIES – four volumes

Paice, M.
  1 The lucky fall
  2 The secret of Greycliffs

Paine, A. B.
HOLLOW TREE STORIES – nine volumes

Palmer, G., *and* **Lloyd, N.**
  1 Mystery in Sherwood 1962
  2 The greenwooders 1963
  3 Greenwooders' triumph 1964

Palmer, L. [M. L. Peebles]
HONOUR SERIES:
  1 A question of honour
  2 Where honour leads

MARGARET STORIES:
1 Drifting and steering
2 One day's weaving
3 Archie's shadow
4 John Jack

Pansy *pseud.* [**Mrs. G. M. Alden**]
Note – This author has written about 200 stories. Hereunder are some of the sequels.
CHAUTAUQUA SERIES – two volumes
ESTHER RIED SERIES – seven volumes
RUTH ERSKINE SERIES – two volumes

Pardoe, M.
BUNKLE SERIES:
1 Bunkle began it
2 Bunkle butts in
3 Bunkle bought it
4 Bunkle breaks away
5 Bunkle and Belinda
6 Four plus Bunkle
7 Bunkle baffles them
8 Bunkle went for six
9 Bunkle gets busy
10 Bunkle scents a clue
11 Bunkle's brainwave
12 Bunkle brings it off 1961
MACALISTER CHILDREN SERIES:
1 Argle's mist
2 Argle's causeway 1958
3 Argle's oracle 1959
Stories in which a modern family is projected back into the past.
□
1 Charles arriving
2 May madrigal
BOAT SERIES:
1 The ghost boat
2 The boat seekers
3 The Dutch boat
4 The nameless boat 1956
5 The Greek boat mystery 1960

Parish, P.
AMELIA BEDELIA SERIES:
1 Amelia Bedelia 1964
2 Thank you, Amelia Bedelia 1965

Parker, R.
PIPER SERIES:
1 A valley full of pipers

2 Perversity of pipers

Parry, E. A.
1 Katawampus
2 The first book of Krab
3 Butterscotia

Patchett, M. E.
BREVITT SERIES:
1 Undersea treasure hunters
2 Caribbean adventurers
3 The quest of Ati Manu
4 Treasure of the reef
5 Return to the reef 1956
6 Outback adventure 1957
7 Call of the bush
8 The golden wolf 1962
JELF JAMES SERIES:
1 Warrimoo
2 Dangerous assignment
3 The Venus project 1963
JOEY MEEHAN:
1 The Brumby 1960
2 Brumby come home 1961
3 The circus Brumby 1962
4 Stranger in the herd 1964
5 The Brumby foal 1965
AJAX SERIES:
1 Ajax the warrior 1953
2 Tam the untamed 1954
3 Return to the reef 1956
4 Call of the bush
5 The end of the outlaws 1961
6 The golden wolf 1962
8 Ajax and the drovers 1963
9 Ajax and the haunted mountain 1965

Paternoster, G. S.
1 The motor pirate
2 The cruise of the *Conqistador*

Patchin, F. G.
BATTLESHIP BOYS SERIES – eight volumes
PONY RIDER BOYS SERIES – 12 volumes
RANGE AND GRANGE SERIES – four volumes

Patrick, M.
TOMMY HAWKES SERIES:
1 Tommy Hawkes' first case
2 Tommy Hawkes' second case
3 Tommy Hawkes' third case

Patten, G.
CLIFF STIRLING SERIES:
1 Cliff Stirling, captain of the nine
2 Cliff Stirling behind the line
3 Cliff Stirling, stroke of the crew
ROCKSPUR SERIES:
1 The Rockspur nine
2 The Rockspur eleven
3 The Rockspur rivals

Paull, Mrs. G. A.
PRINCE DIMPLE SERIES:
1 Prince Dimple and his everyday doings
2 Prince Dimple's further doings
3 Prince Dimple on his travels

Paull, M. A.
MARJORIE SERIES – three volumes

Paull, M. E. K.
RUBY SERIES – four volumes

Pearce, A. H.
1 Porpoise bay
2 Hyok inlet
3 Rattlesnake range

Pearl, I.
JANEY SERIES:
1 Janey
2 Janey and her friends

Peck, G. W.
PECK'S BAD BOY SERIES – 13 volumes

Peel, H. M.
ANN AND JIM HENDERSON SERIES:
1 Pilot the hunter 1961
2 Fury son of the wilds 1962
3 Pilot the chaser 1963
4 Easter the show jumper 1965

Pendexter, H.
ALONG THE COAST SERIES:
1 The young fisherman
2 The young sea-merchants
CAMP AND TRAIL SERIES:
1 The young timber-cruisers
2 The young gem-hunters
3 The young woodman

4 The young trappers
5 The young loggers

Penrose, M.
DOROTHY DALE SERIES – 13 volumes
MOTOR GIRLS SERIES – ten volumes
RADIO GIRLS SERIES – four volumes

Perkins, L. F.
TWINS SERIES:
1 American twins of 1812
2 American twins of the Revolution
3 Belgian twins
4 Cave twins
5 Chinese twins
6 Colonial twins of Virginia
7 Dutch twins
8 Eskimo twins
9 Filipino twins
10 French twins
11 Indian twins
12 Irish twins
13 Italian twins
14 Japanese twins
15 Norwegian twins
16 Pioneer twins
17 Scotch twins
18 Spanish twins
19 Spartan twins
20 Swiss twins
21 Puritan twins
22 Mexican twins
Continued by D. Rooke
23 South African twins
24 Australian twins

Perry, N.
1 A flock of boys and girls
2 Another flock of girls
3 A flock of girls and their friends

Pertwee, R.
STORY OF PATRICK FARADAY:
1 The Islanders
2 Rough water
3 Operation wild goose
4 An actor's life for me

Peterson, H.
MAGNUS SERIES:
1 Magnus and the squirrel
2 Magnus and the van horse

3 Magnus in the harbour
4 Magnus in danger
5 Magnus and the ship's mascot

Peyton, K. M.
1 Stormcock meets trouble 1962
2 The hard way home 1963
3 Brownsea silver 1964

Phipson, J.
THE BARKERS SERIES:
1 Family conspiracy 1962
2 Threat to the Barkers 1963

Pier, A. S.
ST. TIMOTHY'S SERIES:
1 Boys of St. Timothy's
2 Dormitory days
3 The jester of St. Timothy's
4 Harding of St. Timothy's
□
1 His father's son
2 Grannis of the fifth

Pierson, C. D.
MILLERS SERIES:
1 Three little Millers
2 The Millers at Pencroft
3 The Millers and their playmates
4 The Millers and their new home

Pilkington, R.
BRANXOME FAMILY SERIES:
1 Jan's treasure 1956
2 Chesterfield gold 1957
3 The missing panel 1958
4 The Dahlia's barge 1959
5 Don John's ducats 1960
6 Nepomuk of the river 1961

Pinkerton, K.
1 Hidden harbour
2 Second meeting
3 The secret river 1958

Plant, J.
RUSTY MASON SERIES:
1 Sky trail to danger 1962
2 The league of the purple dagger 1963

Plummer, M. W.
ROY AND RAY SERIES:
1 Roy and Ray in Mexico
2 Roy and Ray in Canada

Pocock, D.
HALLOWDENE FARM SERIES:
1 The secret of Hallowdene Farm
2 Summer at Hallowdene Farm

Porteous, R. K.
1 Tambai Island 1957
2 Tambai treasure 1958
3 The silent isles 1963

Porter, B. C.
TRUDY AND TIMOTHY SERIES:
1 Trudy and Timothy
2 Trudy and Timothy and the trees

Porter, E. H.
MISS BILLY SERIES:
1 Miss Billy
2 Miss Billy's decision
3 Miss Billy – married

Prentiss, E.
LITTLE SUSY SERIES – four volumes

Price, E.
JANE SERIES:
1 Meet Jane
2 Just Jane
3 Enter – Jane
4 Jane the fourth
5 Jane the unlucky
6 Jane the popular
7 Jane the sleuth
8 Jane the patient
9 Jane gets busy
10 Jane at war

Price, W.
HAL AND ROGER HUNT:
1 Amazon adventure
2 South Sea adventure
3 Underwater adventure
4 Volcano adventure 1956
5 Whale adventure 1960
6 African adventure 1961
7 Elephant adventure 1962

Prime, H.

NINE SERIES:
1 The adventurous nine
2 Nine on the trail
3 Nine afloat

HOLLYS SERIES:
1 The Hollys of Tooting steps
2 The Hollys on wheels

☐
1 Moonface 1962
2 Moonface and Mathew 1963
3 Mathew's ear 1964

Pudney, J.

'FRED AND I' SERIES:
1 Saturday adventure
2 Sunday adventure
3 Monday adventure
4 Tuesday adventure
5 Wednesday adventure
6 Thursday adventure 1955
7 Friday adventure 1956
8 Spring adventure
9 Summer adventure 1962
10 Autumn adventure 1964
11 Winter adventure 1965

HARTWARP SERIES:
1 The Hartwarp light railway
2 The Hartwarp dump
3 The Hartwarp circus
4 The Hartwarp balloon 1963
5 The Hartwarp bakehouse 1964
6 The Hartwarp explosion 1965

Pugh, N.
1 The miniature mystery
2 The Bradshaws on the trail

Pullein-Thompson, C., *see* Thompson, C. Pullein-

Pulling, N.
1 A little magic for the Browns
2 A little magic for Barbara

Prysen, A.

MRS. PEPPERPOT SERIES:
1 Little old Mrs. Pepperpot
2 Mrs. Pepperpot again
3 Mrs. Pepperpot to the rescue

Pye, V.

THE PRICE FAMILY:
1 Red letter holiday
2 Snow bird
3 Primrose Polly
4 Half term holiday
5 The Prices return
6 The stolen jewels
7 Johanna and the Prices
8 Holiday exchange

Queen, E.

DJUNA AND CHAMP HIS DOG SERIES:
1 Black dog mystery
2 Green turtle mystery
3 Red Chipmunk mystery
4 Brown fox mystery
5 White elephant mystery
6 Golden eagle mystery

Quirk, L. W.
1 The fourth down
2 The freshman eight
3 The third stroke

☐
1 The boy scouts of the Black Eagle Patrol
2 The boy scouts on crusade
3 The boy scouts of Lakeville High

Rae, G.

MARY PLAIN SERIES:
1 Mostly Mary
2 All Mary
3 Mary Plain in town
4 Mary Plain on holiday
5 Mary Plain in trouble
6 Mary Plain in wartime
7 Mary Plain lends a paw
8 Mary Plain's big adventure
9 Mary Plain home again
10 Mary Plain to the rescue
11 Mary Plain and the twins
12 Mary Plain goes bob-a-jobbing
13 Mary Plain goes to America
14 Mary Plain, V.I.P. 1961
15 Mary Plain's whodunit 1965

Ralphson, G. H.

OVER THERE SERIES – six volumes

Rand, E. A.
LOOK AHEAD SERIES:
1 Making the best of it
2 Up North in a whaler
3 Too late for the tide mill
UP THE LADDER SERIES:
1 The Knights of the White Shield
2 The school in the light-house
3 Yard-stick and scissors
4 The camp at Surf Bluff
5 Out of the breakers
ANOTHER SERIES:
1 Her Christmas and her Easter
2 Margie at Harbor Light

Ransome, A.
1 Swallows and amazons
2 Swallowdale
3 Peter Duck
4 Winter holiday
5 Coot club
6 Pigeon post
7 We didn't mean to go to sea
8 Secret water
9 Missee Lee
10 The big six
11 The Picts and the Martyrs
12 Great Northern

Ray, A. C.
BUDDIE BOOKS – two volumes
SIDNEY BOOKS – four volumes
TEDDIE BOOKS – six volumes

Raymond, E.
DOROTHY BOOKS – 11 volumes
JESSICA BOOKS – three volumes

Read, Miss, *pseud.,* **[D. J. Saint]**
1 Hobby-horse cottage 1963
2 Hob o' the horse bat 1965

Reed, H. L.
BRENDA SERIES – six volumes
IRMA SERIES – two volumes

Reid, M.
1 The boy hunters
2 The young voyageurs
☐
1 The bush boys
2 The young yagers

3 The giraffe hunters
☐
1 The plant hunters
2 The cliff climbers
☐
1 Ran away to sea
2 The ocean waifs

Reid, M. M.
TIFFANY SERIES:
1 Tiffany and the swallow rhyme
2 Carrigmore Castle
3 The cuckoo at Coolnean 1956
4 Strangers in Carrigmore 1957
5 The Tobermillin oracle 1962
THE PEYTON CHILDREN:
1 All because of Dawks
2 Dawks does it again
3 Dawks on Robbers' mountain 1957
4 Dawks and the duchess 1958
RATHCAPPLE SERIES:
1 Sandy and the hollow rock 1961
2 The McNeills at Rathcapple 1962
3 With Angus in the forest 1963

Remick, G. M.
SHELDON SERIES – three volumes
GLENLOCK SERIES – four volumes
JANE STUART SERIES – four volumes

Rhoades, N.
1 The little girl next door
2 Little Miss Rosamund
☐
1 Winifred's neighbours
2 The children on the top floor

Rhodes, J. *and* **Gibbs, S.**
TIM AND BETSY SERIES:
1 Badger's Bend 1964
2 Adventure at Badger's Bend 1965

Richards, F.
BILLY BUNTER SERIES:
1 Billy Bunter of Greyfriars school
2 Billy Bunter's banknote
3 Billy Bunter's barring-out
4 Billy Bunter in Brazil
5 Billy Bunter's benefit
6 Billy Bunter among the cannibals
7 Billy Bunter's postal order
8 Billy Bunter and the Blue Mauritius

Richards, F. (*contd.*)
9 Billy Bunter butts in
10 Billy Bunter's beanfeast
11 Billy Bunter's Christmas party
12 Billy Bunter's brainwave
13 Billy Bunter's first case
14 Billy Bunter the bold
15 Bunter does his best
16 Lord Billy Bunter 1956
17 Bucking up Billy Bunter 1956
18 The banishing of Billy Bunter 1956
19 Billy Bunter afloat 1957
20 Billy Bunter the hiker 1958
21 Billy Bunter's bargain 1958
22 Bunter out of bounds 1959
23 Bunter comes for Christmas 1959
24 Billy Bunter's bolt 1959
25 Billy Bunter's double 1959
26 Billy Bunter keeps it dark 1960
27 Bunter the bad lad 1960
28 Bunter the ventriloquist 1961
29 Billy Bunter's treasure hunt 1961
30 Billy Bunter at Butlin's 1961
31 Bunter the caravanner 1962
32 Billy Bunter's bodyguard 1962
33 Just like Bunter 1963
34 Big chief Bunter 1963
35 Bunter the stowaway 1963
36 Thanks to Bunter 1964
37 Bunter the sportsman 1965
38 Bunter's last fling 1965
Bunter appeared in the Greyfriars school series in the periodical 'Magnet' for over 30 years.
☐
1 Jack's the lad
2 Jack at the circus
☐
1 Tom Merry and Co.
2 Tom Merry's triumph
Tom Merry appeared in the periodical 'Gem' for many years. These are the only publications in book form.

Ridge, A.
1 Endless and Co.
2 Galloping Fred
3 Hurrah for Muggins!

Roberts, G. D.
1 Heron's Island
2 Herons of Pikey's steep
3 Winter at Pikey's steep

Robinson, E.
LITTLE PURITAN SERIES:
1 A little puritan bound girl
2 A little puritan rebel
3 A little puritan's first Christmas

Robinson, M.
MALTY SERIES:
1 First act
2 Malty in films
3 Malty on television 1959
☐
1 The vet's family 1964
2 The vet's son 1966

Rock, N.
1 The hat
2 Bobo and the crocodile 1961

Rockwood, R.
DAVE DASHAWAY SERIES – five volumes
DAVE FEARLESS SERIES – three volumes
SPEEDWELL BOYS SERIES – five volumes

Roland, B.
1 The forbidden bridge 1962
2 Jamie's discovery 1963
3 Jamie's summer visitor 1964

Romany, *pseud.*, *see* Evans, G. K.

Rooke, D., *see* Perkins, L. F.

Ross, D.
THE LITTLE RED ENGINE SERIES:
1 Story of the little red engine
2 Little red engine gets a name
3 Little red engine goes to market
4 Little red engine goes to town
'MISS PUSSY' SERIES:
1 The enormous apple pie
2 The bran tub

Roy, L. E.
FIVE LITTLE STARRS SERIES – eight volumes
POLLY BREWSTER SERIES – seven volumes

Roy, O. F.
THE STEWARTS SERIES:
1 The hill war
2 Orders to poach
3 Steer by the stars

4 House in the hills
5 Wandering star

Ruff, A.
1 Adventures of Pinkie 1958
2 More adventures of Pinkie 1959

Russell, I.
1 Princess Susan
2 The rival clubs

Russell, S.
BULLDOZER BROWN SERIES:
1 Bulldozer Brown
2 Bulldozer Brown in Africa

Ruthin, M.
1 Reindeer girl 1960
2 Lapland nurse 1962

Rutley, C. B.
COLIN AND PATRICIA SERIES:
1 Colin and Patricia in Canada
2 Colin and Patricia in South Africa
and Rhodesia

Sabin, E. L.
BAR B BOYS SERIES – six volumes
GREAT WEST SERIES – four volumes
TRAIL BLAZERS SERIES – six volumes

Saint, D. J., *see* Read, Miss, *pseud.*

Salmon, R.
POYO, THE INDIAN BOY:
1 High jungle
2 Mountain trek

Salten, F.
BAMBI SERIES:
1 Bambi
2 Bambi's children

Samuels, A. F.
DICK AND DAISY SERIES:
1 Adrift in the world
2 Fighting life's battles
3 Saved from the street
4 Grandfather Milly's luck
DICK TRAVERS ABROAD SERIES:
1 Little Cricket
2 Palm Land

3 The lost tar
4 On the wave

Sandberg, I.
ANNA SERIES:
1 Anna and the magic hat
2 What Anna saw
3 What Anna saved

Sanderson, M. L.
THE CAMP FIRE GIRLS SERIES – seven
volumes

Sandler, M.
1 Young horse dealers 1957
2 Steep farm stables 1958

Saunders, M.
BEAUTIFUL JOE SERIES:
1 Beautiful Joe
2 Beautiful Joe's paradise
□
1 True Tilda
2 Tilda Jane's orphans

Saville, M.
SUSAN AND BILL SERIES:
1 Susan, Bill and the wolf dog
2 Susan, Bill and the ivy-clad oak
3 Susan, Bill and the vanishing boy
4 Susan, Bill and the golden clock
5 Susan, Bill and dark stranger
6 Susan, Bill and the *Saucy Kate*
7 Susan, Bill and the Bright Star circus
1960
8 Susan, Bill and the pirates bold 1960
SIMON SERIES:
1 Three towers in Tuscany 1963
2 The purple valley 1964
3 Dark danger 1965
MICHAEL AND MARY SERIES:
1 Trouble at Townsend
2 Riddle of the painted box
3 Flying fish adventure
4 Secrets of the hidden pool
5 Young Johnny Bimbo 1956
6 The fourth key 1957
LONE PINE FIVE CLUB SERIES:
1 Mystery at Witchend
2 Seven white gates
3 Gay Dolphin adventure
4 Secret of Grey Walls

Saville, M. (*contd.*)
5 Lone Pine five
6 Elusive grasshopper
7 Neglected mountain
8 Saucers over the moor
9 Wings over Witchend
10 Lone Pine London 1957
11 Secret of the gorge 1958
12 Mystery mine 1959
13 *Sea Witch* comes home 1960
14 Not scarlet but gold 1962
15 Treasure at Amory's 1964
NETTLEFORD SERIS:
1 All summer through
2 Christmas at Nettleford
3 Spring comes to Nettleford
4 Secret of Buzzard Scar
JILLIES SERIES:
1 Redshanks warning
2 Two fair plaits
3 Stranger of Snowfell
4 Sign of the Alpine Rose
5 Luck of Sallowby
6 Ambermere treasure
BUCKINGHAMS SERIES:
1 Master of Mary Knoll
2 Buckinghams at Ravenswyke
3 The long passage
4 A palace for the Buckinghams 1963

Sawyer, R.
LUCINDA SERIES:
1 Roller skates 1964
2 Lucinda's year of Jubilo 1965

Sawyer, W. L., *see* Standish, W., *pseud.*

Saxby, J. M. E.
SHETLAND SERIES:
1 The lads of Lunda
2 The Yarl's yacht
3 The Viking boys
4 The saga-book of Lunda

Schultz, J. W.
1 Sinopah, the Indian boy
2 With the Indians in the Rockies
3 The quest of the fish-dog skin
4 On the warpath

Scott, G. F.
JEAN CABOT SERIES:
1 Jean Cabot at Ashton
2 Jean Cabot in the British Isles
3 Jean Cabot in cap and gown
4 Jean Cabot at the house with the blue shutters

Scott, I.
1 Two cadets
2 Two sub-lieutenants
3 Two lieutenants

Scott, M.
OAKDALE ACADEMY SERIES – six volumes

Scott, P.
ALGY, PETER AND JEREMY SERIES:
1 Galleon's Bay
2 The negro's ring

Scott, W.
CHERRYS SERIES:
1 The Cherrys of River House
2 The Cherrys and company
3 The Cherrys by the sea
4 The Cherrys and the Pringles
5 The Cherrys and the galleon
6 The Cherrys and the double arrow
7 The Cherrys on Indoor Island
8 The Cherrys and the silent room
9 The Cherrys' mystery holiday
10 The Cherrys on zig-zag trail
11 The Cherrys famous case 1962
12 The Cherrys to the rescue 1963
13 The Cherrys in the snow 1964
14 The Cherrys and the blue balloon 1965

Scudder, H. E.
THE BODLEY FAMILY SERIES:
1 Doings of the Bodley family in town and country
2 The Bodleys telling stories
3 The Bodleys on wheels
4 The Bodleys afoot
5 Mr. Bodley abroad
6 The Bodley grandchildren and their journey in Holland
7 The English Bodley family
8 The Viking Bodleys

Sea-lion, *pseud.* [**G. M. Bennett**]
DESMOND DRAKE SERIES:
1 Meet Desmond Drake
2 Damn Desmond Drake
JOHN PRENTICE SERIES:
1 Phantom fleet
2 Sink me the ship
3 Cargo for crooks
4 Sink when danger threatens
MIDSHIPMAN 'TIGER' RANSOME SERIES:
1 The pirate destroyers 1954
2 Wrecked on the Goodwins 1955
3 Detective Tiger Ransome 1956

Seligman, A.
1 Thunder reef
2 Thunder in the bay

Serraillier, I.
1 They raced for treasure
2 Flight to adventure

Seth, R.
CAPTAIN BRIAN GRANT SERIES:
1 Operation retriever 1954
2 Operation lama 1955
3 Operation ormo 1956
4 The spy and the atom-gun 1957
5 Rockets on moon island 1958
6 Smoke without fire 1959

Severn, D.
'CRUSOE' SERIES:
1 Rick afire
2 Cabin for Crusoe
3 Wagon for five
4 Hermit in the hills
5 Forest holiday
WARNER SERIES:
1 Ponies and poachers
2 Cruise of the *Maiden Castle*
3 Treasure for three
4 Crazy castle
5 Burglars and bandicoots

Sewell, H.
1 Away goes Sally
2 Five bushel farm
3 Fair American

Shaw, J.
1 Penny foolish

2 Twopence coloured
3 Threepenny bit
4 Fourpenny fair
5 Fivepenny mystery
SUSAN SERIES:
1 Susan pulls the strings
2 Susan's helping hand
3 Susan rushes in
4 Susan interferes
5 Susan at school
6 Susan muddles through 1960
7 Susan's trying term 1961
8 No trouble for Susan 1962
9 Susan's kind heart 1965
□
1 Anything can happen
2 Nothing happened after all
□
1 The moochers
2 The moochers abroad

Sheldon, Mrs. G.
1 A girl in a thousand
2 A thorn among roses
□
1 The golden key
2 A heritage of love
□
1 The magic cameo
2 The Heatherford fortune

Sheppard, W. C.
RAMBLER CLUB SERIES – 15 volumes

Sherman, C. L.
DOT SERIES – four volumes

Sherman, V. T.
1 Boy scouts with Joffre
2 Boy scouts in the war zone
3 Scouting the Balkans in a motor boat
4 Capturing a spy
5 The runaway balloon
6 A lost patrol
7 The boy scout signal
8 An interrupted wig-wag
9 The call of the Beaver Patrol
10 The perils of an air ship

Sherwood, E.
BOYS AND GIRLS FRIEND SERIES – eight
volumes

Shirley, P. [S. J. Clarke]
BOY DONALD SERIES – three volumes
LITTLE MISS WEEZY SERIES – three volumes
SILVER GATE SERIES – three volumes

Shute, H. A.
REAL DIARY OF A REAL BOY – six volumes

Sidney, M. [H. M. Lothrop]
FIVE LITTLE PEPPERS SERIES – 12 volumes

Silvers, E. R.
1 Dick Arnold of Raritan College
2 Dick Arnold plays the game
□
1 Ned Beals, freshman
2 Ned Beals works his way
□
1 At Hillside High
2 Jackson of Hillsdale

Simpson, C.
1 Adam in ochre
2 Adam with arrows
3 Adam in plumes
A trilogy on Australia

Sindall, M. A.
'THE WARREN' SERIES:
1 The children of The Warren
2 Strangers at The Warren
3 Holidays at The Warren
4 Caravan at The Warren 1957
5 Surprises for The Warren 1960

Singmaster, E.
SARAH SERIES:
1 When Sarah saved the dog
2 When Sarah went to school

Sinopy, H.
1 Family gold rush 1956
2 Both sides of the medal 1957

Sleigh, B.
1 Carbonel
2 The kingdom of Carbonel

Smedley, E.
THE JAYS SERIES:
1 The Jays
2 A job for the Jays

Smee, D.
JEREMY SERIES:
1 Jeremy Smith to the rescue 1958
2 Jeremy Smith investigates 1959
3 Jeremy Smith in trouble 1960
4 Jeremy Smith shows the way 1961

Smith, C. C.
BOB KNIGHT SERIES:
1 Bob Knight's diary at Poplar High School
2 Bob Knight's diary camping out
3 Bob Knight's diary with the circus

Smith, C. F.
1 Ship aground
2 Painted ports

Smith, D. J.
1 Into the happy glade
2 By a silver stream

Smith, E.
1 Seven sisters at Queen Anne's
2 Septima at school

Smith, E. Y.
JENNIFER SERIES:
1 The Jennifer wish 1958
2 The Jennifer gift 1959
3 The Jennifer prize 1960
4 Jennifer is eleven 1961
5 Jennifer dances 1962
6 High heels for Jennifer 1965
An Illinois family in the early years of this century.

Smith, H. L.
1 The girls of Friendly Terrace
2 Peggy Raymond's vacation
3 Peggy Raymond's school days
4 The Friendly Terrace quartette
5 Peggy Raymond's way
Note – For the 'Pollyanna series' see Porter, E. H.

Smith, Mrs. M. P. W., *see* Thorn, P.

Smith, R. P.
THE RIVAL CAMPERS SERIES:
1 The rival campers
2 The rival campers afloat

3 The rival campers ashore
4 The rival campers among the oyster
  pirates

Smyth, Sir J.
ANN SHELTON SERIES:
1 Paradise Island 1958
2 Troubles in Paradise 1959
3 Ann goes hunting 1960

Smythe, P.
THREE JAYS SERIES:
1 Jacqueline rides for a fall 1957
2 Three Jays against the clock 1958
3 Three Jays on holiday
4 Three Jays go to town
5 Three Jays over the border 1960
6 Three Jays go to Rome 1960
7 Three Jays lend a hand 1961

Snedeker, Mrs. C. D.
1 Downright Dencey
2 Beckoning road

Snell, R. J.
RADIOPHONE BOYS SERIES – four volumes

Sommerfelt, A.
1 The road to Agra
2 The white bungalow

Southall, I.
SIMON BLACK SERIES:
1 Meet Simon Black 1951
2 Simon Black in peril 1952
3 Simon Black in Coastal Command
  1954
4 Simon Black in China 1955
5 Simon Black in the Antarctic 1956
6 Simon Black takes over 1959
7 Simon Black at sea 1961

Spain, N.
1 The tiger who couldn't eat meat
2 The tiger who went to the moon
3 The tiger who won his star
4 The tiger who saved the train
5 The tiger who found the treasure

Sparhawk, F. C.
DOROTHY BROOK SERIES:
1 Dorothy Brooke's schooldays

2 Dorothy Brooke's vacation
3 Dorothy Brooke's experiments
4 Dorothy Brooke at Ridgemore
5 Dorothy Brooke across the sea

Speed, N.
CARTER GIRLS SERIES – five volumes
MOLLY BROWN SERIES – eight volumes
TUCKER TWINS SERIES – six volumes

Spyri, J.
1 Heidi's early experiences
2 Heidi's further experiences
  Modern editions are in one volume.
  Continued by Tritten, C.
1 Heidi grows up
2 Heidi's children

Stables, G.
1 Cruise of the *Snowbird*
2 Wild adventures round the Pole

Standish, B. L.
BIG LEAGUE SERIES – 13 volumes
FRANK AND DICK MERRIWELL SERIES –
  17 volumes

Standish, W. *pseud.* [**W. L. Sawyer**]
JACK LORIMER SERIES:
1 Captain Jack Lorimer
2 Jack Lorimer's champions
3 Jack Lorimer's holidays

Stanhope, D.
'SEA URCHIN' SERIES:
1 *Sea Urchin's* first charter
2 *Sea Urchin's* second charter
3 *Sea Urchin's* third charter
4 *Sea Urchin's* last charter

Steiner, C.
KIKI SERIES:
1 Kiki dances 1960
2 Kiki is an actress 1961
3 Kiki loves music 1963
4 Kiki's playhouse 1963
5 Kiki skates 1964
6 Kiki goes to camp 1964
7 Kiki and Muffy 1964
KAROLEENA SERIES:
1 Karoleena 1964
2 Karoleena's red coat 1964

Stephens, C. A.
CAMPING OUT SERIES:
1 Camping out
2 Left on Labrador
3 Off to the geysers
4 Lynx-hunting
5 Fox-hunting
6 On the Amazon
KNOCKABOUT CLUB SERIES:
1 Knockabout Club alongshore
2 Knockabout Club in the Tropics, Mexico and South America
3 Knockabout Club in the woods: Maine and Canada
4 Knockabout Club in search of treasure
5 Knockabout Club on the Spanish Main
6 Knockabout Club in North Africa
7 Knockabout Club in Spain
8 Knockabout Club in the Antilles
9 Knockabout Club in the Everglades

Stevens, F. H.
KORONGLEA SERIES:
1 Koranglea Cobbers 1961
2 Koronglea ponies 1962
3 Koronglea adventures 1965
Sheepfarming in Australia.

Stevens, M.
JACK LIGHTFOOT SERIES – 14 volumes

Stevens, W. O.
1 'Peewee' Clinton, plebe
2 Messmates

Stevenson, B. E.
1 The young section-hand
2 The young train dispatcher
3 The young train master
4 The young apprentice
   □
1 The Holladay case
2 The Marathon mystery
3 That affair at Elizabeth

Stevenson, R. L.
1 Kidnapped
2 Catriona. *Same as* David Balfour
   Note – 'Porto Bello gold', by A. D. H.
   Smith, is in the form of a prelude to
   'Treasure Island', and 'Back to Treasure
   Island', by H. A. Calahan is a sequel.

*'Alan Breck again', by A. D. H. Smith,
is a sequel to 'Catriona'.
There is a sequel to 'Treasure Island'
'The return of Long John Silver', by
John Connell, (J. H. Robertson).
Adventures of Ben Gunn by R. F.
Delderfield. Not a sequel to 'Treasure
Island' but a foreword. Tells how Silver
lost his leg and the treasure was buried.*

Stewart, J. L.
CAMP-FIRE GIRLS SERIES – six volumes

Stirling, Y.
1 A United States midshipman afloat
2 A United States midshipman in China
3 A United States midshipman in Japan
4 A United States midshipman in the South Seas

Stockum, H.
1 Jeremy Bear 1962
2 Little old bear 1962
3 Bennie's new baby 1963
4 The new baby is lost 1964

Stoddard, W. O.
COWBOY AND COLLEGE LIFE SERIES:
1 Dab Kinzer
2 The quartet
REVOLUTIONARY SERIES:
1 Dan Munroe
2 Two cadets with Washington

Stokes, K.
THE MOTOR MAIDS SERIES – six volumes

Stone, G.
JANE SERIES:
1 Jane and the owl
2 The adventures of Jane

Stone, S.
CONWAY SERIES:
1 Conway, K.C.
2 Bookmaker's body

Storr, C.
POLLY AND THE WOLF:
1 Clever Polly and the stupid wolf
2 Polly the giant's bride
3 Adventures of Polly and the wolf
MARIANNE SERIES:
1 Marianne dreams

2 Marianne and Mark
LUCY SERIES:
1 Lucy
2 Lucy runs away

Strang, H.
RUSSO-JAPANESE WAR SERIES:
1 Kobo
2 Brown of Mukden
STORIES OF THE GREAT WAR SERIES:
1 Burton of the Flying Corps
2 Fighting with French
2 A hero of Liége
4 With Haig on the Somme
5 Tom Willoughby's scouts
6 The blue raider

Stratemeyer, E.
BOUND TO SUCCEED SERIES – two volumes
COLONIAL SERIES – six volumes
DAVE PORTER SERIES – 11 volumes
LAKEPORT SERIES – six volumes
OLD GLORY SERIES – six volumes
PAN-AMERICAN SERIES – six volumes
ROVER BOYS SERIES – two volumes
SHIP AND SHORE SERIES – two volumes
SOLDIERS OF FORTUNE SERIES – four volumes

Stratemeyer, E. and Otis, J. see Otis, J.

Streatfield, N.
1 The Bell family 1958
2 New town 1959

Striker, F.
LONE RANGER SERIES:
1 Lone Ranger and the mystery ranch
2 Lone Ranger and the gold robbery
3 Lone Ranger and the outlaw stronghold
4 Lone Ranger on gunsight mesa
5 Lone Ranger and the Bitter Spring feud
6 Lone Ranger and the code of the West
7 Lone Ranger on Red Butte trail

Strutton, B.
DR. WHO SERIES:
1 Dr. Who 1964

2 Dr. Who and the Zarbi 1965

Stuart, G.
BOY SCOUTS OF THE AIR SERIES – 14 volumes

Stuart, Mrs. R. M.
SONNY SERIES:
1 Sonny: a Christmas guest
2 Sonny's father

Stuart, S. J.
ALISON SERIES:
1 Alison's highland holiday
2 More adventures of Alison
3 Alison's Christmas adventure
4 Well done, Alison
5 Alison's Easter adventure
6 Alison's poaching adventure
7 Alison's kidnapping adventure
8 Alison's pony adventure
9 Alison's island adventure
10 Alison's spy adventure 1955
11 Alison and the witch's cave 1956
12 Alison's yacht adventure 1957
13 Alison's riding adventure 1958
14 Alison's cliff adventure 1959
15 Alison's caravan adventure 1960

Stuart-Young, J. M., see Young, S. J. Stuart-

Styles, S.
MIDSHIPMAN QUINN SERIES:
1 Midshipman Quinn 1957
2 Quinn of the navy 1958
3 Midshipman Quinn wins through 1961
4 Quinn at Trafalgar 1963
Stories of the Napoleonic Wars.
SIMON AND MEG SERIES:
1 Ladder of snow 1960
2 The shop in the mountain 1962
3 A necklace of glaciers 1963
□
1 The flying ensign
2 Byrd of the 95th 1962
Stories of the Peninsular War.
□
1 Tiger Patrol
2 Tiger Patrol wins through 1958

Styles, S. (*contd.*)
1 Kidnap castle
2 Traitor's mountain
3 Gideon Hazel

Suddaby, D.
ROBIN HOOD SERIES:
1 New tales of Robin Hood
2 Robin Hood's master stroke

Sullivan, J. F.
1 Here they are!
2 There they are!
3 Here they are again!

Sutcliffe, R.
1 The eagle of the ninth
2 The silver branch 1957
Stories of the Roman army in Britain.

Sutton, M.
JUDY BOLTON SERIES:
1 The vanishing shadow
2 Haunted attic
3 Invisible chimes
4 Seven strange clues
5 Ghost parade
6 Yellow phantom
7 Mystic ball
8 Voice in the suitcase
9 Mysterious half cat
10 Riddle of the double ring
11 Unfinished house
12 Clue in the patchwork quilt
13 Living portrait
14 Mark on the mirror
15 Midnight visitor
16 Name on the bracelet
17 Rainbow riddle
18 Secret of the barred window
19 Secret of the musical tree

Sweet, S.
PENNYPACKERS SERIES:
1 The six little Pennypackers
2 How the Pennypackers kept the light

Swinburne, D.
JEAN SERIES:
1 Jean tours a hospital 1957
2 Jean becomes a nurse 1958
3 Jean at Jo's hospital 1959

4 Jean, S.R.N. 1960
5 Jean's new junior 1964

Symons, B.
JANE CARBERRY SERIES:
1 Jane Carberry investigates
2 Jane Carberry detective
3 Magnet for murder

Taggart, M. A.
BETH SERIES:
1 Beth's wonder winter
2 Beth's old home
DOCTOR'S LITTLE GIRL SERIES:
1 The Doctor's little girl
2 Sweet Nancy
3 Nancy, the Doctor's little partner
4 Nancy Porter's opportunity
5 Nancy and the Coggs twins
SIX LITTLE GIRLS SERIES:
1 Six girls and Bob
2 Six girls and the tea room
3 Betty Gaston, the seventh girl
4 Six girls and Betty
5 Six girls grown up
6 Her daughter Jean

Tannenforst, U.
1 The thistles of Mount Cedar
2 Heroines of a schoolroom

Tarrant, E.
HIGHLANDS SERIES:
1 Summer term at Highlands
2 New girl at Highlands
3 Lodgers at Highlands
4 The amazing affair at Highlands

Tatham, J., *see* Wells, H.

Taylor, E. C.
TED STRONG SERIES – 43 volumes

Taylor, R.
ANDY SERIES:
1 Andy and the mascots
2 Andy and the water crossing
3 Andy and the display team
4 Andy and the sharpshooters
5 Andy and the secret papers
6 Andy and the miniature war
7 Andy and the royal review

Temple, W. F.
1 Martin Magnus
2 Planet rover
3 Martin Magnus on Venus
4 Martin Magnus on Mars 1956

Thatcher, D.
TOMMY SERIES
1 Tommy's new engine
2 Tommy and the onion boat
3 Tommy and the lighthouse

Thompson, C. Pullein-
DAVID AND PAT SERIES:
1 The first rosette 1956
2 The second mount 1957
3 Three to ride 1958
4 The lost pony 1958
☐
1 The empty field
2 The open gate
☐
1 Giles and the elephant
2 Giles and the greyhound
3 Giles and the canal
SANDY AND LAWRENCE SERIES:
1 We hunted hounds
2 I carried the horn
3 Goodby to hounds
MAJOR HOLBROOKE AND HIS PONY CLUB:
1 Pony club
2 The Radney riding club
3 One day event
4 Pony club team
5 Pony club camp 1957
EASTMAN SERIES:
1 The Eastmans' in Brittany
2 The Eastmans' move house

Thorn, I.
1 Quite unexpected
2 A flock of four
3 Geoff and Jim
4 Captain Geoff
5 Jim
6 The Harringtons at home

Thorn, P. [Mrs. M. P. W. Smith]
JOLLY GOOD TIME STORIES – eight volumes
OLD DEERFIELD SERIES – three volumes
YOUNG PURITANS SERIES – four volumes

Thorndyke, H. L.
HONEY BUNCH SERIES – three volumes

Thurston, Mrs. I. T.
1 The bishop's shadow
2 The big brothers of Sabin Street
☐
1 The scoutmaster of Troop 5
2 Billy Burns of Troop 5

Thwaite, A.
JANE AND TOBY SERIES:
1 A seaside holiday for Jane and Toby
2 Toby stays with Jane
3 Toby moves house
4 Jane and Toby start school

Timlow, E. W.
CRICKET SERIES:
1 Cricket
2 Cricket at the seashore
3 Eunice and Cricket

Titus, E.
ANATOLE SERIES:
1 Anatole
2 Anatole and the bat
3 Anatole and the rabbit

Todd, B. [Euphan, J., *pseud.*]
WORZEL GUMMIDGE SERIES:
1 Worzel Gummidge
2 Worzel Gummidge again
3 Worzel Gummidge and Saucy Nancy
4 Worzel Gummidge takes a holiday
5 More about Worzel Gummidge
6 Earthy Mangold and Worzel Gummidge
7 Worzel Gummidge and the treasure ship 1958
8 Worzel Gummidge again 1959
9 Detective Worzel Gummidge 1963

Todd, H. E.
BOBBY BREWSTER SERIES:
1 Bobby Brewster and the winker's club
2 Bobby Brewster
3 Bobby Brewster's camera
4 Bobby Brewster's shadow
5 Bobby Brewster's bicycle
6 Bobby Brewster's wallpaper

Todd, H. E. (*contd.*)
7 Bobby Brewster's conker
8 Bobby Brewster's detective
9 Bobby Brewster's potato

Tomlinson, E. T.
COLONIAL SERIES – four volumes
FLAG AND COUNTRY SERIES – five volumes
FOUR BOYS SERIES – six volumes
REVOLUTIONARY STORIES – five volumes
ST. LAWRENCE SERIES – three volumes
WAR OF 1812 SERIES – eight volumes
WAR OF THE REVOLUTION SERIES – four
volumes
WARD HILL SERIES – two volumes
WINNING SERIES – three volumes

Tomlinson, P. G.
FOUR CLASSMATES SERIES:
1 To the land of the Caribou
2 In camp on Bass Island

Townsend, J.
1 Rocket ship saboteurs 1960
2 A warning to Earth 1961
3 The secret of Puffin Island 1962

Townsend, J. R.
1 Gumble's yard 1964
2 Widdershins' Crescent 1965

Townsend, V. F.
1 Sirs, only seventeen!
2 Dorothy Draycott's tomorrow
3 Dorothy Draycott's todays

Tozer, K.
1 Wanderings of Mumfie
2 Here comes Mumfie
3 Mumfie's Uncle Samuel
4 Mumfie the admiral
5 Mumfie's magic box

Tranter, N.
KEN AND FIONA SERIES:
1 Spaniard's isle
2 Border riding
3 Nesta the master
4 Birds of a feather
□
1 Something very fishy
2 Give a dog a bad name

Travers, P. L.
MARY POPPINS SERIES:
1 Mary Poppins
2 Mary Poppins comes back
3 Mary Poppins opens the door
4 Mary Poppins in the park
5 Mary Poppins from A to Z

Treadgold, M.
1 The heron ride 1961
2 Return to the heron 1963

Trease, G.
1 No boats on Bannermere
2 Under Black Banner
3 Black Banner players
4 Black Banner abroad
5 Gates of Bannerdale
MIKE AND SANDRA SERIES:
1 The Maythorn story 1961
2 Change at Maythorn 1962

Treece, H.
VIKING TRILOGY:
1 Viking dawn
2 The road to Miklagard
3 Viking's sunset 1960
*There are three other Viking novels, but
they are not part of this trilogy.*
□
1 Legions of the eagle
2 The eagles have flown
□
1 Ask for King Billy
2 Don't expect any mercy
□
1 The golden strangers 1956
2 The dark Island 1952
3 Red queen, white queen 1956
4 The great captains 1958
*A series of novels on early Britain.
1 describes the last days of the Picts, 2
the Roman conquest, 3 Roman occupation, and 4 the Arthurian period.*
GORDON STEWART SERIES:
1 Killer in dark glasses 1964
2 Bang, you're dead 1966

Treece, H., *see also* Defoe, D.

Trevor, E.
WUMPUS SERIES:
1 Wumpus
2 More about Wumpus
3 Where's Wumpus

Trevor, E.
1 The island in the Pines
2 Squirrel's island
□
1 Into the happy glade
2 By a silver stream
3 Green glade

Trick, E. H.
TOMMY TAD AND POLLY WOG SERIES:
1 Adventures of Tommy Tad and Polly Wog
2 More adventures of Tommy Tad and Polly Wog

Tring, A. S., *pseud.* [L. Meynell]
PENNY SERIES:
1 Penny dreadful
2 Penny triumphant
3 Penny penitent
4 Penny puzzled
5 Penny dramatic 1956
6 Penny in Italy 1957
7 Penny and the pageant 1959
8 Penny says goodbye 1961
BARRY SERIES:
1 Barry's exciting year
2 Barry gets his wish
3 Barry's great day

Tritten, E. C., *see* Spyri, J.

Trowbridge, J. T.
BRIGHT HOPE SERIES:
1 Old battle ground
2 Father Brighthopes
3 Hearts and faces
4 Ironthorpe, the pioneer preacher
5 Burcliff
JACK HAZARD SERIES:
1 Jack Hazard and his fortunes
2 A chance for himself
3 Doing his best
4 Fast friends
5 The young surveyor
6 Lawrence's adventures

SILVER MEDAL STORIES:
1 His own master
2 Bound in honour
3 Young Joe
4 The silver medal
5 The pocket rifle
6 The jolly rover
START IN LIFE SERIES:
1 The start in life
2 Biding his time
3 The kelp gatherers
4 The scarlet tanager and other bipeds
5 The lottery ticket
6 The adventures of David Vane and David Crane
TIDE MILL STORIES:
1 Phil and his friends
2 The Tinkham Brothers' Tide Mill
3 The satin-wood box
4 The little master
5 His one fault
6 Peter Budstone
TOBY TRAFFORD SERIES:
1 The fortunes of Toby Trafford
2 Woodie Thorpe's pilgrimage; and other stories
ANOTHER SERIES:
1 Cudjo's Cave
2 Three scouts

True, J. P.
1 Scouting for Washington
2 Morgan's men
3 On guard against Tory and Tarleton
4 Scouting for Light Horse Harry

Tunis, J. R.
1 Iron Duke
2 Duke decides
□
1 Keystone kids
2 Rookie of the year
□
1 Kid from Tomkinsville
2 World series
3 Kid comes back

Turley, C. [C. T. Smith]
GODFREY MARTEN SERIES:
1 Godfrey Marten, schoolboy
2 Godfrey Marten, undergraduate

Turner, E. [Mrs. H. R. Curlewis]
1 Seven little Australians
2 The family at Misrule
3 The Cub
4 Captain Cub
5 Brigid and the Cub

Turner, L. [Mrs. F. L. Tompson]
1 Paradise and the Perrys
2 The Perry girls

Unnerstad, E.
THE LARSSON FAMILY SERIES:
1 The saucepan journey 1962
2 The Pip-Larssons go sailing 1963
3 The urchin 1964
4 Little O 1965

Upton, B.
GOLLIWOG PICTURE SERIES – several volumes

Uttley, A.
LITTLE GREY RABBIT SERIES:
1 Squirrel goes skating
2 Wise Owl's story
3 Little Grey Rabbit's party
4 The knot Squirrel tied
5 Fuzzypeg goes to school
6 Little Grey Rabbit's Christmas
7 Moldy Warp the mole
8 Hare joins the home guard
9 Little Grey Rabbit's washing day
10 Water Rat's picnic
11 Little Grey Rabbit's birthday
12 The speckledy hen
13 Little Grey Rabbit to the rescue (play)
14 Little Grey Rabbit and the weazels
15 Little Grey Rabbit and the wandering hedgehog
16 Little Grey Rabbit makes lace
17 Hare and the Easter eggs
18 Grey Rabbit and the circus
19 Grey Rabbit's May day
SAM PIG SERIES:
1 Adventures of Sam Pig
2 Sam Pig goes to market
3 Six tales of Sam Pig
4 Sam Pig and Sally
5 Sam Pig at the circus
6 Sam Pig in trouble

7 Yours ever, Sam Pig
8 Sam Pig and the singing gate
9 Sam Pig at the seaside
LITTLE BROWN MOUSE SERIES:
1 Snug and Serena meet a queen
2 Snug and Serena pick cowslips
3 Going to the fair
4 Toad's castle
5 Mrs. Mouse spring-cleans
6 Christmas at the Rose and Crown
7 The gypsy hedgehogs
8 Snug and the chimney-sweeper
9 Snug and Serena count twelve 1959
10 Mr. Stoat walks in 1957
11 Snug and the silver spoon 1957
TIM RABBIT SERIES:
1 Adventures of no ordinary rabbit
2 Adventures of Tim Rabbit
3 Tim Rabbit and company
4 Tim Rabbit's dozen
LITTLE RED FOX SERIES:
1 Little Red Fox and wicked uncle 1955
2 Little Red Fox and Cinderella 1956

Vaile, C. M.
1 The Orcutt girls
2 Sue Orcutt

Vallance, R.
TIMMY SERIES:
1 Timmy Turnpenny
2 Timmy and Janet
3 Timmy and Roger
4 Timmy in the country
5 Timmy and Bingo
6 Timmy moves house 1956
7 Timmy Turnpenny's secret 1957

Vandercook, M.
GIRL SCOUT SERIES – five volumes
RANCH GIRL SERIES – eight volumes
RED CROSS GIRLS SERIES – ten volumes

Vandercook, M. *and* **Frey, H. C.**
CAMP FIRE GIRLS SERIES – 22 volumes

Van Dyne, E.
AUNT JANE'S NIECES SERIES – ten volumes
MARY LOUISE SERIES – eight volumes

Vaughan, C.
MATILDA SERIES:
1 Missing Matilda 1964
2 Two foals for Matilda 1965

Vereker, B.
CAROLINE SERIES:
1 Caroline at the film studios 1955
2 Adventure for Caroline 1956
3 Caroline in Scotland 1957
4 Caroline in Wales 1958

Verne, H.
BOB FAWCETT SERIES:
1 Bob Fawcett and the Moran mystery 1956
2 Bob Fawcett and the pirates of the air 1957
3 Bob Fawcett and the sunken galley 1957
4 Bob Fawcett and the buccaneer's boat 1957
5 Bob Fawcett and the valley of hell 1958
6 Bob Fawcett and the fiery claw 1958

Verney, J.
THE CALLENDAR FAMILY:
1 Friday's tunnel 1960
2 February's road 1961
3 Ismo 1964

Verill, A. H.
1 The cruise of the *Cormorant*
2 In Morgan's wake
□
1 The trail of the cloven foot
2 The trail of the White Indians
BOY ADVENTURE SERIES – four volumes
DEEP SEA HUNTERS SERIES – three volumes
RADIO DETECTIVE SERIES – five volumes

Victor, R.
THE BOY SCOUTS SERIES – eight volumes
COMRADES SERIES – ten volumes

Vipont, E.
1 The lark in the morn
2 The lark on the wing
3 The spring of the year 1956
4 Flowering spring 1960
Not strictly sequels, though the same
characters reappear. Carnegie Medal winner, 1950.
DAWBIGGINS SERIES:
1 Family at Dawbiggins
2 More about Dawbiggins
3 Changes at Dawbiggins 1960

Voegeli, M.
ADVENTURES OF ALI!:
1 The wonderful lamp 1959
2 Prince of Hindustan 1960

Walker, A. P.
SANDMAN'S SERIES – seven volumes

Walker, D. E.
PIMPERNEL SERIES:
1 The fat cat Pimpernel
2 Pimpernel and the poodle

Walker, R.
1 Pickles of the lower fifth
2 The fifth form detective

Wallace, I. L.
POOKIE SERIES:
1 Pookie
2 Pookie puts the world right
3 Pookie in search of a home
4 Pookie and the gypsies
5 Pookie believes in Santa Claus
□
1 The young Warrenders 1961
2 Thanks to Peculiar 1962
3 Strangers at Warrenders Halt 1963
4 The snake ring mystery 1965

Walsh, G. E.
TWILIGHT ANIMAL STORIES – 14 volumes

Walters, H.
CHRIS GODFREY SERIES:
1 Blast-off at Woomera 1957
2 The domes of Pico 1958
3 Operation Columbus 1960
4 Moon base one 1961
5 Expedition Venus 1962
6 Destination Mars 1963
7 Mission to Mercury 1965
8 Journey to Jupiter 1965

Warde, M. [*pseud.* **E. K. Dunton**]
BETTY WALES SERIES – eight volumes
NANCY LEE SERIES – four volumes

Warner, F. A.
BOBBY BLAKE SERIES – 11 volumes

Warner, P.
1 Buddy Christmas
2 Jessie growing up

Warner, P. M.
FRANCES SERIES:
1 A friend for Frances 1956
2 If it hadn't been for Frances 1957

Warner, S. [**E. Wetherell**]
GIVING HONOUR SERIES:
1 Little Camp
2 Willow Brook
GIVING SERVICE SERIES:
1 Sceptres and crowns
2 Flag of truce
GIVING TRUST SERIES:
1 Bread and oranges
2 The rapids of Niagara
WIDE WIDE WORLD SERIES:
1 The wide wide world
2 Ellen Montgomery's bookshelf
☐
1 What she could
2 Opportunities
3 House in town
4 Trading
☐
1 Daisy
2 Daisy of the field
3 Melbourne House

Warwick, A.
CARROLL FAMILY SERIES:
1 Pets in the barn
2 Hunt the Piggies

Watson, H. H.
1 Peggy, D. O.
2 Peggy, S. G.

Watson, J.
HOGGIE SERIES:
1 Hoggie
2 Hoggie and bear

Wayne, J.
THE WINCHESTER FAMILY SERIES:
1 The day the ceiling fell down
2 The night the rain came in
3 Merry by name 1964
4 The ghost next door 1965

Weir, R.
1 The secret journey 1956
2 The secret of Cobbet's farm 1957
☐
1 No. 10 Green Street 1959
2 Great days in Green Street 1960
ALBERT THE DRAGON SERIES:
1 Albert the dragon 1962
2 Further adventures of Albert the dragon 1964

Wellard, B.
THE DIPPERS SERIES:
1 The Dippers and Jo
2 The Dippers and the high-flying kite

Wells, A. E.
1 Tales from Arnhem Land
2 Rain in Arnhem Land

Wells, C.
BETTY SERIES:
1 Betty's happy year
2 Story of Betty
DICK AND DOLLY SERIES:
1 Dick and Dolly
2 Dick and Dolly's adventures
DORRANCE SERIES:
1 The Dorrance domain
2 Dorrance doings
MARJORIE SERIES – six volumes
PATTY SERIES – 17 volumes
TWO LITTLE WOMEN SERIES – three volumes

Wells, H.
CHERRY AMES SERIES:
1 Cherry Ames student nurse
2 Cherry Ames senior nurse
3 Cherry Ames flight nurse
4 Cherry Ames cruise nurse
5 Cherry Ames chief nurse
6 Cherry Ames boarding school nurse
7 Cherry Ames visiting nurse
8 Cherry Ames private duty nurse

9 Cherry Ames department store nurse
10 Cherry Ames mountaineer nurse
11 Cherry Ames camp nurse
12 Cherry Ames island nurse
13 Cherry Ames army nurse
14 Cherry Ames at Hilton Hospital
   Continued by J. Tatham
15 Cherry Ames clinic nurse
16 Cherry Ames at Spencer
17 Cherry Ames night supervisor
18 Cherry Ames rest home nurse
19 Cherry Ames country doctor's nurse
20 Cherry Ames dude ranch nurse
   □
1 Silver wings for Vicki
2 Vicki finds the answer
3 Hidden valley mystery
4 Secret of Magnolia Manor

Welsh, R.
THE CAREY FAMILY SERIES:
1 Knight crusader
2 Captain of dragoons
3 Mohawk Valley 1958
4 Captain of foot 1959
5 Escape from France 1960
6 For a King 1961
7 Nicholas Carey 1963
   *The story of an English family from the
   Crusades to the 19th century.*

West, J.
NEW ZEALAND SERIES:
1 Drovers' road 1963
2 Cape lost 1964
3 The golden country 1965

West, M.
MOTOR RANGERS SERIES:
1 Motor rangers' lost mine
2 Motor rangers through the Sierras
3 Motor rangers on blue water
4 Motor rangers' cloud cruiser
5 Motor rangers' wireless station
6 Motor rangers touring for the trophy

Westerman, P. F.
CADET ALAN CARR SERIES:
1 His unfinished voyage
2 Cadet Alan Carr
SEA SCOUTS SERIES:
1 Sea scouts all

2 Sea scouts abroad
3 Sea scouts up channel
4 Sea scouts at Dunkirk
   □
1 The mystery of Stockmere school
2 Sinclair's luck
   □
1 The pirate submarine
2 Captain Cain

Westwood, A. M.
KITTIWAKE ROCK SERIES:
1 The riddle of Kittiwake Rock 1959
2 Trouble at Kittiwake Rock 1960

Wetheroll, E., *see* Warner, S.

Wevil, L. F.
BETTY SERIES:
1 Betty's first term
2 Betty's next term

Wheeler, F. W. R.
UNITED STATES SERVICE SERIES – 21 volumes

Wheeler, J. C.
BILLY BRADLEY SERIES – five volumes
CAPTAIN PETE SERIES – three volumes

White, C. A.
1 The ballet school mystery
2 Dancer's daughter

White, C. M.
JOANNA BRADLEY SERIES:
1 Cadet nurse at St. Mark's 1961
2 Junior nurse at St. Mark's 1962
3 Nurse at St. Mark's 1963

White, P.
JUNGLE DOCTOR SERIES:
1 Jungle doctor
2 Jungle doctor on safari
3 Jungle doctor operates
4 Jungle doctor attacks witchcraft
5 Jungle doctor's enemies
6 Jungle doctor meets a lion
7 Jungle doctor to the rescue

White, P. (*contd.*)
8 Jungle doctor's case-books
9 Jungle doctor and the whirlwind
10 Eyes on Jungle doctor
11 Jungle doctor looks for trouble
12 Doctor of Tanganyika
13 Jungle doctor hunts big game 1956
14 Jungle doctor's monkey tales 1957
15 Jungle doctor on the hop 1957
16 Jungle doctor's crooked dealings 1958
17 Jungle doctor stings a scorpion 1959
18 Jungle doctor's tug of war 1960
19 Jungle doctor spots a leopard 1961
20 Jungle doctor pulls a leg 1962

White, P. *and* **Britten, D.**
1 The mystery miler 1960
2 Ructions at Ranford 1961
3 Ranford goes fishing 1962

White, T. H.
THE ONCE AND FUTURE KING: AN ARTHU-
RIAN EPIC:
1 The sword in the stone
2 The witch in the wood
3 The ill-made knight
4 The candle in the wind

Whitehill, D.
POLLY PENDLETON SERIES – seven volumes
TWINS SERIES – four volumes

Whitlock, J.
BUNYIP SERIES:
1 The green Bunyip 1962
2 Bunyip at the seaside 1962
3 Bunyip and the Brolga bird 1963
4 Bunyip and the bushfire 1964
5 Bunyip and the tiger cats 1965

Whitlock, R.
COWLEAZE FARM SERIES:
1 Cowleaze Farm
2 Harvest at Cowleaze
3 Cowleaze Farm in winter

Whittle, T.
1 Spades and feathers 1955
2 The runners of Orford 1956
3 Castle Lizard 1957

Wilcox, B.
BUNTY BROWN SERIES:
1 Bunty Brown; probationer
2 Bunty Brown's bargain
3 Bunty Brown of the Flying Squad

Wilder, L. T.
LAURA INGALL SERIES:
1 Little house in the big woods 1955
2 Little house on the prairie 1957
3 On the banks of Plum Creek 1959
4 By the shores of Silver Lake 1960
5 Long winter 1961
6 Little town on the prairie 1963
7 These happy golden years 1964
8 Farmer boy 1965

Wilkinson, Sir N.
TITANIA'S PALACE SERIES:
1 Yvette in Venice
2 Grey Fairy
3 Yvette in Italy
4 Yvette in Switzerland

Willard, B.
1 Snail and the Pennithornes 1957
2 Snail and the Pennithornes next time 1958
3 Snail and the Pennithornes and the Princess 1959

Williams, D.
WENDY SERIES:
1 Wendy wins a pony 1961
2 Wendy wins her spurs 1962
3 Wendy at Wembley 1963
4 Wendy goes abroad 1964

Williams, J. L.
1 The adventures of a freshman
2 Princeton stories
   □
1 The stolen story, etc.
2 The day dreamer
3 The girl and the game

Williams, U. M.
BINKLEBYS SERIES:
1 The Binklebys at home
2 The Binklebys on the farm

Williamson, M.
JOHN AND BETTY SERIES:
1 John and Betty's English history visit
2 John and Betty's Scotch history visit
3 John and Betty's Irish history visit

Willson, R. B.
SARAH AND ALASTAIR SERIES:
1 A seraph in a box 1963
2 Pineapple palace 1964

Wilson, A. C.
NORMAN AND HENRY BONES SERIES:
1 Norman Bones detective
2 Norman and Henry Bones
3 Norman and Henry Bones investigate
4 Norman and Henry solve the problem 1957
5 Norman and Henry follow the lead 1959

Wilson, J. F.
TAD SHELTON SERIES:
1 Tad Shelton, boy scout
2 Tad Shelton's Fourth of July

Winfield, A.
PUTNAM HALL SERIES – six volumes
ROVER BOYS SERIES – 28 volumes

Wingate, J.
1 Submariner Sinclair
2 Jimmy-the-one
3 Sinclair in command
4 Nuclear captain 1962
5 Sub-zero 1963

Wood, A.
1 Mystery cruise
2 Noah's Ark river

Wood, L.
HAG DOWSABEL AND THE LINDLEY CHILDREN:
1 People in the garden 1955
2 Rescue by broomstick 1956

3 The Hag calls for help 1957
4 Seven-league ballet shoes 1959
5 Hags on holiday 1960
6 Hag in the castle 1962

Woolf, B. S.
THE TWINS SERIES:
1 The twins in Ceylon
2 More about the twins in Ceylon

Woolley, L. T.
FAITH PALMER SERIES:
1 Faith Palmer at the Oaks
2 Faith Palmer at Fordyce Hall
3 Faith Palmer in New York
4 Faith Palmer in Washington

Wrightson, P.
THE COLLINS CHILDREN:
1 The crooked snake 1956
2 The Bunyip hole 1958

Wyman, L. P.
GOLDEN BOY SERIES – eight volumes

Yates, E.
1 Patterns on the wall 1943
2 Hue and cry 1953
New England family life in the early 19th century.

Young, C.
JACK RANGER SERIES – three volumes
MOTOR BOYS SERIES – 22 volumes

Young, E. H.
1 Caravan island
2 River holiday

Young, J. M. Stuart-
1 Johnny Jones, gutter-snipe
2 What does it matter?

Zinkin, T.
RISHI SERIES:
1 Rishi 1960
2 Rishi returns 1961

WHITE CRESCENT PRESS LTD, LUTON